John Shertzer Hittell

Hittell's Hand-Book of Pacific Coast Travel

John Shertzer Hittell

Hittell's Hand-Book of Pacific Coast Travel

ISBN/EAN: 9783337211448

Printed in Europe, USA, Canada, Australia, Japan

Cover: Foto ©Andreas Hilbeck / pixelio.de

More available books at **www.hansebooks.com**

HITTELL'S

HAND-BOOK

OF

PACIFIC COAST TRAVEL.

By JOHN S. HITTELL,

Author of "The Commerce and Industries of the Pacific Coast," "The Resources of California," "The History of San Francisco," "A Brief History of Culture," etc.

SAN FRANCISCO:
THE BANCROFT COMPANY, Publishers, History Building
1887

PREFACE.

The main purpose of this book is to present, in a small space, such information as will be of most interest to travelers generally, visiting the Pacific Slope of North America. The notable views along the line of the Union and Central Pacific railroads, from the Mississippi River to the Pacific, are pointed out; the various climates of the vast region west of the Rocky Mountains, from Panama to the Arctic Ocean, are described; and the tourist is taken through the different districts and supplied with such explanation of the features of local nature and art as will enable him to enjoy them readily and to converse about them understandingly.

The work is not designed exclusively for the pleasure tourist from abroad. Special attention has been paid to the needs of invalids, especially those of the consumptive class, and the chapters on the climates and mineral springs of our slope, (the former copied from the *Commerce and Industries of the Pacific Coast*, by the same author, and issued by the same publishers), are the most comprehensive essays ever prepared on their respective subjects. The opinions of the highest medical authorities, on the therapeutical effects of different classes of natural medicinal waters, and on the influence of meteorological conditions on diseases of the respiratory organs though not quoted here, as unsuited to a brief compendium like this, justify the assertions that the best climate in the world for consumptives, and the best mineral springs in the United States, so far as a judgment can be formed from published statistics, are in California.

Besides the wants of invalids and stranger tourists, those of a third class have been kept in view—the residents who wish to know the best places for picnics, camp grounds, summer idling, and country walks and drives. The wild and romantic cañons of the San Mateo, Pilarcitos, San Leandro, San Pablo, Wild Cat, Nicasio, Reed, Lagunitas and San Geronimo creeks, within twenty miles of San Francisco, are unknown to many old residents of San Francisco, even to rich pleasure seekers who have made the tour of Europe. Attention is called to them here. Camping is one of the specialties of California, and a chapter has been devoted to it.

The area of which the work treats, is the entire region west of the summit of the Rocky Mountains, from Panama to the Arctic Ocean; but a large share of the space is given to the metropolis, for the reasons that it is the home or chief stopping place of a majority of the tourists; that most of the travel for pleasure is within 100 miles of it; and that the information is fuller and more precise in reference to it, than to other districts.

The publishers expect to issue every spring a new edition, with such corrections and additions, as will make it one of the most complete works of its kind.

TABLE OF CONTENTS.

CHAPTER I.—NEW YORK TO SAN FRANCISCO.

	Page.
ROUTES	11
SOUTHERN PACIFIC	11
ATLANTIC AND PACIFIC	12
NORTHERN PACIFIC	12
CENTRAL-UNION PACIFIC	12
OMAHA TO CHEYENNE	12
CHEYENNE TO CRESTON	14
CRESTON TO GRANGER	15
GRANGER TO EVANSTON	17
EVANSTON TO OGDEN	18
YELLOWSTONE PARK	20
SALT LAKE CITY	21
FROM SALT LAKE SOUTHWARD	25
FROM OGDEN TO PALISADE	26
PALISADE TO BATTLE MOUNTAIN	28
BATTLE MOUNTAIN TO RENO	29
SOUTH FROM RENO	30
A SILVER MILL	32
CARSON AND COLORADO R. R.	33
RENO TO TRUCKEE	36
LAKE TAHOE	36
THE DONNER TRAGEDY	38
SUMMIT TO EMIGRANT GAP	39
SCENERY BELOW EMIGRANT GAP	41
HYDRAULIC MINING	42
SACRAMENTO TO SAN FRANCISCO	43

CHAPTER II.—THE CLIMATES.

	Page.
COMPARATIVE METEOROLOGY	45
STANDARDS OF TEMPERATURE	46
METEOROLOGICAL REGIONS	46
SAN FRANCISCO SUMMERS	47
HOT DAYS	48
COOL NIGHTS	49
WARM WINTERS	49
THE EARLY SPRING	51
SAN FRANCISCO RAINS	51
FOG	53
RELATIVE HUMIDITY	54
WARM BELT	57
SACRAMENTO CLIMATE	59
LOS ANGELES CLIMATE	62
OREGON CLIMATE	64
UTAH AND ARIZONA	64
ALASKA'S CLIMATE	65

Chapter III.—CENTRAL CALIFORNIA.

	Page.		Page.
The Pacific Slope	66	Clubs and Libraries	87
Pleasure Resort Districts	66	San Francisco Drives	88
Characteristics	68	San Francisco Picnic Grounds	89
A Mountainous Country	69	Golden Gate Park	89
Geological Convulsions	70	Presidio Reservation	91
Mineral Wealth	70	Point San Jose	91
Peculiar Vegetation	70	Cliff House	92
Flowers	71	Woodward's Garden	93
Field for Sportsmen	71	San Francisco Cemeteries	93
The Californians	72	Chinatown	94
Romance of the Present	72	Joss Houses	95
The Name California	73	Sunday in Chinatown	96
The Missions	73	Chinese Holidays	97
Mexican Dominion	74	Funerals	98
American Settlers	74	Chinese Theatres	99
American Conquest	75	Merchants	100
Rapid Progress	75	Restaurants	100
Californian Agriculture	76	Chinese Missions	100
San Francisco	76	Conveyances	101
The City's Origin	77	Alameda County	101
A City of 100 Hills	77	Oakland	101
Telegraph Hill	79	Lake Merritt	102
San Francisco at Night	80	Sunday Parks	102
A Treeless City	80	Berkeley	102
A Great Seaport	81	Piedmont	103
A Pleasure Resort	81	High Peaks	103
The Streets	82	Drives	103
Architecture	82	Moraga Pass	103
Notable Buildings	83	Telegraph Pass	103
Mint	84	Laundry Farm	104
City Hall	85	Haywards	104
Hotels	85	Alameda	104
Safe Deposit	85	Fruit Vale	105
Stock Exchange	85	Contra Costa	105
Nob Hill	86	Mt. Diablo	105
Churches	87		

TABLE OF CONTENTS.

	Page.		Page.
SAN MATEO	108	VOLCANIC OVERFLOWS	123
PALO ALTO	108	SONOMA VALLEY	124
SUMMER RESORTS	108	RUSSIAN RIVER	125
SANTA CLARA	109	GUERNEVILLE	125
SANTA CLARA TOWNS	110	FORT ROSS	125
PLEASURE RESORTS	111	SONOMA SPRINGS	125
SANTA CRUZ	111	NAPA VALLEY	125
CITY OF SANTA CRUZ	112	NAPA CITY	126
SANTA CRUZ BIG TREES	112	ST. HELENA	126
SANTA CRUZ MOUNTAINS	113	CALISTOGA	127
SANTA CRUZ RUINS	114	MT. ST. HELENA	127
FATA MORGANA	114	EAST-NAPA RIDGE	128
VARIOUS RESORTS	115	LAKE COUNTY	129
MONTEREY	116	CLEAR LAKE	129
TOWN OF MONTEREY	116	BORAX LAKE	129
MONTEREY GROVES	116	THURSTON LAKE	130
HOTEL DEL MONTE	116	COBB VALLEY	130
PACIFIC GROVE RETREAT	117	BLUE LAKES	130
CARMEL MISSION	117	SULPHUR BANK	130
SAN BENITO	118	BARTLETT SPRINGS	130
SAN LUIS OBISPO	118	ADAMS' SPRINGS	131
SAN JOAQUIN VALLEY	118	HARBIN'S SPRINGS	131
MARIN	118	HIGHLAND SPRINGS	131
SAUCELITO	119	OTHER LAKE COUNTY SPRINGS	131
POINT BONITA	119	MENDOCINO	131
SAN RAFAEL	119	HUMBOLDT	131
TAMALPAIS	119	SACRAMENTO	131
VARIOUS RESORTS	120	TEHAMA	132
SONOMA	121	THE FOOTHILLS	132
GEYSERS	121	SHASTA	134
PETRIFIED FOREST	123		

CHAPTER IV.—SOUTHERN CALIFORNIA.

TERRITORY INCLUDED	135	SAN GABRIEL VALLEY	138
LOS ANGELES	136	SIERRA MADRE VILLA	138
SAN GABRIEL MISSION	137	PASADENA, ETC	138

TABLE OF CONTENTS.

	Page.
SANTA BARBARA	139
SANTA BARBARA MISSION	140
MONTECITO	140
HOLLISTER'S RANCHO	141
COOPER'S RANCHO	141
SANTA INEZ VALLEY	141
SANTA BARBARA ISLANDS	141
VENTURA	141
OJAI	142
MATILIJA	142
SAN BERNARDINO	142
SAN BERNARDINO TOWN	144
RIVERSIDE, ETC.	144
SAN BERNARDINO SPRINGS	145
SAN DIEGO COUNTY	145
SAN DIEGO CITY	146
MUD VOLCANOES	146
BELOW SEA LEVEL	147
MISSION OF SAN DIEGO	147
MISSION OF SAN LUIS REY	147
LA JOLLA	147

CHAPTER V.—THE SIERRA NEVADA.

	Page.
THE CHAIN	149
YOSEMITE	151
GENERAL EFFECT	152
A STATE PARK	154
ROUTES	154
PROGRAMME	156
TRAILS	158
THE WALLS	158
THE RIVER	158
FIRST VIEW OF THE VALLEY	159
RIBBON FALL	159
THE CAPITAN	159
THE BRIDAL VEIL	160
CATHEDRAL ROCKS	160
THE THREE BROTHERS	161
THE YOSEMITE FALL	161
SENTINEL ROCK	164
SENTINEL DOME	164
GLACIER POINT	164
ELEVATIONS	164
THE HALF DOME	166
ROYAL ARCHES	166
WASHINGTON COLUMN	166
NORTH DOME	166
MIRROR LAKE	166
VERNAL FALL	166
THE NEVADA FALL	168
CAP OF LIBERTY	168
MT. STARR KING	168
CLOUD'S REST	169
TOOLOOLWEACK FALL	169
SNOW AND HAIL	169
SADDLE HORSE CHARGES	170
CARRIAGE CHARGES	170
GUIDE AND TRAIL CHARGES	170
GUIDES	170
HORSES	171
GUARDIAN OF THE VALLEY	171
YOSEMITE VALLEY	172
METHOD OF FORMATION	172
OTHER YOSEMITIES	173
MOUNTAIN TOPOGRAPHY	174
THE CALIFORNIAN ALPS	175
BIG TREE STATION	176
MARIPOSA BIG TREES	177
THE SIERRA FOREST	178

TABLE OF CONTENTS. 9

	Page.
CALAVERAS BIG TREES	178
OTHER GROVES	180
SHASTA	180
ASCENT OF SHASTA	181
VIEW FROM MOUNT SHASTA	181
DESCENT FROM SHASTA	182
BERRYVALE	182
SCENERY NEAR SHASTA	183
MT. LASSEN	183
SNAG LAKE	183
CINDER CONE	184
RECENT VOLCANIC ACTION	184
BOILING LAKE	185
LASSEN BASALTIC COLUMNS	185
LASSEN GEYSERS	185
ASCENT OF LASSEN	186
COTTONWOOD CAVE	186
REDDING CONES	186
CEDAR PETRIFIED FOREST	186
SIERRA LAVA BEDS	186
MONO LAKE	186
GLACIERS	187

CHAPTER VI.—OREGON, WASHINGTON, ETC.

SCOPE OF CHAPTER	189
COLUMBIA RIVER	189
CASCADE RANGE	189
HOOD RIVER	190
TILLAMOOK BAY	190
CLATSOP BEACH	190
WILHOIT SPRINGS	190
MYSTIC LAKE	190
WASHINGTON	190
PUGET SOUND	192
SNOQUALMIE FALL	192
SEATTLE RESORTS	192
OLYMPIA RESORTS	192
GRAY'S HARBOR	193
ILWACO	193
OYSTERVILLE	193
BRITISH COLUMBIA	193
ALASKA	193
NEW MEXICO	194
ARIZONA	194
RUINS	196

CHAPTER VII.—CAMPING.

OUTDOOR LIFE	197
CAMPING TOURS	198
TIME FOR CAMPING	198
SADDLES	198
TENTS	200
PERSONAL OUTFIT	200
PROVISIONS	200
COOKING UTENSILS	201
TABLE WARE	201
BEDDING	201
TOOLS	201
BOOKS ON CAMPING	201
THE CAMPING PARTY	202
SANTA CRUZ CAMPING TOUR	202
MARIN CAMPING TOUR	203
HUNTING	204

TABLE OF CONTENTS.

	Page.		Page.
BEAR	205	TURKEY	206
BUFFALO	205	GROUSE	207
DEER	205	QUAIL	207
RABBITS, ETC.	206	PIGEONS	207
WILD HOGS, ETC.	206	WATER FOWL	207
CARNIVOROUS ANIMALS	206	FISH	208

CHAPTER VIII.—HAWAIIAN ISLANDS.

THE GROUP	209	MOLOKAI	212
HONOLULU	209	LANAI	213
TOUR OF OAHU	210	HAWAII	213
MAUI	211	KAUAI	216

CHAPTER IX.—MINERAL SPRINGS.

MEDICINAL VALUE	218	THERMAL SPRINGS	225
LOCALITIES OF SPRINGS	219	THERMAL SPRINGS, TABLE OF	226
CHEMISTS	219	SULPHUR SPRINGS	226
ALKALINE SPRINGS	219	SULPHUR SPRINGS, TABLE OF	227
ALKALINE SPRINGS, TABLE OF	220	OTHER SPRINGS	228
PURGATIVE WATERS	222	GENERAL REMARKS	228
PURGATIVE SPRINGS, TABLE OF	223		

CHAPTER X.—DISTANCES, PRICES, ETC.

EXPLANATIONS	230	STEAMBOAT ROUTES	266
DISTANCES FROM SAN FRANCISCO	232	RULES FOR TRAVELERS	267

CHAPTER I.

NEW YORK TO SAN FRANCISCO.

Routes.—Six main rail routes connect the Atlantic slope of the continent with the coast of the Pacific—the Southern in latitude 32°; the Atlantic and Pacific in 35°; the Central in 40°; the Union Short Line in 44°; the Northern in 48°; and the Canadian in 50°. The Southern, Northern, and Canadian extend eastward to the meridian of New Orleans or beyond; the others reach only to about the meridian of Salt Lake, connecting there with numerous other roads, including the Union Pacific, Denver and Rio Grande, Atchison, Topeka, and Santa Fé, Missouri Pacific, etc. The terminal seaports on the waters of the Pacific are Vancouver, Tacoma, Portland, San Francisco, Wilmington, San Diego, Guaymas, and to this list Yaquina will soon be added by the Oregon Pacific.

The Steamer Route.—The trip from New York to San Francisco, by way of Panamá, occupies from 25 to 28 days, there being a difference of several days in the length of the alternate trips. One steamer touches at a certain list of intermediate ports on the Western Coast of Mexico and Central America, and the next one visits another list, so that all are accommodated within a month. The traveler should make careful inquiry about the time to be spent on the Isthmus, and select the trip that hurries him through or gives him a day or two of delay there, according to his wishes. The scenery along the line of the Panamá Railway is very luxuriant in some of the most brilliant forms and colors of tropical vegetation; and the city of Panamá is an interesting sample of Spanish-American life in a hot climate. The charge for first-class passage is usually the same on the steamer from New York to San Francisco as on the railroad, but on the latter the traveler must pay for sleeping car and meals in addition. The charge in steamer steerage is the same as in the emigrant car on the rail. The steamer passenger can take 200 pounds of baggage in the cabin and 150 in the steerage—and here he has another advantage over the traveler by rail.

Southern Pacific.—The Southern Pacific has its main terminations at San Francisco and New Orleans, the distance being 2449 miles, and the time 5 days and 22 hours, without regard to the differences of meridian. The apparent duration of the trip is 6 days and one hour going eastward; and 5 days and 19 hours going westward. The greater part of the route is through a dry, desolate, and uninteresting country; but in Southern California there is much most beautiful scenery.

Atlantic and Pacific.—The main line of the Atlantic and Pacific extends from the Rio Grande to Mojave, so that the company is dependent at present on other roads for access to the main terminal points at the east and the west. The Grand Canyon of the Colorado near the road, and the peculiar villages of the Pueblo Indians, some of them built on the face of steep cliffs are among the most noted scenes on the route. The region traversed is arid and very unattractive in general character.

Northern Pacific.—The Northern Pacific has its main terminations now at Minneapolis and Tacoma. The scenery from the Mississippi westward is more varied and interesting on this route than on any of the other transcontinental roads, the region traversed being better supplied with rains, rivers, grass, and timber. Clarke's Fork east of Pend d'Oreille Lake, and the Columbia River from Des Chutes westward, has each, for a distance of more than a hundred miles, a constant succession of views, remarkable for their beauty and their grandeur. The abundance of verdure and forest, the number of large and impetuous streams, and the snow-covered cones rising in solitary grandeur a mile and a half above the level of the adjacent ridges, are notable features of this route, and will ever command the favor of sight-seers.

Central-Union Pacific.—Of the various routes from New York to San Francisco, the shortest, by way of Chicago, Omaha, and Ogden, is 3332 miles in length, and requires 6 days and 10 hours for the trip by the express trains. Some remarks about railroad time will be found in the last chapter.

Omaha to Cheyenne.—At Council Bluffs your baggage will be re-checked, and crossing the Missouri on an iron bridge 2750 feet long, in 11 spans of 250 feet each, supported by 10 high piers—a structure that cost $2,650,000—you reach Omaha, a thriving city of 30,000 inhabitants, in Nebraska.

From Omaha the Union Pacific Railroad runs in the Platte basin for nearly 500 miles. The name "Platte" is the French for flat, and was given by Canadian hunters because the stream for much of its length is broad, shallow, and flows but little below the wide, level valley. It is pre-eminently the flat river. From Valley station, 35 miles west of Omaha, the Omaha and Republican Valley Railroad branches off south-westerly, running to Lincoln and Stromsburg, distances of about 75 and 100 miles respectively. From Duncan, 64 miles further west, a branch road is built about 125 miles in a north-westerly direction to Willow Springs, and another about 50 miles north of Norfolk. At Grand Island Station, 154 miles from Omaha, connection is made with the St. Joseph Line, and also with the Grand Island and St. Paul Road, running northwest about 100 miles to New St. Helena.

The track, at the Omaha station, 966 feet above the sea, ascends with an average grade of about 6¾ feet to the mile to Denver Junction, 3,500 feet above the sea. For 200 miles from the Missouri the road runs through a district of rich and moist soil, well tilled in productive farms; then the country becomes poorer, the farms smaller and rarer, and at Denver Junction we have reached the pastoral region.

Although we are at a high elevation, and are ascending the Rocky Mountains, we see no high peaks, no forests, nor indeed anything that reminds us of the proximity of a great continental divide, though in length, number of high peaks, and many other respects, the one we are approaching is the greatest on the globe. The country about us is less mountainous in appearance than in the Alleghanies, the summit of which on the Pennsylvania Railroad is below the level of Denver Junction. From the last named station, which is 371 miles from Omaha, a branch road, running about 200 miles in a south-westerly direction, connects Denver, Colorado, with the Union Pacific Railroad.

Julesburg, or Weir, 377 miles from Omaha, is the residence of Mr. Iliff, who has a herd of 26,000 head of neat cattle, which pasture over a district 150 miles long. About 5,000 head of fat cattle are sold annually, bringing an average of $140,000. From Sidney, 43 miles west of Denver Junction, stages run to Deadwood, 267 miles distant, and much freight is sent to the Black Hills mines. Journeying on 89 miles, we pass a small station called Atkins, and on a clear day can begin to see the high peaks of the Rocky Mountains. Southward 160 miles is Pike's Peak, whose summit, 14,147 feet above the sea, is 12 miles west of the meridian of Cheyenne, and 156 miles south of its latitude. This peak is not on the main ridge of the Rocky Mountains; the waters from all its sides flow to the Atlantic. South-westward is Long's Peak, 14,271 feet high, and the highest point on the main divide of the continent visible from the road. It is 75 miles south-west of Cheyenne, and occupies the angle in the most notable bend of the chain. From the Mexican boundary the divide runs for 600 miles to the east of north, till it reaches this peak, when it turns to the north-west, which general direction it follows till it reaches Alaska. The mountains to the north are the Black Hills; and in a southerly direction, the Spanish Peaks, respectively 13,620 and 12,720 feet in height, are seen lower in the horizon and more distant. We cross the Nebraska line about 470 miles from Omaha, shortly before reaching Pine Bluffs, and enter Wyoming at its south-east corner. The peaks seen to the south are in Colorado; Elk is in Wyoming, and the Black Hills in Dakota. In this region intense cold prevails in the winter, and snow falls in sufficient quantity to give much trouble to the railroad superintendents. The road in this vicinity is protected in many places by fences built on its windward side, and under their lee the drifting snow collects before it reaches the rails. A short distance east of Cheyenne we go through the first snow-shed, a building which in winter, when covered with snow, looks like a tunnel, and in summer, like a bridge built in a dry cut.

Cheyenne to Creston.—Since leaving Denver Junction the ascent of the mountain slope has become steeper, averaging for 139 miles 18 feet to the mile, until 516 miles from the Missouri, and 6,041 feet above the sea, we reach Cheyenne, the largest and busiest town on the line of the main road between Omaha and Sacramento. This town owes its prosperity to the combined influences of the junction of the Denver Pacific and Colorado Central roads with the Union Pacific, the extensive workshops of the company owning the road last mentioned, the terminal business of an important wagon road from the Black Hills, the proximity of the national military post, Fort Russell, 3 miles distant, and its selection as the Territorial capital of Wyoming. Cheyenne is also connected by railroad with Fort Laramie, 89 miles to the north, and is distant 106 miles from Denver, the capital of Colorado. It has 5,000 inhabitants, an active business, and many substantial buildings. It is situated exactly half way between Omaha and Ogden.

At Cheyenne commences the longest stretch of steep ascending grade on the road in our westward course. For 33 miles the average ascent is $66\frac{1}{2}$ feet to the mile, ending at Sherman, the highest railroad station on the continent, 8,242 feet, or more than one and a half miles above the sea. When first opened in 1868 this was the highest railroad station in the world; but others still higher have since been constructed in South America. Sherman is 549 miles from Omaha, and its superior height might lead the tourist to infer that it is on the summit of the main divide; but it is on a spur which runs out to the northward, between the headwaters of the South Platte and of the Laramie rivers, the latter a tributary of the North Platte. Two miles west of Sherman the road crosses the canyon of Dale Creek on an iron bridge or trestle work 650 feet long and 130 feet high. Near Sherman are some piles of granite known as Skull Rocks.

From Sherman we descend with an average grade of $46\frac{1}{2}$ feet to the mile, for 24 miles to Laramie; the direction of the road having changed from the west, to north-north-west, which direction we take for about 60 miles.

Red Buttes Station, 15 miles from Sherman, is so named because of some pinnacles of fantastic shape, north of the road. They rise to a height of 600 or 800 feet above the level of the adjacent land and probably owe their elevation to superior hardness, the softer material that surrounded them in a remote past having been washed away.

The Medicine Bow Range and its chief peak, Sheep Butte, 9,722 feet high, are visible in the west. At Red Buttes we have reached the Laramie plain, from 6,500 to 7,500 feet high, and 60 miles long by 40 miles wide. It is the most northerly of a series of similar high valleys in the Rocky Mountains, surrounded by ridges considerably higher. The most notable of the sister valleys, the others being called "Parks," are superior in timber and scenery, but inferior in indigenous pasturage. The town of Laramie has a population of 4,000, and the only rolling-mill between Omaha and Ogden. Looking westward from Laramie we see Sheep Butte with Mount Agassiz on its left. Besides cattle, large flocks of sheep graze on the adjacent plains.

Cooper's Lake Station, 27 miles west from Laramie, is named from a lake about 2 miles long and half a mile wide, visible from the water tank.

At Lookout, about 5 miles further on, we may observe a grayish green shrub, with a trunk which appears as if it had been split by twisting, and leaves which have an unpleasant odor. This is the sage brush, a common feature in the landscape for the next 1,000 miles. Soon after leaving Lookout, we get a view of Laramie Peak, 10,000 feet high, to the northward; and, at the same time, the Medicine Bow Range is in plain sight on the other side of the road, Elk Mountain, its principal peak, being 11,511 feet high.

After passing Aurora Station, 55 miles from Laramie, the traveler can see Como Lake, 3 miles long and 1 mile wide. It is fed by warm springs, and abounds with newts—lizard-like amphibia, which can breathe under water, and live in the open air. They attain a length of 18 inches, and sometimes may be caught on the rocks.

Medicine Bow River, which we cross beyond Aurora, runs northward, and is a tributary of the North Platte. Beyond Medicine Bow Station we get a good view of Elk Mountain, which, however, is seen to the best advantage from Percy, 15 miles beyond.

Carbon derives its name from valuable coal mines in its vicinity. The principal vein is 10 feet thick and the annual product is about 100,000 tons.

At Separation, 722 miles from Omaha, water is obtained from an artesian well 860 feet deep. There are many of these wells along the line. Approaching Creston we have a good view, and the last one, of Elk Mountain and of the Black Hills. Shortly after leaving it, we see the Wind River Mountains, with Fremont's Peak, 13,570 feet high, to the northwestward. Pilot Butte is visible to the west.

Creston to Granger.—West of Creston 2½ miles, and 89½ miles from Sherman, we reach the main divide between the two oceans at an elevation of about 1,140 feet less than that of the last named station. As the water flowing eastward from Creston reaches the Atlantic through the North Platte, 1,200 feet of ascent could have been saved by following up the canyon of that stream, but the greater distance, the more costly grading and the steeper grades on that route, in the opinion of the railroad engineers, more than counterbalanced all its advantages in other respects. The waters flowing westward from Creston go to the Green River, a tributary of the Colorado, and so find their way to the Gulf of California. Of all the large rivers of the temperate zone, the Colorado is the one that has the greatest amount of desert and the smallest proportion of land suitable for tillage, in its basin. It receives all the waters flowing down the western flank of the Rocky Mountains through 10 degrees of latitude, and has not anywhere a tract 10 miles square of fertile and moist soil suitable for tillage in all its basin. Indeed, through a great part of its length it has no valley, but instead, an immense if not an unparalleled canyon, more than a mile deep between nearly vertical walls of rock for a long distance. The scenery about Creston does not suggest the summit of a great mountain range. The road is not steep, nor when it has reached the top does it find a narrow gateway. Looking southward from Creston we seem to be in a wide plain, but this is Bridger's Pass, and Bridger's Station is on the old stage road at the base of the distant hills.

Red Desert Station is in a little alkaline basin with a scanty rainfall and no outlet to the sea, at least none in ordinary seasons.

Table Rock Station is named after a steep bluff, 600 feet high, with a level top, south of the road.

Bitter Creek Station is in a valley which we follow down 60 miles to Green River. The waters of Bitter Creek derive their name from their alkaline taste which is strongest when the stream is low. The scenery in some parts of the valley is interesting.

When approaching Black Buttes Station, observe the large, loose rock north of the road, and about 20 yards distant. The station derives its name from some hills that may be seen to the southward.

Point of Rocks is named from some columns of stone, the summits of which are 350 feet above their bases, and 1,100 feet above the road. At the base of these columns there are 7 springs of sulphur and several of iron-water. From an artesian well, 1,000 feet deep, water is pumped by steam to supply the station. There are productive coal mines near Point of Rocks, and also strata of rock containing remarkable petrifactions of oyster shells, and of the leaves of elm, maple and fan-palm trees.

Rock Spring has an artesian well 1,145 feet deep, and in the vicinity there are productive coal mines. Here the cars enter the deeper portion of the gorge of Bitter Creek, where we are in sight of wild scenery for 13 miles ending at Green River.

The village of Green River, at the crossing of that stream, has 500 inhabitants. Here moss agates and samples of petrified wood and fish may be found for sale in the stores. East of the river and north of the bridge are remarkable cliffs of sandstone. This rock formation consists of thin strata in which numerous petrifactions occur. In many places near the river, rock columns of singular shape have been left by erosion. Among these the most notable are Castle Rock, the Twin Sisters, the Giant's Club and the Giant's Teapot.

When approaching Bryan, 13 miles from Green River Crossing, by looking to the south and southeast, we obtain a view of the summit of the Uinta Mountains, a high ridge running nearly east and west from the Wasatch to the Rocky chain, except where intersected by Green River, and about 70 miles south of the road. At Bryan we strike Black's Fork of Green River, and follow it up with an ascending grade for 30 miles. Near Marston may be seen hills with vertical sides, looking like towers.

Granger to Evanston.—The Oregon Short Line, branching off from the Union Pacific at Granger, runs northwestward to Umatilla on the Columbia River, where it connects with the Northern Pacific route. The distance is 757 miles. After passing Granger, excellent views of the snow-covered Uintas are obtained.

Church Buttes Station is named from a remarkable hill about 10 miles south of the road, with vertical walls worn by the water to resemble long lines of columns. Moss agates are more abundant here and at Granger than at any other stations.

Within a radius of 20 miles from Carter are numerous coal beds and springs of sulphur and chalybeate waters. Fort Bridger, a national military post, is 10 miles from this station to the southward. In the neighborhood there is much game, including grouse, deer and bear. Bridger Station, and also the Fort, are named after a noted trapper and guide, who died in 1875, when nearly 80 years of age, after spending most of his life in the Rocky Mountains.

After leaving Piedmont look out on the left to see the track and the snow-sheds. The longest shed on the Union Pacific, more than half a mile in length, is found on the summit, two miles west from Aspen, which has an elevation of 7,835 feet. The ridge which we cross here—the eastern boundary of the Utah Inclosed Basin—called by some persons the Uinta range, is properly the Wasatch. It is worthy of note that this mountain is higher on the line of the railroad from Omaha to San Francisco than either the Sierra Nevada or the main divide of the Rocky chain.

Aspen Station is named from Quaking Aspen Mountain, 8,688 feet high, seen in the north.

At Hilliard Station the train passes under a V flume, the first on the road. It has a current of water which conveys timber, lumber and firewood from the forest on the side of the mountains, a distance of 24 miles, in which it descends 2,000 feet.

Many Sulphur Springs are found at distances within 20 miles from Hilliard. Soon after leaving Millis, four miles west of Hilliard, we come to Bear River, which we follow for two miles and then cross. This stream rises on the western slope of the Wasatch

Mountains, flows nearly due north 200 miles, and then making a sharp turn runs as far nearly due south, and empties into Salt Lake, of which it is an important tributary. A branch of Bear River widens out into Bear Lake, 15 miles long and 7 wide, one of the few fresh water lakes in the Utah Basin. From the Bend to Snake River the distance is only 50 miles, and there is no high intervening ridge.

Evanston to Ogden.—Evanston, on the bank of Bear River, just half way between Omaha and San Francisco, 957 miles from either terminus, has 1,500 inhabitants, most of whom obtain their support from lumbering and coal mining industries. The chief coal mines are 3 miles from the Union Pacific to the northward, and are reached by a branch road. The line between Wyoming and Utah crosses the road west of Evanston, and is marked by a sign which stands on the south side of the track, and has "Wyoming" on one side and "Utah" on the other.

The Utah Inclosed Basin, one of the remarkable features of the world's topography, has no outlet for its waters. Its rivers flow into salt lakes, which rise every winter on account of the rains, and fall every summer under the influence of evaporation. There are also irregular periods, that may last from 5 to 20 years of predominant rise, alternating with other periods of fall. Not more than 2 per cent. of the whole area is covered by water. This great basin is divided into many smaller subordinate basins, which never, since they were observed by white men, have sent any water to the sea, or to any of the adjacent basins, and never will, so long as the present climatic conditions continue.

The most notable of the subordinate basins are those of Salt and Sevier lakes in Utah; of Humboldt, Pyramid and Walker's lakes in Nevada; of Owens, Mono, Amargosa, Mojave, Seven Palms and Honey lakes in California, and of Harney in Oregon. Some of these lakes are also called "sinks" of their streams, the water of which spreads out in the winter over a considerable space of flat ground, and in August or September, after a dry summer, almost disappears. Our road takes us through the basins of Salt, Humboldt and Pyramid lakes, for a distance of 631 miles. The soil and atmosphere are too dry for vigorous vegetation, except in a few places where there are facilities for irrigation, and the Utah Basin, as a whole, is a desert. It includes portions of California, Oregon, Idaho, Utah and Nevada, but not all of any one of these political divisions.

At Castle Rock, 20 miles from Evanston, we enter the canyon of Echo Creek, which we follow down 30 miles to the larger canyon of Weber River, and in that we have an equal distance to travel, making 60 miles of canyon, with steep rock walls, which have many strange forms and colors, with a height that often rises to nearly 2,000 feet. The crooked course of the canyon, and the wildness of its rocky scenery, make this one of the most interesting portions of the road. We enter the canyon nearly on a level with the top of its walls, and gradually descend as it gets deeper. It is customary at Castle Rock to attach an observation car at the end of the train, so that passengers can have a view not obstructed in any direction, save in front where the other cars are. Castle Rock is so named from a rock resembling a tower with a large gateway east of the station, and near it are some needle-shaped rocks. Perhaps a mile west of the station are The Swallows' Nests, a name given to some holes high up in the rocky wall of the canyon. Most of the attractive scenes are on the north side of the canyon. Near Emory is Hanging Rock, a point at the summit of a high cliff, projecting several hundred feet over the valley beneath. Seven miles below Hanging Rock we come to Steamboat Rock, or the Great Eastern, a high point which bears some resemblance to the prow of a large

PULPIT ROCK.

ocean steamer. Just before reaching Echo Station, and near the bend of a bluff called Bromley's Cathedral, on the right of the road is Pulpit Rock, the summit of which is about 60 feet above the track. It derives its name from its supposed resemblance to an old-fashioned pulpit.

Echo Station, at the mouth of Echo Creek, is noted for the echoes which suggested the name. A square column of rock, perhaps 50 feet thick and 250 high, styled the Monument, is one of the remarkable features of the canyon. Branch railroads run from Echo south to Coalville and to Park City. Coal-beds'are worked in this vicinity and yield at present about 400 tons daily. Some irregular columns, yellow, reddish and gray in color, about 100 yards north from the road, and as far above its level, are known as the Witches' Rocks. Four miles below Echo, the train enters the Narrows, and soon passes a solitary fir tree with a sign "1,000 miles from Omaha." Below this tree the road crosses to the south bank of the river, and oack again to the north bank, and then we come in sight of the Devil's Slide, where two parallel, vertical strata of rock, each about 15 feet in thickness, and as far apart, project in places 100 feet or more from the steep side of the canyon, leaving a deep trough between them.

At Weber Station, 25 miles east of Ogden, the traveler may observe a sign, "Z. C. M. I," which is prominent in many of the Mormon towns. It means "Zion's Co-operative Mercantile Institution." The Latter-Day Saints have made a remarkable success in trading on the co-operative principle, and a branch of this "institution" is to be found in all their large towns. Devil's Gate, at the lower end of Weber Canyon, is one of the grand scenes on the route, and then we emerge out into the valley of Salt Lake, and 13 miles beyond we reach Ogden, the point where the Union Pacific road ends and the Central Pacific begins. It is, moreover, a terminus of the Utah and Northern Railroad, which is completed as far as Silver Bow, Montana, 400 miles; and of the Utah Central which runs south 280 miles, to Frisco, Utah, making 689 miles of road nearly on the meridian, crossing the line of the Union and Central Pacific at right angles. Ogden has a population of 6,000, most of whom are Mormons. Situated at the southern base of steep mountains, the summits of which are covered with snow most of the year, it is 4340 feet above the sea, and 1,032 miles west of Omaha. A small canyon in the mountains back of Ogden, has pleasant scenery and deserves a visit from the tourist having a day at his disposal.

Yellowstone Park.—Ogden is also the best point from which to reach the Yellowstone Park, a National Reservation, containing within its limits many natural wonders. The visitor leaving Ogden by the Utah and Northern Railway, crosses the Ogden River, and after a ride of 9 miles reaches Hot Springs Station, where there are several mineral springs, the temperature of the water being 125°.

About 3 miles north of Richmond, and 74 miles from Ogden, we cross the line separating Utah from Idaho.

At Arimo, 125 miles north of Ogden, we find a stage running to the Great Soda Springs, 35 miles east of the railroad, and near the bend of Bear River. There are about a dozen of these springs, all of them surrounded with a whitish deposit of lime. One of the springs blows out steam at intervals. The waters are considered valuable for their medicinal qualities, and it is expected that when better known, they will attract a great number of people. A small hotel provides accommodation for visitors.

At Eagle Rock, 204 miles from Ogden, the road crosses Snake River, which here, 250 feet deep, affords fine salmon-trout fishing. Near Spring Hill Station, 300 miles from Ogden, we enter Montana.

At Dillon, 348 miles from Ogden, we take stage for Virginia City, 84 miles distant, each passenger being allowed 40 pounds of baggage.

From Virginia City to the hotel in the park, the distance is 95 miles, and the time 16 hours by stage.

The park embraces an area of about 3,400 square miles, being rectangular in shape, with sides 54 by 64 miles; the east and west line being the shorter one. On entering by the Virginia City Road the visitor first comes upon hot springs, and then sees the lower group of the Fire Hole River Geysers, the upper group being about 10 miles distant from the lower. Between the two groups is the Midway Basin where are some of the largest hot springs known. The Upper Basin contains the principal geysers which are 8 in number, with jets, in some instances, 18 feet in diameter, 250 feet high, bursting out at intervals of an hour or more, and lasting from 20 to 30 minutes. We then go to Yellowstone Lake, a sheet of water 20 miles long, over 15 wide, and 7,427 feet above the sea. It is studded with tree-clad islands, and abounds with fish. On the western shore of the lake are hot springs, one of which is so near the lake that it is possible for an angler to catch a trout, and, turning in his tracks, drop the fish into the hot water and cook it there. The outlet of the lake—the Yellowstone River—is at its northern extremity, and passing down the stream 18 miles, we come upon the Upper Fall, measuring 140 feet in height. Near this point Cascade Creek falls 129 feet. Less than a mile below the Upper Falls we reach the Great Fall, where the river makes a descent of more than 350 feet, and then flows for 30 miles through a canyon whose walls are 1,500 feet high in places. Near the northern line of the park are the Mammoth Springs, the most remarkable group of hot springs known. Good views of mountain peaks, over 10,000 feet high, can be had at several points.

Salt Lake City.—Ogden, however, is a point of interest to many travelers, chiefly on account of its position at a terminus of the Utah Central Railroad, which leads to the Holy City of the Latter Day Saints, 37 miles to the southward.

At Summit Station, 8 miles from Ogden, we are in the region from which Salt Lake Valley derives its supply of coal.

At Centreville, 26 miles from Ogden, the lake approaches nearest to the mountains.

The road from Ogden to Salt Lake City is nearly level, and runs half way between the mountains and the lake, which are about 10 miles apart. The soil is fertile, but some of it, not provided with water for irrigation, is covered with sage brush. Most of the small towns along the road are supported by agricultural regions, and orchards are plentiful in all settlements. The following extract from *Through the Rocky Mountains*, by A. K. McClure, is introduced as being here pertinent. "One of the first duties required [of a Mormon] when a new farm is opened, is the planting of all kinds of fruit, and the result is that in every settlement the houses are first recognized by the clusters of green foliage or fragrant blossoms that surround them. As an industrial system the Mormon Church is a positive success, and challenges the admiration of the most embittered foes of this peculiar religious faith. I did not see a single home of a Mormon where there were signs of dilapidation or decay."

Salt Lake City "lies at the north-west base of a spur of the Wasatch Mountains, 12 miles from the south-east extremity of the Great Salt Lake, with an expansion to the south of more than 100 miles of plains." It has an area of 5,730 acres, with 25,000 inhabitants, and an elevation of 4,300 feet above the sea, and 50 feet above the level of the lake. The straight streets, 132 feet wide, cross each other at right angles, and most of them have a small current of clear water and a row of trees along the edge of each sidewalk. The blocks, containing 10 acres each, are about 700 feet square, and their greater part, except in the business portion of the city, is occupied with gardens and orchards. The houses have a look of solidity and comfort; the business of the city is active, and there are many evidences of growth. The most notable building is the Tabernacle, 250 feet long by 150 feet wide, with an arched roof 65 feet high in the middle. On the main floor and its galleries there is space for 8,000 people, and in its acoustic design it is superior to any other large hall in the United States, and probably on the globe. A good speaker, even if his voice is not strong, can be distinctly heard in all parts of the hall. It contains a fine organ, made in the city, and mostly of material produced in Utah. The Tabernacle is the principal place of Mormon worship, and tourists spending Sunday in the city should not neglect to attend the services.

On the same block with the Tabernacle is the Temple, which is to be 184 feet long by 116 wide, and about 96 feet high, exclusive of the towers, the spires of which will reach an elevation of 192 feet. The interior is to be 120 by 80 feet, and the building will cost, it is said, $15,000,000. A quarter of a century has elapsed since its foundation was laid, and at least three-fourths of the work are still to be done. The Stake Tabernacle, the Theatre, the City Hall, and the building of the Zion's Co-operative Mercantile Institution, are among the most prominent buildings. The principal hotels are the Townsend and Walker houses. Within the city limits, and only a mile from the principal hotels, and accessible by horse-cars for those who do not wish to walk, are some warm springs, supplied with comfortable bath-houses, where the Russian or Turkish baths can be obtained by those not content with the natural water, which has common salt and sulphate of magnesia among its mineral constituents, and a luke-warm temperature. A mile beyond the Warm Springs are the Hot Springs, which have a temperature of 200°.

Camp Douglas, a national military post, 2 miles east of the city, on elevated ground, commands a beautiful view.

The high mountains are near the city, and grand in their forms. One of the favorite pleasure resorts for the people of Salt Lake City, is Lake Point, on the shore of the lake, 20 miles distant. It has a hotel, bath-houses, a nice beach, and is reached by the Utah Western Railway, which is completed to Stockton, 19 miles beyond the Point. A small pleasure steamer makes the tour of the lake when parties so desire.

Great Salt Lake is 80 miles long, about 50 wide, and 4,200 feet above the sea. It has mountain views on three sides, and several islands dot its surface. Advantage has been taken of the density of its waters, and from 10,000 to 15,000 tons of excellent salt are annually produced by evaporating the brine in tanks, into which the water is lifted by pumps.

The tourist when visiting Salt Lake City, will be led naturally to reflect upon the strange religion of the people among whom he finds himself. Mormonism is one of the wonders of the XIXth century, and a most unnatural product of a skeptical age, in a land of the highest average of popular intelligence. Many forms of ancient superstitions may have been the natural and innocent developments of imaginative ignorance and credulity, but every intelligent person who carefully reads the history of the founder of Mormonism without becoming a convert to his doctrines—this expression admits that intelligent and sincere men are to be found among its converts—is satisfied that his so-called revelations are a studied fraud, devised to aggrandize himself by giving him control of the faith and money of his followers. His scheme was well devised for his purpose, and partly on account of the sound judgment, steadfast courage, and eminent tact of his successor, Brigham Young, it has secured a foothold that seems to be permanent. But prejudice against Mormonism should not blind the observer to the good points of the Mormons. No other community has done more, with equal means, in the same space of time. After they had been persecuted and mobbed in Illinois and Missouri, they determined to establish a home beyond the Rocky Mountains, where they would have the predominance and could defend themselves. On the 24th of July, 1847, Brigham Young, with 151 other Mormons, encamped on the place now occupied by the Mormon Temple, in Salt Lake City, when the territory still belonged to Mexico, or at least had not been ceded to the United States. There the Mormon President determined to build the Holy City of his Church, and there it has been built. Poverty, privation and arduous toil have been the lot of his followers generally, but they have enjoyed peace and increasing prosperity. Their numbers and productive industries have shown a constant and large growth. In their methods of settling disputes by arbitration, and of conducting mercantile business by co-operation, they are unequaled. They have less drunkenness, less gambling, and fewer public women than any other American community. These are undeniable and important facts. Their "plural marriages," as they call it, objectionable as it may be, is not associated with slavery, concubinage and the seclusion and gross ignorance of the women, as in Mohammedan countries. They have a good common school system, and do not discourage free inquiry. Their church members are allowed to read, and their bookstores to sell books attacking their creed; they even go so far as to open their churches for discussions with Christian clergymen. They have few lawyers, and few criminals. The administration of justice is prompt and cheap; the Courts do not make themselves ridiculous by trying cases over half a dozen times. Their leaders have been men of serious character and of superior capacity. When President Buchanan devised a plan for diverting attention from the slavery question, by getting up a Mormon war, Brigham defied, outwitted and frightened him. The Mormons have been accused of general responsibility for numerous murders and thefts, but such charges when made against an extensive community, living in laborious poverty, with unexampled harmony and mutual helpfulness, rebound against the malignity or prejudice of the accusers. The loudest denouncers of the Mormons are men who have never examined the evidence needed to support their assertions, and do not understand the importance of weighing both sides with an impartial mind. Until the tourist finds conclusive proof that the Mormon community, or its leaders, as a body, are responsible for serious crimes, let him look upon the error of belief here established as one of the singular phases of humanity—as on Mohammedanism—a step in the march of our race, not necessarily indicative of any moral obliquity or grave mental inferiority on the part of its adherents. Some Mormon women dislike polygamy, but generally they avoid conversation with strangers on the subject, for fear that they will have to hear offensive remarks about their religion, and they believe that the women, as a class, are happier in Utah than in any other part of the world. The signs of poverty are far more abundant than those of discontent.

One chief trouble in the way of the Mormon Church is the promise of our National Government to suppress polygamy, the practice of which, however, does not seem essential to the perpetuation and spread of the creed.

Since the death of Brigham Young, John Taylor has been the head of the Mormon Church. George Q. Cannon, who will probably come next in the order of succession is considerably younger, and by many persons is considered the ablest man now in the hierarchy.

According to a newspaper report, Mr. Cannon gives 2,500 as his estimate of the number of polygamous families in Utah, averaging three wives to each. In a few cases, one husband has twelve wives. Brigham Young had a larger number.

From Salt Lake Southward.—The road bearing the tourist south of Salt Lake City, a continuation of the one that brought him into it, is known as the Utah Southern Railroad. Its general course is up the Jordan Valley and along the eastern shore of Utah Lake. The scenery is varied; to the east the peaks of the Wasatch range, and on the other hand a succession of cultivated farms, with thriving villages interspersed.

At Junction, 12 miles south of the Mormon metropolis, the Bingham Canyon and Camp Floyd Narrow Gauge Railroad leaves our line and leads to the south-west about 20 miles, to the Bingham Canyon mines. The principal business is transporting ores, and the traveler can visit the silver mines by this route without discomfort.

Sandy, a mile further south, is the point of junction with the Wasatch and Jordan Valley Railroad, also a narrow gauge line. This road runs into Little Cottonwood Canyon, 17 miles in an easterly direction to Alta. Between Wasatch Station and Alta the grade is so steep, in one place (nearly 600 feet to the mile), that a locomotive engine cannot be used, and the cars are drawn by animals. Returning, the descent is made under the impulse of gravity. This portion of the road is completely covered by snow-sheds. There are falls in the canyon, and the general scenery is wild.

In places where the approach to a mine is too steep for the use of ordinary vehicles, ore is brought down in a sack of ox hide, drawn by mules. The granite for the temple at Salt Lake City is quarried near Wasatch. Between Draper and Lehi, both farming villages, the tourist comes in sight of Utah Lake, 30 miles long, 6 to 10 wide, and 500 feet above Great Salt Lake. To the south is Mount Nebo, 11,992 feet high, the loftiest peak of the Wasatch range.

At a distance of 34 miles from Salt Lake City we reach American Fork, an incorporated city having about 2,000 inhabitants. From this point a narrow gauge road formerly ran 17 miles to Deer Creek in American Fork Canyon, but the mines with which it connected having proved unprofitable, the rails were taken up. The canyon, with steep walls, 3,000 feet high in places, and wild scenery, is well worth a visit. The wagon road in the canyon is good.

Provo, 48 miles from Salt Lake City, is a city of 5,000 inhabitants, situated on the Provo River, a tributary of Utah Lake. Here are the largest woolen mills between Omaha and San Francisco.

Springville, the terminus of the Utah and Pleasant Valley Narrow Gauge Railroad, running to the Pleasant Valley coal mines, has a population of 2,500, and is 53 miles from Salt Lake City.

From Santaquin, our next station, it is about 15 miles to the Tintic silver mining district, where several stamp mills and smelters may be seen in operation.

At Nephi, 91 miles south of Salt Lake City, we have an excellent view of Mount Nebo.

After leaving Juab we enter the Sevier River Valley, and crossing the river follow down on its left bank. This stream, rising in the Wasatch range, flows northward about 100 miles, then making a bend runs southward 50 miles to Sevier Lake, a sheet of salt water 20 miles long, 10 miles wide at its widest point, and 4,600 feet above the sea.

At Milford, 226 miles from Salt Lake City, our road tends to the westward, and 17 miles beyond we reach the present end of the track.

Frisco (named after San Francisco by an abbreviation in common use), a mining town, situated at the eastern base of the San Francisco Mountains, is chiefly notable as being the nearest point to the celebrated Horn Silver Mine, a vein of ore remarkable for its size, general uniformity of assay, and large production.

We are now in a subtropical climate, and the surrounding valleys produce cotton, tobacco, rice, grapes, and fruits ranging from the apple to the pomegranate.

From Ogden to Palisade.—From Ogden westward to San Francisco the trains run on Pacific standard time, which is one hour behind that used from Omaha to Ogden. After going 8 miles we pass the Hot Springs, the stream of which rising at the foot of the mountain, may be seen from the cars in cold weather. Corinne, 25 miles from Ogden, is a Gentile town (all persons not of their faith are termed by the Mormons Gentiles), and the only one of note in Utah under gentile control.

Promontory, 53 miles from Ogden, is the place where the last spike was driven, May 10th, 1869, connecting the Central and Union Pacific railroads, and completing the track from the Sacramento to the Missouri rivers. Communication with the wires at the roadside was so made that the blows of the hammer with which the spike was driven were telegraphed to the expectant people in all the great cities of the nation. A sign-board, 4 miles west of Promontory, at the side of the road, says: "Ten miles of track in one day." The day was April 29th, 1869, and 4,000 men were employed to put 2,000 tons of rails, spikes, fish-plates and bolts, together with the ties, in place. The two companies had been racing, each expecting to hold all it could build, but after the meeting at Promontory, President Grant decided that the two roads should meet at Ogden, and the Union surrendered all west of that place to the Central Company. The Union had extended its grade 53 miles to the westward of Promontory, with the expectation of building so far. Between Rozel and Lake Station a sign-board shows the western limit of the 10 miles of track laid in one day.

Monument is the last station near the lake, but the view is not so good as from a higher elevation a few miles west of Kelton, enabling us to see the further shores of the lake, and the Wasatch and Oquirrh mountains. Beyond Kelton is the terminus of an important wagon road used by much of the freight and travel of Southern Idaho. The great Shoshone Falls of the Snake River, 190 feet high and 700 feet wide, are 110 miles from Kelton and 10 from the Rock Creek Station (on the Idaho stage road), where a carriage can be obtained. The landscape is desolate, but the scenery grand.

At Matlin Station we are near the northern border of a bare flat, that seems to have been the bed of a lake, the beach line of which may be seen at the base of the hills on the right. Beyond Terrace we obtain a view of Pilot Peak to the south-west, one of the prominent landmarks of this region. It is 36 miles south of Tecoma, shortly before reaching which station we see a granite monument at the roadside marking the boundary between Utah and Nevada.

Since leaving Kelton the road has been rising gradually to cross the Pequop Mountains, which have an elevation of 6,184 feet at Pequop station. On this ridge half a dozen snow-sheds are necessary for the protection of the track. We descend into Independence Valley, obtaining some fine views as we go down the winding road, and then ascend to Moore's, 6,166 feet high, in Cedar Pass. Leaving the summit we enter the basin of the Humboldt River, and remain in it with a continuous descent for 318 miles. We enter the valley of the river soon after leaving Cedar. Wells, 676 miles from San Francisco, the end of the Salt Lake Division of the Central Pacific, and a place for changing conductors and locomotives, is named from a score of well-like springs half a mile west of the station. They do not overflow, and though not warm, never freeze over, though the thermometer goes to zero in the winter. The ground round them is elastic, and some of the residents express a confident opinion that this soil is merely a thin shell covering a subterranean lake, the water of which fills the crater of an extinct volcano. It is said that sounding with a line 1,500 feet long failed to find bottom. The facts that the wells contain indigenous fish, and that the water never freezes in the intense cold of winter, nor becomes offensive to the taste or smell in the heat of summer, are evidences of the lake theory. Southward from Wells the traveler will observe a mountain ridge, the northern end of which is called Castle Peak, and is snow-capped through much of the year. This ridge, like most of those in Nevada, runs parallel with the meridian.

Bishops is named from Bishop Creek, which enters the Humboldt from the north, through the canyon which attracts attention on the right.

Camp Halleck, a National military post which gives its name to Halleck Station, is at the base of the mountains, distant 13 miles to the southward. After passing the station, we see Elko Mountain on our right, but the road turns and the mountain then appears on our left, to the southward, and stays there, till out of sight.

Below Peko, the North Fork of the Humboldt enters the Humboldt River, breaking through the mountains in a large canyon. It is about as large as the main stream. From this point westward, the Humboldt River grows smaller under the influence of evaporation and absorption in the summer and fall. The Osino Canyon begins near the mouth of the North Fork, and before entering it, we cross that stream. The canyon is remarkable for its sharp curves.

Elko is an "eating station," and some travelers assert that it is the first place on the westward line where you can get first-rate bread made in Californian style. The town is supplied through pipes with water from the hills, 17 miles to the north. Here we see for the first time the Piute Indians, a filthy and degraded race. Near the town, to the northwest, are mineral springs, three hot and three cold. One of the hot springs has a temperature of 185°, another is a "chicken soup" spring, being thickened naturally with an unctuous clay, to the thickness and color of restaurant chicken-soup, and the resemblance in taste is complete approximately, when well seasoned with salt and pepper. The springs have a bath-house. A daily stage runs northward from Elko to Tuscarora, Cornucopia, Cope, and other mining towns; and southward to Bullion there is a semi-weekly stage. A few miles west of Elko, in cool weather, the steam may be seen rising from hot springs on the south side of the river near a bridge on a wagon road. The canyon on the left is that of the South Fork of the Humboldt. After leaving Moleen we enter the Five Mile Canyon, and near the entrance are some eroded ledges of tower-like forms known as the Moleen Rocks. Carlin has the repairing shops of the Humboldt Division of the Central Pacific Road, and before the construction of the railroad to Eureka, was the terminus of the main wagon-road to that place.

Palisade to Battle Mountain.—Below Carlin the track enters the 12-mile, or Palisade Canyon, which has steep rock walls from 500 to 1,000 feet high, and much wild scenery. In this canyon is the Palisade Station, where the narrow-gauge railway, 90 miles long, starts for Eureka—now, in spring of 1885, the most productive silver mining district in Nevada. Its ores are argentiferous galena, which is reduced by smelting, the first product being base bullion, or lead, containing usually from $300 to $400 of silver in a ton. Some of the mines send their base bullion to San Francisco to be refined; the Richmond refines at the mine. At Curo we emerge from the Palisade Canyon, and soon see the Cortez Mountains to the northward.

Beowawe, said to be the Indian title meaning "friendly gate,"—and the topography of the vicinity renders the term suitable—is a station at Copper Canyon where the Humboldt breaks through a ridge, crossing its course at right angles. Below Beowawe, willow thickets line the river for 20 miles, and pelicans are numerous there in the summer. It is said that some of these birds, while breeding, go every day to Humboldt Lake, more than 75 miles distant, and bring back a load of fish in their pouches for their consorts and young. It is a good story, whether true or not. On the southern border of the valley below Beowawe, there is a cluster of 100 hot springs, the steam of which can be seen from the cars in cold weather, especially when they have one of their spouting fits, during which, besides steam, they throw up water and mud to a height of 30 feet. At Shoshone, Rock Creek enters the Humboldt from the north, and is its last tributary worthy of notice. The stream has increased little in size in the last 50 miles—we have followed it for 220—and below this point the quantity of water decreases under the influence of evaporation and absorption. Between Shoshone and Argenta, Dunphy and Hildreth of San Francisco, have a cattle ranch, measuring 20,000 acres, and their cattle kept here and in Southern Idaho number 40,000 head. West of Argenta we pass the outlet of Reese River, a tributary of the Humboldt, but its tribute is never paid, except in seasons of exceptional rainfall. At all other times the waters of Reese River evaporate or sink into the ground before they come within 20 miles of the Humboldt.

Battle Mountain to Reno.—Battle Mountain is the starting point of the Nevada Central Railway, which extends 93 miles southward to Austin, the chief town of the Reese River mines. The road is of narrow gauge. About 40 miles south of Austin, by wagon road, the tourist can find a natural curiosity, called the Devil's Punch Bowl. At the top of a smooth, rounded elevation, 1,200 feet in diameter at the base and 100 feet at the summit, is a deep, well-like opening, partly filled with boiling water giving off steam.

Battle Mountain was named from a high ridge, the summit of which is about three miles from the station to the southward, and the ridge was so named because of a battle which occurred there about a quarter of a century since, between some Piute Indians and a party of white men whose cattle had been stolen. Many of the noble red men were sent to the happy hunting grounds, and afterwards cattle were more secure property in that neighborhood.

Near Iron Point is the mouth of the Little Humboldt, which drains Paradise Valley lying north of the road. This is the last valley of note opening into the Valley of the Humboldt. There is nothing worthy of mention at Golconda, save some very hot springs west of the station and north of the road. They are used for irrigating gardens, and occasionally for scalding hogs. Since leaving Omaha our general course has been due west, and starting from latitude 41° 15' we have not deviated 50 miles on either side from that parallel, in a distance of 1,450 miles. At Tule we reach the Big Bend of the Humboldt, and for the next 500 miles our general course is to the south-westward, the direction for 150 miles being south-south-westward.

Winnemucca, named for a chief of the Piutes, is 475 miles from San Francisco, and is the end of a railroad division. Here we change conductors and locomotives, and have a good view of the Santa Rosa Mountains to the northward.

Humboldt Station is noted for its orchard and garden kept green by irrigation. South-eastward, distant 10 miles, is the summit of Star Peak, the highest point in the East Humboldt range; north is the Eugene ridge; west is the Trinity ridge; north-west, between the station and the river, are the Lassen or Humboldt Meadows, and in the same direction, 30 miles distant, is the most productive sulphur mine on our continent. We cross the river, 5 miles beyond Oreana, and after leaving Granite Point, looking to the left we see Humboldt Lake, 30 miles long and 10 wide. This lake has an outlet 10 miles long, leading to the sink, 40 miles wide and 25 long, into which the waters of Humboldt and Carson lakes both flow after rains more abundant than the average.

The White Plains Station, west of the sink, has an elevation of 3,894 feet, the lowest point between the Sierra Nevada and the Rocky Mountains, the lowest indeed between Colton, on the Union Pacific, and Shady Run, on the Central Pacific, a distance of 1,296 miles.

Mirage Station, 366 miles from San Francisco, is so named from the frequency of the atmospheric illusions seen in the vicinity. An enlargement in the channel, connecting Humboldt Lake with the sink below it, is called Mirage Lake.

At Hot Springs Station we can see the steam rising from springs about half a mile from the track on the left.

Wadsworth, in the basin of the Truckee, was the terminus of an extensive freighting business, by mule teams, to the region on the south until the Carson and Colorado Railroad was built in 1880. The stretch of 250 miles between Palisade and Wadsworth, is very unpleasant to travelers in hot, dry weather. The heat in midsummer is intense, and the dust is alkaline and acrid, causing soreness of the nose and chapping of the lips.

At Wadsworth we reach the banks of the Truckee River, which we are to follow 30 miles, going up stream. The Truckee has no existence except between Lake Tahoe, 22 miles long, 10 wide, and 1,700 feet deep, fresh, and 6,167 feet above the sea, and Pyramid Lake, 35 miles long, and 12 wide, saline, with an elevation of 4,890 feet. The river is 97 miles long, and serves to drain one lake and feed the other. With an average fall of 13 feet to the mile, it is for most of its length an impetuous stream, and often carries a very large quantity of water. Usually all its water goes to Pyramid Lake, (so-called from the shape of a rock rising from its midst 600 feet above its surface), but when the lake is high, part of the supply flows into Winnemucca Lake, which is 8 miles distant, and separated by a high ridge from Pyramid.

South from Reno.—Reno, near the middle of the Truckee Valley, with much fertile soil and water for irrigation in its vicinity, has one of the best situations in the state for a town. Practically,

Reno, 50 miles from the summit, is the eastern base of the Sierra. It is the point which has been selected by the railroad builders as the best place from which to start railroads running to the northward and to the southward. The Virginia and Truckee Railroad is 52 miles long, and so crooked that its curves put together are equivalent, it is said, to 17 complete circles. This unsurpassed crookedness suggested a fiction, that an engineer, scared at night by the proximity of two red lights on the track, jumped from his locomotive to escape a collision, though the lights were those on the rear end of his own train. The general course of the road is southward for 31 miles from Reno to Carson on the bank of the Carson River, and then northeastward 21 miles, with an ascent of over 100 feet in a mile to Virginia City, 6,205 feet above the sea. The distance from Reno to Virginia City, by the Geiger Grade wagon road, is 21 miles, and in a direct line 16 miles. Four miles from Reno, beyond Anderson's Station, we come to a V flume which brings lumber down from the mountain side, 15 miles above. At Huffaker's, 3 miles beyond, we come to another flume, and at Brown's another, and there are others at Washoe, Franktown and Carson. Steamboat Station, 11 miles from Reno, derives its names from Steamboat Springs, which issue from a mound, 1,200 feet long by 400 wide. Fissures in the mound about 12 inches wide and of irregular shape, emit puffs of steam. The temperature of the water varies from 60° to 212°, and it is impregnated with sulphur. Bathing-houses, with a hotel and cottages are built on the premises, the altitude of which is 4,500 feet above the sea. The springs have neither so much steam nor so much water as they had 20 years ago, and the decrease is explained by many persons on the theory that the water comes from the Comstock Lode, the surface of which at Virginia is nearly 2,000 feet above the level of the springs. The miners find water with a temperature of 160° in the lower workings. Steamboat is not far from the course of the vein. Much of the water of the Comstock mines runs off through the Sutro Tunnel, and there has been no decrease in the water supply of other hot springs in the vicinity, so the theory is not without plausibility. The water supply at Steamboat has fallen away so much that borings were made to increase it, and the result was successful.

Washoe, 16 miles from Reno, once a busy town—its name was used to designate the mines at Virginia City for years after their discovery—is in a valley which contains a lake 4 miles long and a mile wide. West of the southern end of the valley is Mount Rose, 6,448 feet high. Washoe has a picnic ground on Capt. Dall's place near the lake, and another at the Bowers' Mansion. When the rich deposit of auriferous quartz was discovered at Gold Hill, about 1860, Sandy Bowers, an uneducated miner, owned a good slice of the vein, and he soon became a millionaire. He built a magnificent dwelling, obtained furniture and upholstery from France at enormous expense, planted the grounds with beautiful shrubbery and had the most elegant home in the State. His fortune went as it came, swiftly; his widow survives in poverty; the garden has disappeared and the dwelling is a curiosity. After leaving Mill Station, we rise to the summit of the ridge south of Washoe Valley, and have a comprehensive view of the valley and lake. At this ridge we cross the line of the Virginia City water-pipe, the most remarkable work of its kind in the world. It is of sheet-iron, seven miles long, and sustains a pressure of more than 1,700 vertical feet of water. The pipe is a foot in diameter, and the quantity of water delivered daily is 20,000,000 gallons. Soon after leaving Lake View Station we can look down on Carson Valley and Carson City, the Capital of the State, and the site of a National Mint. A favorite picnic ground near Carson City, used also by the people of Virginia, is the Treadway Place on the banks of the Carson River. It has a green lawn, fruit trees, and pleasant shades. About a mile west from Carson City are Swift's Springs, which have a hotel, bathhouse, swimming bath, and an abundant supply of natural hot water in the midst of a plain covered with sage brush. One of the springs is of the kind known as "Chicken Soup," described on page 28. A coach makes regular trips from the principal hotels and the railroad station to the Springs, and the charge for a bath with a ride both ways is 50 cents. A hot spring in the State Prison Grounds, a mile from Carson, is not open to the use of the general public. Genoa, in the vicinity of Carson, has some hot springs, one of the features of which is a mud-bath. There is a hotel to accommodate visitors.

A Silver Mill.—Three miles east of Carson, on the line of the railroad, is Empire, which has a large silver mill on the bank of the Carson River. A silver mill pulverizes the ore under heavy iron stamps, which are arranged usually in sets of 5, side by side, in an iron box or battery, and they are lifted and then allowed to drop successively, making a loud, rattling noise. A stream of water running into the battery on the upper side, and out through a wire or sheet-iron screen on the lower side, carries off the ore as fast as it is sufficiently pulverized, and deposits it in tubs from which it is shoveled into cast-iron pans, about 5 feet across and 2 feet deep, in which it is mixed with common salt, sulphate of iron, quicksilver, and enough water to make a thin mud. It is stirred around for 6 hours, by which time the silver is sufficiently amalgamated or mixed with the quicksilver, and the pulp runs off to a settler in which the amalgam falls to the bottom and the water and worthless material escape. The amalgam is pressed out in a canvass bag to get rid of the loose quicksilver, and the thick, remaining mass is heated to redness which drives off the quicksilver, and leaves a spongy mass of precious metal. This is melted and run into bars. The processes of pulverizing, amalgamating and separating the precious metal from the amalgam, are all included under the general term of reduction, which is the business of silver milling, while the mining department has charge of the extraction, which finds the ore and brings it to the surface. The ore reduced at the Empire Mill is brought down from Virginia City by rail. There are other silver mills, below the Empire, on the Carson River, and each has its chute on which ore is sent down from the cars. The Santiago Mill is 500 feet below the road.

Carson and Colorado Railroad.—Mound House, 41 miles from Reno, is the terminus of the Carson and Colorado Railroad, 3 feet gauge, which extends to Keeler, 293 miles in a southerly direction, and accommodates the traffic of Bodie with its gold mines, Columbus with its borax deposits, Cerro Gordo, Owens Lake and vicinity. Mound House is also the station nearest to Sutro, the outlet of the Sutro Tunnel, which is 19,790 feet long, and cost $4,500,000, without interest, for construction. It strikes the Comstock 1,898 feet below the croppings of the Gould and Curry mine, and is of great service for the drainage and ventilation of the lode. Unfortunately, since its completion in 1879, the mines have produced relatively little. The Carson and Colorado Railroad crosses the Carson River at Dayton, 6 miles from Mound House, ascends Churchill Canyon, a tributary of the Carson, crosses over into Mason Valley, in the basin of the Walker River, follows that stream to Walker Lake, a sheet of water 25 miles long, 7 wide, and 3,840 feet above the sea, skirts the lake on the west, and passes on beyond to the region of the borax deposits. Hawthorne, 100 miles from Mound House and 4 miles south of Walker Lake, is the station where the trains connect with the wagons and stages of Bodie.

Virginia City.—Eleven miles northward by rail from the Mound House we arrive at Virginia City, the terminus of the road. Virginia City stands on the side of a steep hill, and offers little opportunity for the construction of level roads. The only pleasant drive is that to Steamboat Springs, 8 miles distant, on the Geiger grade, over a romantic mountain, with wild rocky scenery, but no trees near the road. The city, with its suburb, Gold Hill, has about 7,000 inhabitants, and for its existence depends on the Comstock Lode, one of the largest and richest argentiferous veins in the world, and without exception the most productive in the last half of our century. It has been distinctly traced for a distance of 3 miles, and has an average width of 20 feet, though in one place where the ore was very rich it spread out to 300. The deepest workings are 3,000 feet below the surface, in the Belcher and Yellow Jacket mines, 2,800 in the Imperial, 2,700 in the Crown Point, 2,600 in the Ophir, Mexican and Union, and 2,500 in the Consolidated Virginia, California and Sierra Nevada mines. The total yield since 1860 has been about $325,000,000. The lode crops out on the eastern slope of a ridge, which culminates in Mount Davidson. The engraving on the next page is intended to show a vertical section of the Comstock Lode, drawn on a scale of 2,000 feet to the inch, as seen in imagination from the east, looking westward. The base line is 3,000 feet below the level of the Gould & Curry Mill;

the top line follows the level of the surface where the main works were originally established. The little marks at the base line indicate the limits of the different mines, which are numbered consecutively, beginning at the north, and the name of each mine is placed with its number beneath the engraving. Between the Belcher and Alta Mines, a distance of 3,000 feet, no mines are mentioned as there is a dispute about the course of the vein. The dark strips in the engraving show the barren portions of the vein; the middle tint indicates the supposed situation of "pay chutes" in which rich ore bodies may be found; the light tints respresent the rich ore bodies; and the white lines running down from the surface are the main shafts and inclines. Five pay chutes each nearly a quarter of a mile long horizontally, appear in the engraving, and between each adjacent pair there is a barren chute of equal length. The first pay chute commencing at the north, contained a body of rich ore in the Sierra Nevada and Union Mines, but produced neither dividends nor any considerable quantity of mineral. The second pay chute discovered at the surface in 1860, was very profitable for three years, then yielded nothing for ten years, and for six years, from 1874 to 1879, was profitable. It paid $140,000,000 gross, to the Mexican, Ophir, California and Consolidated Virginia companies. The third, appearing in the Gould and Curry, Savage, Hale & Norcross and Chollar Mines, has turned out $55,000,000. The fourth, known as the Gold Hill bonanza, was worked at first at the surface as a gold placer, then mills were established to save the gold, losing most of the silver, and silver mills have succeeded them. The ground now owned by the Imperial, Yellow Jacket, Kentuck, Crown Point and Belcher has produced $110,000,000. The fifth pay chute has yielded several millions, but has paid no dividends.

Auriferous quartz is generally, and argentiferous quartz sometimes found in pay chutes, the remainder of the veins being nearly or quite barren ; but many intelligent miners familiar with the Comstock Lode believe that it has no pay chutes, and that the ore bodies are scattered in it without discoverable system. Most of the rich deposits so far found have in general form approached the shape of beans, standing upright or nearly upright, but many of them were too small to be shown on the engraving.

The Comstock Lode is, in many respects, the most remarkable silver-bearing vein in the World. The *Veta Madre*, or Mother Vein, at Guanajuato, Mexico, and the great vein at Cerro Pasco, Peru, are similar to it in length, width and great production, but in three centuries neither has yielded much more than did this lode in twenty years. Potosi, in Bolivia, has turned out considerably more silver, but it has no one large vein equal to the Comstock,

This ridge has a north-north-east, and a south-south-west course, and its eastern side has a descent of about 25° from the horizontal, while the lode dips at an angle of 45°. The first streets of the town run along the mountain sides near the croppings, and the

NEW YORK TO SAN FRANCISCO. 35

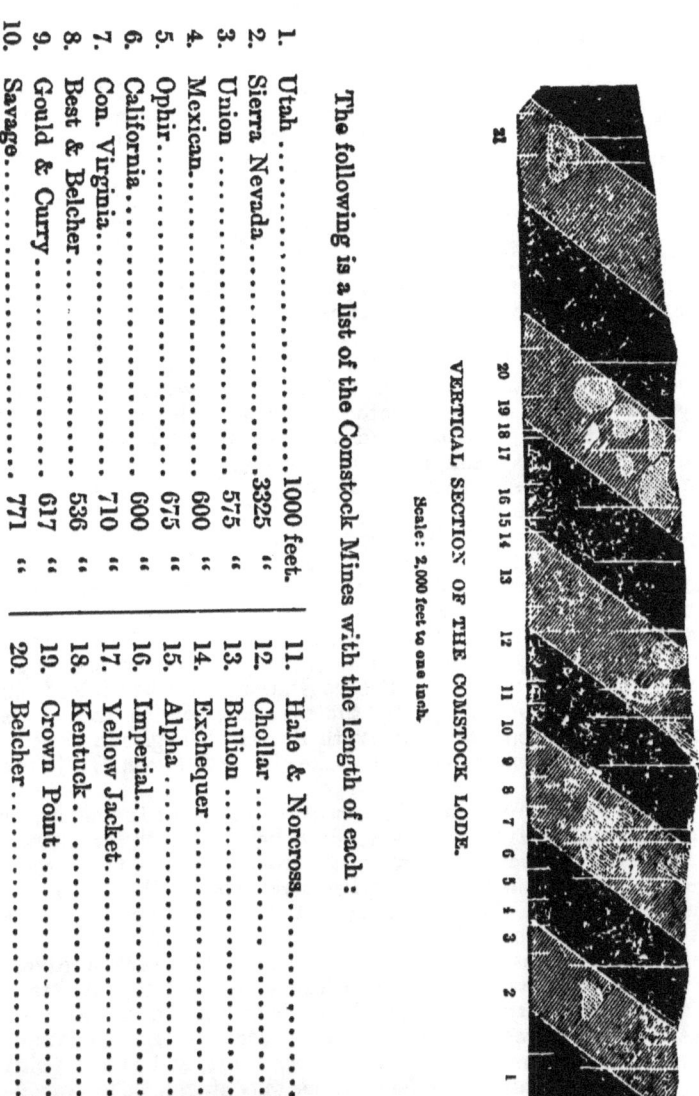

VERTICAL SECTION OF THE COMSTOCK LODE.

Scale: 2,000 feet to one inch.

The following is a list of the Comstock Mines with the length of each:

1. Utah............................	1000 feet.	11. Hale & Norcross...........	400 feet.
2. Sierra Nevada.................	3325 "	12. Chollar.....................	1400 "
3. Union...........................	575 "	13. Bullion.....................	943 "
4. Mexican.......................	600 "	14. Exchequer..................	400 "
5. Ophir...........................	675 "	15. Alpha.......................	306 "
6. California.....................	600 "	16. Imperial....................	685 "
7. Con. Virginia.................	710 "	17. Yellow Jacket.............	957 "
8. Best & Belcher...............	536 "	18. Kentuck....................	93 "
9. Gould & Curry...............	617 "	19. Crown Point...............	541 "
10. Savage.........................	771 "	20. Belcher.....................	1008 "

deeper the shafts the farther down hill the hoisting works and mills were built. The summit of Mount Davidson, 7,827 feet above the sea, commands a view of an extensive region, most of which consists of numerous mountain ranges, rocky in their material, steep and angular in their forms, dull and monotonous in their colors, and bare of vegetation. Virginia City, only 2 miles to the eastward, shows no gardens, grass-plots or trees. The meadows of the Truckee, 25 miles to the northward; the farms and pastures of the Washoe Valley, 15 miles to the westward, and of the Carson Valley as far to the southward, have distinct green tints, which are much modified by the haze of distance. The coniferous forest of the western slope of the Sierra is dark brown rather than olive in its color. To the eastward, we see the lower part of Carson Valley and the Humboldt Desert, both as cheerless as wild sage and bare sand. The higher portions of the mountains visible from Mount Davidson are covered with snow through much of the year. The scene, though not without its grand features, is always desolate. Among the prominent features of the landscape are Mount Lincoln, Silver Mountain and Job's Peak, and the Humboldt range may be discerned on the eastern horizon. Geneva and Dayton may be seen, but Carson City is hidden.

Reno to Truckee.—Returning to Reno we notice the Nevada and Oregon Railroad, the construction of which has been commenced recently. The road connects with the Central Pacific, and the main reliance of its projectors in the near future is the transportation of timber from a magnificent forest about 30 miles from Reno. Taking an overland train again, we resume our westward journey. Shortly after passing Bronco Station, about 285 miles from San Francisco, we see a sign by the roadside, bearing the words "State Line," and marking the 120th degree of longitude west of Greenwich, the boundary north of Lake Tahoe between California and Nevada.

Boca, 267 miles from San Francisco, is situated at the mouth of the Little Truckee River, the name Boca being Spanish for mouth. The town has lumber mills, extensive ice-houses, and the largest lager beer brewery on the coast. Prosser Creek is chiefly notable as the terminus of a V flume. Ice is cut and stored here in winter for the San Francisco market.

Lake Tahoe.—Truckee is the point where the Truckee River, after running northward from Lake Tahoe for 15 miles, makes a rectangular bend to the east, and where the railroad in its westward course leaves the river and begins its steep ascent of the mountain. Truckee is the centre of an active lumber trade, and is the point where most of the tourists for Lake Tahoe take stages. The wagon-road leads southward and upward in the canyon of the Truckee, between steep hill-sides, in some places covered with timber, and elsewhere spotted with stumps. The outside seat with the driver is desirable for the scenery is interesting, and cannot be seen so well from the inside of the stage. The driver, if requested, will point out a log-slide, where logs or bolts of wood are sent sliding down the steep mountain side, in a channel made with the trunks of small trees. At the lower end of the slide, the wood jumps with a tremendous splash into a pool of water, which protects it from being split by the concussion, and holds it in readiness to be carried down to Truckee by the V flume, alongside of which the stage-road runs. The canyon, though it has no large bend, has many little ones, each of which makes a change in the landscape. The forms of the hills, rocks and trees, the colors of the foliage, the dark green of the still water, and the white foam of the rapids, present many beautiful scenes. The willows and aspen-like cottonwood, on the edge of the river, are light green in the spring and summer, and red and yellow under the autumnal frosts, and here and there some other deciduous tree serves as a contrast to the more sombre colors of the conifers. Every minute brings some new object of interest into sight, until the stage drives into a village called Tahoe City, at the northwestern corner of the lake, where we find a wharf from which we can step aboard the steamer *Governor Stanford*, bound for different parts on the lake shores, or we may stop at the hotel.

Lake Tahoe is 22 miles long, 10 wide and 1,700 feet deep. Its surface is 6,247 feet above the sea; its waters are clear and cold, and abound with large trout of fine flavor. Steam and sail-boats on its waters, and hotels on the shores, offer their accommodations to the pleasure seeker, and the locality is much visited during the summer. There are hot springs on the shore near the north-east corner of the lake, on the line between the two States, supplied with a hotel and bath-houses. When the steamboat leaves the shore for a trip round the lake we look down with astonishment. The boat appears almost as if suspended in the air. The bottom, distinctly visible to a depth of 50 or 60 feet, instead of being mud or sand, as is usual in lakes, is composed of clean gravel, showing that no slime is carried into the lake from the surrounding mountains. The rock of the lake basin is nearly all granite, and when it disintegrates, usually takes the form of a clean sand. The color of the water, when the depth is not over 20 feet, is of a delicate yellowish green, and under a clear sky, the rays of the sun are collected in streaks of brightness by the waves, and the lights and shades thus formed, dance over the bed of the lake with singular effect. When the boat passes over greater depths—the deepest point is 1,500 feet—the color of the water, as seen from the sunny side, passes to a light indigo blue. As seen in the shade, the color, in places a deep black near the boat, at a distance shows deep blue, and rich purple hues near the middle of the lake. At the immediate edge there is a seam of brilliant emerald, even where there is nothing in the bank or sky above to furnish any similar tint by reflection. At the southern end of the lake there is an extensive shallow, ranging from 5 to 20 feet deep, and suddenly the bottom pitches off to a depth of

500 feet or more, the position of the sharp and crooked edge of this under water cliff being clearly indicated by the light green water on one side and deep purple on the other.

The route of the boat is, the greater part of the way, near rocky shores, with abundant forests of pine, and occasional fringings at the water's edge of deciduous foliage. Here and there on the mountain sides, at elevations of 7,000 feet or more above the sea, snow is visible in patches. The last port touched in the round of the lake is Glenbrook, on the eastern shore. This place is the site of several saw-mills, and the terminus of a railroad, on which timber is carried to the top of the mountain, and thence sent in a flume down to Carson City, whence it goes by rail to Virginia City, there to be used in bracing up the great excavations made in mining, or as fuel. The trees are cut on all sides of the lake, and made into rafts, to be towed by steam to Glenbrook, which thus is an immense base of supplies. The shores of the lake abound with delightful nooks and valleys, and there are comfortable houses for the accommodation of visitors. Lake Tahoe is remarkable from the fact, that notwithstanding the intense cold of winter, its water never freezes, and it remains so cold through the summer that the bodies of persons drowned in it never decompose, and therefore never come to the surface. At least 12 white persons have been drowned in it. We now return again to the Central Pacific. Truckee is 5,819 feet and Summit 7,017 feet above the sea, and the distance by road is 15 miles, an average ascent of 79 feet to the mile. This may be a good place to say that the word Sierras, as applied to these mountains, is incorrect. The primary meaning of the Spanish *Sierra* is saw, and the term is applied to high mountain chains, the comb or edge of which, seen from a distance, suggests saw-teeth. As it would be improper to say "the Rocky Mountain chains," so it is improper to say "the Sierra Nevadas," or "the Sierras."

The Donner Tragedy.—Leaving Truckee, with a new conductor and a fresh locomotive, we are on the Sacramento Division of the road. Northwest of Truckee, and 2½ miles distant, is Donner Lake, a beautiful little sheet of water, 3½ miles long, a mile wide, and 250 feet deep. Aside from its natural attractiveness, the locality has a tragic interest as the site of a camp where the Donner party of emigrants, (so styled from their captain, George Donner,) on their way with ox-teams from Illinois and adjacent States to the Sacramento Valley, were arrested by snow, in October, 1846, and detained until many died of starvation. They arrived at the lake on the 28th of October, and, after spending a few days there, came to an understanding that they would kill all their cattle for food, and start afoot to cross the mountains; but that night snow began to fall, and continued falling for several days, covering up their camp and causing their animals to wander off and get lost in the deep drifts. Several of the cattle were recovered alive and the carcasses of others were dug out of the snow; but by the middle of December provisions were getting low and it became necessary to take immediate steps to prevent starvation. One bear had been shot and this appears to have been the result of their attempts to live on the country, although as the lake abounds in excellent trout it seems strange none were taken through the ice. Accordingly on the 16th of the month a party of 17, several of whom were women, was formed to seek relief in the valley to the westward. The survivors of this party, 2 men and 5 women, reached the first house on the western slope of the Sierra, on the thirty-second day after starting. Their sufferings on the way were terrible. Traveling through a trackless waste amid snows from 12 to 60 feet in depth, without shelter at night and often without fire, their scanty supply of provisions soon gave out, and life was only supported by cannibalism. A relief party was soon formed to rescue the remainder of the unfortunates at the lake, but such were the difficulties of travel that, although this party was followed by a second, and the second by a third and a fourth, it was not until after the middle of April that the undertaking was accomplished. The party that went into camp near the lake, in October, consisted of 81 souls, of whom 23 males and 24 females lived to reach the valleys of California, and 34 died of cold and starvation.

Summit to Emigrant Gap.—Summit Station is surrounded by interesting scenery, and is the best stopping place for those who wish to spend a few days in the High Sierra near the railroad. Lake Angeline is only a mile distant. Lake Donner is two miles, and Lake Tahoe 22 by the trail, and numerous small lakes, some of them beautifully situated amidst the timber on little benches or flats in the mountain side, are found within 5 miles. The Summit Soda Springs, a pleasant resort with a hotel for the accommodation of visitors, is 6 miles distant, by a good wagon-road. The chief attraction of the vicinity, however, is Mount Stanford, called by some writers "Castle Peak," and by others, "Fremont's Peak," 9,175 feet high, only 4 miles north from the station. This is one of the loftiest peaks between Lake Tahoe and the Oregon line, and commands the most extensive view to be found near the railroad. Within the range of vision, with the unaided eye, on a clear day, are the Coast Range, the Marysville Buttes, Downieville Peak, Mount Lincoln, Mount Davidson, and extensive regions in the basins of the Truckee, Carson, Humboldt and Sacramento, besides all of Donner Lake and half of Tahoe. The high slopes of Mount Stanford are covered with loose stone, and at the top there are pinnacles of rock so difficult of ascent, that very few persons have reached the summit. The ascent to excellent points of view can be made on horseback, but good walkers will find it more satisfactory to go afoot. Mount Lincoln, about six miles south of the railroad, is next to Mount Stanford the highest peak in the vicinity. Carriages can be obtained for trips to Donner Lake, Summit Valley, (2 miles long by one wide, and drained by a tributary of the Yuba River,) and other interesting points in the vicinity. At Summit we pass through a tunnel 1,659 feet, and then begin to descend to Emigrant Gap, which has an elevation of 5,225 feet The difference in the height of the two ends of the line of sheds indicates the greater snowfall on the western slope of the Sierra. In an average winter, 55 feet of snow fall at the Summit, 45 at Emigrant Gap, and 35 at Strong's Canyon, but at the latter place the cold is more severe than at Emigrant Gap, the snow drifts more and does not melt so soon. The 55 feet of snow, when old and packed down, will not measure more than 20 feet and perhaps not so much. An ordinary train can not run through fresh snow 2 feet deep, but a snow-plough, pushed by three or four heavy locomotives, will easily go through 10 feet of soft snow, even if not very fresh. When the snow is dry and loose, so that it can drift, it fills up the track almost immediately behind the plough, so that the only secure way of keeping the track clear is to cover it with sheds. These, in some places are intended to protect the track against the fall or drift of snow; in other places they are designed also to guard the trains against avalanches which are common on the steep mountain slopes. The strength of the sheds is proportioned to the immense weight and strain to which they are exposed; they are 34 miles in length, and cost about $10,000 a mile. From Soda Springs Station another wagon road leads to the Soda Springs already mentioned.

Scenery below Emigrant Gap.—As the snow sheds almost completely shut off the view, we do not get a chance to see much of the country between Strong's Canyon and Emigrant Gap, but after leaving the latter station, the most impressive scenery on our route begins to come into view. We are 5,000 feet above the sea, and at turns in the road we can look down over the tidewater, 75 miles to the southwest, and see the Coast Range, 150 miles away to the west and southwest. But wide as is the prospect, with the naked eye we can see little distinctly in the distance. The mountains near us sink down into hills, beyond which are plains darkened in places with timber. The Coast Range, if its edge were horizontal, might be mistaken for the ocean, so dim does it appear. The vicinity of the road claims the greatest part of the traveler's attention and admiration. He is in a wilderness of sharp ridges, separated by steep canyons, 2,000 or 3,000 feet deep, covered in many places with magnificent forests, and even when clothed with chaparral, or bare, rich in color and interesting in form. We look down from the top of one of these ridges into a canyon so deep, that its bottom is dim in the haze, and the sun, still high in the heavens, strikes the mountain side a thousand feet from the base. The American River, 2,500 feet below, looks like a rivulet; the trees are like shrubs; the gardens like figured napkins, and the houses like pigeon boxes. Far down in the canyon is a narrow-guage railroad, with rails that seem no larger than telegraph wires. Directly in front of us are other mountain ridges, and beyond them the Coast Range with the intervening valley. The whole panorama forms a sublime spectacle, in which is mingled a touch of terror when the train runs along a narrow track, cut from the edge of a vertical cliff, 1,000 feet high, with a curve so sharp that the engines are out of sight, and rounds the headland of Cape Horn. Another element, that takes a strong hold on the thoughts of the traveler, is the rapid advance into a region of exceptional fertility of soil and geniality of climate. For more than 1,000 miles he has been passing through a desert. On the summit, if he comes in the winter or spring, he may see the snow 10 feet deep along the road which for months in the average winter would be impassable for 30 miles, if it were not protected by snow-sheds and cleared, where there are no sheds, by snow-plows. This subarctic climate gives character to the vegetation. No oak, no maple, no buckeye, no laurel greets the eye. The fir, the pine and a few other conifers that delight in the snow, are the only trees. But the train descends at the rate of 1,200 vertical feet in an hour, and as there is a rapid succession of varied, interesting scenes, the hours seem to be very short. The vegetation changes rapidly, the soil assumes richer tints and becomes more abundant; wild flowers and oak trees make their appearance; orchards with apple, pear and peach trees are seen near the road; then comes the vine, the almond, the orange, the eucalyptus, and a multitude of flowers that thrive only in places where snow is rare, and frost never severe. It is this change from the desert to a region blooming with flowers in all seasons; this descent from the snow of the high Sierra to the eternal spring of a sunny valley, that gives delight to the traveler, when he crosses the continent on the Union and Central Pacific route. None of the rival transcontinental routes now under construction, can equal this one in the mountain scenery near the western end of the road, or in the swift succession of changes from the climate of eternal winter to that of eternal summer. Charles Nordhoff says : " A grander or more exhilarating ride than that from the Summit to Colfax, you cannot find in the world. The scenery is various, novel, magnificent. * * * The entrance to California is as wonderful and charming as though it were the gate to a veritable fairyland. All its sights are peculiar and striking; as you pass down from Summit, the very color of the soil seems different from and richer than that you are accustomed to at home; the farm-houses with their broad piazzas speak of a summer climate; the flowers, brilliant at the roadside, are new to eastern eyes; and at every turn new surprises await you."

Soon after leaving Strong's Canyon, 7 miles from Truckee, and 6,317 feet above the sea, we enter a snow-shed, which is so dark that it looks almost like a tunnel. Immediately after leaving it we enter a genuine tunnel, and then shed and tunnel alternate, but mostly shed, for 28 miles. This magnificent scenery, however, is all hidden from the traveler who takes the first-class passenger train going in either direction. There is only one such train daily each way, and all that portion between Rocklin and Reno, including everything in the Sierra Nevada, will be hidden by darkness at all seasons of the year to the travelers on the regular passenger train, until the time-table shall be changed. The emigrant train, going westward, leaves Emigrant Gap at 5:45 A. M., so that in the summer the traveler taking it can see the finest of the mountain views. The emigrant train going eastward arrives at Shady Run at 7:35 P. M., allowing the traveler to see many of the grandest scenes on the western slope of the Sierras. The tourist, however, should not leave the express train without consulting the conductor, who will tell him whether there has been a change in the time-table, and whether he can certainly find an emigrant or freight train to accommodate him.

The old emigrant wagon-road, passing below us at Emigrant Gap, 235 miles from San Francisco, gives that station its name. Blue Canyon Station is a point where much lumber, sawn in the adjacent mountains, is placed on the cars for shipment to points east and west. The snow does not remain during the winter below this point. At Shady Run we obtain an excellent view of the great American Canyon, on the south of the road, where most of the fine views are to be seen.

Hydraulic Mining.—Dutch Flat, on the north side of the road, is the site of extensive hydraulic washings, which are now forbidden by the courts. The elevation of the road here is 3,395 feet; the town is several hundred feet lower, and that is above the level of the Dead Blue River, which runs north and south across the tops of the ridges made by the streams of the present day crossing it at right angles. The channel of the dead river is a half mile wide or more, and filled up to a depth of 300 feet with auriferous gravel, which has been traced and washed from Forest Hill, in Placer County, to Eureka, Sierra County, a distance of more than 50 miles. This dead river was very rich in gold throughout its length, and where it has been washed away by the living rivers, these were rich too. The American, Yuba, Bear rivers and their tributaries were poor above and rich below the points where they crossed the great Dead Blue River, and washed along its gravel. A large hydraulic mine is one in which the water is thrown through a nozzle not less than 7 inches in diameter, under a pressure at least 250 vertical feet, against a bank of auriferous gravel 100 feet or more, high; and this stream, carrying as much water as would be required for domestic purposes by a city of 100,000 inhabitants, digs down and carries away more gravel than could 10,000 men with picks, shovels and wheelbarrows. If the gravel contains 10 cents of gold in a ton it can be washed with profit.

Gold Run, two miles west of Dutch Flat, works the same channel, and about 15 years ago was the most productive hydraulic mining camp in the State. The views after leaving Gold Run are some of the most interesting on the road. Soon after passing the next station, Cape Horn Mills, at which trains usually do not stop, we come to Cape Horn, where the road runs along a narrow track cut into a bluff, 2,000 feet high, and for 1,000 feet nearly vertical. Colfax, 2,422 feet above the sea, is the terminus of a narrow-guage railroad to Nevada City and Grass Valley; the latter being the leading gold quartz mining town in California. From an area six miles square, of which the town is the centre, the miners have obtained $80,000,000 in gold. At Colfax we reach the "foothills," the region in which orchards and vineyards appear, and at Auburn, 1,360 feet above the sea, they are numerous. Newcastle, with an elevation of 956 feet, and 182 miles from Sacramento, is in a district where oranges are cultivated for profit, and they ripen here in December, about six weeks earlier than at Los Angeles.

Roseville, called Junction on the railroad time-table, 169 feet above the sea, and 18 miles from Sacramento, is a terminus of the Oregon branch of the Central Pacific Railroad, which extends 152 miles northward to Redding, at the head of the Sacramento Valley.

Sacramento to San Francisco.—Sacramento, the State Capital, on the left or eastern bank of the Sacramento River, and just below the mouth of the American River, has a population of 20,000, an active business, and is the chief railroad centre in the interior of the State. Here we cross the Sacramento River, and after passing through Davisville, on the bank of Putah Creek, the centre of an extensive horticultural district, we reach Suisun, where we come into the swamp land, covered with tule, a reed abundant in the shallow waters of California. To the south of us is Suisun Bay and beyond it Mount Diablo. At Benicia, 33 miles from San Francisco, and the site of a National arsenal, barracks, store-houses, etc., we reach the Strait of Carquinez, or Silver Gate, half a mile wide at the narrowest, separating the Bays of Suisun and San Pablo, and accessible for ships drawing 23 feet. To the southeastward from the shore of this strait we see the town of Martinez. An immense ferryboat, the largest ever built, 424 feet long and 116 wide, the *Solano*, is ready to take the entire train on board, and it carries us across to Port Costa, where the locomotive pulls us ashore. On the *Solano's* main deck 4 tracks are laid, measuring more than a quarter of a mile in the aggregate, and a train of 48 freight cars or 24 passenger coaches can be ferried across at a trip. At Port Costa, as at Benicia, there are wharves and warehouses from which numerous ships are loaded with wheat for Europe every year. Three miles from Port Costa we arrive at Vallejo Junction, a wharf for the accommodation of the ferry-boat running to Vallejo, which may be seen to the northward distant about 4 miles.

We now follow the shore of San Pablo Bay to the south-westward, then strike across the point separating that bay from the northern arm of San Francisco Bay, which soon comes into sight on the west, and beyond it is Mount Tamalpais, which will be spoken of again.

We skirt along the western borders of the City of Oakland, run out a mile and a half into the Bay of San Francisco, on a mole built of stone, reach a large, commodious and elegant station, and thence pass to the ferry-boat, which deserves attention for its large size, its nice furniture and its cleanly condition. From the open galleries of this boat we see San Francisco, on its hills, four miles distant, Goat, Alcatraz and Angel islands on our right, the Marin peninsula beyond them, the Golden Gate to the left of Alcatraz, the peninsula of San Francisco south of the city, and the southern arm of San Francisco Bay to the south of us. Behind Oakland is the Contra Costa Ridge of mountains. In 20 minutes the ferryboat runs from wharf to wharf, and we are at the end of the journey, for the purposes of this chapter.

CHAPTER II.

THE CLIMATES.

Comparative Meteorology.—One of the most potent aids to individual comfort and national progress, is an equable and genial climate. Within historical times no nation has risen to greatness, no man to eminence in literature or industrial art, in a torrid or frigid region. The leadership of progress, the custody of the highest culture, predominance in political and military power belong to the temperate zone. Tropical heat and arctic cold depress the mental and physical energies, diminish ambitions, reduce the field of activity, and cut off many sources of enjoyment. To a less extent these unfavorable influences are exercised also by meteorological extremes, within the temperate zone. C. L. Brace, who has traveled extensively in different parts of the world, and whose attention has been called to this subject by his stay in California, wrote that "of all human conditions next to civilization and its advantages, the most important is climate; perhaps, for personal happiness, it is more than all other material circumstances." Yet our geographies, cyclopedias, and books of travel generally, give no adequate idea of the climatic advantages and disadvantages of the main meteorological divisions, and of the differences of temperature, rainfall and humidity between New York, London, San Francisco and Los Angeles. The thermometrical means of January in those 4 cities are respectively: 31°, 37°, 49°, and 52°; and of July, 75°, 62°, 60°, and 75°. These figures indicate vast differences, in the suitability of temperature, to the healthy development of our bodies, and the active use of our mental and physical powers. As superiority of climate is to a nation one of the most valuable of all possessions, so an understanding of climatic differences is to an individual one of the most desirable of all kinds of knowledge. The clearness of the sky and the height of the mercury determine whether the weather is to be pleasant or unpleasant, and often whether the day shall pass agreeably or disagreeably. Our coast, as a whole, and especially the Californian part of it, has much to gain, and nothing to lose, by the diffusion of knowledge about comparative meteorology.

Standards of Temperature. — Annual thermometrical means have very little value, in conveying correct ideas of temperature. According to the National Signal Service Report, the annual mean for 1877-78 was 54° for New York, and 57° for San Francisco, but January was 21° warmer, and July 14° cooler in the latter, than in the former city. The difference between the means of the months was 42° at Hell Gate, and 7° at the Golden Gate; and between the respective extremes 81° and 37°. These figures show that the annual means have very little value, except to conceal the disadvantage of climates, which run from extreme cold in midwinter to extreme heat in midsummer. A similar objection can be made, with good reason, to the means showing the average temperature of the four seasons; they serve to hide the pivotal figures which are the thermometrical means of January and July, and these are in most places the coldest and hottest months, or the extremes connected by gradual changes, so that he who knows those two, knows the whole year. The mean of July in any one place varies very little from year to year, and so of January; but it is better to have the mean of many years, so as to avoid mistake from the exceptional character of any one season. Such means are the pivotal figures and best standards of temperature.

Meteorological Regions. — In its meteorology, as in its botany, that part of our slope which lies west of the Sierra Nevada Range — including its continuation far into Alaska — bears much more resemblance to Western Europe than to the Atlantic side of our continent in the same latitudes. Alaska is the counterpart of Norway in climate. British Columbia, Washington and Oregon, in general character are like England and Scotland; and California is like Spain or Italy. France, as a whole, has no equivalent on our coast, Nevada and Utah must seek for their parallels in Turkistan and the high lands of Persia. Idaho, Eastern Oregon and Washington are much like New York in temperature, though they have less rainfall. We have no complete meteorological statistics for the two slopes of Mexico, and therefore cannot compare them in that respect, but it is well known that the Pacific shores of our continent are free from yellow and black fevers, frequent and swiftly fatal at many points near the Gulf of Mexico.

Our slope has a number of distinct meteorological regions, the principal of which are those of Alaska, Western Oregon, San Francisco, Sacramento, Utah, Los Angeles, Arizona and Western Mexico. These regions will be considered separately, beginning with that of San Francisco, including the country west of the main ridge of the Coast Mountains, from the 35th to the 40th parallel, with a length of 350 and a width of 30 miles; the metropolis occupying a position on its western edge, nearly midway between the northern and southern borders. This region, within 10 miles of the ocean, has the most equably cool climate on the globe, and makes the nearest approach to the temperature in which active physical labor can be performed with the least discomfort at all seasons of the year. Nowhere else is the sky so favorable to the toiler.

San Francisco Summers.—The thermometrical mean of July, 60°, 5° or 10° below the degree of warmth that is comfortable to the idler, demands heavy woolen clothing and active movement from those who spend much time in the open air. It is the best of all temperatures for the man engaged in productive industy, spurring him to continuous exertion. It is a tonic, that becomes part of his system; a perpetual stimulant, that has no intervals of depression. All book-writing travelers, who have visited San Francisco and commented ably on the climate, have spoken in its praise. C. L. Brace said: "Here, it seems to me, you have it as near perfection as man can attain without enervation." In another place he tells his readers that "the climate is the great charm of the city. It is the most exhilarating atmosphere in the world. In it a man can do more work than anywhere else, and under it he feels under a constant pressure of excitement." Fitzhugh Ludlow speaks of the "divine days" and "heavenly climate" of the Golden Gate. Samuel Bowles says: "The evenness of the climate, * * * and the indescribable inspiration of the air, are the great features of life." Sir Charles Dilke remarks, that "the peculiarity of climate carries with it great advantages. It is never too hot, never too cold, to work—a fact which, of itself, secures a grand future for San Francisco. The effect upon national type is marked. At a San Francisco ball you see English faces, not American." B. F. Taylor sings of the city—

"Where Winter keeps watch and ward,
With Summer asleep at its feet ;
Stands guard with a silver sword,
Where the Junes and Decembers meet."

In July San Francisco is cooler than London by 2°, than Olympia by 3°, than Portland by 7°, than San Diego by 9°, than Paris by 10°, and than Genoa, Naples, Jerusalem, Cincinnati or New York by 17°. This peculiar coolness, unexampled at the level of the sea, in the same latitude, is attributable mainly to the prevalence of the trade wind, blowing nearly every day from April to October over the Kurosiwo, which, after sweeping round under the islands of Alaska, reaches our shores with a temperature never varying, near the Golden Gate, more than 3° from 55.° This vast ocean stream, bringing subfrigid waters into a subtropical latitude, is a great factor in the life of California, influencing its pleasures and its business in many ways. The Atlantic in the 40th parallel is warm enough on both sides in summer for pleasant bathing, but not so the Pacific near its eastern shore in the same latitude. San Francisco, within her city limits, has a magnificent beach, but the air and water there, on the average July day, are more than cool—they are chilling.

The intense heat in the interior of the continent is the main cause of the trade wind, prevailing along the coast, in the warm season. Throughout a region 1,000 miles long by 500 wide, the dry soil, under a burning sun, causes a vast extent of rarefied atmosphere into which the breezes rush from the west and north-west. If the plains and mountains of central California, Nevada, Utah, Arizona and northern Mexico were covered with forests, the rainfall would be greater, the sun would not strike the earth in the same manner, evaporation would keep down the temperature, the quantities of air warmed to a high degree would be much smaller, and the breezes from the ocean much weaker. We have no meteorological statistics to prove the direction or strength of the main air currents, that supply the region east of the Sierra Nevada; but we know, from the heat of the soil there in the summer days, that a large supply of air must be needed to replace that which rises. There is a better opportunity and there are more stations to observe the currents blowing into the great interior valley, or Sacramento-San Joaquin basin of California. Every average summer day these currents pass eastward from the Pacific, over the Coast Range, sometimes carrying flecks of cloud or fog 20 or 30 miles inland, to mark their track. The current is especially strong at the Golden and Silver gates, where it finds the only opportunity to travel near the level of the sea, and its influence is clearly discernible along its route, as we shall have occasion to remark in other paragraphs.

Hot Days.—The highest temperature recorded by the signal service in San Francisco for July, 1877, was 76°, not high enough to be uncomfortably warm. The average of the maximum observations for each day in the month was 66°; while the similar average for New York City was 83°. In 25 out of the 31 days, the mercury on Manhattan Island rose to 80°, at which figure oppressive heat begins. An examination of the meteorological tables, kept in San Francisco by Thomas Tennent for 32 years ending October 1, 1881, shows that the thermometer reached 80° on 209 days in that period, or less than 7 days in a year, on the average; in some years not once. In 1855, an exceptional season, there were 20 hot days. In 1861, 1862, 1863, 1873 and 1881, there was not one.

Not only are the hot days few, but they are scattered. It is a very rare occurrence for more than 3 to come together; but as the San Franciscans, accustomed to their chill climate, dress in heavy woolen suits through the summer, a day which they call hot would not receive such a title in Sacramento or New York. Summer heat at the Golden Gate, is always associated with an arrest of the trade wind; so long as that blows briskly, with its temperature of 55° or 60° at the beach, the thermometer can not raise to 75° in the city. Let it stop, however, for 6 hours in daylight and the sun's rays will soon become oppressive. The trade wind blowing from the west supplies cool air to the heated surface of the Sacramento basin. However, there are occasions when, for a few days, a strong wind blows from the north through that basin. At such times the trade wind has little to do at the Golden Gate, and a period of heat follows. Whenever a strong north wind prevails in the Sacramento Valley, for several days, then a lull in the trade wind and a warm day may be expected. In the climate of San Francisco the phrase "dog-days" is not applicable to any portion of the summer, as in the cities on the Atlantic slope. One result of the cool temperature and constant trade wind at San Francisco is, that a person with weak lungs can not drive out comfortably, in an open carriage, to the ocean beach in July, unless the day is exceptionally still and warm.

It is a singular feature of the shore climate of the San Francisco region, that July is not the hottest month, nor is August, but September. Thus, according to the signal service records, the mean of July in 1877 was 59°, and of September 61°. The means of a number of years give 58° to July, August and October, and 59° to September. In St. Louis, of July, August and September, the respective means are 78°, 76° and 70°, and in New York City, 74°, 74° and 66°. The greater heat of September, as compared with July, in San Francisco, is presumably caused by the cooling of the Sacramento basin, so that there is not such a draft of cold air pouring through the Golden Gate in the autumn as in the summer. At Sacramento City the temperature of September is 7° less than that of July; at Red Bluff, 6° less, and at Visalia, 9° less. These figures indicate a considerable decrease in the demand of the great interior valley for cooling breezes. As the mean temperature of July is less than that of September, so is the average number of hot days. Thus, in the 32 years ending October 1, 1881, June had 36 hot days (of 80°); July, 17; August, 19; September, 57, and October, 41. September had three times, and June and October each twice as many as July.

Cool Nights.—The nights are always cool at the Golden Gate. On rare occasions, the early part of the night has been warm, but the latter part, never. The lowest observation taken in July, 1877, was 53°. The mean of the minimums was 55°. All the signal service figures are, however, a little higher than those taken by unofficial observations. The mean temperature of the July sunrise in San Francisco is, according to Dr. Henry Gibbons, 52°—cool enough to make a fire desirable.

Warm Winters.—The Kurosiwo, which moderates the summer's heat, also tempers the winter's cold, on our coast, carrying such a mass of water, and spending so much time in its grand circuit, that the change of the seasons has little perceptible effect on its temperature, when it reaches California. It is almost as warm in January as in July, and almost as cold in the latter as in the former month. Not so swift in its current nor so narrow along the Asiatic coast as is the gulf stream near Florida, it has greater width, probably greater depth, and a longer course. Off San Francisco, it seems to be 500 miles wide, and is perhaps a mile deep. The temperature of the water at the Golden Gate is in July about 53°, 7° less than that of the air; 200 miles out it is 58°, 10° less than that of the air; and 600 miles out it is 67°, 3° less than that of the air. This change in the temperature of the water, in the same latitude, can not be explained satisfactorily upon any theory, save that the ocean current has a width of 500 miles or more. The normal mean temperature of July, in the 38th parallel of latitude, is about 75° on land and 70° in the water.

The mean temperature of January in San Francisco is in average years about 49°. According to the United States signal service records, the mean of the month in 1878 was 53° and the lowest observation, 39°. The mean for the same month at 2 P. M., was 57°, and at sunrise, 49°. According to the self-registering thermometer of Thomas Tennent, in the 32 years ending October 1, 1881, the mercury fell to the freezing point on 155 nights, or not 5 nights in a year, on the average. The greatest number in a year was 21, in 1862; but there was not one in 1852, 1853, 1860, 1866, 1871 or 1877. Of these 155 freezing nights, December had 58; January, 50; February, 19; November, 16; March, 7; April, 4 and May, 1. The mercury has not been so low as 32° between sunrise and sunset on more than 10 days in 32 years.

Snow is sometimes seen to fall in San Francisco, but almost invariably melts within 5 seconds after touching the ground, which has never been white with it within 25 years, except once. On several occasions the streets have been white or whitish with sleet or fine hail. Ice has formed to the thickness of an inch, but usually disappears before noon. The coldest temperature ever observed in San Francisco was 25°, or 7° below the freezing point. Although in the average winter there are not more than five nights in which the thermometer, as usually placed, 4 feet from the ground, records a figure so low as 32°, yet there are probably 20 mornings in which a white frost may be seen on the ground, especially in places where it is covered by grass, straw, or woody fiber. The frosts, however, are never severe, and delicate subtropical ornamental plants, including the heliotrope, fuchsia, floripondio, geranium, and French roses, live and often bloom through the winter in the open air.

Associated with the small range of temperature between the means of January and July, and between the means of the maximums and minimums of either month, is also a small range in the temperature of the days considered separately. Thus the greatest difference between the maximum and minimum of any one day was 20° in July and 17° in January, whereas in New York, the difference was 22° in July and 28° in January; in St. Louis it was 26° in July and 22° in January. It must be remembered that these oscillations in San Francisco are on both sides of the temperature of comfort, while in New York and St. Louis they belong, for July, to the domain of oppressive heat, and for January to that of intense cold.

The remarks about the climate of San Francisco apply, with slight modification, to Santa Cruz, Monterey, and all places on or very near the ocean beach, between the 35th and 40th parallels. San Francisco is a little cooler in summer than other points, because of the draft of cool air from the ocean passing through the Golden and Silver Gates to the Sacramento Valley. Santa Cruz is a little warmer than Monterey in summer, because it is protected by a hill from the trade wind. There is less frost on the beach than there is a mile away; less within a mile than 4 miles away. The heat of summer and the cold of winter increase, as we leave the ocean, and as we get beyond into the shelter of any range of hills, that breaks the force of the ocean breezes. Thus Vallejo, at the Silver Gate, only 25 miles from San Francisco, has a July 8° warmer, and a January 1° colder; St. Helena, about as far from the ocean as Vallejo, but shut in by a mountain ridge 2,000 feet high, is 19° warmer in July and 7° colder in January. The valley towns in the San Francisco region, though much warmer in the summer than the metropolis, can not grow the same tender plants in their gardens. As a general rule, it may be said, January is about 2° colder, and July 10° warmer 30 miles from the ocean than on the beach. Among the valley towns in the San Francisco region are San Jose, Santa Clara, Gilroy, Watsonville, Salinas, Soledad, Hollister, Haywards, San Rafael, Santa Rosa, Healdsburg, Cloverdale, Ukiah, Calistoga, St. Helena, Napa, Sonoma, Clayton, Livermore and Pleasanton, and the summer and winter temperatures of each are much influenced by the amount of sea breeze reaching them.

The Early Spring.—The pleasantest season of the average year in California is the early spring, a period of about 6 weeks, commencing sometimes in the middle of February, when the heaviest rains and the cold of winter have passed; when the summer heats have not commenced in the interior, nor the winds and fogs on the coast; when the breezes are balmy and the temperature genial; when the sky is free from clouds, and the atmosphere from haze, when the hills and valleys are gorgeous in varied tints of green, the wild flowers abundant, and the colors and shapes of the far distant mountains distinctly discernible. In this region, all seasons of the year are pleasant, but this is pre-eminently beautiful. In June, if not in May, the surface of the soil becomes dry, the landscape turns brown, the flowers die, the roads and the lower strata of the air become dusty, and the mountains dim. Beautiful as is the Indian summer on the Atlantic slope, it is far inferior in brilliancy and attractiveness to the early spring of California, and especially of Southern California, where, in addition to the charms of the season in other portions of the State, we then see the orange orchards loaded with the ripe fruit of one crop, and with the fragrant blossoms of the next one, at the base of grand mountains, and within 10 or 20 miles of their snow-crowned summits.

San Francisco Rains.—The average amount of rain in San Francisco is 23 inches in a year, about half as much as falls at New York or London. The Californian rainfall, however, is confined to the winter half of the year, and is called the rainy season, although there are not more rainy days, nor is there more rainfall, than during the same months in New York. We speak of the rainy season, not because we then have continuous rain, but because it is the only period when we have rain. The average rainfall, in the 6 months from May to October, inclusive, is an inch and a half; in the other 6 months it is 21½ inches. In the 4 months from June to September, inclusive, the average is less than a third of an inch, and less than a twentieth of an inch for each of the months of June, July and August. Though the amount of the rainfall varies greatly in different parts of the State, there is much resemblance in the relative proportions of the different seasons, everywhere save in the Colorado basin, which belongs to the Arizona meteorological region, having its rain in the summer, while the winter is usually dry.

The scarcity of summer rain in California and Nevada, is doubtless due mainly to two causes: First, the California trade winds are so cold that they will not take up much moisture from the ocean; that is, they take up much less than hot winds would; and, second, so soon as they reach the land, they encounter a much higher temperature, so that their moisture, instead of being condensed, is absorbed by hot currents, which rise and pass in a clear sky to the eastward and northward, until in Oregon, Idaho, or Montana, they encounter currents cool enough to cause precipitation. Prof. John Le Conte says: "This remarkable feature of the climate of this coast is clearly due to the excess of temperature of the adjacent land, during the summer, above that of the cool ocean on the west. This condition of things, while it argument the force of the west winds, renders the precipitation of the aqueous vapors of small tension, which they sweep from the cool ocean to the hot interior, a physical impossibility, since they are being carried to a region of higher temperature. Further north, along the coasts of Oregon, Washington Territory and Alaska, the presence of a comparatively warm ocean renders the conditions more favorable for summer rains."

No hurricane has ever visited California, or the ocean near its shore, and thunder storms are very rare, year after year passing in the valleys without one brilliant flash of lightning. The deaths by lightning in the State have been 2 in 30 years, whereas, in England, 25, and in the American States east of the Rocky Mountains, 145 are killed by it annually. In a region where there are no hurricanes, where summer rains are almost unknown, and where the winter rains are announced usually 24 hours in advance by a change in the direction of the wind (it blows from the north, north-west, or west for clear weather, and from south-west, south, or south-east for rain), there is comparatively little use for the barometer.

There is more irregularity in rainfall than in temperature. The mean of the thermometer for any one month is about the same in one year as in another, a variation of 5 per cent. being rare; and year after year will pass without a difference of 2 per cent.; whereas, a variation of 50 per cent. in the rain-gauge is not unfrequent. If we count years of flood, as those with more than 30 inches of rain, we have had 7 in the 32 years from 1849 to 1881; and estimating 17 inches or less as a drought, we have had 6 in the same period, making 13 years of extremes out of the 32, or more than one in 3. It is estimated that 12 inches of water is sufficient, with skillful management, to secure a good crop of wheat, but the rain often comes at such times. that a large part of it is lost to the farmer; and the fall is less in the wheat-growing valleys than in San Francisco.

As a general rule, the rainfall in California is 2 inches greater for each degree of latitude, as we go northward from the southern boundary of the State. It is greater near the ocean shore than inland; greater in the mountains than in the valleys; and greater on the western, than on the eastern slopes of the mountains. A comparison, for example, of the rainfall at San Francisco with that at Niles, 15 miles to the eastward, and at Livermore, 10 miles east of Niles, will show the decrease in proportion to distance from the ocean. According to the figures recorded at the stations of the Central Pacific Railroad Company, the amounts at the 3 places were in 1871-72, 28, 23 and 19 inches respectively; in 1872-73, 16, 14 and 11; in 1873-74, 23, 14 and 12; in 1874-75, 18, 12 and 12; in 1875-76, 26, 26 and 20; in 1876-77, 9, 9 and 6; in 1877-78, 32, 25 and 17; in 1878-79, 23, 15 and 10; and in 1879-80, 25, 18 and 16. The average at San Francisco, is 69, and at Niles 38, per cent. more than at Livermore. All studies so far undertaken to discover a regular periodicity in the variations of the Californian rainfall, or an increase and decrease, concurrent with the progress of the sunspots or with some astronomical cycle, have been unsuccessful.

There are 66 days with rain in a year at San Francisco, including 12 in December; 10 in January; 9 in February; 9 in March; 7 in November; 5 in April and 2 in October. In London there are 140 such days in a year; in New York there are 90. Many portions of the San Francisco region, beyond the range of the ocean fogs, have 220 clear days, without a cloud to obscure the sunlight. New York has not half, and London not a third so many.

Fog.—The shore of San Francisco's meteorological region is visited by frequent sea fogs, and they are especially abundant at the Golden Gate, as there they have a chance to travel inland at the level of the sea. Usually they do not rise to a height of more than 1,500 or 2,000 feet, and the summits of the Coast Mountains may be in clear sunlight while the valleys below are hid in the fog. In the City of San Francisco the summer nights are usually foggy, and a warm clear moonlight evening is a rarity; but after sunrise the land radiates out so much heat, that before the middle of the forenoon the fog is absorbed. The wind continues to blow with a velocity of about ten miles an hour, but the immense bank of fog over the ocean seems to be stationary, being converted into invisible moisture so soon as it gets to the land. At night, however, when the heat decreases, the fog can advance 10 or 20 miles inland, and may maintain its position until midnight, then vanish, to appear again in the morning. This fog is especially abundant in the summer, and is one of the main features of the climate of San Francisco, contributing to make the evenings cold and dark.

Relative Humidity.—These summer fogs give a dampness to the atmosphere, along the shore of the San Francisco region. The amount of moisture in the air is measured by placing 2 thermometers side by side, one of them having its bulb covered with a wet cloth. When the air is saturated with moisture, there is no evaporation from the wet cloth, and the 2 thermometers register the same temperature. When, on the other hand, the air is very dry, the evaporation is rapid, and as evaporation causes cold, the wet bulb thermometer marks a lower temperature than the other. The difference between the two figures furnishes a basis for calculating the relative humidity; that is, the amount of moisture, in proportion to the capacity of the air at that temperature, to carry moisture, visible or invisible. The best method of stating the relative humidity is to divide the year into two semesters, or periods of 6 months; the warm semester from May to October inclusive, and the cold semester from November to April inclusive. This relative humidity is a matter of little moment to a healthy person in a temperature of pleasant warmth, but, even in such a temperature, it is important to the invalid suffering with pulmonary disease, and when the weather is either hot or cold, may have a great influence on the comfort of the most robust. The preponderance of recent medical authority has condemned the custom of sending consumptives to moist tropical places, like Havana, St. Augustine, Bahia, and Honolulu, and now recommends in preference, mountain health resorts in the temperate zone, with an elevation not less than 1,500, nor more than 3,000 feet above the sea, with a mean temperature not lower than 40° in January, nor warmer than 75° degrees in July, and a relative humidity not exceeding 60 in the warm, nor 70 in the cold semester. Such places, however, are rare. An examination of all the accessible meteorological statistics, justifies the assertion that nowhere on the globe is there a better combination of low humidity with pleasant warmth, and desirable elevation above the sea, than can be found at various places in the Coast Mountains of California. New Mexico, Nevada and Arizona have lower relative humidity, over considerable districts at least, but their summers are too hot, or their winters too cold. The following table includes the statistics of the best climates in the United States, Europe and Africa, for persons suffering with diseases of the respiratory organs; and also of various American cities which represent the meteorological conditions of populous districts. The figures have been obtained by extensive research, not only through books, but also by correspondence with the meteorological bureaus of various governments, and the table, as a whole, is the most comprehensive of its kind ever published :—

THE CLIMATES. 55

PLACES.	Relative Humidity.			Mean Temp're.		Elevation.	Latitude.
	Warm Semester.	Cold Semester.	Year.	January.	July.		
Atlas Peak, Cal.............	39	51	45	50°	74°	1500ft.	38°25'
Blake's, Cal................	44	70	57	45	73	2100	38 35
Santa Fe, New Mexico......	35	46	41	32	69	6851	35 41
Pignerol, Italy..............	58	68	63	38	76	950	44 50
Caltanisetta, Italy..........	48	74	61	45	78	1871	37 27
Beziers, France.............	62	64	63	43	75	300	42 38
Potenza, Italy..............	53	71	62	36	71	2756	40 39
Murcia, Spain..............	57	63	60	50	80	141	37 59
Foggia, Italy...............	53	73	63	43	80	286	41 27
Denver, Colorado...........	41	50	45	24	76	5269	39 45
Kimberly, South Africa.....	69	71	70	74	49	4400	28 55
Umatilla, Oregon...........	44	71	58	35	75	460	45 55
St. Paul, Minnesota	66	70	68	10	69	795	44 53
Jacksonville, Florida	70	69	70	56	83	23	30 24
Ashville, North Carolina....	79	65	72	32	75	......	35 35
Visalia, Cal................	42	72	57	45	88	348	36 20
Los Angeles, Cal...........	66	64	65	52	75	318	34 3
Santa Barbara, Cal..........	71	67	69	53	68	60	34 25
San Diego, Cal.............	75	69	72	51	72	65	32 44
San Francisco, Cal..........	74	72	73	49	58	120	37 47
San Rafael, Cal.............	65	83	74	48	67	60	37 58
Red Bluff, Cal..............	70	74	72	47	83	337	40 10
Sacramento, Cal............	68	78	73	45	73	75	38 35
Salt Lake City, Utah........	31	58	45	30	78	4362	41 10
Villaviciosa, Spain..........	51	68	59	42	79	2247	40 21
Madrid, Spain..............	61	75	68	40	73	2148	40 24
Balboa, Spain...............	83	76	80	51	69	32	43 15
Coimbra, Portugal..........	76	75	76	50	67	462	40 14
Pioche, Nev................	26	59	42	14	72	5778	37 57
Camp Apache, A. T.........	57	36	46	38	84	5000	33 47
Boise City, Idaho	44	63	54	32	75	2877	43 40
Camp Verde, A. T..........	38	41	40	37	88	3500	34 23
Llandudno, England........	79	83	81	37	62	......	......
Virginia City, Montana	49	41	45	19	64	5479	45 20
Boston, Mass.............,..	69	70	70	24	73	140	42 21
New York City.............	66	68	67	27	77	60	40 42
Chicago, Ill................	69	71	70	22	73	650	41 52
New Orleans, La............	69	70	70	53	83	56	29 58
Portland, Oregon...........	66	77	71	42	66	97	45 30
Olympia, W. T.............	72	83	78	38	64	36	47 2

This table includes only a few of the stations from which statistics of relative humidity and temperature are obtainable, the large majority being excluded, because their climatic conditions are not favorable for consumptive invalids. For this reason, all the stations in Germany, Russia, New Zealand, New South Wales and Canada, and most of those on the Atlantic slope of the United States, are omitted. Of all the stations in France, Beziers has the driest climate; of all in Italy, Caltanisetta; of all in the Spanish peninsula, Murcia; of all in South Africa, Kimberly; of all in Colorado, Denver; of all in Minnesota, St. Paul; and of all in Florida, Jacksonville. The table was drawn up for the purpose of enabling students to make a fair comparison of the climatic advantages of the best health resorts for consumptives, so far as obtainable meteorological statistics supply the material. The figures here given show that Atlas Peak and Blake's in the Coast Mountains of California, respectively, 20 and 30 miles north of Silver Gate, are unequaled in their combination of dry atmosphere, with a mild temperature in winter and summer, and a desirable elevation. No observations for relative humidity have been kept at any other part in the Coast Mountains, but there are, doubtless, many places in that range, south of the Silver Gate, with conditions equally favorable, as will probably appear within a few years. The relative humidity in winter is 62 at Cannes, 68 at Mentone, 71 at Nice and 80 at Pau, and those are the only figures within reach for those towns, considered among the best winter resorts for consumptives in Europe. In their combination of dry atmosphere with elevation, they are far inferior to various Californian stations in the winter; and physicians agree that most, if not all, are decidedly objectionable in the summer. Visalia, Camp Apache and Camp Verde are dry, but too hot in the summer; Salt Lake, Santa Fe, Denver, Pioche, Boise City and Virginia City, in Montana, are dry, but too cold in winter.

In 1877, Dr. F. W. Hatch, permanent secretary of the Californian State Board of Health, addressed a circular letter to physicians, requesting a report of their experience and opinions, as to the suitability of the various climates near them, to the needs of consumptives. The result was a strong preponderance of testimony in favor of the eastern portion of the Coast Mountains, at elevations ranging from 1,200 to 1,800 feet above the sea; and especially for that portion of the Coast Range north of the Silver Gate. In his official report of that year, Dr. Hatch said : " The fact, however, has been abundantly verified, that for the large majority of consumptives— those in a condition to endure the inconvenience of camp life—this mountain region is better suited than are the Sierra Nevada Mountains."

In 1879, the State Medical Society of California, at its annual meeting, unanimously adopted a resolution requesting the legislature to establish a State Hospital for consumptives. The legislature instructed the State Board of Health to make a report on the subject, and in 1880, the Board, in its annual report, recommended that such an institution should be established, and selected Atlas Peak as the preferable place for it. They also stated that a good site for such an institution in Southern California could be found at the Sierra Madre Villa.

Warm Belt.—Although the Californian lowland has a subtropical climate, it is not anywhere free from frost. The leading subtropical fruit trees, including the orange, lemon, fig, olive and date, when of mature age, can endure 12 degrees of frost—that is 12 degrees below the freezing point—if occurring only occasionally and lasting but a few hours, without serious injury; and to such cold they are exposed, in many of the Californian valleys, perhaps once in five years on an average. In the ordinary winter the mercury does not fall below 28° in San Francisco. The situations least troubled by frost are not the lowest lands, in the most southern part of the State as might be expected, from the fact that climate becomes warmer as we approach the equator, and that there is an average decrease of one degree of temperature for every 300 feet of elevation. These rules apply in California as well as elsewhere, but there are certain other facts which must not be overlooked.

Frosts are not rare at the level of the sea, near the tropics. The trade winds, blowing from the Pacific with a temperature of 55° over the coast of California, north of latitude 35°. during a large part of the year, render frost rare near the shore, but its chilly influence continuing through the summer is more damaging to fruit than an occasional frost.

The parts of California best suited for fruit sensitive to frost are portions of the "warm belt," a general term applied to portions of the hills, usually not less than 200 nor more than 2,000 feet above the level of adjacent valleys. It is important that there should be an adjacent valley, into which the cold air can flow down at night; otherwise the benefits of the elevation are lost. Frosts are more severe in the lower situations, and especially on moist soil, than on the dry hillsides; and more severe in enclosed valleys, with peaks covered with snow in their vicinity, than in open plains, far from the snow.

At the Sierra Madre Villa, 1,700 feet above the sea, on the hillside above the valley of the San Gabriel, there is much less frost than in the low land, 10 miles distant. The same relative exemption is enjoyed by the upper Ojai, as compared with the lower Ojai Valley in Ventura County. In Santa Clara County the hillsides about Los Gatos are found to have far less frost than the bottom lands near San Jose. At the Napa Soda Springs, at Atlas Peak, at Howell Mountain, and at various other places, the East-Napa Ridge has far less frost than has the fertile Napa Valley at its base. The plain of Santa Rosa, and the mountain side above it, show similar differences. As a general rule, the warm belt enjoys a much greater relative exemption from frost in the autumn and early winter than in the spring. In the hills, places which in ordinary seasons are exempt from frost from September till November inclusive, will, in April and May, have frosts almost as frequent and severe as those observed in the low lands.

In a paper read before the San Francisco Academy of Sciences, B. B. Redding said: "The zone in the Sierra, known as the 'foothills,' is as warm for the year, and as warm for the coldest month, as the Sacramento Valley in the same latitudes. This warm belt certainly extends to an elevation of 2,500 feet. Colfax, with an elevation of 2,422 feet, has a mean for the year of 60°, and a mean for the coldest month of 45°, while, for the same periods, Sacramento has, for the year, 60°, and for the coldest month 46°. Fort Tejon, on the Tehachapi Mountains, elevation 3,245 feet, for the year is but 6° colder than Tulare, in the center of the valley 3,000 feet below; while the temperature for the winter months is nearly the same."

Dr. James Blake discussed the same subject, a few weeks later, in a paper read before the same academy, and produced meteorological statistics to prove that the minimum temperatures in winter are less on the hillsides than in the valleys. For instance, he showed that during the first 5 days of the previous December, (1878), the mercury stood, in Sacramento, at 50° at 9 P. M.; and at 41° at 7 A. M.; indicating a decline of 9°; whereas, at Colfax (2,421 feet) and Emigrant Gap (5,221 feet high) there was no variation. At the latter place the mercury stood at 52° at 9 P. M., and 7 A. M. During those 5 days the air was quiet; but in the 5 days from the 11th to the 15th of the same month, while a strong wind was blowing, the temperature at the higher stations was considerably colder than at Sacramento, and it declined in the course of the night. Dr Blake found that January of 1878, a rainy and stormy month, had a mean of 49° at Sacramento, 45° at Colfax, and 34° at Emigrant Gap; while the following December, a calm and clear month, had a mean of 45° at Sacramento, 47° at Colfax, and 41° at Emigrant Gap. Among other things he said : "The only explanation that can be offered of this anomalous distribution of temperature is, that during a calm state of the atmosphere, the lower stratum of air that has been heated in the valleys during the day, gradually rises up *en masse*, its place being supplied by the cold air flowing down into the valleys, over the surface of the ground, that has been cooled by radiation during the long winter nights. This can only take place when there is a calm state of the atmosphere, and when radiation is not obstructed by clouds or fogs, conditions that prevailed to a great degree during December [1878]. Under these circumstances the heated body of air gradually ascends, and as our temperature curves show, can reach an elevation of at least 5,000 feet, and probably much higher. * * The fact is a most important one in its relation to the cultivation of semi-tropical fruits. The only time at which they are liable to be injured, at least up to an elevation of 3,000 feet, is during calm and cold nights, and on such nights, as has been plainly shown, it is the more elevated places that are the warmer. During our stormy weather, even in midwinter, the temperature never falls low enough at the elevations above given to injure them. At my residence, [2,100 feet above the sea, near Mt. St. Helena], most of the orange-trees that were planted out only last season, are uninjured. They certainly have suffered less than at Los Angeles, where a temperature of 23° has been reported, while at my residence the thermometer has not been lower than 29 degrees."

In a private letter, dated in 1881, Dr. Blake says: "I find on clear, calm nights that the thermometer at my place begins to rise about 3 A. M., and rises until 5 A. M., at which time it is 1° or 1.5° higher than at 9 P. M. From 5 A. M., to 7 A. M., there is generally a fall of about 2°, the minimum being reached at sunrise. During the early frost (November 15) last year, the thermometer at Calistoga [elevation 300 feet] was 21°; at Sacramento, 18°; and at my place, 44°."

Sacramento Climate. — The Sacramento region includes the basins drained by the Sacramento and San Joaquin Rivers. On the west it is sheltered from the ocean breezes by the ridges of the Coast Range, which may average 3,000 or 3,500 feet in height. As compared with the San Francisco regions, these basins have less fog, in the winters more cold, in the summers more heat, and in the low lands less rain, less timber, and more clear days. A prominent feature of the sky of the Sacramento and San Joaquin Valleys, as well as of Southern California, is the paucity of clouds. Week after week will pass, in the summer, without a film of mist near the earth, or a speck of cloud in the heavens. California, as a whole, is pre-eminently a sunny land, offering a great contrast in this respect to England, and to the western divisions of Oregon, Washington, and British Columbia. In London there are 2 hours of sunshine in the average day from October to December inclusive, and not more than 5 hours on the average in the year; in Sacramento the corresponding figures are about 7 and 10.

The temperature in the valley land is largely influenced, if not mainly controlled, by exposure to the breezes from the ocean. At the northern and southern ends it is bounded on the west by mountains 4,000 or 5,000 feet high; while near the middle, it is intersected by a considerable gap, and the mountains for 30 miles on each side are lower than they are to the north and the south. If we move northward from the Silver Gate, on the west side of the Sacramento Valley, we find a mean for July of 72° at Fairfield; 78° at Woodland; 81° at Williams; and 85° at Redding, an increase of 13° of temperature in 2° of latitude. If we move southward on the eastern side of the San Joaquin Valley we shall find a mean for July of 74° at Stockton; 79° at Merced; 86° at Tulare; and 90° at Delano, indicating a difference of 16° of temperature in 2° of latitude. Traveling eastward, on the line of the Central Pacific Railroad from the middle of the valley, we have 74° in Sacramento; 75° at Auburn, with an elevation of 1,360 feet; 75° at Alta, 3,607 feet above the sea; 62° at Cisco, 5,934 feet above the sea; and 60° at Summit, 7,017 feet above the sea, as means for July. Thus we see that, as we go northward or southward from the center of the valley, we get into greater summer heat; as we ascend the Sierra Nevada, the temperature of July remains the same, until we reach a point nearly 4,000 feet above the sea, and above that elevation it falls about one degree for every 200 feet. The valley is very hot at midday for several months in the summer. The mean of the July maximums in Sacramento in 1877 was 92°. On 3 days the thermometer reached 100° or more, the highest being 103°; on 7 other days the mercury went to various figures between 95° and 99°. In 22 out of 31 days in the month the heat was 90° or more. If we compare this with the same month in New York City, we find that it is 10° hotter. The mean of the month was about the same, but the mean of the maximums was 10° less on Manhattan Island. On only 2 days out of 31, did the mercury there reach 90°, and the highest figure was 93°,

At Red Bluff, which represents all the northern part of the Sacramento Valley, and presumably the sides of the adjacent mountain, to an elevation of 3,000 feet, the mean of the maximums for July, 1877, was 101°. The highest temperature of the month was 108°. The thermometer rose to 100° or more in 13 days of the month; and in 14 other days to some figure between 90° and 99°—leaving only 4 days with less than 90°. Visalia, representing the southern end of the San Joaquin Valley, had about the same intense heat in July. The mean July temperature of Red Bluff, in latitude 40°, 10', is the same as that of New Orleans in 29°, 58', but in the latter city the mercury does not rise above 96°.

Fortunately for the residents of the Sacramento-San Joaquin Valley, its intense heat at midday is counterbalanced by a relatively low temperature at night. Thus at Sacramento the mean of the July minimums is 58°, a figure implying that blankets must be used on the bed for comfort. New York, which has 10° less of heat at 2 P. M., has, on the other hand, 10° more heat at night, the mean of the minimums for the month being 67°. According to figures published in the New York *Tribune* at the time, the mercury at midnight in the 30 days ending July 21, 1877, fell only 3 times below 75°; and 8 times it stood at 80° or more. No approach to that heat has ever been observed in Central California. The mean of the July minimums is 69° at Red Bluff, and 77° at New Orleans.

The days when the thermometer rises above 100° at Red Bluff or Visalia, and above 95° at Sacramento, are usually days when a strong north wind blows. It might be supposed that a wind from that direction would be cool, but the north wind of the Sacramento Basin is hot, sometimes scorching hot, and always intensely desiccating in its influence, so that it blasts vegetation and fruit, occasionally kills small animals by sunstroke, and causes a serious depression in spirits in persons of nervous temperament. Such winds come, perhaps, a dozen times a year, and sometimes last 10 days, but not more than 3 usually; and the average intervals between them may be 2 weeks. The hot wind often blows in the Sacramento Valley with a temperature little above 80°, but it does not become very oppressive until it has a temperature of 90°; it then evaporates an inch of water within 24 hours. While it continues, cows give a third less milk than under ordinary circumstances; and if the wheat is "in the milk" the crop is destroyed. The hottest wind ever known in Central California was observed in Stanislaus County on the 23d of June, 1859, when the thermometer rose in the shade to 113°. It is said that this wind gives relief to asthmatics, but makes consumptives worse.

The oppressiveness of the midday heat in the interior of California, as well as in other parts of our slope between the 20th and 42nd degrees of latitude, is mitigated by the extreme dryness of the atmosphere, which carries away the perspiration rapidly, and thus counteracts the effects of the heat. As a consequence, there is less feeling of discomfort at Red Bluff, when the thermometer reaches 100°, than in New York, when it goes to 85°. In the former place, the mean relative humidity of the 4 months from June to September, inclusive, is 32, while in New York, during the same months, it is 71; in New Orleans, 67; and in St. Louis, 63. At all points east of the Mississippi it is more than double as much as in the northern end of the Sacramento Valley. In Sacramento City the relative humidity for these four months is 46, and at Visalia, 40. This extreme atmospheric dryness in California is a protection against sunstroke, the cases of which are rare, averaging not 5 per cent. of the number that occur in the American States, east of the Mississippi River. There have been, presumably, 120 fatal cases in California, within 30 years; and of these, 10 occurred in Colusa County in June, 1876. There are 4 annually on an average in the State. In St. Louis there were 135 deaths by sunstroke in the week ending July 19, 1878; in New York City there were 79 in the 24 hours ending at noon on July 1, 1880; in Great Britain there are 90 deaths by sunstroke annually. Hydrophobia, which is frequent in countries that have intense summer heat in a moist atmosphere, is rare on the Pacific slope north of Mexico; indeed, there is reason to doubt whether there is one genuine case on record.

Two or three sandstorms visit the middle and southern part of the San Joaquin Valley every year, and sometimes fill the air with dust to such an extent that lamps must be used in the houses while the sun is above the horizon.

The mean January temperature of Sacramento City is 49°; of Red Bluff, 47°; and of Visalia, 48°, showing a remarkable uniformity. On 5 days in January, 1878, the mercury fell below 32°, the lowest observation being 28°. On 6 days at Red Bluff it went down to the freezing point, the lowest being 25°; and in 7 days it went to 32° at

Visalia, the lowest being 24°. The frost is more frequent and severe at the ends of the great valley than in its middle. The mercury has fallen as low as 12° in the southern part of the San Joaquin Valley, the proximity of the Californian Alps, with their great masses of snow, making the frost more severe there than in any other part of the State near the level of the sea. At Red Bluff the mercury has fallen to 14°; at Sacramento to 16°, and at Sumner to 12°; but such cold does not occur more than once in 10 years, on an average.

There are 5° of latitude between Sumner, at the southern end of the San Joaquin Valley, and Redding, at the northern end of the Sacramento Valley. The average annual rainfall at the two towns, and at various intervening places, was thus calculated by B. B. Redding from statistics accessible in 1878 : Sumner, 4 inches; Delano, 4; Tulare, 5; Borden, 3; Merced, 9; Modesto, 10; Stockton, 13; Sacramento, 19; Marysville, 17; Chico, 22; Tehama, 16; Red Bluff, 18; and Redding, 29. These figures imply that in the Sacramento-San Joaquin Valley each degree of latitude brings 4 or 5 inches of additional rain. The towns in the San Joaquin Valley, from Sumner to Stockton are on its eastern side; the western side, in the same respective latitudes, has not half so large a rainfall.

As we ascend the Sierra Nevada, the amount of rain increases rapidly with the elevation. Thus, on the line of the Central Pacific Railroad, the mean annual rainfall for 8 years was 19 inches at Sacramento; 43 at Colfax, at an elevation of 2,422 feet; 47 at Alta, 3,607 feet above the sea; 55 at Cisco, 5,934 feet high, and 58 at the Summit, 7,017 feet high. This indicates an additional inch of rain for each increase of 200 feet in elevation. In these figures, one foot of fresh snow is counted as equivalent to an inch of rain, and above 2,000 feet there is some snow every winter; above 5,000 feet more snow than rain; above 6,000 feet nearly all the precipitation is in the form of snow, which near the summit is not unfrequently 20 feet deep, after much has melted, and the remainder has been packed into a hard mass.

Los Angeles Climate.—The Los Angeles meteorological region includes Santa Barbara, Ventura, and those portions of Los Angeles, San Bernardino, and San Diego counties, at the western base of the Coast Range, and on their western slope, fronting 280 miles on the Pacific, and extending on an average 40 miles inland. The entire region lies south of latitude 35°, and beyond the influence of those cold summer fogs and strong breezes which give a peculiar coolness to San Francisco in the summer. Los Angeles City lies only 14 miles from the ocean, without the shelter of any intervening hill, but it has a warm climate, the mean of July being 71°; the mean of its maximums being 80°, and of its minimums 62°. The mean of its January is 54°, the lowest temperature recorded for the month in 1878 being 37°. It is, however, not exempt from frost; for the mountains to the eastward, within 20 miles, rise to an elevation of 10,000 feet, and in the winter have much snow, which helps to send the mercury down occasionally as low as 24°, causing serious damage among the nurseries of orange and lemon trees. The cold is not severe enough to injure the old trees, or the fruit which is usually of full size and ripe, when the frost comes. San Diego, at the southern end of the Los Angeles region, has a mean temperature of 69° in July and 55° in January. Santa Barbara, near the northern end of this district, has a mean of 71° in July and 54° in January. These figures give a general idea of the temperature of the whole region. The climate, though not exempt from occasional severe frosts, is subtropical in its main features, and the fruits and ornamental plants include many varieties that belong to the warmest borders of the temperate zone. Going eastward from Los Angeles, at a distance of 50 miles we reach the San Bernardino Valley, from 800 to 1,200 feet above the sea, with about the same mean temperature as near the ocean shore; but occasionally with greater heat in July, and harder frost in January.

The greater part of this Los Angeles region has occasional hot north winds and sand storms in the summer. A hot wind at Santa Barbara, on June 17, 1859, had a temperature of 133°. Trees were blasted; fruit was blistered and killed; and calves, rabbits, and birds died from exposure to the wind. In the last 22 years no wind approaching that one, in heat or damaging effects, has been felt in any part of the State.

The average annual rainfall is about 15 inches at Santa Barbara, 12 at Los Angeles, 10 at San Diego, and 9 at Colton. The climate at Los Angeles has been marked by periods of large and small rainfall. Thus in the 4 seasons ending June, 1864, the highest rainfall was 13 inches, and the aggregate of the 4 years was only 28 inches, or an average for the period of 7 inches; while in the 3 years ending June, 1876, the lowest fall was 21 inches, and the average, according to one rain-gauge, was 24 inches. The average of the 10 years ending June, 1870, was 10 inches; of the 10 years ending June, 1880, 14 inches. The smaller rainfall in San Bernardino Valley is claimed to be advantageous to all those places supplied with abundant water for irrigation, on the theory that the dryness of the atmosphere protects the orange and other fruit-trees from destructive insects.

One feature of the climate of the Los Angeles, Utah and Arizona regions, and of the southern part of the Sacramento region, is the occasional occurrence of "cloud bursts," or extremely heavy rains, in which the water pours down, as if a reservoir had broken in the sky. The consequence is, that sometimes ravines, previously dry, are suddenly filled with water, which sweeps everything before it, not giving people time to escape. There is no trustworthy record of a cloud burst in or near any of the larger towns of California; they are of rare occurrence anywhere, and are never observed in the large valleys.

Oregon Climate.—The western Oregon region includes all those portions of Oregon, Washington and British Columbia, north of latitude 43°, and west of the summit of the Cascade Range. It has an abundant rainfall in summer, as well as in other seasons of the year, a moist atmosphere, a cool summer, a mild winter, little ice or snow, and a dense growth of coniferous trees over most of its area. The mean temperature of July is 69° at Portland, and 63° at Olympia; of January, 42°, at Portland, and 41° at Olympia. The climate of Puget Sound bears a close resemblance to that of England, but is 4° warmer in winter. At Porland, the highest temperature in July, 1877, was 91°, and the mean at 2 P. M., was 81° while the mean of the minimums, was 55°, indicating that the nights are always cool. The mean at 2 P. M., in January was 46°, and the mean of the minimums 36°. On 8 different days, the thermometer fell to the freezing point, the lowest figure reached being 18°. Only once did the thermometer remain so low as the freezing point for 24 consecutive hours. At Olympia the thermometer rose to 80° or more on 8 different days in July, 1877, and to 75° or more on 16 days. The mean of the minimums in that month was about 50°. The highest observation in January, 1878, was 52°, and the mean of the minimums was 36°. The lowest temperature was 25°, and on 8 different days the mercury fell to the freezing point, but never was so low as that at midday. No thick ice ever forms near the level of the sea on the Pacific side of the continent, in the latitude of Boston. The temperature is about the same on Vancouver Island as at Olympia.

The annual rainfall of the Western Oregon region is about 80 inches near the ocean, and from 40 to 60 inches 50 miles inland. On the eastern shore of Vancouver Island and in Southern Oregon it is less; and in the northern part of British Columbia more. There are no tornadoes. The mean relative humidity of the warm semester is 67 at Portland, and 76 at Olympia; of the cold semester, 77 at the former and 82 at the latter place.

The Eastern Oregon meteorological region includes the country between the 42nd and 55th parallels of latitude, and between the summits of the Cascade Chain and the Rocky Mountains. The temperature in the southern part of this region is nearly the same as in New York City; the mean of July being from 72° to 75°, and of January 30° to 35°. The annual rainfall, however, is only a third so much as at Manhattan Bay, not averaging more than 15 inches, but this is enough to secure good crops in the agricultural districts, the soil being moister than in California. The northern part of this meteorological region has a higher elevation, more cold in the winter, and more rain.

Utah and Arizona.—The Utah meteorological region, including nearly all of Utah and Nevada, and part of California east of the Sierra Nevada, has a temperature differing little from that of New York, the mean temperature of January being 30°, and that of July,

78°. The rainfall ranges from 18 inches, at Salt Lake City, to 4 inches, near Humboldt Lake. The average for the region is not more than 7 inches, and the evaporation, from exposed water surfaces, is more than 4 feet a year.

The Arizona meteorological region, which includes Arizona, Sonora and South-eastern California, has intense heat in the summer; and in the high lands, intense cold in the winter. At Tucson, the mercury is never below 90° at 2 P. M., in July; and the mean of the minimums for that month is 78°, indicating nights too hot for comfort. The elevation is 1,000 feet above the sea, and on 25 of the 31 days in January, 1878, the mercury fell to the freezing point, the lowest point being 24°. Yuma, at the level of the sea, representing the low valleys in Arizona, has a mean of 104°, in July, and 56° in January. In July, 1878, there were only 4 days in which the thermometer did not go to 100°; and in the 5 months, of May, June, July, August, and September of the year 1877-78, the mercury reached that figure on 99 different days. On 23 days in July, the mercury did not fall below 80°. Notwithstanding its broiling summer, the place is visited by frost in the winter. In the mountains the heat and cold vary with the elevation. The average annual rainfall, which occurs from June to September inclusive—the remainder of the year being the dry season—is 4 inches at Yuma, 13 at Tucson, and more in the mountains, running up to 25 inches in the eastern and north-eastern part of the Territory.

Of the climate of Western Mexico, south of Sonora, we have no meteorological statistics; but we know that it is hot, through the year, near the level of the sea, and, south of Sinaloa, the rains are abundant. The rainy season, or the wettest part of the year there, as in Arizona, is in the summer months.

Alaska.—The climate of Southern Alaska is chilly, damp and foggy in the Summer, and about as cold as that of New York in the winter. At Sitka the mean temperature is 30° in January, and 55° in July.

CHAPTER III.

CENTRAL CALIFORNIA.

The Pacific Slope.—The tourist having been brought to San Francisco, and the climate of the Pacific Slope having been described to him, he is now prepared to consider the relative attractiveness of various features of the scenery, business and society of this Coast. There is here much unlike anything to be found elsewhere, much that gains special interest from the fact, that it is situated in a country undergoing a rapid industrial upheaval. Progress is marching over the land with seven-league boots, and the grain which she sows at every step, unlike that mentioned in the Grecian myth, covers the land, not with destroying soldiers, but with peaceful producers. In most other regions, civilization is a plant of very slow growth, and does not blossom, until it has been cultivated and guarded for a thousand years; but here, within a generation, it reaches an unsurpassed luxuriance of bloom. The activity of business, and the surroundings of a prosperous population, make an atmosphere, that contributes much to the enjoyment of sojourners, as well as of permanent residents.

It is not to be supposed that all persons traveling merely for their pleasure, will find equal enjoyment in the same sights; but we may safely assume, that those scenes which have been most attractive in the past, to tourists generally, will also be so in the future.

Pleasure Resort Districts.—Among these, the first place belongs to San Francisco, with her leading business streets; her cable railroads; her ocean beach; her Seal Rocks; her spacious bay, studded with islands; her active stock market; her cemeteries; her park; her Chinatown; and her hundred hills, some of them crowned with palaces. The attractiveness of our Pacific metropolis varies little in the course of a year. The city is a resort of pleasure-seekers in the summer as well as in the winter. It offers a refuge from the heat of July, as well as from the cold of January, in the interior of the continent. The visitor may find almost equal satisfaction whether he comes in May, September or December. The novelties of the topography and architecture, and the main features of public life can be seen within a week, but the city never grows dull, and is the most convenient centre from which to explore the other districts. The second place belongs to Yosemite, with its cliffs, waterfalls, domes, and adjacent mountain peaks, and mammoth groves. The Yosemite requires six days, including the time going and coming, with two days (the shortest reasonable allowance) in the valley; and is entirely exhausted for the average tourist after he has staid there ten days. The best time in an ordinary season for the trip is from May 1st to July 1st. From October 1st to May 1st, the visitor is exposed to the chances of snows, which may interfere with his movements, even if they do not obstruct the roads for more than a few days.

With many persons, however, and especially those suffering from general debility, and desirous of sojourning for months, a favorite portion of the State is Southern California, where they find an inexhaustible charm in living out of doors through the dry warm winters, as well as through the summers, in the midst of ever blooming gardens and orange orchards never without flowers or fruit, and for many months bearing both at the same time. Los Angeles City is a convenient centre from which to visit the other portions of the sub-tropical coast, in the triangle bounded by San Diego, Santa Barbara, and San Bernardino, and is a metropolis possessing many attractions within her limits and in her near vicinity. San Gabriel, Pasadena, Santa Monica, Anaheim, Orange and Westminster can be reached within two hours; and the trip to Riverside—one of the most interesting towns in the State—takes half a day. This district appears to the best advantage in the early spring, from February to April, inclusive, when the hills and plains are green, the sky clear, and the temperature mild. From June to September, the heat is often oppressive, the landscape outside of the orchards, vineyards, and gardens always brown, and the roads are dusty. The traveler passing between San Francisco and New York, on the southern route, should not fail to stop at Los Angeles and see San Gabriel.

Another district that has many visitors, perhaps more than any other on the coast, is that of Santa Cruz and Monterey, situated within four hours ride from the metropolis, accessible by sea as well as land, supplied with numerous excellent houses of entertainment, and possessing a great variety of natural scenery and pleasant resorts, including bathing beaches, drives, mineral springs, great trees, and beautiful summer homes on the mountain tops. They continue to grow in favor as they are better known. The Santa Cruz district borders on the ocean, and preserves its verdure, outside of the gardens and cultivated fields, till late in the summer, and the tourist season at Monterey never closes, though the patronage is much larger from May to October inclusive, than during the other six months. Three days may suffice for a hasty glance by the hurried traveler.

The counties of Alameda, Santa Clara and Contra Costa may be considered another district, which includes the remarkable mountain summits of Mt. Diablo and Mt. Hamilton, the mountain passes and canyons back of Oakland, and the extensive gardens and orchards covering a large part of the plain from Oakland to Los Gatos, a distance of more than fifty miles.

Crossing the Golden Gate, we come to what may be called the San Pablo district, north of San Pablo Bay, including Napa, Sonoma, Petaluma, Russian and Clear Lake Valleys, with Mt. St. Helena, Howell Mountain, the Geysers, the Petrified Forest, the Sulphur Bank Quicksilver Mine, numerous excellent medicinal springs, and a large number of extensive vineyards. The San Pablo and Alameda districts appear to the most advantage from March to June inclusive, and, while a general idea of each can be obtained within three or four days, they are more varied in their attractions than Los Angeles, and will furnish entertainment for as long a period to those who have the leisure.

These six districts, which may be designated by the names of San Francisco, the Yosemite, Los Angeles, Santa Cruz, Alameda and San Pablo, include the most attractive features of Californian scenery, business and society; and for the average tourist, any one considered separately, has more interest than any portion of Oregon, Washington, Arizona, Nevada, Alaska, Idaho or Mexico, all of which, however, have their own attractions. It is not improbable that after a few years, Mazatlan, or some other town on the western coast of Mexico, will have many visitors every winter, from the northern portions of our Coast; but as yet, there is a lack of accommodations, amusements and society. The wonders and beauties of the Columbia River, of the snow peaks of Mt. Hood, Mt. Rainier, Mt. Adams and Mt. St. Helen's, and of the great peaks, and the inter-island channels of Alaska, will have many thousands of visitors every summer, after they are better known and are made more conveniently accessible.

The Canyon of the Colorado, and the ruins of ancient cities in Arizona, may also in a few years become far more prominent in the public estimation than they are at present.

We shall have something to say in subsequent chapters about Oregon, Washington, British Columbia, Alaska and Arizona, for the present, our attention will be limited to the Golden State.

Characteristics.—Now that we are in California, let us make a brief statement of her main characteristics. Many of these will be observed separately when we visit different districts, but it may be well to get a general view of them before starting out. We find a combination of rich resources and attractive features, such as can not be found elsewhere. Other lands, like Great Britain and France, New York and Pennsylvania, may be better fitted to maintain a dense population, but if they have much which California has not, on the other hand, she has much in which they are lacking. She has many peculiarities of climate, topography, scenery, geology, botany, zoology, industry and population. Her rainfall measures 20 inches, and the number of rainy days is limited to about 60 days in the year; or half as many as in the Atlantic States or Central

Europe. The scarcity of rain, between May and October, and of snow and ice in the winter, relieves life from many of the annoyances and discomforts experienced elsewhere. Thunder, hail and fierce windstorms are great rarities. The summers are cool near the ocean and hot in the interior, where the air is remarkably dry, and the sky, except in the rainy season, almost cloudless. Different climates are found at various latitudes, elevations and distances from the Pacific, and every meteorological condition may be found that is needed for comfort or health.

A Mountainous Country.—Numerous steep and high mountain ranges, most of them parallel with the ocean shore, cut the State into narrow strips of valley. More than 100 different peaks rise to an elevation exceeding 10,000 feet. The mountains are everywhere in sight, and the views not only from their summits, but from the intervening valleys, present a landscape that is grand and beautiful. The hills, generally bare of timber, have a beauty of modeling unseen in those regions where the heights are covered with forest. In the yellow or brown tinge of their midsummer garb there are charms little inferior to the verdure of spring. The sunlight has a peculiar warmth of color, in harmony with the tints of plain and mountain.

At the northern end of the State is Mt. Shasta, an immense volcanic cone, rising a mile and a half above the level of the ridges in its vicinity, covered with a complete mantle of snow, for more than a mile of vertical height, through nine months of the year, and visible from an immense area. It has no equal in the north temperate zone, and nothing that approaches it in Europe. Mt. San Bernardino and its associate snow peaks, supply a magnificent distance and contrast to the orange groves in the valleys of the Los Angeles, San Gabriel and Santa Ana; less elevated, but more remarkable for the territory which it commands, is Mt. Diablo, rising in the midst of the State, as in an amphitheatre, and looking down on an area of 40,000 square miles, and on the homes of 500,000 people. From its peak, the spectator can see the western slope and summit of the Sierra Nevada, from Mt. Lassen to Mt. Whitney, a distance of 350 miles, while in its immediate vicinity are fertile farms, and a little further the bays tributary to the Golden Gate, and the cities of San Francisco, Sacramento and Stockton.

The Californian Alps, as we call the highest portion of the Sierra Nevada, between latitudes 35° and 38°, have four great chasms, the most remarkable of which, the Yosemite, on the headwaters of the Merced, has a world-wide reputation for its cliffs, half a mile high, for half a dozen waterfalls, one measuring, vertically, a third of a mile, and for its peculiar dome-shaped granite peaks. Within a few miles are several groves of the *sequoia gigantea*, reaching a height of 300, and a diameter in the trunk of 30 feet. The Tuolumne, King's and Kern Rivers have each a chasm similar to that of the Merced, but less accessible as well as inferior in the combination of attractive features.

Geological Convulsions.—The marks of great geological convulsions are numerous, and include hundreds of extinct volcanoes. One of these, Mt. St. Helena, is visible from San Francisco, and the hills that bound Sonoma and Napa Valleys, on both sides, are mainly composed of igneous rocks. From the summit of Mt. Lassen, one of the highest and most prominent crater cones in the State, 35 others of less note can be counted. Thousands of square miles are covered with basalt, which in several cases filled up the beds of rivers, without covering the adjacent banks; these being of softer material, were gradually eroded in the course of ages, leaving the lava to stand like a huge serpent winding down through the landscape, the more remarkable, when, as at Cherokee and Columbia, it covers rich beds of auriferous gravel. There are numerous mineral springs, hot and cold, in various parts of the State, and in Sonoma and Plumas Counties, especially, there are canyons abounding with hot and steaming mineral springs.

Mineral Wealth.—California is striped longitudinally with valuable mineral deposits. Near the ocean is asphaltum, associated with petroleum. Next to this comes quicksilver, found from Trinity to San Luis Obispo County. Then we have the coal measures, and these are followed by large deposits of copper, at the western base of the Sierra Nevada. A little higher on the mountain side is a belt of placers and auriferous quartz; on the eastern slope is silver, and at the eastern base of the chain, borax. In gold the State is now more productive than the Australian Colony of Victoria, which long took the lead of the world.

Peculiar Vegetation.—In vegetation, California is unlike any other portion of the globe, though more akin to Europe than to the Atlantic States. We have no hickory, beech, white-walnut or basswood; our oaks, maples, black-walnuts, buckeyes, pines and firs, are species not found on the other side of the continent: our redwood, evergreen oak, valley oak, madroño, laurel, manzanita, ceanothus, chamiso, poison oak, alfilerillo and bur clover, the predominant plants in the indigenous vegetation near the ocean, are not found elsewhere.

Our agriculture is peculiar. Wheat occupies two-thirds of the cultivated area, and barley ranks next in the list of cereals. Usually, grain is cut with the header, taken immediately to the threshing machine, and left lying in sacks on the open field for weeks or months. Neither stack nor barn is needed for it. Maize occupies an insignificant place. The annual wool crop amounts to about 22,000 tons. Most of the domestic animals are never housed, and require no food but wild herbage. In fine wool and fast horses California excels. The European grape covers about 70,000 acres; the orange 10,000; the apple 6,000; the peach and apricot 2,000; the plum, prune and nectarine, 1,000; and the pear as many. The drying of raisins, plums, prunes, apricots and figs, and the canning of apricots, plums, prunes and pears, are extensive and growing industries. No country surpasses this State in the large size and brilliant color of the fruit, in the quantity produced in proportion to the number of inhabitants, in the length of the season for which it is found in the market, or in the enterprise and skill of its orchardists.

Flowers.—A resident of the Atlantic Slope who came to California several years since, with a party of editorial visitors, wrote thus of the flowers in the gardens of San Francisco and vicinity: "Like everybody else, I had heard much of the marvelous beauty and wealth of blossom of the flowers of California, and although the season of their glory and pride is far advanced, I was not prepared to see such wonderful exhibitions and floral display as was spread out on all sides, upon taking a drive into the residence portion of the city, on the afternoon of the first day of our stay here. Our carriage load of Eastern travelers had none of them been to the Pacific coast before, and one might well have thought that we were all jolly green in the matter of flowers, upon hearing our exclamations of suprise and admiration, as we drove about the city. Such fuchsias, trained up to and covering the second story windows of the houses, or standing out in trees of many feet high, and weighted with richly colored buds and blossoms. Such vines of ivy geranium, one solid mass of leaf and flower. Such roses of every imaginable name and kind. Such ivies, with leaves large enough for mother Eve to have covered herself with quite comfortably, if they grew as large in her day. Such beds of verbenas and such patches of heliotrope. I thought I had seen fine specimens of all these beauties before, but I had never seen anything like these, and I shall look at my own little handful of flowering plants and shrubs, which I have heretofore tended with so much gratification, as most feeble attempts at the cultivation of flowers. A sight of the flowers of California cannot but have the effect of seriously dwarfing the home productions of those who have seen the floral products of the Pacific coast, at least as far as regards size of vine and wealth and profusion of blossoms. The geraniums, which flourish equally well here with other flowers, a few of which I have named, and scores of others as rich and beautiful, not enumerated, are past their prime, and now fading in blossom, but after a short respite, they will again renew their life when the rainy season commences, and thus keep up their round of almost perpetual bloom and beauty."

Field for Sportsmen.—There are few portions of the United States, and there are not many countries in the world, that offer a better field of operation to the sportsman than can be found in California. Those who like sport combined with danger, will find all the excitement they wish in portions of the Coast Range, and on the western slope of the Sierra, where grizzly and cinnamon bears and Californian lions are plentiful. Deer, hare, rabbit and quail abound in most portions of the State. During the winter and early spring, large flocks of wild ducks and geese frequent the rivers and sloughs, and are shot in such numbers, by persons who hunt for a livelihood,

that they sometimes have little or no value in the market. There
is fine salmon fishing in various parts of the State, and notably in
the Sacramento River. There is good trout fishing in many of the
streams, and for those who are fond of deep sea fishing there is excellent sport in the harbor of San Francisco and the Bay of Monterey.

The Californians.—The Californians are, as a rule, well edu-
cated. Nearly all the leading men are natives of the Atlantic States
or of Europe, and many of them possess the best commercial and
industrial talents, together with culture and acquirements of the
most polished nations. Whatever has been done elsewhere to ac-
cumulate experience, to train observation, to enlighten the judgment, to aid the human muscle, to facilitate production, to protect
right, or to promote comfort, has been adopted here in its best form
—speaking in general terms—and, in many respects, has been improved. Numerous inventions made by Californians in the washing
of gold, the metallurgy of silver, the manufacture and transportation of lumber, the conveyance of water, the communication of information by the help of electric currents, and the traction of street
railroads, are, in their influence, imperishable additions to progress.
The most comprehensive system of codified law is that now in force
in this State.

The people of California have undertaken and successfully managed a multitude of great enterprises. Though our information in
regard to other countries is not full, there is reason to claim that
we have the largest dairy of the globe for the production of milk,
the largest butter dairy, the largest cheese dairy, the largest vineyard, the largest almond orchard, the largest orange orchard, the
largest mining ditch, the most productive placer mine, the most
productive auriferous quartz mine, the most productive silver mine,
the largest mining pump, the most remarkable pipe for conveying
water across a deep valley, (the silver mine, pump and pipe, are in
Nevada, but owned and managed by Californians,) the largest hotel,
and the corporation which has built the greatest number of miles of
railroad.

Romance of the Present.—California has few ruins, and those
few not grand in size, nor beautiful in design, nor rich in historic associations. The oldest buildings are the mission churches, rude in
architecture and coarse in material. The Indian mounds, the ac-
cumulations of ages, contain little save dirt, coal, and the remnants
of shells and bones. There is nothing to compare in archæological
interest with the kitchen heaps of Denmark, the lake dwellings of
Switzerland, the Indian mounds of the Mississippi Basin, or the
buried cities of Greece, Italy and Asia Minor. California's romance
belongs not to the past but to the present. It is the building up of
a populous, intellectual and wealthy community within a single
generation upon a basis of permanence, with skillful mining, manufacturing and agricultural industries, a world-wide commerce, a

brilliant newspaper press, an excellent educational system, and luxurious homes.

The Name California.—The word California was first used as the name of an imaginary island of the Pacific Ocean, in an obscure Spanish romance, published early in the sixteenth century; and when, subsequently, the Spaniards, sailing northward on a voyage of discovery from Acapulco, found a peninsula, which they supposed to be an island, they called it California. More than a century and a half later, Jesuit missionaries took possession of the peninsula, to which the name California was restricted, until 1769, when a party of Franciscan friars was sent to build missions on the coast, from San Diego northward. The territory thus occupied was called New or Upper California, while, what was simply California before, became Older Lower California. The two were considered different provinces, and were called, the Californias; sometimes under a single governor in military and a mission president in ecclesiastical affairs.

When the Americans obtained possession of upper or Alta California in 1846, they adopted its Spanish name, in official and popular use, and continued to do so until after the discovery of the gold mines of the Sierra Nevada. Then the territory became so important, that the peninsula fell into relative insignificance, and when the Constitutional Convention adopted a name for the State, they called it California, as it then did not need a qualifying adjective to prevent people from mistaking it for the region to the southward.

The Missions.—The present State of California was first seen by a white man in 1542, when Cabrillo, a Portuguese navigator, in the service of Spain, visited the coast on a voyage of discovery. On April 11th, 1769, the first white settlers of California arrived at San Diego, in the brig San Antonio; and on July 16th, 1769, the Mission of that place was founded by Franciscan Friars, under the presidency of Junipero Serra. The Mission of San Carlos, near Monterey, was founded in 1770; those of San Gabriel and San Antonio in 1771; that of San Luis Obispo in 1772; those of San Francisco and San Juan Capistrano in 1776; that of Santa Clara in 1777; that of San Buenaventura in 1782; that of Santa Barbara in 1786; that of Purissima in 1787; that of Soledad in 1791; those of San Fernando, San Miguel, San Juan Bautista, Santa Cruz and San Jose in 1797; that of San Luis Rey in 1798; that of Santa Inez in 1804; that of San Rafael in 1817; and that of Sonoma in 1823. The last was the most northern, and the only one established under the Mexican dominion. San Francisco de Asis, San Francisco Solano, San Antonto, San Luis Obispo, San Luis Rey, San Buenaventura, Santa Clara and Santa Barbara, were saints of the different branches of the Franciscan Order; San Diego, San Carlos and San Fernando, were national saints of Spain; San Gabriel, San Rafael and San Miguel, are archangels; La Purissima, Concepcion, Santa Cruz and Soledad, may be claimed as mysteries of the faith. Every mission had a sacred title.

From 1709 until the Spanish authority was overthrown, April 9th, 1822, the predominant authority was that of the friars. They held nearly all the land in trust for the missions, but had exclusive control. From San Diego to San Francisco, the estates of the missions were considered to occupy a continuous strip. The power of the friars over the Indians, who made up 90 per cent. of the population, was practically unlimited, but was not abused. The red men had no separate property, and could not select their residences or occupations. They began to diminish in numbers soon after the establishment of the missions, but had kinder treatment than they received after the authority of the friars was overthrown. The distance from San Diego to Sonoma is 500 miles; and, as there were 21 missions, they were, on an average, 25 miles apart; but, as they were not on a straight line, and the average distance from one to another, by the traveled roads, was about 40 miles. The sites were well selected, being usually in fertile valleys at the base of mountains, in situations well supplied with water. The sites of San Francisco and San Diego, selected on account of proximity to the anchorages, on the only deep bays, had the least agricultural advantages.

Mexican Dominion.—The friars were a self-denying set of men. They had little education or ability, but they were sincere, and generally managed the missions in a manner consistent with the principles of their order—the most ascetic and humble of all regular orders in the Catholic Church. Not one of the Spanish friars in California was ever the subject of any serious public scandal. Soon after the Mexican revolution began, the annual subsidy of $400 for each friar, from the government, was interrupted; the soldiers and Indians became insubordinate, and the civil authorities hostile; and the mission property began to decrease. In 1828, five of the Spanish friars left California, and those remaining alive, withdrew to the missions from San Luis Obispo to San Diego, in 1832, when a party of Mexican Franciscans arrived. In 1835, the missions were secularized; that is, the friars were deprived of the control over the lands and herds, which were to be divided among the Indians and white residents; but, as a matter of actual fact, the Indians got or kept nothing—all passing into the possession of the whites. During the next 11 years, California was in a condition of almost continuous revolution. The natives were not satisfied with the rule of governors sent to them from Mexico; nor, after they expelled the strangers, could they agree among themselves. Many of the leading men were disposed to favor the idea of an American, British, or French protectorate; and the probability of a change of flag, was a subject of frequent conversation.

American Settlers.—Before the end of the last century, American whalers visited the Pacific; and when the Mexican revolution began, the Americans had more ships in the North Pacific than any other nation. The overthrow of the authority of Spain opened the ports to trade, which fell mainly into the hands of Americans.

Young men from the Atlantic States settled at Los Angeles, Santa Barbara, and Monterey, for the purposes of trade. In 1826, the first party of American trappers arrived by land in California; and the first party of emigrants who came in wagons, arrived in 1844. In 1846, the majority of the white settlers north of a line drawn from the Golden Gate by way of Carquinez Straits and the American River, were Americans. It was estimated by D. Marsh, that there were in that year 7000 whites of Spanish blood, 10,000 mission Indians, 700 Americans, and 200 British, Irish, French, Germans, and Italians, in California. The Americans were confident in the advance of their country, as well as preponderant in numbers over the other foreigners. They believed that their government intended to obtain possession of California, and were anxious to hurry up the event, from which they expected a great benefit to the country.

American Conquest.—On the 7th of July, 1846, the American flag was hoisted at Monterey, and California became a part of the United States. Some resistance was made, but it was because of the bad management of the volunteer forces, not because of any affection on the part of the people for Mexico. The treaty with Mexico, transferring the dominion, was not ratified till May 30th, 1848; but before that day, an event, destined to change the business and population of the territory, had occurred. Gold was discovered at Coloma, January 19th, 1848. It was a great event, not only for California, but for the world. The placers proved to be very rich, and they covered an area of 10,000 square miles. There was room for hundreds of thousands of laborers, and they came promptly. The report of the discovery gained little confidence in the valleys of California until May, and was not generally credited in the Eastern States until the end of the year. In 1849, 80,000 immigrants came to California, and more than half as many for each of the three following years, so that the white population had increased more than twenty fold within three years. In 1849, a constitution was framed by a convention, which was in session six weeks, and adjourned on October 13th. On November 13th it was submitted to popular vote, and ratified; and at the same time a set of executive officers and a State Legislature were elected. This State Government had no legal authority until recognized by Congress, but under instructions from Washington, the Military Governor, Gen. Riley, issued a proclamation December 20th, relinquishing the administration of civil affairs to the State Officials, who had been installed five days before. It was not until September 9th of the next year that the State was admitted into the Union.

Rapid Progress.—Since the year 1850, California has made steady and rapid progress in many directions. The shallow placers have been nearly exhausted, so that now they do not yield more than $3,000,000 yearly, whereas they yielded $50,000,000 in 1853. The present annual gold production is about $18,000,000, of which sum more than half is from deep placers worked by the hydraulic process; and a third from quartz mines. The decrease in the gold yield, has been more than counterbalanced by the development of agricultural resources. California is now the leading American State in wool and wine, and one of the first in wheat. A great system of railroads connecting us with the Mississippi Valley, measuring 6,000 miles of road, west of the Rocky Mountains, has its chief ownership and transportation centre in San Francisco. Regular steamship lines connect us with Panama and Sitka and intermediate ports, and with China, Japan, Australia and Honolulu. California has become a centre of pecuniary enterprise, and a source of emigration for our slope, and has exercised a potent influence in Oregon, Washington, Idaho, Nevada and Arizona.

Californian Agriculture.—When the American gold hunters descended the western slope of the Sierra Nevada, or crossed the Sacramento Valley, in the fall of 1849, they said to one another that the country was unfit for cultivation, and would never be desirable for the permanent home of civilized men, though it might be an excellent place to stay for a few years, until enough gold could be accumulated to secure a comfortable residence in the Atlantic States or Europe. Every year brought evidence that they had undervalued the agricultural resources of the land, and that they had made a serious mistake in measuring its capacities by its appearance in the dryest part of the year. The introduction of the varieties of fruit trees, grape-vines, kitchen vegetables, ornamental plants, timber trees, sheep, cows and horses, better than any known to the native Californians, and the arrival of farmers, gardeners, orchardists, winemakers, shepherds and dairymen, possessing the highest skill of the most enlightened communities, contributed to make a rapid succession of changes, until now the agriculture of California is in many respects, inferior to that of no other country; and in many respects it has no equal. The *Westminster Review* says, that she was "first the treasury and then the garden of the world." Some other authority says she is "the cornucopia of the continent." She is competing with Spain in the production of raisins, with Sicily in oranges, with France in wine and prunes, and has not yet taken a fair start in olives and figs, lemons and limes.

San Francisco.—Though San Francisco had only 233,000 inhabitants in 1880 and, therefore, must be classed as to size with cities of the third or fourth grade, she may fairly claim a place in the first rank in point of interest to the traveler and student. She possesses a happy combination of advantages in her situation, the agreeable nature of her climate, the activity of her business, the rapidity of her growth, the cosmopolitan character of her population, and the abundance and variety of her public amusements. Nature and art have united their powers to make it the metropolis of this side of our continent. Her position is midway on the western coast; and topographical, industrial and climatic influences unite, with established routes of travel, and financial and social considerations, to make her the converging point of the entire slope. Her chief business district is 6 miles from the Pacific Ocean, on the eastern side of the head of a peninsula, 30 miles long, that separates the southern arm of San Francisco Bay from the sea. This bay, covering with its branches more than 600 square miles, has been aptly described as "a miniature Mediterranean," and in beauty and convenience for commerce, is not unworthy of its magnificent entrance, the Golden Gate.

The City's Origin.—The city is the successor and heir of two villages, those of San Francisco and Yerba Buena. The former occupied about 150 acres near the mission church, on the corner of Dolores and Sixteenth Streets, the mission having been founded by Franciscan Friars, October 8th, 1776. For 59 years the authority of the mission was dominant, at least nominally, but it was overthrown in 1835 by the decree of secularization, and then the village of San Francisco succeeded. In that same year W. A. Richardson, an Englishman, who had been residing for 13 years at Saucelito, erected a tent at 811 Dupont Street, as the place is now designated, to trade in hides and tallow. This was the beginning of the village of Yerba Buena, which in 1845 occupied about 40 acres of land on the shore of Yerba Buena Cove. The two villages were separated by 3 miles of sand hills, covered with dense chaparral, and the only communication was by a horse trail. San Francisco was Spanish-American and lived by the sale of hides and tallow; Yerba Buena was American and British, and lived by trading. A great change was made in July, 1846, when the American flag was hoisted, and San Francisco Bay became the headquarters of the American Navy on the Pacific. In July of the next year, the village of Yerba Buena assumed the name of San Francisco; and in July, 1848, six months after the gold discovery, had about 500 residents, or perhaps one-fifteenth so many people as the average annual increase of the population for the last 32 years. Every house not standing within 2 miles from the business centre of the city has been built within 36 years; and every house of the better class within 30 years. The face of nature has been changed, so that those who saw the site in 1848, no longer recognize it. Then there was scarcely level space enough for 500 people; now there is room for 500,000 people. Hundreds of hills and ridges have been cut down; and large tracts of ravine, swamp, mud flat and bay, filled up.

A City of 100 Hills.—Notwithstanding all that has been done by industrial art to reduce the steepness of the natural grades of streets and lots, including the transfer of 20,000,000 cubic yards of earthy material, San Francisco is still remarkably hilly, and may properly be termed "The City of 100 Hills." The highest point, a mile and a quarter south-eastward from the Mission Peaks, is 938 feet high. The Mission Peaks, twin hills of equal height, perhaps 200 yards apart, are 925 feet; Reservoir Hill, a mile north-west from the Mission Peaks, 920; Park Peak, 570; Bernal Hill, 480; Lone

Mountain, 468; Strawberry Hill, in the Golden Gate Park, 426; Russian Hill, a mile long, and the most prominent hill in the densely settled part of the city, 400; Potrero Hill, 326; Telegraph Hill, 294; South San Francisco Hill, 260; and Rincon Hill, 120. These are all within the city limits, and are but a few of many, the others being less notable because of remoteness from the settled districts or smaller elevation. Russian Hill, Telegraph Hill and Rincon Hill are covered with dwellings. Almost as numerous as the hills are the valleys, some of which are in the shape of amphitheatres, nearly surrounded by heights, from which the spectator looks down on a densely populated territory, interesting by day and brilliant at night when numerous long rows of gas lights and lighted windows are spread out, reaching to the hill-tops in the remote distance. Such amphitheatres are seen looking from Telegraph Hill to the south-westward, from Rincon Hill to the westward, from Mission Peaks to the north-eastward, from Russian Hill to the westward, and from its southern end to the southward, the last being the most attractive of these views, and also the most conveniently accessible. The city, as seen from the approaching Oakland ferry-boat, makes an impressive appearance, especially at night, when ablaze with lines of light climbing its hills. A clergyman from Ohio, the Rev. G. W. Pepper, thus expressed himself:

"Inconceivably beautiful is the first glimpse of San Francisco. This city is the grandest embodiment of the American mind! the most modern type of the ancient cities, which fancy dreams of in the past! American genius covered that sandy ground with a throng of business temples, sacred edifices, palatial residences—the comeliest assemblages of structures the sun has ever gilded. The public buildings—the Mint, the California Bank, the Merchants Exchange, the hotels—Baldwin, Occident, Lick House, and the Palace, are marvels of architecture. * * San Francisco has no rival in the United States. We may contrast, but not compare it with Eastern or even European cities. London is grand but not beautiful. Paris is beautiful but not grand. Constantinople is picturesque, but has no architectural splendor. But San Francisco has all these attributes. It has been compared to Cleveland, city of beautiful avenues, Cleveland is charming; San Francisco is stupendous, romantic; Cleveland is lovely; San Francisco is grand; Cleveland is American; San Francisco is Cosmopolitan; Cleveland is a garden made by man; San Francisco looks as if it were built by the gods."

A. E. D. Rupert, who wrote a book about his travels in the United States, says: "San Francisco is a city of wondrous sights. It is the most picturesque town in America—not even excepting Quebec—and also one of the most beautiful. Its streets, whether on the level plain or running up and down hills of various heights, are well laid out—wide and straight. They are well paved and extremely clean in summer, being almost daily or nightly swept by the trade winds—

by the way, the most faithful blowers I have ever met—and carefully sprinkled."

Telegraph Hill.—In the north-eastern corner of San Francisco is Telegraph Hill, so called because in 1849 and for some years afterwards, it was occupied by a Telegraph Station, with arms attached to a pole, and when a vessel entered the harbor, these were moved to indicate the character of the new arrival. The signal for a side-wheel steamer, about the time when the New York Mail, by way of Panama, was expected, attracted great attention. The hill is 296 feet high, and from its summit the best view of the water front and business portion of the city can be obtained. All the wharves, from Rincon Point to North Point, are in sight; with the shipping at anchor, either in the stream or in the slips. The Golden Gate and the Pacific Ocean, nearly all of both arms of San Francisco Bay, part of San Pablo Bay, the Contra Costa Mountains for a distance of thirty miles, Monte Diablo, the Suscol Hills, the hills beyond Napa Valley, the range between Napa and Sonoma, the plains of Alameda and San Pablo, Oakland, Brooklyn, Alameda, San Leandro, San Lorenzo, Hayward's, and various other villages, are visible. It is important to select a very clear day. The view is so extensive that a slight haze, scarcely noticed, when looking at objects within a mile or two, hides much of beauty in the distance. The wind on the hill is often cold and strong. The best time for going to the hill is about nine o'clock on a clear morning.

The following are the directions and distances of various points:

	Distance.	Directions.
The Farallones	35 miles	W.
Pt. Bonita Light House	6½ "	Nearly W.
Alcatraz	1½ "	N. N. W.
Yerba Buena Island	2½ "	E.
Saucelito	5 "	N. W.
Red Rock	9 "	N.
Two Brothers	11 "	N.
Two Sisters	13 "	N.
Fort Point	3½ "	W.
Oakland	7 "	E.
Monte Diablo	29 "	N. N. E.
Tamalpais	12 "	N. W.

Monte Diablo and Tamalpais are the two most prominent peaks visible from the hill.

Mr. Rupert says: "A good view of the city and its splendid surroundings can be had from several of the hills, especially from Telegraph Hill and California Street Hill. From these heights the traveler sees at a glance the whole city; a forest of houses, with domes and steeples towering above them; the busy wharves and the Bay, the largest, the most commodious and the safest harbor in America. Alcatraz and Goat Islands are near by. The former is not a smiling island. On the contrary, it frowns, and at times its thunders awaken the echoes of the surrounding mountains, for it is fortified and garrisoned by United States troops. * * * The beautiful city of Oakland, the Brooklyn of San Francisco, the villages of Berkeley and Alameda are there in full view, cast, just across the bay, some seven or eight miles distant, smiling under a blue and cloudless heaven; and almost under the shadows of a range of treeless mountains, green in winter and yellow in summer, that frame the panorama at whatever points of the compass the eyes may be directed."

San Francisco at Night.—A consequence of the topographical situation of San Francisco, on hills which enclose several amphitheatres, is that the city, as seen from various points, presents a most brilliant appearance at night. The best view is found on the corner of California and Jones Streets looking to the southward, eastward and westward, looking over many square miles intersected by lines of street lamps. The other portions of Russian Hill, north of California Street; and Telegraph Hill, have similar views, but less extensive. As seen from the bay, when approaching from Oakland at night, San Francisco presents a brilliant spectacle, of which Mr. Rupert says: "Your eyes seem riveted on something in the distance ahead. It is a strange, novel, wierd, fascinating sight, that something. It is a mountain looming out of the water some three miles in length and all ablaze with lights running upwards in close parallel lines, and losing themselves in the cloudless horizon above, among twinkling stars. Silvery stars above and golden stars below—splendid contrast! This miniature firmament profusely decked with stars of gold, and seemingly floating over the waters of the bay, is San Francisco, sleeping."

A Treeless City.—On account of the poverty of the soil on the peninsula, and the strength of the winds, large indigenous trees never grew on the San Francisco peninsula within 15 miles of the Golden Gate. Scrub oaks, more like bushes than trees, were abundant, but most of those have been cut down, and little has been done to find substitutes for them. The average temperature in midsummer being unpleasantly cool, the people want all the sunshine obtainable, and dislike trees which obstruct the solar rays. Moreover, trees are costly because of the lack of rain in the summer, and the expense and trouble of irrigation and, therefore, the residence streets are without those beautifully shaded avenues seen in other cities. The most common varieties are the eucalyptus, the Australian acacia in many varieties, the Monterey and Lawson cypresses, the Monterey and Norfolk Island pines, and various dwarf palms. Frequently when they become large enough to cast much shade, they are cut down to make room for smaller ones. Horse chestnut, linden, maple, Lombardy poplar, silver poplar and elm of eastern cities are, if not lacking, very rare here.

The glory of San Francisco's vegetation, is in her ornamental gardens, green, luxuriant and bright, with flowers throughout the year. Large, blooming, sub-tropical shrubs, such as cannot be cultivated in the open air, in places where the temperature is often fully 10° below the freezing point, are here abundant; including fuchsias, brugmansias, heliotropes, French roses, flowering verbenas, and geraniums; the calla lily, though of a different class, deserves to be mentioned with them. Many of the flowers of New York and Illinois are rare in California, and most of our flowers cannot live there, in the open air, through the winter.

A Great Seaport.—San Francisco is a great seaport, sending many large cargoes to distant countries, receiving others in return, and almost monopolizing the foreign commerce of the coast north of Mexico. Every ocean steamer line touching our continent, between Sitka and Panama, has its terminus here. She is the only point which the traveler cannot avoid when passing round the globe by regular lines of steam communication. She is the chief centre of the railroads west of the Rocky Mountains. Her exports, including treasure, exceed $100,000,000, annually. The bulk of the precious metals turned out by the mines of California and Nevada since 1848, amounting in value to nearly $2,000,000,000, has been forwarded to San Francisco. Much of it has been produced by mines owned here, and it has, therefore, helped to enrich the city. The most active of all stock markets was that in which the shares of the Nevada mines were sold from 1871 to 1877, while the Comstock Lode was in its most productive condition. San Francisco has one-fifth of the population and one-third of the wealth, and owns most of the banking capital, rich mines and railroads of the Coast. She counts more than 50 millionaires among her citizens; she has a large share of the manufacturing industry of the slope; and has the only sugar refineries, paint mills, glass works, brass foundries, and the largest rolling mills, foundries, machine shops, woolen mills and factories for the production of clothing, shoes, gloves, harness, cigars, furniture, carriages and woodenware. Her vicinity is more densely populated, and yields more valuable agricultural produce, in proportion to area, than any other part of the slope.

A Pleasure Resort.—A metropolis is necessarily, to some extent, a pleasure resort. It combines many attractions which cannot be found in small towns. Within a little space, it has a large number of men eminently successful as bankers, underwriters, merchants, lawyers, editors, manufacturers and contractors. It is a center of intellectual and fashionable society, of musical, dramatic, and pictorial art, and of educational influences. It has commodious hotels, in which the stranger can live with comfort, and public amusements to occupy his attention every evening in the year. In all these respects, San Francisco is not inferior to other metropolitan cities. Her cool summer attracts those who dislike intense heat; its warm winter attracts those who seek a refuge from intense cold. Extensive portions of our slope are so wild, that the metropolis appears the more brilliant by contrast with them. As a pleasure resort, no city on our continent is entitled to so high a position.

There are no nationalities in Europe, and few in the world without representatives in San Francisco. Her inhabitants are not marked by the staid habits, grave demeanor and cautious reserve of older communities. The enterprise and intelligence of many races are blended among her population, and the dullard, the slothful, and the faint-hearted seldom find here an abiding place. There is probably no city in the Union, where so many men, starting in life with no capital, but their own brains and industry, have achieved a marked success; and there are few better fields for honest well-directed effort, than can be found to-day in the metropolis of this coast. The wages of labor are still 15 to 30 per cent. higher than on the other side of the continent, and 50 to 100 per cent. higher than in European cities; while the cost of living is lower than in either. There are few parts of the world where money can be earned so easily, or will purchase so much.

The Streets.—The visitor lands in San Francisco at the foot of Market street, which runs about north-east and south-west, and is the dividing line between the two main systems of streets. The other streets cross at right angles, and are numbered from the water front, or from Market street, 100 numbers being assigned to each block. There are numerous avenues, but most of them are in portions of the city which are not yet built up. The principal ones are Montgomery avenue, which connects Montgomery street with the northern portion of the city, and Van Ness avenue, 125 feet wide, and containing some very handsome residences, extending from Market, just beyond Eleventh street, in a northerly direction towards Black Point. The principal wholesale houses of the city are north of Market street, on Sansome, Battery, Front and Davis, and the streets that intersect them at right angles; the territory between First street, and the water front, south of Market, is mainly occupied by iron foundries, machine shops, planing mills and lumber yards. Most of the banks, insurance companies and offices are located on Montgomery or California streets, and a few on Sansome street. The principal retail stores are on Kearny street, the southern portion of Montgomery street, and the part of Market street, lying between Second and Fifth.

Architecture.—The business portions of San Francisco contain many handsome and imposing structures, and, year by year, the wooden buildings, that form the landmarks of earlier days, are being crowded out by substantial brick and iron edifices. The residence quarters, however, are occupied almost exclusively by frame houses, the mild climate and the liability to earthquakes giving them the preference over any other description of dwelling. On Van Ness avenue, and the streets lying to the west of it, the visitor may see a larger number of handsome frame residences than he will find elsewhere, within the same space, in any city in the world.

One feature that the visitor will notice in the prevailing style of architecture, is the multiplicity of bay windows, which are to be seen in almost every private house; and, in many buildings, as the Palace Hotel, stud the entire front, adding much to the comfort of the inmates, if marring somewhat the external appearance of the edifice. A large proportion of the permanent population live at hotels or in furnished apartments, and one bay window at least, with a sunny aspect, is considered essential in rooms occupied by ladies. In the principal streets of other large cities, most of the sunshine is excluded by walls of brick and mortar, but this is not the case in San Francisco. The sidewalks are mostly of plank, but there are many of asphaltum, and not a few of cut or artificial stone. Stone sidewalks are rapidly coming into use in the business portions and fashionable residence quarters of the city. The streets on which the heavy business teaming is done are paved with cobbles or rectangular blocks of basalt; most of the others are planked or macadamized.

Notable Buildings.—Among the notable buildings of San Francisco are the following:

New City Hall, S. E. corner of McAllister and Larkin streets.
Old City Hall, S. E. corner Kearny and Washington.
U. S. Mint, corner Fifth and Mission.
National Treasury, Commercial near Montgomery.
Main Post-office, corner of Washington and Battery.
U. S. Appraiser's Building, corner of Washington and Sansome.
Palace Hotel, Market and New Montgomery.
Occidental Hotel, Montgomery and Bush.
Lick House, Montgomery and Sutter.
Baldwin Hotel, Market and Powell.
Grand Hotel, Market and New Montgomery.
Russ House, Montgomery and Bush.
Brooklyn Hotel, Bush, near Sansome.
American Exchange, Sansome, near California.
California Theatre, Bush, near Kearny.
Standard Theatre, Bush, near Montgomery.
Bush Street Theatre, Bush, near Montgomery.
Grand Opera House, Mission, near Third.
Tivoli, Eddy, near Powell.
Panorama Halls, Mason and Eddy; Market and Tenth.
Vienna Garden, Stockton and Sutter.
Mercantile Library, Bush, near Sansome.
Mechanics' Institute, Post, near Montgomery.
Odd Fellows' Hall, Montgomery, near California.
Free Library, Bush, near Kearny.
Law Library, 27 Montgomery Block.
French Library, 120 Sutter Street.
San Francisco Verein, Sutter and Dupont.
Mechanics' Pavilion, Larkin and Hayes.
Hammam Baths, 11 Dupont street.

Safe Deposit Building, Montgomery and California.
Art School, 430 Pine street.
Bohemian Club, 430 Pine.
Union Club, Stockton and Post.
Pacific Club, Post and Grant avenue.
State Mining Bureau, 24 Fourth street.
Railroad Building, Fourth and Townsend.
California Market, California, near Kearny.
Fish Market, Clay, near Sansome.
Pioneer Building, 24 Fourth street.
Bancroft's Building, Market, near Third.
Leland Stanford's Residence, California and Powell.
Charles Crocker's Residence, California and Taylor.
Mrs. D. D. Colton's Residence, California and Taylor.
Mrs. Mark Hopkins' Residence, California and Mason.
Mission Church, Dolores, near Sixteenth.
Stock Exchange, Pine, near Montgomery.
J. C. Flood's Residence, California and Mason.
Unitarian Church, Geary and Franklin.
Calvary Church (Presbyterian), Stockton and Powell.
Trinity Church (Episcopalian), Post and Powell.
Synagogue Emanu-El, Sutter, near Powell.
St. Ignatius Church (Catholic), Hayes and Van Ness.
St. Patrick's Church (Catholic), Mission near Third.
Hop Wo Joss House, 751 Clay street.
Ning Wong Joss House, 230 Montgomery avenue.
Kong Chow Joss House, 512 Pine.
Dan San Fung (Chinese) Theater, 623 Jackson.
Ann Quai Yuen (Chinese) Theater, 814 Washington.
Chinese Merchants' Exchange, 739 Sacramento.
Cliff House, Geary and Beach.
Fort Point, Narrows of Golden Gate.

Other notable places or structures in the city are, the Oakland Ferry Landing, at the foot of Market street, (the boats for Oakland, Alameda, Saucelito and San Rafael, all have their slips together); the Pacific Mail Wharf, at the foot of Brannan street; the Long Bridge, from the Potrero to South San Francisco; and the Stone Dry Dock, 450 feet long and 31 feet deep, at Hunter's Point.

Mint.—The United States Mint, fronting 161 feet on Mission and 217 feet on Fifth street, is one of the handsomest public buildings in San Francisco. It is built in the Doric style of architecture, with massive fluted columns at the entrance. The basement and steps are of Californian granite, and the upper walls of freestone, obtained from Newcastle Island, in the Gulf of Georgia. The machinery is of the latest pattern, and is equal in efficiency to any used in the United States. When working to its full capacity, the Mint can coin nearly 1,000,000 ounces per month. For the year 1878, the total coinage was $50,186,000. Visitors are admitted daily between 9 and 12 A. M.

New City Hall.--The New City Hall on Park avenue, McAllister and Larkin streets, is not yet completed, although work was commenced on it in 1871, and over $3,000,000 have already been expended on the building. The cost of the entire structure is estimated at $4,500,000. The foundation which is of broken stone and cement, 6 feet in thickness, cost $600,000. When completed, the main entrance will front on a wide avenue, leading into Market, opposite Eighth street. The main tower is over 260 feet high.

Hotels.—The first-class hotels in San Francisco are the Palace, the Occidental, the Baldwin, the Lick and the Grand. The Palace and Grand Hotels, located on the south side of Market street, and on opposite sides of New Montgomery street, are connected by a covered bridge. The Grand does not, at present, furnish board to its patrons, and many of the guests take their meals at the Palace which, besides its large dining-rooms, contains a restaurant where meals are served to order. The Palace is the largest hotel in the world, and cost, with all its equipments and furniture, about $7,000,000. It is 7 stories in height, fronts 275 feet on Market street, with a depth of 350 feet, contains 755 rooms above the ground floor, and is capable of accommodating 1,200 guests. The building is solid, massive and simple in its style of architecture. More than 30,000,000 bricks were used in its construction.

Safe Deposit.—Another building that may interest the visitor is that of the Safe Deposit Company, on the south-east corner of Montgomery and California streets, in the basement. Here are steel vaults of burglar proof metal, and inclosed in fire-proof casing, containing 4,600 small safes, built in tiers, each one being furnished with a combination lock. Surrounding the vault is a corridor, where men keep guard day and night, and communicate every half hour with the headquarters of the police. Here travelers, stopping for a short time in the city, can deposit money, jewelry, securities or valuable papers, at a very moderate charge by the day, week or month. Packages containing valuables, can be left over for a single night at a charge of 50 cents.

Stock Exchange.—To many strangers, one of the most interesting and amusing experiences in San Francisco is a visit to the Stock Exchange. When mining stocks are lively, whether they are going up or down, the conduct of the brokers seems to verge on lunacy. Their movements, gesticulations and shouts resemble the fury of a violent mob more than the conduct of sharp business men engaged in making important pecuniary contracts. It is difficult for the visitor to distinguish, amid the babel of sounds and the excited gesticulations of the bulls and bears, a single word that is uttered, and he will wonder how the caller manages, amid the uproar, to note each transaction with such accuracy that, though thousands of shares may have changed hands, when the list of sales is afterwards read off by the clerk, the caller's decision is seldom disputed. Around the oval is a walnut railing, on the outer side of which on the main floor, are seats for spectators who pay for the privilege, and are usually occupied by persons who want to buy or sell stock. In 1876, when the mining stock excitement ran high, it cost $30,000 to be admitted to membership in this exchange.

The building was erected at a cost of nearly $900,000, and is over 80 feet in height, with a cupola rising 85 feet above the roof. The front is composed of alternate layers of dark and light colored granite; and the entrance is flanked with pillars of polished granite, and floored with English tiles; the walls being wainscoted with marble. The visitor passes through elaborately carved doors of walnut that cost $1,000 each, into the vestibule, on the right of which is a committee room, and on the left, the members' private room. The board room is wainscoted with black Belgian marble, above which is a panel of gray Tennessee marble, and above this again a border of carved primavera wood. The caller's desk is at the farther end of the room, facing the entrance, and in the center is an oval space where the brokers buy and sell, as each stock is named by the caller.

Nob Hill.—A ride of less than 5 minutes, from the terminus of the California street cars, and the expenditure of 5 cents, will bring the tourist within sight of the 3 largest and most costly residences in San Francisco, the property of the railroad magnates, who control the Central Pacific. The sum expended in their erection, with all the improvements and furniture, is probably not short of $6,000,000. Alighting from the car at Taylor street, the visitor may see, in the course of an hour's stroll, the principal edifices on Nob Hill, while enjoying a view that presents some very striking features. They are all wooden buildings, and are probably among the largest frame residences in the world.

On the north-west corner of California and Taylor streets, is the site of the Crocker mansion. The grounds are enclosed by a low wall of Penryn granite, surmounted by iron railings. A double flight of polished granite steps, 18 feet wide, leads up to a portico with Romanesque frieze and pediment, supported by fluted columns. In the picture gallery is a frieze which illustrates the progress of art, history and science, and many works of noted masters.

The mansion of the late Mark Hopkins is on the south-east corner of California and Mason streets. The gateway and doorway are flanked with pillars of polished granite. In the grounds are hothouses, arbors, grassy lawns, fountains, and almost every decoration that art can invent or wealth supply. At the top of the house is an observatory 140 feet in height, and adjoining the breakfast room is a conservatory containing some rare tropical plants.

The Stanford mansion, on the south-west corner of California and Powell streets, adjoins the Hopkins residence. There are other very expensive, and some elegant buildings on Nob Hill. The house built by the late General Colton, on the north-east corner of California and Taylor streets, is admired on account of the neat style of its architecture.

The dwellings of the millionaires, on Nob Hill and in San Mateo County, contain many interesting works of art, but are not open, as some of the European palaces are, to strangers.

Churches.—The handsomest and largest church building of San Francisco is the Jesuit College of St. Ignatius, occupying the block between Van Ness, Franklin, Hayes and Grove streets. A large part of the structure is used for educational purposes. The church hall is 200 feet long and will accommodate 6,000 people. Over the altar is a large oil picture by Tojetti, representing St. Ignatius Loyola at his reception in Heaven. The spires are 275 feet high, the highest in California. St. Patrick's (Catholic) Church on Mission street, near Third, has a chime of bells presented by Peter Donahue, and the largest organ in California. St. Mary's (Catholic) Cathedral has a picture of the Immaculate Conception by Capatti, not a work of great merit. The Synagogue Emanu El, on Sutter street, near Powell, is one of the finest buildings of its kind on our continent. The new Unitarian Church, on the corner of Geary and Franklin streets, will presumably be a handsome structure.

The oldest building in San Francisco, and the one most notable, considered historically, is the Mission Church, on the corner of Dolores and Sixteenth streets. The mission was founded October 8th, 1776, and we have no record of the time when the structure was commenced or finished, but the date of completion was probably not earlier than 1786. The adobe walls are 3 feet thick, resting on a low foundation of rough stone, not laid in mortar; and the roof was covered with heavy semi-cylindrical tiles. The floor was of earth, except near the altar, and the entire structure was rude in character. The walls remain, a shingle roof gives better protection against the rains than the tiles ever did, and the church is still used for purposes of worship. Adjoining it is the old Mission Cemetery, not used for purposes of interment since 1858. Most of the inscriptions are in Spanish, and among the tombs are those of James P. Casey, an ex-convict from the New York penitentiary, at Sing Sing, executed in 1856 by the Vigilance Committee for murder. He was one of a gang of unscrupulous ballot-box stuffers, who disgraced San Francisco from 1852 to 1856. His monument prays for mercy to his "persecutors," but does not suggest his own crimes. The grave of Don Luis Argüello, the first governor of California, under the Mexican dominion, is also here.

Clubs and Libraries.—San Francisco has seven public libraries, with about 200,000 volumes in the aggregate. The principal of these are the Free, the Law, the Mercantile, the Mechanics, the Odd Fellows, the San Francisco Verein, and the French. The largest is the Mercantile, with 50,000 volumes. There are half a dozen clubs, including the Pacific, the Union, the Bohemian (including many journalists and artists), the San Francisco Verein (German), the La Ligue Nationale Française (French), the Society of California Pioneers, (membership is limited to those who arrived in California before January 1st, 1850, and their descendants), the Society of Territorial Pioneers (membership limited to those who came before September 9th, 1850,) and the various German Turnvereins. The City has German, French, British, Italian, Spanish, Portuguese, Scandinavian, Swiss, and Dalmatian societies of mutual aid, and many of them render assistance to poor immigrants of their respective nationalities.

San Francisco Drives.—Among the drives in San Francisco most worthy of attention are the following:

First.—The Golden Gate Park.

Second.—The Hill Park.

Third.—The Cliff House, which can be reached either through the Park or by way of Geary street.

Fourth.—The beach, accessible by Geary street or through the Golden Gate Park. This beach is three miles long, and is in the best condition for driving at low tide, wet sand being much more compact than is dry.

Fifth.—The Mission Pass road, leading from the mouth of Merced Creek (the outlet of Lake Merced,) eastward to Market street, across the hills, and surmounting the ridge at Mission Pass which is 600 feet high, and has a good view of the city and bay. After leaving the ocean, this road, for nearly a mile, follows Merced Creek, and a mile and a half from the beach is the Ocean House, near the bank of Lake Merced, which is shaped like a V, one arm being a mile, and the other a mile and a half long, the average width being about a sixth of a mile. The water is fresh, and when the reservoirs of the Spring Valley Company, in San Mateo County, threatened to run short, has been pumped up to furnish part of the water supply of San Francisco.

Sixth.—Lone Mountain Cemetery.

Seventh.—The Alms House road. This leads southward from the middle of the Golden Gate Park, by way of the Lake Honda Reservoir, and south-eastward to the Mission Pass road.

Eighth.—The road from the Golden Gate Park south-westward to the Ocean House. This road has no attractions and part of it has been covered with drifting sand.

Ninth.—The Presidio Reservation roads.

Tenth.—Along the water front, from Powell street to the South San Francisco Dry Dock, including a visit to the Rolling Mill at Potrero Point. A Rolling Mill, for a person who has never seen one, is a very interesting sight.

Eleventh.—A drive to the top of Mt. San Bruno, ascending at the north-western corner of the mountain. The summit (seven miles from the New City Hall in San Mateo County, and 1,325 feet high), cannot be reached with a wagon, but the distance to walk is not more than a quarter of a mile. There is no shade on the mountain, and the chief attractions are its elevation and accessibility. From the Baden station on the Southern Pacific Railroad, the distance to the mountain top is about two miles.

The most attractive drives in adjacent counties near enough to be enjoyed without absence from the city over night are Pilarcitos Reservoir, San Mateo Canyon, the vicinity of Belmont, the vicinity of Menlo Park, and La Honda, in San Mateo County; Penitencia Canyon, and Pacific Congress Springs in Santa Clara; Berkeley, Wild Cat Canyon, the Fish Ranch, San Pablo Canyon, Piedmont, the circuit of Piedmont Hill, Moraga Valley, Haywards, the Laundry Farm and the Oakland Cemetery, in Alameda County; Alhambra Valley in Contra Costa County; Blithedale, White's Hill, Nicasio, by the Petaluma Road, and Ross Valley, by the hill from San Rafael, in Marin County; Napa Soda Springs, in Napa County, and the Sonoma vineyards in Sonoma County. Many of these places are accessible to good walkers, who leave the city in the morning and return in the evening. Among the points within reach from San Francisco, without staying away more than one night, are Mt. Diablo, Mt. Hamilton, Mt. Tamalpais, (by horseback,) Mt. St. Helena, (by horseback,) the Magnetic Springs, Pescadero, Howell Mountain, Pope Valley, Bolinas, and the petrified forest of Sonoma. Of these drives in adjacent counties, mention will be made hereafter.

San Francisco Picnic Grounds.—The places preferred for Picnics by the San Francisco people, are Woodward's Gardens, the Harbor View Garden and the Golden Gate Park, and the Ocean Beach in the city; Badger's Park, Shell Mound Park, Berkeley, Piedmont, and Strawberry Canyon, in Alameda County; Fairfax Park, Laurel Grove, Lagunitas Station and Saucelito Canyon, in Marin County; and Belmont, in San Mateo County. Woodward's Gardens, Harbor View, Badger's Park and Shell Mound Park, are usually crowded on Sunday in the summer, so that quiet people prefer to go there on week days. On pleasant Sundays in the summer, the Lone Mountain Cemetery, the Golden Gate Park and the Alameda Baths attract large numbers of visitors.

Golden Gate Park.—San Francisco has several public parks, the largest being the Golden Gate Park, three miles long and half a mile wide, with an area of 1,013 acres. It extends from the ocean beach eastward to Stanyan street; and from that street to Baker, two-thirds of a mile, there is an avenue 500 feet wide. This is one of the largest city parks. The New York Central Park has 862 acres; Fairmount Park, at Philadelphia, 2,706; Druid Hill Park, at Baltimore, 550; Prospect Park, Brooklyn, 550; Hyde Park, London, 389; Regent's Park, 473; and the Bois de Boulogne, near Paris, 2,158 acres. There are several large English Parks not far from London. Cincinnati and St. Louis have no large parks. The improvement of the Golden Gate Park was commenced in 1874, and in the last eight years about $650,000 were spent in its improvement. The greater portion of its area was bare sand dune, and to fix the drifting sands, to obtain good soil, and to make trees grow, under the strong breezes of the Golden Gate, were not easy tasks. A very respectable success was made, and San Francisco can boast that, in some respects, her park is unequaled. The mountain surroundings are beautiful. The Peaks west of the Mission are only a mile distant, and are 925 feet high. Strawberry Hill, within the limits of the Park, has an elevation of 426 feet; and Lone Mountain, in the vicinity of 468. There are places in the Park from which Mt. Diablo, Mt. Tamalpais, and the Golden Gate can be seen. The Park fronts on the Ocean for half a mile, and the beach for a length of two miles, is one of the most attractive of all beaches. The surf there is always beautiful and often grand.

The drives in the Park are numerous and in excellent condition. They are hard, smooth, free from dust in summer, and from mud in winter. In laying them out, the natural undulations of the ground were used with much skill, so that they should wind about, with gentle ascents and descents, as well as level stretches, and obtain a succession of pleasing landscapes. Trees, mostly eucalyptus, Monterey cypress and Monterey pine, have been planted out in large numbers, and if their growth has not been so rapid or beautiful, as in the fertile valleys of the State, it has, nevertheless, done much to beautify the place, and give shelter against the winds.

Near the eastern end of the Park, where nature had provided a small area of fertile soil, in what was formerly known as Sans Souci Valley, are a number of plats planted with flowers and ornamental plants, with intervening patches of grass and clumps of trees. Between 250,000 and 300,000 trees or shrubs are now in various stages of growth. A considerable portion of the ground has been graded and sown with suitable grasses; and by the aid of plentiful irrigation, fine grass plats and flower beds have been formed. There are also several grottoes, arbors, and artificial mounds, and numerous rustic seats.

On a plateau about a quarter of a mile from the entrance of the Park, is a conservatory 250 feet in length, the main attractions of which are the orchid house, which is not yet fully stocked, but contains some handsome plants, and the fernery, where is a fine specimen of the Victoria Regia or Amazon Water Lily, some of its leaves being 6 feet across. There are many miles of drive and walk laid out in the Park, and the main avenues are kept well watered every day during the dry season. The favorite drive leads down to the Pacific ocean, and brings the visitor in sight of the sea within less than a mile from the entrance. The Geary street cars, which start at intervals of 3 minutes from the junction of Geary, Market and Kearny streets, will convey the visitor to the Park in about 20 minutes for a 5 cent fare. Southward two blocks from the eastern end of the wide portion of Park avenue is the Hill Park, which is half a mile long from north-east to south-west, and a quarter of a mile wide, with an area of about 160 acres. An elevation of 570 feet at the highest point, commands an extensive view of the city, bay and ocean, gives it some attractions not to be found in any other public park.

Presidio Reservation.—Fronting on the Golden Gate for 2 miles on each side of Fort Point, and extending southward nearly 2 miles from the Point, with an area of about 1500 acres, is the Presidio Reservation, the property of the National Government, established for military purposes. Presidio is the Spanish name for a principal military station; and near Fort Point, Spain, and afterwards Mexico, maintained a presidio, and the name has been preserved by the Americans. The Presidio Barracks have the largest military force on the western slope of the United States. Fort Point, situated at the narrowest portion of the Golden Gate, is a brick building, supplied with many heavy guns. Gen. McDowell, commanding the Pacific Military Division of the National Army, has made fine roads through the Presidio Reservation, planted trees, and commenced other improvements, so as to convert it into a public park, which, in time, may rival the Golden Gate Park in its attractions.

One of the pleasantest walks in the suburbs of the city, is through the military reservation of the Presidio. Taking the California street cars at the intersection of Kearny and California streets, the visitor should ride out to the terminus, and from that point the road leads off to the right towards the Presidio. After ascending a small hill, he will come in sight of the Pacific ocean in two directions, and will obtain a fine panoramic view of the bay and its encircling hills. At the foot of the hill three roads meet. The one to the right leads back to San Francisco, and after passing through the eastern gate of the Presidio, at a distance of about a mile from the starting point, you meet the cars that run to the foot of Montgomery street. The two roads to the left (at the foot of the hill), meet each other at a sharp angle, and lead through the barracks, now occupied by the First Artillery, out towards Fort Point. The upper one will take the visitor through the officers' quarters, near which the band of the regiment, one of the finest in the service, plays every week day afternoon at 2 P. M., except on Thursdays and Saturdays. If time permit, the walk may be extended a distance of about a mile from the barracks, to Fort Point, with its large fortress of brick, earthworks, and fine view of the Golden Gate.

Point San Jose.—Another pleasant and shorter stroll in the neighborhood of the city, is through the reservation of Point San Jose, which can be reached by the cars that leave the foot of Montgomery avenue. The visitor should stop at Polk street, and from this point the path leads off to the right towards the reservation. After passing through the entrance, close to which are the Pioneer and Mission Mills, the largest woolen factory west of the Missouri River, the road skirts the grounds of the officers' quarters, at the gate of which are a couple of Spanish guns of very antiquated pattern. A few yards further you reach a fort, near which are 3 15-inch Rodman guns, the largest ever cast in the United States for general use, the exceptions being a few of 20-inch bore, made experimentally. They weigh about 25 tons, require a charge of 100 pounds of powder, and throw a solid projectile of 450 pounds, or a shell of 432 pounds. The site commands a very fine view of the bay; and the band of the Second Artillery plays at the officers' quarters every Thursday at 2.30 P. M. Returning towards the entrance, the road leads off to the right to the western boundary of the reservation, a short distance from which you again meet the Montgomery avenue cars, or, by following the line of the cars for a short distance in a westerly direction, the walk may be extended through the Presidio.

Cliff House.—One of the chief attractions and most famous places of California is the Cliff House, situated at Point Lobos, or the South Head, at the entrance of the Golden Gate. The house is a hotel built on a cliff at the edge of the ocean, and perhaps 100 feet above its level. Within 200 yards from the cliff, are 7 rocky islets projecting from the sea, and these, or the 4 nearest the Cliff House, are covered every summer day with sea lions, which are near enough to be seen and heard distinctly, for they keep up a continuous barking. The animal is a large seal, sometimes reaching a length of 11 feet, and is very active in the water. Thousands of them swimming in the water and climbing over the rocks offer a singular sight, not to be seen elsewhere so near a city. They could easily be shot from the shore, but the law protects them; though the fishermen complain that the sea lions greatly reduce the supply of salmon. The name of the sea lion in Spanish is *lobo marino* (literally, sea wolf), and the Spanish name of the place was *La Punta de los Lobos Marinos* (the Point of the Sea Lions).

The Cliff House is at the end of Geary street, called also Point Lobos avenue, and the Cliff House road. The Geary street cable road connects with a steam railroad which runs to the Golden Gate. When the steam car reaches First avenue, it turns to go southward to the park. At this bend, persons going to the ocean leave the steam car and take a horse car which runs out to within a mile of the Cliff House, and they can walk the remainder of the distance, or take an omnibus. Very near the Cliff House the beach commences, and half a mile southward is the Golden Gate Park. On a clear day there is an unbroken view from the Cliff House of the Pacific Ocean for 30 miles, with the Farallone Islands lying low on the western horizon, and a fine sweep of the coast line both north and south, with the promontory of Point Reyes stretching away towards the north. Attached to the house are long sheds, where horses and buggies are taken in charge by a hostler. The visitor can take lunch at the Cliff House, and afterwards drive back to San Francisco, by way of Golden Gate Park, which fronts on the sea beach, or he may return along the beach as far as the Ocean House, and return by way of the Mission Pass or the Alms House.

Woodward's Garden.—This favorite resort occupies a space of 6 acres, on Mission street, between Thirteenth and Fourteenth, and can be reached by several lines of cars. The charge for admission is 25 cents for adults, and 10 cents for children. This garden has many strong attractions, and as a cheap place of amusement for the multitude, has no equal in the United States. It includes a menagerie with grizzly bears, Californian panthers, coyotes, lions, tigers, kangaroos, and many other wild animals; a pond of sea-lions, which should be seen while getting their afternoon meal; an excellent aquarium; a conservatory with many tropical plants; a pavilion used for musical and theatrical performances on Saturday and Sunday afternoons, and occasionally for dancing and roller skating; a gymnasium; a picture gallery; a library; numerous amusements for children; a large variety of rare plants; and a restaurant.

San Francisco Cemeteries. — There are eight public burial grounds in San Francisco; of which three belong to the Hebrews, one each to the Masons, Odd Fellows, and Catholics, one to the City (used mainly for Chinamen and paupers), and the Lone Mountain Cemetery, as it is generally known, though the name adopted by the Company managing it, is Laurel Hill. Lone Mountain is a hill near by, but not within the limits of the tract. This cemetery, about two miles west from the corner of Montgomery and Post streets, is on hilly ground. The soil is sandy, and 30 years ago was covered with evergreen scrub oak trees, many of which still remain, and contribute much to its beauty. The grounds have been laid off, and the lots improved, with great expense and fine taste. Costly and elegant vaults and monuments, and plats covered with flowers and ornamental plants, in excellent condition, are numerous and varied. From the higher points, views of the City and Golden Gate can be obtained. The vault and monuments of W. C. Ralston, M. S. Latham, John P. Jones, W. F. Babcock, D. C. Broderick, Dr. E. S. Cooper, Gen. E. D. Baker, N. Luning, Horace Hawes, John Young, Judge Lyons, Thomas H. Williams, Charles McLaughlin, Thomas H. Selby, Judge Lorenzo Sawyer, Hiram Pearson, J. W. Tucker, Dr. H. H. Toland, Wm. Pierce, Sisson, and Patten, are a few among a multitude worthy of attention. Sir Charles Dilke expressed an opinion, common among travelers, when he said Lone Mountain is "the loveliest of all American cemeteries."

The visitor to Lone Mountain may be interested in seeing the *Yerba Buena* (Spanish for good herb), a kind of creeping mint, from which the village of Yerba Buena (changed in January, 1847, to San Francisco), obtained its name.

The Catholic (Calvary) Cemetery, adjoining the Lone Mountain Cemetery on the south, and a little farther east, in general appearance is much inferior to the Lone Mountain, but has some very large and costly monuments, well worthy of a visit. The vault of

W. S. O'Brien (of Flood & O'Brien) is of polished granite, elaborately carved. The monument of Mrs. Wm. Sharon is of chiseled marble, and was imported from Rome. The vault of W. Dunphy, built in imitation of the altar in the Cathedral of Notre Dame, and surmounted by a figure of Hope, was erected at a cost of $40,000, if rumor be true. Other notable monuments are those of John Dillon, Michael Hayes, Lynch and Sheehy.

The entrance to the Masonic Cemetery, a handsome and well kept burial ground, is on Point Lobos avenue, and on the line of the Geary street cars. The broad, serpentine walks, the fountain playing in the center, the profusion of flowers, and the large number of handsome monuments, make it well worth a visit. Near the entrance is a tall castellated tomb. The Brittan monument, a white marble obelisk, on the top of which is a statue of Grief, and one of polished Aberdeen granite, in memory of Dr. Hill, are among the many beautiful decorations. Besides these are the monuments of J. B. Fargo, Monroe Ashbury, Jas. Savage, Spreckels, Piper and Garratt.

The Odd Fellows' Cemetery, which adjoins the Masonic burial ground, fronts on Point Lobos avenue. One plot, of 2,400 square feet, is owned by the Grand Army of the Republic, and contains a beautiful monument, on which are inscribed the words "Mustered Out." The railing is flanked with pieces of artillery. On a hillock, planted with trees, is an obelisk, erected at the expense of $16,000, in honor of Past Grand Master Parker, who introduced Odd Fellowship into California.

Chinatown.—The Chinese population of California, numbers at least 75,000, and of San Francisco about 22,000. It is estimated that there are, in San Francisco, 13,000 Chinese laborers and factory operatives, 5,000 house servants, 3,000 laundrymen, and 1,000 merchants, storekeepers, traders, peddlers, and idlers. The female population is about 2,000, and there are but a few hundred children.

Chinatown proper, that is, the portion of the city occupied almost exclusively by Chinamen, extends from Stockton street, almost to the border of Kearny, and from Sacramento to Pacific streets, including all the lanes and alleys that lie between. The most densely populated portion of the quarter is the block on Dupont street, which is bounded by Jackson and Pacific. Here one finds himself in a labyrinth of passages, where none but the Chinamen themselves, and a few of the police officers can thread their way with certainty. The main artery in this network is termed Sullivan's alley, and midway in the block is a passage 2 feet wide, connecting Sullivan's alley, with narrow lanes, called Li Po Tai's alleys, from the fact, that the greater portion of the property is owned by a Chinese physician of that name. On the north side of Pacific street, and above Sullivan's alley, comes Ellick's alley, where are displayed some of the grosser features of Mongolian life. There are also in this neighborhood, many nameless holes and corners through which the visitor will not care to pass.

Joss Houses.—Of the 6 principal Joss houses in San Francisco, one belonging to the Hop Wo Company is located at 751 Clay street; one belonging to the Ning Wong Company at 230 Montgomery avenue; one is at 35 Waverly place; one at 512 Pine street, (the Kong Chow); one is situated in a lane on the north side of Sacramento street, 3 doors below Stockton; and one on Jackson street, between Stockton and Dupont. There are also many small temples, some of them belonging to private parties, and others supported by the companies or trades to which they belong. The laundrymen have one of their own, in connection with which is a sort of benevolent association. There are others belonging to the cigar makers and to different crafts.

Except a few tinsel ornaments on the balcony, and a figure or two perched on the balustrade, there is nothing to distinguish the exterior of any of the pagan temples from the better class of buildings in Chinatown; nor is the interior decorated with anything approaching to the splendor of an Oriental edifice. John is too practical to expend his hard earnings in erecting costly houses of worship in a land where he finds no abiding place. The wealthier Chinamen have, moreover, an idol of their own, before which they perform their devotions in their private apartments. In the Joss house, on Waverley Place, are several alcoves, in one of which are seated three gods, forming a sort of Chinese Trinity. The middle one is named "Yum Ten Tin;" or, the "God of the Sombre Heavens." He is supposed to control all the waters of the earth and above the earth; to have the power of extinguishing fire, and putting an end to drought. He is a vegetarian, and only vegetables and tea are offered on his shrine. On his right sits the Chinese god of war, named "Kowan Tai." His image may frequently be seen in stores and dwellings, and in San Francisco he is the favorite deity, being supposed to have the power of settling disputes, quelling riots, and intimidating the most lawless of hoodlums. The third of the trio is worshipped as "Nam Hoi Hung Shing Tai," or the "God of the Southern Seas." He is believed to have the control of fire, and when Chinamen, or their effects, are rescued from the flames, offerings are made to him of meat, vegetables, wine and tea.

In other alcoves are "Wah Tair," the "God of Medicine," who holds in his hand a large golden pill, and when invoked by certain mysterious incantations, is supposed to cure all manner of diseases, and "Tsoi Pah Shing Kwun," the "God of Wealth." The last mentioned holds in his hand a bar of bullion, and has, of course, many earnest votaries; the coolie and the capitalist alike bend the knee before his shrine. There are other images in the temple, all of wood or plaster, and some of them representing evil deities, which are also propitiated. The gods are never allowed to go hungry or thirsty. Food, tea, and sometimes wine, are always set within easy reach. A large bell, cast in China, and an immense drum, are used to rouse them when their slumbers are too protracted. In front of the altars are incense jars, filled with sand or ashes, where are kept, slowly burning, sticks of lighted incense, punk or sandal-wood. In the Clay street Joss house, are some copper screens, elaborately carved by hand, and representing scenes from early Chinese history. These are offerings presented as donations, by wealthy Chinamen.

In the Chinese mode of worship there is a remarkable lack of reverence and formality. They enter the temple as they would enter a lodging house, chatting and smoking and with covered head. Without uncovering, or ceasing their conversation, or even removing from their lips the cigar or pipe, they approach their favorite deity, go through the "chin-chinning process;" (bowing low three times) as rapidly as possible; leave their offering if they have one to leave; and go about their business without further ceremony. The female worshippers are more devout, often prostrating themselves before the deity, and giving utterance to their supplications with due reverence. The prayers and offerings of either sex, are nearly all for some worldly good; for success in business and in gambling, protection in journeys, freedom from calamity, recovery from sickness, etc. They have, however, a dread of purgatory, and their biggest worship days are when they pray the souls of their friends out of that supposed place of punishment.

The priests obtain their livelihood from the sale of paper money, incense tapers, and other articles required by worshipers. It is also customary for white visitors to purchase from them some trifle as a curiosity.

Connected with some of the Joss houses are hospitals, each able to accommodate 25 to 30 patients. Here the sick are treated and nursed without charge. Few Chinamen care, however, to avail themselves of this opportunity, preferring when sick, to remain among their friends. Even the indigent sick have a decided objection to being treated in a public building. The most interesting time for strangers to visit these temples is on the Chinese New Year, when grand services are held, offerings of all kinds are made, and large crowds of Chinamen gather for prayer. There is no special time for supplication, and all during the day (at New Year), some pious-minded Chinamen may be seen performing their devotions.

Sunday in Chinatown.—Sunday is perhaps the best time to see Chinatown in full blast. On that day the many factories, where Chinamen are employed, contribute their quota to increase the swarm; and most of the domestic servants spend part of the day there. The sight is an instructive, but not a pleasing one. In the Chinese workshops, there is no cessation of toil. In the multitude of their shops and cellars they make cigars, or boots and shoes, or bend over sewing machines, with backs that never tire. The cobbler is at work, seated on his box on the sidewalk, while a customer waits near by until his shoes are repaired. The barbers' shops are still busy shaving and shampooing the polls of their countrymen.

The shaving process is elaborate. The skin is scraped and washed, from the shoulders upwards, excepting only the portion of the scalp from which the queue depends. The queue is washed, combed, oiled and braided, and the eyelashes trimmed and sometimes tinted. The Chinaman as a rule is very careful about his person and especially about his ablutions. The veriest vagabonds, or thieves or jail birds, that hang around the gambling saloons, or lie two deep on and under the shelves of opium dens, are cleaner and more decently clad than many of the Barbary Coast denizens of San Francisco.

Chinese notions regarding the exclusion of women, forbid gentlemen being invited into their domestic apartments, but their families are visited daily by ladies connected with the Chinese missions. There are many family rooms in the rear of stores, and the majority of them are neatly and comfortably furnished, though in far too many instances they are overcrowded. The women brought here from China are often taken by their own countrymen as secondary wives, and the children born of them are, by Chinese law and usage, perfectly legitimate. The time of the women is occupied in needle work, the making of fancy ornaments and similar light occupations.

The children are healthy-looking, and appear to be well cared for. Their plump red cheeks, dark expressive eyes, and intelligent features, are in marked contrast with the sad, stolid, indifferent gaze of the adult Chinaman.

One may walk through the whole Chinese quarter without meeting more than half a dozen women; one or two of them perhaps, holding children by the hand, and hurrying across the street as if they had no business there. Young children are seldom seen on the streets, and never alone. In their attire, the women can hardly be distinguished from the men. Their garments are the same in pattern, but wider, and of better material. Their principal ornaments are worn in the hair, which, in front, is oiled and pasted close to the head, and at the sides and back is sometimes rolled and puffed, and decorated with gilt ornaments and lofty combs. The coiffure of the women indicates whether they be married or single, and is changed at different ages. Rings of bone or ivory are worn around the wrists and ankles. Ear-rings and finger rings, gilt, or of brass, are also commonly used.

At all hours of the day, and at most hours of the night, there is a kind of sluggish activity in Chinatown, but late in the evening, one may witness the most striking scenes. A walk of a few blocks from the most brilliantly lighted portion of Kearny street, will take the visitor to the dingiest portion of the Chinese quarter, where the streets are narrowest and most gloomy.

Chinese Holidays.—Festivals are almost as numerous among the Chinese as with the Russians; but there is only one that is universally observed as a holiday, and that is the Chinese New Year, which begins with the first new moon after the sun has entered the sign of Aquarius, and may, therefore, come at any time between January 21st and February 18th. In his mode of celebrating New Year, the Mongol is, in some respects, superior to the white man; he is never intoxicated, and he pays his debts. To be in debt on New Year, is considered disgraceful, and if there should be any laggard debtor who has not fulfilled his obligations, his creditors besiege him on the previous eve and threaten and worry him until he has made a settlement. Otherwise, the festival is celebrated in Chinatown very much as the white population, but with a little more noise. There is the same visiting from house to house, the same handshaking, the same kind wishes, and the same feasting. Instead of "Happy New Year," they exclaim, "New joy! new joy! get rich." Friendly salutations are exchanged on the streets. Cards of neat, red paper, with the name of the visitor inscribed in Chinese characters, are left at each house. The oldest friends receive the first visits, and then the more intimate among their comrades. Bunting and lanterns and placards decorate the walls and windows; bombs and fire-crackers are exploded (the police permitting), and gongs and kettle-drums are beaten to drive away from earth all the bad spirits that may have collected on the scene during the past twelve-month, and to usher in the new year without the presence of any evil influences. Other Chinese holidays are the day for the worship of the dead, usually in the first week in April; the feast of the goddess of Heaven in the last week of April, and the distribution of moon cakes in the second week of September.

Funerals.—Among Chinamen there is often much apprehension that a suitable coffin may not be provided for the repose of their remains; hence, a present of a handsome and well-made burial casket is no uncommon gift. At the better class of funerals, the body is usually dressed in new garments and covered with a white cloth. Different kinds of meat—cooked and uncooked, with vegetables, fruit, cakes, confections, tea and wine, are placed on tables at the feet of the corpse, and some of the food is presented to its mouth by the nearest relative. Sometimes fish and fowls, and even hogs are roasted whole for the occasion. The hired mourning women, dressed in white, then gather around, and on their hands and knees, utter their lamentations and eulogies over the deceased. Fire crackers are exploded, and drums and gongs are beaten to scare away the evil spirits. The body is then placed in the hearse, and on the way to the burying-ground strips of paper, in imitation of Chinese money, purchased from the priest of the Joss house, are scattered with a liberal hand, in order to propitiate the bad spirits that may be hovering around the route. Paper money is also strewn and burnt around the grave. After the corpse has been deposited in the tomb, and the earth heaped upon it, candles and sticks of punk are lighted and placed around the spot. The food, wine and tea are brought out to the grave. A portion of them are strewn about the place, and the party return to town and consume the remainder. There are no further ceremonies until a fortnight after the interment, when a day of special mourning is solemnized, if the deceased was a man of wealth or distinction, and especially if he was a parent. In such cases the ceremonies are very elaborate, and the memory of the dead is perpetuated for many years. At the burial of women and infants, and also of men who, during life, were poor and without influence, there is little formality observed.

On the second month of the Chinese year, and on the 24th day of the month, occurs the festival named Tsing Ming—the pure and resplendent. On that day the Chinese believe that the dead come forth from their graves and revisit the earth. Banquets, including all manner of delicacies, such as the living delight to partake of, are prepared for the ghostly visitors, and taken out to the burial ground. The graves are repaired; the trees and shrubs are trimmed; and ceremonies performed similar to those held at funerals. The party then returns to the city, and a feast is spread, in which all participate.

Chinese Theatres.—San Francisco has 2 Chinese theatres—the only ones in America—one at 623 Jackson, the other at 814 Washington street. The charge for admission is 25 cents for Chinamen, and 50 cents for white persons, who, however, if they wish to be comfortable, should have a box, which, in the Jackson street Theatre—the only one worthy of a visit—costs $3 additional, and will hold from 6 to 10 persons. The performance runs from 4.30 till 12 P. M., but the white visitor can see enough between 8 and 10 to satisfy his curiosity. The stage is narrow, without curtain or shifting scenes, footlights, or pictorial art of any kind. A sign on the wall back of the stage with the words, *Dom Quai Yuen* in Latin letters announces, that this is "The Elegant Flower House." Under tnat sign are the seats of the musicians, whose music, if that name can properly be applied to their noise, continues through all the plays, which seem to be semi-operatic in character.

Two doors, one on each side of the stage, with their openings directly in front of the auditory, are used for all the entrances and exits. There is no division of a play into acts, and a scene lasts while there are actors on the stage. After a man is slain, he soon afterwards gets up and walks off. The idea of a change of place is conveyed by symbols. A little bush on the top of a chair, brought to the front of the stage, conveys the idea that the actors are in a forest. And the street, the sea-shore, a field, and the interior of a palace or a hut, are suggested by similar devices. On the English stage, three centuries since, it was the custom to hang up a little sign stating the name of the town, or the kind of a place in which the event was supposed to occur. As in Shakespeare's time, so now in the Chinese theatre, spectators are allowed to go on the stage when there is not room elsewhere. The orchestra has half a dozen performers, using instruments unknown to the English dictionary, but bearing some resemblance to violins, guitars, drums and gongs. Their concert, a succession of squeaks, rattles and bangs, ludicrous in its quieter intervals, and hideous in its more violent fits, provokes wonder at the taste of the nation, which could invent, tolerate, and enjoy such discord. It has so little, of either melody or harmony, that it sounds more like a caricature than a serious attempt to gratify the ear. The acting is all done in front of the orchestra. The play often runs through several days, and usually represents prominent scenes in the life of some military hero, noted in the ancient history of China; a fellow of superhuman strength, rare courage, and wonderful success in all his achievements.

Merchants.—At 739 Sacramento street, are the new rooms of the Chinese Merchants' Exchange. They are fitted up in the ordinary Chinese style, and though presenting no special attraction to the visitor, the business transacted there is of considerable importance. A Chinese merchant, contractor or speculator, never starts on any enterprise alone. He always has at least one partner and in most cases, several. He makes no secret of his transactions, but converses about them at the Exchange, and often goes there in search of capital, when his own means are insufficient. He sometimes applies to that institution to find him a capable man to manage a new business, which he is about to start. If, as often happens, one be selected who is in debt to other members, they make arrangements which will not interfere with the new enterprise; and the debtor is not unfrequently released from his obligations.

Restaurants.—The Hang Fer Low Restaurant, on Dupont street, between Clay and Sacramento, is the Delmonico's of Chinatown. The second floor of this and other leading restaurants is set apart for regular boarders, who pay by the week or month. The upper floor, for the accommodation of the more wealthy guests, is divided into apartments by movable partitions, curiously carved and lacquered. The chairs and tables, chandeliers, stained window panes, and even the cooking utensils used at this restaurant were nearly all imported from China. Here dinner parties, costing from $20 to $100 for half a dozen guests, are frequently given by wealthy Chinamen. When the latter sum is paid, the entire upper floor is set apart for their accommodation, and the dinner sometimes lasts from 2 P. M. till midnight, with intervals between the courses, during which the guests step out to take an airing, or to transact business. Among the delicacies served on such occasions are bird's nest soup, shark's fins, Taranaki fungus (which grows on a New Zealand tree), Chinese terrapin, Chinese goose, Chinese quail, fish brains, tender shoots of bamboo, various vegetables strange to American eyes, and arrack, (a distilled liquor made of rice,) champagne, sherry oysters, chicken, pigeon, sucking pig, and other solids and liquids familiar to the European palate, also find their places at the feast. The tables are decorated with satin screens or hangings on one side; the balconies or smoking rooms are illuminated by colored lanterns; and Chinese music adds to the charms of the entertainment.

Chinese Missions.—There are several Missions in California, whose special objects are the conversion of Chinamen to the Christian faith, their education, the visiting of Chinese families, and the reformation of Chinese women. In San Francisco the principal associations are the Presbyterian Mission, 800 Stockton street, under the care of the Rev. A. W. Loomis; the Mission of the Methodist Episcopal Church, 916 Washington street, in charge of the Rev. Otis Gibson; and the Woman's Union Mission, at the northwest corner of Jackson and Dupont streets. In connection with them are evening schools, where classes are instructed in the English branches, by competent teachers. On Sacramento street is a Home and Reformatory for Chinese women and children, who have been rescued from slavery. The average attendance at all the evening schools, in California, is about 900, and the number of Chinese baptized in the Christian faith about 550.

Conveyances.—The means of public conveyance about San Francisco, and from the city to the surrounding country are excellent, and the fares generally are relatively low. The street railroads are numerous, the trips frequent, the cars clean and the conductors attentive. The ferry-boats on the bay are large and elegant. The railroads lead to many wild places in the mountains of Santa Cruz and Marin, and other places equally wild (and also within three hours from the metropolis), can be reached by stages from stations in those counties, as well as in San Mateo, Alameda, and Contra Costa. So wild is the country that in 1880, a wild cat was killed in the Golden Gate Park of San Francisco; and deer are found within two hours travel from the city. Having considered San Francisco, let us look at the neighboring counties, beginning with Alameda.

Alameda County.—Alameda, on the eastern shore of San Francisco Bay, is, in wealth and population, the second county of California. Distant from the metropolis only 6 miles, and connected with it by 3 lines of ferry steamers, its suburban population numbers 40,000. It has, besides, a remarkably fertile and warm soil, and contains some of the best land for orchards and gardens in the State. The city of Oakland, and the towns of Alameda, Berkeley and Haywards, have many attractions for strangers. The number of visitors who cross the bay, from San Francisco, on a pleasant Sunday in the spring is very large, often numbering, probably, more than 20,000. The four lines of horse cars run to the foot of the mountains, back of Oakland; and the canyons on both sides of the first spur, abound with romantic drives and places for picnics. The highest summits of the ridge near the western side of the county are about 2,000 feet above the sea.

Oakland.—Oakland is one of the handsomest cities in the United States. It is, in the main, a large collection of handsome suburban residences, each surrounded by a spacious and luxuriant garden. The ride across the Bay in the fine, large, airy and comfortable ferry boats; the short trip by steam cars into the city; the cheapness of the passage, considering the distance traveled, and the accommodations afforded; the frequent trips of the boats, making a return to

San Francisco every half hour always easy; the great safety and convenience of the passage; the facilities for traveling by nine lines of street cars, and by private conveyance when Oakland is reached; the number and variety of resorts and places worth visiting; the mild yet exhilerating climate and genial sunshine; the beauty of the city, and the charm of the grounds and residences of prosperous citizens, all combine to make a visit to Oakland one of the most agreeable experiences within easy reach of the tourist in California. The hotels are inferior, though there is one near Broadway Station which is a first-class house.

Lake Merritt.—Lake Merritt, a favorite place for boating in the eastern part of the city, a shallow sheet of water about a mile long by half a mile wide, was formed by throwing a dam at Twelfth street across the San Antonio estuary. Both sail and row-boats are kept for hire, 50 cents an hour for sail-boats, and 25 cents for row-boats being charged. There is no danger in boating on Lake Merritt. The waters are usually placid as a mill-pond, and never deeply agitated on account of the shallowness of the water.

Sunday Parks.—Shell Mound Park, a favorite resort for marksmen, lies three miles from the Oakland City Hall, in the north-eastern part of the city, and is accessible by the Berkeley steam cars, (fare, 10 cents.) It contains 5 acres and has two dance halls, shade trees, walks, swings, etc. No admission is charged except when the grounds are rented to picnics.

Badger's Park, in East Oakland, on the line of the Central Pacific local train, (on which no fare is charged within the city limits,) may be reached by the street cars which run on Twelfth street, 3 blocks distant, fare, 6¼ cents. It contains 5 acres, is a popular Sunday resort, and has a theatre and dance halls, refreshment stands, swings, shady walks and some fine trees. It is open without charge, except when rented to picnic parties.

Berkeley.—Berkeley, 4½ miles north of Oakland, is the seat of the State University. Steam cars (fare 10 cents) from the ferry landing, and horse cars (fare 15 cents) every hour from Broadway, Oakland. The carriage drive is fine. The elevation of the site of the University is about 400 feet above the sea, with a commanding outlook to the west. Facing the Golden Gate, the eye takes in the whole San Francisco peninsula at a sweep, with its hills crowned with houses, its forest of masts in the foreground, and the bold islands that deck the bay, while to the north-west towers the peak of Tamalpais. The walks through the grounds, which embrace 200 acres, are delightful, and the interest is augmented by the many foreign trees, shrubs and vines, as well as all the domestic varieties, making an extensive botanical garden, which are cultivated here.

A panoramic view of great interest and variety greets the eye of the visitor from the hills east of Oakland. In the foreground are Berkeley, Oakland and Alameda, then the glistening bay beyond, and the city of San Francisco, climbing the hills on the other side, the Golden Gate in the west, and the bold shore line of Marin on the north.

Piedmont.—Piedmont, in the hills, 3 miles north-east of Oakland, is a favorite resort. It has a good hotel, a mineral spring, avenues of trees, winding walks, shady lounging places, and many delightful outlooks. The Broadway and Piedmont street cars run every hour from Washington street (Broadway Station), to Piedmont.

The Oakland Cemetery lies in the upper end of a valley to the north-east of Oakland, 2 miles distant, has handsome walks and monuments. It contains 60 acres of diversified surface, and is well laid out and highly ornamented. A great variety of trees, shrubs, vines and flowers are cultivated in the grounds, making the place attractive. It is reached in 20 minutes by street cars, fare, 6¼ cents, from Broadway.

High Peaks.—East of Berkeley, and partly within the limits of the University grounds, is Strawberry Canyon, which has many nice places for picnics, and at the head of this canyon, a little more than a mile from the University in a direct line, is Brush Peak, 1,742 feet. The road to it is open, and there is pleasant shade on the way as well as at the top. Two miles south-east from Piedmont is Redwood Peak, which rises to an elevation of 1,639 feet. A wagon road used by farmers leads nearly to its top, on which grow whortleberry bushes.

Drives.—Oakland has many pleasant drives in its streets and vicinity, including those to the Cemetery, Piedmont, Fruit Vale, Berkeley, Alameda, the Fish Ranch, the Laundry Farm, San Leandro and Moraga Valley.

The most romantic short drive near Oakland is around Piedmont Hill. This leads out Broadway and Webster streets, to the terminus of the Piedmont horse car track, then turns to the right and follows the main road until it meets the car track at a short turn, there continues in an eastward course (while the car goes southward to the Piedmont Hotel), and follows the main road to the right, making a complete circuit and entering East Oakland on Thirteenth avenue. Wild canyons are seen on both sides of the hill. The length of the drive is about 5 miles.

Moraga Pass.—A longer drive and one still more romantic, may be found by turning sharply to the left, after getting about half way around Piedmont Hill, and going eastward over the Thorn Toll Road. This leads through Moraga Pass, crossing the mountain at an elevation of about 1,400 feet, and descending on the other side into Redwood Canyon, a tributary of San Leandro Creek. The road is steep and narrow but otherwise good, and leads through very romantic scenery. San Leandro Creek runs about 10 miles to the southward, through a canyon all the way, before it turns to the westward, and issues into the open plain. Those who want to take a long drive can follow the canyon down till it turns sharply to the left, while the main road turns at a right angle to the right. This right hand road leads out into the Alameda plain.

After the driver has followed Redwood Canyon in its eastward course down to where the stream bends to the southward, he can turn to the north-eastward and return by the Telegraph road, of which mention will be made in next paragraph.

Telegraph Pass.—By following the Berkeley horse car track from Berkeley out to Temescal, and there turning to the right, a romantic drive will be found crossing the mountain by Telegraph Pass, so called because the first telegraph running from Oakland eastward was built on this route. The summit, 6 miles from Oakland, has an elevation of 1,350 feet, and commands an extensive view to the east and west. About 2 miles beyond the summit is the Fish Ranch, a summer resort, where a good meal can be obtained. The water flowing past the Fish Ranch belongs to San Pablo Creek, and after flowing northward through a wild canyon, turns to the west and comes out into the plain. The drive from Oakland through the canyon is about 35 miles long, and, with a good team, carriage and driver, furnishes very pleasant occupation for a long summer day. The drive to Oakland from the Fish Ranch by way of Moraga Pass is 14 miles; or, by the Ranch road and Moraga Pass, 17 miles. The post-office address of the proprietor of the Fish Ranch is "J. H. Olive, of the Fish Ranch, Oakland."

Wild Cat Creek, a tributary of the San Pablo, rises east of Berkeley, and makes a canyon which can be reached by driving north from Oakland about 5 miles, and then going eastward 3. It has some pleasant scenery, but is smaller and less interesting than the San Pablo Canyon.

Laundry Farm.—Laundry Farm, 6 miles south-east of Oakland, is a favorite place for private picnics. It is in the hills, and its attractions are the great oaks, the rolling hills, the shady ravines, secluded nooks and fresh water. Sunday School picnics and quiet people generally go to Laundry Farm. It is reached only by private conveyance, going out on the San Leandro road to Mill's Seminary lane, and thence past the Seminary to the farm.

Haywards.—Haywards, 15 miles south-east of Oakland, a summer resort much patronized by visitors from San Francisco and Oakland, may be reached by steam cars on the Central Pacific Railroad. The town is of a quiet and orderly character, and is located in the midst of a superior farming community, where the farms are kept in a high state of cultivation. There are pleasant drives and walks in the vicinity.

Alameda.—Alameda is visited by many San Franciscans, especially on pleasant Sundays, on account of its abundance of trees, profusion of flowers, nice rambles in open grounds, and the various places of resort on the narrow-guage railroad, including the swimming baths and Schutzen Park, which contains 4 acres of ground covered with fine trees, and has a bowling alley, dancing hall and shooting gallery. Trains run to Alameda every hour, connecting with ferry-boats from San Francisco.

The Alameda Swimming Baths, which have a large patronage in the summer, are on the south side of the Alameda peninsula. There are 7 establishments, which occupy about 2,000 feet in length on the beach, and have an average width of 200 feet within their enclosures, and outside there are 3 miles of open beach of the same character for bathing purposes. The beach is a fine sand, firmly packed, and has a gradual slope, the water being only 5 and 6 feet deep 200 feet from the shore. The diving pools in the basins are from 10 to 12 feet deep, having been excavated for that purpose. There are in all 1,125 dressing rooms at the several establishments, and as many as 3,000 and 4,000 bathers have been accommodated on a Sunday. Hot salt water baths are provided for all who prefer them. The price of a bath, either hot or cold, is 25 cents. The average number of visitors on week-days, in good weather, is about 1,000, one-third of whom are ladies.

Fruit Vale.—Fruit Vale, 3 miles north-east of Oakland, is a delightful suburb of the city, in which are some fine residences of wealthy citizens, and many of the finest fruit farms in the county. Street cars run to this quiet retreat from Broadway, Oakland, and from the railroad station in East Oakland.

Contra Costa.—Contra Costa, so named, because, when originally organized as a county, it included most of the opposite side or counter coast of the bay, as seen from San Francisco, was afterwards divided, the southern portion of its territory being taken to make up the County of Alameda. The chief points of interest to the pleasure-seeker in Contra Costa are Mt. Diablo, Pine Canyon, San Pablo Canyon, Mitchell's Canyon, the Fish Ranch, and the town of Martinez. San Pablo Canyon and the Fish Ranch, though in Contra Costa, are most conveniently accessible for most of their visitors from Oakland, and have been mentioned in connection with that place. Pine Canyon at the western, and Mitchell Canyon at the northern base of Mt. Diablo, are places in favor with campers, having an abundance of shade, water, wood and pleasant scenery. Martinez is a pleasant town, well sheltered against the winds and fogs, by high hills on the west. The climate is similar to that of San Rafael, and is much better in summer than that of San Francisco, for people with weak lungs. The favorite drives of the Martinez people are to Alhambra, Pacheco, Ignacio, and Diablo Valleys; the picnic grounds are in Pine Canyon and Cox's Grove, San Ramon Valley. From Antioch there is a nice drive to Marsh Creek. Two miles from the railroad station of Byron, there are warm springs, which are supplied with a hotel and bath houses for visitors.

Mt. Diablo.—Mt. Diablo, 3,848 feet high, directly east from the Golden Gate, and 30 miles in a direct line from San Francisco, is seen every clear day by 500,000 people, and on account of its central position, rising like a cone in the midst of a large basin, is the most prominent mountain in California. Prof. Whitney says: "The most interesting short excursion, however, which can be made from San Francisco, is the ascent of Mt. Diablo. * * * From the summit the view is panoramic, and perhaps unsurpassed in extent. Owing to the peculiar distribution of the mountain ranges of California, and the position of Mt. Diablo in the centre of a great elliptic basin, the eye has full sweep over the slopes of the Sierra Nevada to the crest, from Lassen's Peak [in latitude 40° 30',] on the north, to Mt. Whitney [in latitude 36° 32',] on the south, a distance of fully 325 miles. It is only in the clearest weather that the details of the snowy range [the summit of which at the nearest point is 130 miles away,] can be made out; but the nearer masses of the Coast Range, with their innumerable waves of mountains and wavelets of spurs, are visible from Mt. Hamilton and Mt. Oro on the south, to Mt. St. Helena on the north. The great interior valley of California, the plains of the Sacramento and San Joaquin, are spread out under the observer's feet, like a map, and they seem illimitable in extent. The whole area thus embraced within the field of vision, as limited by the extreme points in the distance, is little less than 40,000 square miles, or almost as large as the whole State of New York."

From Mt. Diablo the spectator can see San Francisco, Sacramento, Stockton, Martinez, Vallejo, Benicia, Sonoma, Petaluma, San Rafael, San Mateo, Redwood City, and a hundred towns of less note. Among the most remarkable sights obtainable from the mountain, is its shadow in the evening as it advances across the San Joaquin plain, and gradually climbs from its base to the summit, ascending 8,000 feet, and reaching to a distance of more than 100 miles. Perhaps even more remarkable is the shadow as thrown at sunrise, in the midsummer, on the fog overhanging San Francisco. That part of the fog in the sunlight is brilliant white; while that in the shadow is a dark gray, conveying the idea, at first glance, that it is a large black mountain between the eye and the fog bank.

The following is a list of the principal points visible from Mt. Diablo, with their distances and general directions:

San Francisco	30	miles	S. of W.
Farallone Islands	63	"	S. of W.
Grizzly Peak	20	"	S. of W.
Mt. San Bruno	30	"	W. S. W.
Redwood City	30	"	S. S. W.
Loma Prieta	66	"	S.
Mission San Jose Peak	27	"	S.
Mt. Hamilton	42	"	S. S. E.
Mt. Oso	39	"	S. E.
Mt. Whitney	175	"	S. E.
Mt. Ritter	115	"	S. of E.
Stockton	35	"	N. of E.
Mt. Stanford	130	"	N. N. E.
Sacramento	54	"	N. N. E.

CENTRAL CALIFORNIA.

Downieville Peak	135	miles	N. N. E.
Marysville	90	"	E. of N.
Mt. Lassen	180	"	E. of N.
Marysville Buttes	90	"	N.
Suisun	25	"	W. of N.
Mt. St. Helena	66	"	N. W.
Martinez	12	"	N. W.
Benicia	14	"	N. W.
Napa	20	"	N. W.
Vallejo	16	"	N. W.
Petaluma	48	"	W.N.W.
San Rafael	32	"	N. of W.
Tamalpais	36	"	N. of W.
Golden Gate	35	"	S. of W.

These directions will be more satisfactory to the general reader than if given in the technical terms used by surveyors.

The views from the tops of high mountains are generally very unsatisfactory because, though the eye may range over a great distance, it cannot distinctly see anything of much interest. In the remote distance are seen dim outlines of mountains, and valleys, and the situations of towns and rivers, while the foreground and middle ground contain nothing but bare rocks and dark forest. It is the peculiar advantage of Mt. Diablo that it occupies a central position in the midst of a fertile country, so near that the dwellings, trees, wagons, fields and villages, at the level of the sea in the adjacent valleys, the streets of the metropolis, the steamers plying in its harbor, and the ships entering or leaving the Golden Gate, can be plainly seen. In the extent of fertile land within 30 miles, and the number and combination of towns, villages, bays, islands, rivers, valleys and snow-covered mountains visible from its summit, no other peak equals Diablo.

The view from every mountain top, however, is often indistinct on account of either the cloudiness or the haziness of the atmosphere. In California the tourist seldom has to complain of the clouds, but often of the haze, which seems to increase from the end of one rainy season till the beginning of another. The sky may be clear and the air dry, yet the lower strata of the atmosphere, as seen from an elevation, appear to be full of a reddish dust, which is thicker in the afternoon than in the morning, and thicker to the leeward of districts where there are many inhabitants, than to the windward. The best time to climb the mountains for the view is on a spring morning soon after a rain.

A wagon road to the summit ascends on the south-west, the steep rise being four miles long on the Pine Canyon route, and five miles by the Green Valley route. The two routes unite a mile and a half below the summit. The Pine Canyon road has a grade of 16 feet in 100, making it very hard for horses; and livery-stable keepers rarely let horses go to the summit, unless in charge of their own drivers. The distance from Martinez is 18 miles by tne Pine Canyon road; from Haywards, 21 miles by the Green Valley road. From Oakland the distance is 32 miles, and the aggregate of the ascents made is 5,400 feet. A horse trail leads to the mountain top from Clayton, by way of Mitchell Canyon and Deer Flat. The best way to go to Mt. Diablo, is to spend the night at Martinez or Hayward's, and start early in the morning. Each place has a livery stable, supplied with good wagons for large or small parties.

San Mateo.—San Mateo County occupies the greater part of the peninsula between the southern arm of San Francisco Bay and the ocean. Its most interesting features, as considered from the standpoint of this book, are the country residences of the millionaires near Menlo Park, Belmont and Millbrae, the Palo Alto horse farm, the summer hotels of Pilarcitos, La Honda and Pescadero; the camp grounds in the basin of the San Gregorio Creek.

Country Homes.—The plain between the mountain ridge which occupies the western portion of San Mateo County and the bay, is the nearest fertile district to San Francisco, accessible without crossing salt water. Here is a favorite place for the summer homes of Californian millionaires. The most luxurious of these places are the estates of Leland Stanford, D. O. Mills, Wm. Sharon, J. C. Flood and John Parrot. Their dwellings are in the midst of spacious grounds, which are planted with a large variety of ornamental plants, intersected by extensive drives, open on most of the places to visitors every week day. Menlo Park has more of these elegant country homes in its vicinity than any other station on the railroad running through the county; and a day can be spent there pleasantly driving through the private parks.

Palo Alto.—Palo Alto, Spanish for tall timber, suggested by a redwood tree on the bank of San Francisquito Creek, within a few steps of the railroad, is the name of the rural home of Leland Stanford. His ranch contains 8,000 acres, and for years it was noted as the largest horse farm of the world, having more than 500 thoroughbreds and trotters of the best blood. Its management differed from that of any other horse farm in its system of paddock practice— every colt, after reaching the age of 6 months, being tried on speed daily, except during rainy weather; in "short work," or brief exercise in training; in its system of feeding steamed grain to colts; and in the great care taken of brood mares, with inclosure in small paddocks by day and in stalls by night. Mr. Stanford has now given all this land to the Leland Stanford Jr. University, which is to have one of the largest endowments ever given to an educational institution, and is to be opened to pupils in 1889 or 1890. It is expected that the comprehensiveness of its plan and the excellence of its management will be worthy of the munificence of Mr. and Mrs. Stanford, its founders.

Summer Resorts.—Pescadero, on the ocean beach, 40 miles due south, in a direct line, from San Francisco, but about 53 by the ordinary route of travel, is a favorite summer resort. Its attractions are a commodious hotel with accommodations for 100 guests, a bathing beach near the hotel, moss beach, the pebble beach, and beautiful camping and picnic grounds in the vicinity. The moss beach, 12 miles to the southward, abounds with sea mosses which grow as parasites on the strong, coarse kelp. Many of these mosses are very delicate in their forms and colors, though much care and skill are required to spread them out and dry them in a manner to show their beauties to the best advantage. The pebble beach, 2 miles south of Pescadero, abounds with smooth pebbles, many of them from a quarter to half an inch in diameter, of moss agate, carnelian, opal and other stones, which, though not of much value, are interesting, and visitors lie there for hours in the sun, picking out the nicer specimens. It is said by those who have had opportunities for extensive observation, that no other beach in the United States is equal to this in the quality and beauty of its stones. Many of them have been cut and set in jewelry. There is a romantic road running near the ocean shore from Pescadero to Santa Cruz.

La Honda, about 14 miles west from Redwood City, in the redwood forest, is an attractive place of resort, and has a hotel which can accommodate 30 guests. J. H. Sears is the proprietor.

Pilarcitos Reservoir, 5 miles from the railroad station of Milbrae, and 22 miles from San Francisco, is a favorite resort for fishermen, who must have permits from the Spring Valley Water Company before they can fish. Mr. Ebright, whose post-office is Milbrae, keeps a good house for the entertainment of guests, and has a wagon to carry them to and from the station. The house has beautiful shade, and romantic scenery in its vicinity.

There is a beautiful drive from San Mateo, following San Mateo Creek, about five miles to Crystal Springs, then turning north to San Andres Reservoir, then east to Milbrae, and along the main highway of the county to San Mateo.

Santa Clara.—Santa Clara County occupies a prominent place in the horticulture of California, and contains a large area of fertile and well cultivated land. It has probably more trees in orchard, than any other equal area in the United States, and in 1882 it is pervaded by a fever for planting more fruit trees, not only in the valleys, but high up on the slopes of the mountains. The county may be reached from the metropolis, either by water, or by any one of the three railroads, one west and two east of San Francisco Bay.

The main points of interest to the visitors are Mt. Hamilton, Penitencia Canyon, the Pacific Congress Springs, the Gilroy Hot Springs, the Madrone Springs, the New Almaden Quicksilver Mine, the artesian wells, the strawberry fields, and the towns of San Jose, Santa Clara, Mission San Jose and Los Gatos.

The summit of Mt. Hamilton, in latitude 37° 25′, 4,448 feet high, 14 miles in a direct line, nearly due east from San Jose, and 26 miles by the road, has been selected as the site for an astronomical observatory, which was endowed with the sum of $700,000, by the will of James Lick, who died in 1876. A secondary peak, 140 feet lower than the highest summit, was preferred as the place for the observatory, because it could be graded with less expense. The level space on the observatory peak, is 250 feet long, and about 60 feet wide on the average, the widest place being 120 feet. The small dome of the observatory has been erected, and contains a twelve-inch telescope and a four-inch comet-seeker. The transit-house is supplied with time instruments. A contract has been made with Alvin Clark, of Cambridgeport, Mass., for the construction of a telescope, with a lens 30 inches in diameter, and they are at work on it. It will surpass in size every other refracting telescope.

Mt. Hamilton is situated between two ridges of the Coast Range. Ten miles to the eastward is the main divide of the chain, there about 3,500 feet high; and four miles to the westward is the Contra Costa ridge, there 2,500 feet high. The greater part of the space between these two ridges is filled with rugged mountain, covered with chaparral. Little of the San Joaquin Valley, and nothing of the Santa Clara Valley, within 8 miles, is visible from the summit, but on a clear day the spectator can see the summit of the Sierra Nevada, the Pacific Ocean, a large part of the Santa Clara and Pajaro Valleys, the plains of Alameda and San Mateo, Goat Island, Mt. San Bruno and Tamalpais. The view is inferior to that from Diablo. After Mr. Lick announced his intention to endow an observatory to be established on a mountain top, the French Government established one on the Pic du Midi, and the Italian Government one on Mt. Etna.

The road from San Jose to Mt. Hamilton has a smooth, hard surface and an easy grade, and in winding about the hills it gives a constant succession of charming views of valley and mountain. A hotel is to be opened on the summit in June, 1885, and one is now open at Smith Creek, 7 miles below the summit. A stage leaves the Auzerais House, San Jose, every morning in the tourist season, for the summit, stops there several hours and returns in the afternoon; round trip fare, $4.00. Many of the visitors prefer to make the trip in carriages from the livery stables, taking about 6 hours to drive up and 4 to return. Some make the round trip in one day, with the same team, but this is very hard on the horses, and not very satisfactory to the people. Information about the trip can be obtained at the office of the Lick Trust, in San Francisco.

Santa Clara Towns.—The county seat, San Jose, sometimes called the "Garden City," has 13,000 inhabitants, is a prosperous and beautiful town, embowered in trees, and surrounded by a rich horticultural district. The spaciousness and elegance of the gardens, the cleanness of the streets and roads, and the comfortable appearance of the dwellings, indicate that the people have good means. The county has 500 artesian wells, of which 300 are within 5 miles of San Jose, nearly all of them north of a line drawn east and west through the southern part of the town. These wells are used to irrigate strawberry fields, gardens and orchards. The deepest well in the county is 460 feet deep. The vicinity of San Jose has 1,200 acres in strawberries, and the yield sometimes amounts for short periods to 40 tons daily. The town was established on November 29th, 1777, by order of the Spanish Government, the settlers having been brought by land from Sonora. The town is lighted at night by a central electric light, supported at a height of 150 feet above the ground by a frame of gas pipe.

The town of Santa Clara, three miles west of San Jose, is connected with it by a horse railroad, and by two steam railroads, and by the Alameda, a beautiful wide road lined with large old trees on each side. The oldest buildings are those of the Santa Clara (Jesuit) College, and belonged to the Mission of Santa Clara, founded in 1777.

The Mission San Jose is the name of the town which has grown up about the Mission of San Jose, 14 miles northward from the town of San Jose, at the foot of the ridge east of San Francisco Bay. The adobe church, built about the beginning of the century was used till 1868, when it was so shattered by an earthquake, that it was torn down and replaced by a wooden edifice.

Pleasure Resorts.—Besides Mt. Hamilton, the leading pleasure resorts in Santa Clara County are Penitencia Canyon, six miles east of San Jose; the Pacific Congress Springs, the Gilroy Hot Springs, and the Madrone Springs. Every summer some campers go to the valleys of the Pala, Los Gatos and Calaveras Creeks. The Penitencia Canyon is a public park belonging to the city of San Jose, and is a very attractive place. It has mineral springs, a natural vapor bath and a commodious hotel. The vapor bath is in a tunnel cut into the rock. A mile above the hotel the Penitencia Creek has a cascade 70 feet high, and, half a mile below, another 30 feet high.

The Pacific Congress Springs have long been a favorite place of resort, have a good medicinal water, a beautiful situation, and a commodious and well kept hotel. The elevation is about 700 feet above the sea. The springs are a mile and a half from the village of Saratoga, and six miles north from the Los Gatos Station. The road leads through the hills at the eastern base of the Santa Cruz Mountain, amidst vineyards and orchards. This district has done more than any other part of the State, in clearing up chaparral and timber on the hills, to make room for orchards. Six miles westward from the Pacific Congress Springs, by a good wagon road which leads to Santa Cruz, is the summit of the mountain, commanding an extensive view of the Santa Clara Valley and the Alameda plain on one side, and Monterey Bay and its shores on the other.

Santa Cruz.—To pleasure seekers, Santa Cruz is one of the most attractive counties of California. It has convenient means of access with the metropolis by land and water, abundant accommodations for visitors, numerous mineral springs, umbrageous canyons, and camping and picnic grounds, trout in the streams and game in the hills, wild mountain scenery, great redwood trees which approach the Sierra sequoias in magnitude, and an extensive sandy beach on Monterey Bay, with situations well suited for bathing, boating, driving, clamming and gathering sea moss.

City of Santa Cruz.—The City of Santa Cruz, situated at the northern end of Monterey Bay, under the shelter of a protecting point, has probably a larger number of summer boarders, and of houses open for the reception of boarders, than any other place in the State. It is a beautiful town with neat houses, luxuriant gardens, excellent hotels, numerous pleasant drives and cheerful surroundings. By the South Pacific Coast (Narrow Gauge) Railroad, Santa Cruz is 80 miles from San Francisco; by the Southern Pacific (Broad Gauge) 121; by sea 70. The Broad Gauge route follows the valleys; the Narrow Gauge route, between Santa Clara and Santa Cruz, crosses the mountains. A horse railroad carries passengers, from the center of the city of Santa Cruz to the beach, which is a resort for many people nearly every summer day. The mean temperature of the water is 52° in January and 60° in July, in the bay, and the estuaries and lagoons, with which Santa Cruz is better supplied than any other town on the coast, are still warmer in summer.

Santa Cruz Big Trees.—The Santa Cruz Big Tree Grove, seven miles from Santa Cruz, on the bank of the San Lorenzo River, is one of the most interesting points within a day's journey of San Francisco. The distance is 73 miles from the city, and the Narrow Gauge road runs through the edge of the grove, so that there is no delay or inconvenience in reaching the ground. A party leaving the metropolis at 8:30 A. M., can spend nearly three hours in the Big Trees, and reach home at 7 P. M., the same day. The grove covers an area of about 20 acres, and has a score of redwood trees, 10 feet or more in diameter; one tree of 18 feet; several of 17 feet; many smaller redwoods, besides oaks, firs, and other trees. One stump of a redwood is covered with a summer house, which has seats for fourteen persons. Another stump with nine young trees growing up as sprouts from its sides, (some are 8 inches in diameter,) is 18 long steps in circumference. The Pioneer, of which an engraving is given on next page, is 17 feet through. There are many little redwood trees and other pleasant undergrowth. Numerous tables and benches have been provided; and while there is room for thousands of people, there are also numerous secluded little nooks, suitable for the smallest party.

The redwood is so much like the *sequoia gigantea* in form, foliage, bark, wood, size, and places of growth, that the two were supposed to be of the same species, until a small difference was discovered by an expert botanist: and this grove gives as much satisfaction to most visitors, as do the larger Calaveras and Mariposa Groves, which, if they have larger trees, cannot be visited without much more inconvenience and expense. The grove has a small house built for a hotel, but it is entirely inadequate to the wants of the situation, and in the spring of 1882, has no tenant. If there were a good house, there would probably be many summer boarders; that is, if the attractions of the place can be fairly estimated from the impressions left by repeated visits of a few hours each. Eight miles north of the Big Tree Grove, on the bank of Newell Creek, is another redwood grove, containing trees almost as large.

SANTA CRUZ BIG TREE.

Santa Cruz Mountains.—The ridge separating Santa Cruz from Santa Clara County, there generally known as the Santa Cruz Mountains, is 150 miles long. It starts as a spur from the main ridge of the Coast Range in latitude 36° 20′, serves as a boundary between San Benito and Monterey counties, runs through San Mateo, San Francisco and Marin counties, and disappears near the mouth of Russian River, in Sonoma. Its general elevation is about 2,000 feet, and its most notable peaks are Gabilan, Loma Prieta (Mt. Bache), Mt. San Bruno, Mission Peak and Tamalpais. The ridge in Santa Clara and Santa Cruz counties abounds with situations valuable for horticulture and for pleasure resorts. Vineyards, orchards and summer homes are found on the top as well as on the slopes of the mountains. Wright's Hotel and Reed's Hotel, each about 3 miles, and Redwood Hotel and Ocean View Farm, each 4 miles from Wright's Station, are on the summit there, about 1,600 feet above the sea. Near Wright's Hotel is Skyland, a camping place and summer village, where residents of San Francisco and San Jose have cheap dwellings. The Redwood Hotel, or Hotel de Redwood, is on the wagon road crossing the mountains, one of the pleasantest drives in the State. J. D. Whitney says: "The scenery on this road, from Santa Cruz to San Jose, is hardly surpassed by anything in the Coast Range."

Loma Prieta, 3,780 feet high, nearly east from Santa Cruz, is a prominent feature in the landscape, as seen from Monterey Bay or the Santa Clara Valley. It is a dark olive green mountain, covered with chaparral on its ridges, and with redwood timber in its canyons, with a flat top, rising about 1,200 feet above the general level of the ridge in its vicinity. The peak can be ascended either from Soquel or from Wright's Hotel, the distance from the latter point being 8 miles. On a clear day, the summit commands a view of Monterey Bay and its shores, the Pacific Ocean, the Salinas, Pajaro and Santa Clara Valleys, San Francisco Bay, the plains at its sides, the Coast Mountains for 100 miles to the northward and southward, and the top of the Sierra Nevada. Among the towns visible are Monterey, Salinas, Castroville, Carnadero, Watsonville, Santa Cruz, Soquel, Gilroy, Santa Clara, San Jose and Mayfield.

Santa Cruz Ruins.—Fifteen miles north-east from Santa Cruz, on the farm of D. M. Locke, is a peculiar sandstone formation resembling the columns of a ruined building. Prof. Whitney says:

"Here perpendicular tubes or chimneys of rock are found, from 1 foot to 3 feet in diameter, the sandstone appearing to have been hardened on concentric layers by the infiltration of ferrugineous solutions, and this hardened portion has withstood the action of the elements, while the softer bands and the interior column, or cylindrical masses, have weathered away, leaving a pile of rocks behind, which, by some exertion of the imagination, can be construed in a resemblance to a ruined city on a very small scale."

Fata Morgana.—Occasionally, but usually with long intervening periods, the atmospheric phenomenon known in the Mediterranean as the Fata Morgana, is seen from Santa Cruz. The Santa Cruz *Sentinel*, of April 1, 1871, thus described such a scene:

"Standing on the bluff, near the light-house, we watched the beautiful scene for hour after hour. It was one of those scenes which at times makes its appearance on the coast of Messina. The entire beach, with its narrow line of yellow sand extending from Point Pinos entirely around to this place, and the many landing places and towns, became visible, looming up like gigantic castles.

The houses in Monterey, twenty-two miles distant, appeared to hang in the air, as if gently rocked in a sea of glass. The mountains back of that city, and the light-house, formed a splendid background. Far away on the right could be seen an ocean steamer which, at times, seemed to be four or five stories high, with heavy roll ploughing her way to the Golden Gate, and the bay toward Moss' Landing, the buildings of the landing constantly growing taller and taller, the steamer *Monterey* making her way to this city. In the immediate foreground were five or six schooners, tacking in different directions, and passing and repassing each other, adding to the beauty of the scene. We watched this shifting kaleidoscope while it changed into every imaginable shape. The line of sand-beach became rough, and waves like those seen on the intervening bay seemed to roll along the shore. The opposite shore ran up massive columns, supporting a stupendous entablature, which grew wider at the top, then changed and represented beautiful waterfalls or precipitous bluffs. This would give place to a city, whose magnificent buildings would appear to rock, then rising, would remain a moment suspended high in air, then disappear while another picture was forming on the water's level. A gentle breeze was blowing at the time, and the day was warm and clear."

Various Resorts.—The following is a list of notable places, with their distances and directions from Santa Cruz, and their main attractions:

Isbell Grove, 2 miles N. E. Picnics.
Wood's Lagoon, 1 mile E. Bathing.
Mason's Grove, 5 miles N. E. Picnics; camping.
Ord's Grove, 6 miles E. Picnics; bathing.
Aptos Beach, 6 miles E. Bathing.
Hihn's Grove, 4½ miles N. E. Picnics.
Corcoran's Lagoon, 2½ miles E. Duck Hunting.
Soquel Beach, 4 miles E. Camping; bathing.
Meder's Grove, 4 miles N. W. Picnics.
Moore's Beach, 2½ miles W. Natural Bridge.
The Natural Bridge, 5 miles W. Scenery.
Scott's Creek, 16 miles W. Camping; hunting.
Scott's Falls, 19 miles W. Scenery.
Laguna Falls, 10 miles W. Scenery.

Scott's Fall is 85 feet high, and has a large quantity of water in wet seasons. The Laguna fall is 60 feet high. On the bank of Scott Creek, a grove of laurel trees, said to be the largest in California, is a beautiful camp ground. Two miles up the creek is a redwood tree, 18 feet in diameter. Aptos has a fine hotel.

Three miles from Glenwood Station on the South Pacific Coast Railroad, and 7 from the ocean, in a beautiful little valley, closed in by mountains, is the Summer Home Farm, formerly called the Strawberry Valley. The post-office address of the proprietor is J. W. DeWolfe, Glenwood.

Monterey.—Monterey County, 100 miles long and 33 wide, has many attractions for pleasure-seekers. It has a long bay which abounds with fish, and is well fitted for yachting; a beautiful beach suitable for bathing, and rich in sea mosses; three old missions; several peaks that command extensive views; numerous mineral springs; attractive groves and pleasant drives; excellent accommodations for pleasure-seekers, whether rich or poor; and convenient communication, by land and sea, with San Francisco.

The picnic grounds preferred by the people of Salinas, are in Alisal Canyon, 8 miles distant, and in Gabilan Canyon.

Gabilan Peak, 2,780 feet high, rises like a cone high above the adjacent ridge, and commands an extensive view of the Salinas and San Benito Valleys.

Paraiso Springs, 1,000 feet above the sea, 6 miles from Soledad, are in an umbrageous canyon, in which there are beautiful drives.

Town of Monterey—The town of Monterey is one of the most interesting in California. It was the capital of the territory previous to the American conquest, and here the authority of the United States was first established, July 7th, 1846. The houses are mostly of adobe; and many of the inhabitants are of Spanish blood. The climate of Monterey is nearly the same as that of San Francisco, though the winds are not quite so strong, because there is no gap like that at the Straits of Carquinez, in the Coast Range, to let them through into the great interior valley. The summer temperature is well adapted to the wants of residents, of the warm valleys of the interior, who find a change by coming to the breezes and fogs of the beach; while those who live near the ocean can obtain theirs, by going to the inland resorts.

Monterey Groves.—This vicinity is noted for its groves of indigenous cypress and pine trees, which are now favorite ornamental trees in the valleys of California. Both trees are handsome, hardy and quick of growth. The Monterey cypress (which is not found indigenous anywhere, save in the small grove south-west of the town, bears much trimming and can be trained into low hedges or high walls. The two, pine and cypress, groves are near together, but each kind keeps by itself. At the outer end of the Pine Grove, four miles west of town, is Point Pinos, with a light-house. Two miles south of it is the Moss Beach, where there is a strip of sand nearly half a mile wide, between the lines of high and low tide, and here great quantities and many varieties of algæ or sea moss may be found. Beautiful specimens of these mosses, dried and pressed out, can be bought in the town. At the southern end of the Moss Beach is the Seal Rock, where seals bask in the sun every summer day.

Hotel Del Monte.—The most interesting feature of the town of Monterey, for the tourist, is the Hotel del Monte, erected by the capitalists of the Southern Pacific Railroad Company for the accommodation of visitors. It is one of the most complete buildings on the continent for the accommodation of pleasure-seekers. The length is 385 feet, the width, 115; the height, 3 stories. There are accommodations for 400 guests. The hotel has its own gas works, and is supplied with water from its own artesian well. The grounds of the hotel have an area of 100 acres, partly in beautiful garden and lawn, and the remainder wooded with oak, pine and cypress trees. Near by, and under the same ownership, are 7,000 acres of land, through which there are fine roads, open to the patrons of the hotel. A bathing pavilion contains four tanks, each 50 feet long and 36 wide. These are filled with salt water which is heated to a temperature of about 70°. There are also separate bathrooms. The whole establishment is managed in the best style, and it has done much to attract great numbers of visitors to Monterey. The hotel is within a few yards of the beach, so that those who prefer to bathe in the ocean need not tire themselves by walking to reach it.

Pacific Grove Retreat.—A peculiar institution of Monterey is the Pacific Grove Retreat, a permanent camp ground, where hundreds of people spend months every summer, in tents and lodging houses. The site is near the beach in a grove of Monterey pines, about two miles west from the town. The retreat had its origin in a Methodist camp meeting. The participants were so well pleased with their first experience there, that they formed an association, obtained control of the land, and made arrangements to spend some months there every summer. Lodging houses, a restaurant, and a chapel were built, and lots were leased to campers. The property is now under the control of the Pacific Improvement Company, which pursues the same general policy as that originally adopted by the Evangelical Association; and the "moral and prudential management," is still subject to a board of clerical gentlemen. No wines, no gambling, and no sea bathing on Sunday are permitted. There are sermons and Sunday-school on Sunday, and a devotional spirit is prominent. Furnished tents are provided for those who wish to live cheaply; and lots are leased or sold to those who prefer to provide shelter of their own. The beach in front of the grounds is beautiful. Bathing suits and boats can be hired and croquet grounds and swings, can be used without charge. Coaches run from the Grove to the town, at least four times every day, to carry those who do not wish to walk. The plan of this "Christian Seaside Resort," as it is called by the proprietors, has been a decided success.

Carmel Mission.—Four miles south of Monterey, in the valley of the Carmel River, is the Mission of San Carlos, founded by Junipero Serra, June 3, 1770. This was the second mission founded in what is now California, and being considered the most important, was the place where the president of the missions resided. The mission church, built of sandstone, is now in ruins. Here Serra died in 1784, and in the mission church he was buried. The Mission of San Antonio, founded July 14, 1771, and that of Soledad, founded October 9, 1791, have nothing of much interest to strangers.

San Benito.—The most interesting place to tourists in San Benito is San Juan, which has the Mission of San Juan Bautista. The church was one of the largest built in California, under the dominion of Spain, is one of the best preserved, and noted for its long arched corridor. It was founded June 17, 1797.

San Luis Obispo.—San Luis Obispo is a large county fronting on the Pacific, from latitude 34° 55' to 35° 50'. Having no good harbor and not being connected by rail with the remainder of the State, it occupied a secluded position until the spring of 1887, since when it has made rapid progress. The chief points of interest to tourists in the county are the missions of San Luis Obispo and San Miguel, and the Paso Robles Hot Springs. The Mission of San Luis Obispo was founded September 1, 1772, in a fertile valley about 8 miles from the ocean, Junipero Serra, President of the Missions, officiating as master of ceremonies at the consecration. St. Louis, Bishop of Toulouse, a saint of the Franciscan order, supplied the name—*obispo* being the Spanish for bishop. The Mission of San Miguel in the Salinas Valley, was founded in 1797. The Paso Robles Springs are mentioned in the chapter on mineral springs.

Favorite resorts for the people of San Luis Obispo County, are the Pecho and Newsom Sulphur Springs. Though in different directions, both places are about 15 miles from the county seat; both are in deep canyons with pleasant shade; both have a temperature of about 100° in the warmest spring; and neither has a hotel. The Pecho Springs have a bath-house and attract many campers every summer.

Though smaller than either of half a dozen other counties of California, San Luis Obispo is larger than Rhode Island or Delaware. It is diamond-shaped, with each of its four sides 65 miles long, the western side fronting on the Pacific Ocean, and its eastern the summit of the main ridge of the Coast Mountains.

San Joaquin Valley.—The most interesting places in the San Joaquin Valley are Stockton, its chief city, which does a large business in buying, storing and selling wheat; Fresno, with many irrigated orchards and vineyards, and Bakersfield, in a large district irrigated from Kern River, and cultivated in alfalfa, grain and fruit. At the southern end of the valley, and 3,000 feet above the sea, is the "Loop" in the Southern Pacific Railroad, which there completely encircles the top of a hill, and crosses its own track. That is, the track passes through a tunnel, and, after making a bend, 3,800 feet long, runs over that tunnel, the upper track being 78 feet above the level of the lower one. In mountainous countries the railroads are very crooked, but this loop is the only place where a railroad, in its windings, has crossed its own track.

Marin.—Marin County forms the peninsula between the northern arm of San Francisco Bay and the Pacific, and has an area of 507 square miles, mostly mountainous, and much of it covered with redwood timber. It abounds with wild and shady canyons, and contains numerous places in favor with the San Franciscans, for picnicing and rusticating parties. Its most noted resorts are Saucelito, San Rafael, Bolinas, Camp Taylor, Lagunitas Station, Lagunitas Reservoir, Blithedale, the summit of Mt. Tamalpais, Olema and Bear Valley.

Saucelito.—Saucelito, because of its proximity, and because it attracts more visitors than any other portion of the county, must be mentioned first. It is a village built on the side of steep hills, which are covered with a dense growth of scrub oaks, laurel and other trees. The canyons are visited by picnic parties. The yacht clubs of San Francisco have their club houses at Saucelito; and row-boats are kept for hire to people who want to exercise their muscles.

Point Bonita.—Point Bonita, or the north head at the outer limit of the Golden Gate, has a light-house and a siren or fog-horn, which sounds its warning when the entrance of the harbor is hidden by fog. The place can be reached from Saucelito by two roads. The first, a horse trail 4 miles long, starts southward and follows the water; the second, a wagon road 7 miles, starts northward from Saucelito. The latter route is closed by a gate, which will not be opened without a permit.

San Rafael.—The chief town of Marin County, San Rafael, a beautiful place, near the north-eastern base of Mt. Tamalpais, is 15 miles from San Francisco, and can be reached by boat and rail, either by way of Saucelito or of San Quentin. Being sheltered by the mountains, it has little wind or fog, and having beautiful natural scenery, as well as many elegant dwellings and gardens, and pleasant people, it is a favorite summer residence for San Franciscans, who come and go every day. The drives in the vicinity of the town, are very romantic, especially on the roads to Ross Valley, (over the hill), to Nicasio, (by the northern route), to White's Hill and to the Lagunitas Reservoir. San Rafael was the site of a Franciscan Mission, established in 1817, to convert the Indians. The mission buildings have now disappeared.

Tamalpais.—Mt. Tamalpais, one of the prominent features of the landscape of San Francisco Bay, and the most notable peak in Marin County, is 2,604 feet high, and 15 miles from the city in a direct line. As seen from the eastward, it looks like a cone, but when observed from high ground, to the northward, it appears as the steep western end of a level ridge. A wagon road 12 miles long from San Rafael, enables the tourist to drive to the summit comfortably, in 3 hours and the descent requires 2. Two hours can be spent on the summit, including time given to lunch, so that the round trip can be made in 7 hours from San Rafael, and about 10 from San Francisco, and the most interesting one that can be made from the metropolis in that brief period. The route from Ross Valley enters a canyon without extensive views, but beautiful in the early spring, by the variety of the forms and tints of the foliage on the creek banks and hill sides. The deep rich green of the laurel, loading the air with the pungent perfume of its lemon-colored blooms, the ceanothus often hiding its verdure under the luxuriance of its wild lilac flowers, the manzanita showing white and pink blossoms intermingled with its greyish green leaves, the evergreen oak, the Christmas berry bush, the dark redwood and the light green madroño, all evergreens, are the predominant features in the vegetation; deciduous trees and plants, being comparatively rare. The wild gooseberry, however, is in bloom; the buckeye has opened its leaf-buds, and the wild hazel has hung out its catkins as signs that spring is here. Wild flowers of many kinds appear also, though not in such numbers as to hide the grass. The road, leaving the canyon, ascends the eastern slope of the mountain, covered with chaparral, in which manzanita, ceanothus, hazel, California nutmeg, and scrub oak, are observable. The ziggag course gives charming and ever varying views, gradually becoming more extensive with increasing altitude. The conveyances are obtained at the livery stables.

We look down on an area of at least 5,000 square miles, including the City and Bay of San Francisco, and the rich Alameda plain. The proximity of the most interesting features of the landscape, enables us to see them distinctly. The prospect in every direction is interesting. No other point commands so good a birdseye view of the bay and its surroundings. The ocean for fifty miles out, the Farallones, Point Reyes, Tomales Bay, the northern part of Marin County, much of Sonoma and Napa, Mount St. Helena, a snow-covered mountain (probably Mt. St. John), just at the western point of St. Helena, another long snow mountain, ten degrees further west (probably Mt. Sanhedrim, which, as well as Mt. St. John, is 100 miles from Tamalpais), the towns of Napa and Vallejo, Carquinez Straits, Suisun Bay, Mt. Diablo, Oakland, the southern arm of San Francisco Bay, the city, Mt. San Bruno and the ocean beach, make up the circle, while the Golden Gate, Richardson's Cove, Raccoon Strait, Angel Island, and the south end of Marin County seem to be at our feet.

Tamalpais means the country of the Tamal Indians, who also supplied the name to Tomales Bay. Pais is the Spanish for country.

Various Resorts.—The favorite picnic grounds near San Rafael, are Laurel Grove, 2 miles to the south-eastward; Fairfax Park, 4 miles to the westward, and the banks of the Lagunitas Creek, near the Lagunitas Station, on the North Pacific Coast Railroad. Taylorville, 16 miles from San Rafael, will be mentioned in the chapter on Camping. Bolinas, reached by stage from Saucelito or San Rafael, is a favorite resort for fishermen, hunters and campers. The camp ground is among some willows on the eastern shore of Bolinas Bay. There are attractive camp grounds near Olema, and in Bear Valley. Blithedale is the name of a summer resort kept by Mrs. H. R. Cushing, in a small valley at the south-eastern base of Mt. Tamalpais. five miles from Saucelito. The situation is pleasant and the house is well kept. From the Summit Station, 5 miles from Saucelito, the distance to Blithedale is 2½ miles, and there, Mrs. Cushing's wagon receives and delivers visitors. Her post-office address is Saucelito.

Sonoma.—Sonoma, fronting on San Pablo Bay, and also on the Pacific Ocean, is one of the most interesting counties of California. It is drained by Russian River, and Petaluma and Sonoma Creeks, each of which has a valley, and enclosing mountains with peculiar beauties. Sonoma Valley is noted for its vineyards, Petaluma Valley for its wheat and dairies, and the western shore of the county for its redwoods. Within its limits are the Californian Geysers, the Sonoma, or as it is sometimes called the Calistoga Petrified Forest, and many noted mineral springs.

The Geysers.—The Geysers of Sonoma County are 101 miles by each of the two commonly traveled routes from San Francisco, and the hotel is 1,692 feet above the sea. They are situated on a branch of the Pluton River which empties into Russian River. The Cloverdale stage road to the Geysers has 17 miles of distance and 1,400 feet of ascent; the Calistoga Road has 23 miles of distance, 2,900 feet of ascent and 1,300 of descent. The former is the easier and more expeditious route. Both roads are remarkable for the depth, steepness and crookedness of the canyons, on the sides of which the narrow roads wind their way. The declivities are nearer to the vertical line on the Cloverdale route, but when the horses are going at a rapid pace down hill, over a road so narrow, that in many places there is not room for two wagons to pass, even on the Calistoga road, many travelers prefer not to look into the canyon, and are glad when they arrive safely at the hotel.

The word "geyser," is defined in Webster's Dictionary, to be "a fountain which spouts forth boiling water," and there is no such fountain in Sonoma County. The Geysers of the Pluto basin are a collection of hundreds of springs, many of them scalding hot, most of them strongly flavored with various minerals, differing in their flavors as in their temperatures, and accompanied by blow holes, from which hot steam and sulphurous vapors arise. They are found on what may be considered a solfatara, the soil of which is hot over an area of about a quarter of a mile square. The springs are mostly in the bottom of ravines, while the blow holes, from some of which large quantities of steam issue with a roaring noise, are on the hill sides. With the steam, come vapors which deposit sulphur and other substances on the mouths of the outlets. George Davidson wrote thus of the Geysers: "descending from the hotel about 75 feet, we first meet the spring of iron, sulphur, and soda, temperature 73°. The first spring going up the Geyser gulch is the tepid alum and iron incrusted, temperature 97°, and with a very heavy iridescent incrustation of iron, which forms in a single night. Twenty feet from this, we pass the medicated geyser bath, temperature 88°, and containing ammonia, epsom salts, magnesia, sulphur, iron, etc. We collected crystals of epsom salts two inches in length. Higher up, the spring of boiling alum and sulphur has a temperature of 156°; so, also, the black sulphur, quite near it.

"The epsom salts spring has a temperature of 146°, and within 6 feet of it is a spring of iron, sulphur and salts, at the boiling point. Soon we came upon the Boiling Black Sulphur Spring, roaring and tearing continually. As we wander over rock, heated ground and thick deposits of sulphur, salts, ammonia, tartaric acid, magnesia, etc., we try our thermometer in the geyser stream, a combination of every kind of medicated water, and find it rises up to 102°. The Witches' Cauldron is over 7 feet in diameter, of unknown depth. The contents are thrown up about 2 or 3 feet high, in a state of great ebullition, semi-liquid, blacker than ink, and contrast with the volumes of vapor arising; temperature, 195°. Opposite is a boiling alum spring, very strongly impregnated; temp. 176°. Within 12 feet is an intermittent scalding spring, from which issue streams and jets of boiling water. We have seen them ejected over 15 feet. But the glory of all is the Steamboat Geyser, resounding like a high-pressure seven-boiler boat, blowing off steam, so heated as to be invisible until it is 6 feet from the mouth. Just above this, the gulch divides; up the left or western one are many hot springs, but the scalding steam iron bath is the most important; temperature, 183°. One hundred and fifty feet above all apparent action we found a smooth, tenacious, plastic, beautiful clay; temperature, 167°. From this point you stand and overlook the ceaseless action, the roar, steam, groans, and bubbling of a hundred boiling medicated springs, while the steam ascends 100 feet above them all. Following the usually traveled path, we pass over the mountain of fire, with its hundred orifices, thence through the alkali lake; then we pass cauldrons of black, sulphurous boiling water, some moving and spluttering with violent ebullition. One white sulphur spring we found quite clear, and up to the boiling point.

"On every foot of ground we had trodden, the crystalline products of this unceasing chemical action abounded. Alum, magnesia, tartaric acid, epsom salts, ammonia, nitre, iron and sulphur abounded. At thousands of orifices you find hot, scalding steam escaping and forming beautiful deposits of arrowy sulphur crystals. Our next visit carried us up the Pluton, on the north bank, past the ovens, hot with escaping steam, to the eye-water boiling spring, celebrated for its remedial effects upon all manner of inflamed and weak eyes. Quite close to it is a very concentrated alum spring, temperature, 73°. Higher up is a sweetish iron and soda spring, 15 feet by 8; and 12 feet above are the cold soda and iron spring, incrusted with iron, with a deposit of soda, strong, tonic and inviting; temperature, 56°. It is 12 feet by 5, and affords a large supply. The Pluton in the shade was 61°, with many fine pools for bathing, and above for trout-fishing.

"The Indian Springs are nearly a mile down the canyon. The boiling water comes out clear as ice. This is the old medicated spring, where many a poor aborigine has been carried over the mountains to have the disease driven out of him by these powerful waters. On its outer wall runs a cold stream of pure water, temperature, 66°, and another water impregnated with iron and alum; temperature, 68°. It is beautifully and romantically situated. Chalybeate and sulphur waters have completely taken away our rheumatism."

The Geysers have generally been considered the greatest wonder of California after the Yosemite, and have attracted a large number of visitors, many of whom find less to interest them in the springs and steam vents, than in the drives from Cloverdale and Calistoga. The hotel and springs are in a narrow canyon, where the summer heat is intense, and therefore the stay has usually been brief. In 1881, however, a party of fashionable people spent months there, and returned with favorable reports of their experiences.

Petrified Forest.—Not far from the border of Napa County, and nearer to Calistoga than to any other town, but in Sonoma County, and on a mountain about 1,500 feet above the sea, and in the midst of oak, fir, and other timber, is the Petrified Forest, a name given to a region about 4 miles long and a mile wide, over which are scattered the fragments of perhaps 100 petrified trees. In many cases nothing is left of a tree save numerous chips; or piles of petrified fragments, somewhat like heaps of firewood in small pieces. Besides these separated fragments, there are portions of about a dozen trunks, some of them partly buried in the ground, the largest being about 50 feet long and 6 feet through. All are broken by numerous transverse fractures. The circumstances indicate that a flood of volcanic sand mixed with water, flowed into the ancient forest, and buried it to a depth of perhaps 40 or 50 feet; that the sand hardened into rock; that the trees above the rock decayed and disappeared; that the trunks enclosed in the rock decayed and were replaced by deposits of stony matter; that, in the course of ages, the sandstone, surrounding the trunks, and some of the soil under them, was washed away gradually; that the petrified trunks left without support, fell down and broke transversely by the shock; that a new forest grew up about them; and that by the continuation of erosion, the material of many of these trunks, was moved from the places in which it fell, so that nothing can now be found of them save scattered fragments. There is neither a cluster of petrified trunks near together, nor an erect petrified trunk. The chief attraction is one trunk, about 50 feet long and 6 feet through. A microscopic examination has shown that this tree was akin to the redwood, which grows now in the vicinity.

Volcanic Overflows.—The north-eastern portion of Sonoma was the scene of great volcanic activity in a recent geological era. There was evidently a crater near the site of the present Geyser

Canyon. The mountain on the east side of Sonoma and Santa Rosa Valleys is made up, to a large extent, of volcanic sandstone; while the mountain west of Sonoma Valley is covered with basalt, which, in several places, has columnar crystallizations. All the higher hills, west of Petaluma and Russian Rivers, are covered with volcanic rock, and it is to be presumed that the sites now occupied by the ridge between Sonoma and Napa Valleys, and by that east of Napa, were valleys which were filled up by volcanic streams. These formed rocks harder than the older hills, the sandstone of which was gradually eroded, so that the place, which was hill before the period of the greatest volcanic activity, became valley afterwards. It is not to be supposed that the land was a level plain when the great eruptions of the volcanoes at Mt. St. Helena, Clear Lake and the Geysers, occurred. Nor if there were then valleys and intervening hills, is it likely that the lava would run on the hill tops, where we now find it, and spare the fertile valleys where we find none. The Table Mountain in Stanislaus and Tuolumne Counties is a hill of basalt, 30 miles long and half a mile wide, covering the bed of the dead Stanislaus River, a stream, which, in a former geological age, occupied a position near that of the present Stanislaus River. The lava, seeking the lowest levels, usurped the bed of the ancient river, and, being harder than the slate of the adjacent hills, has, after many ages, been left by erosion, standing above the general level of the surrounding country. The dead river was rich in gold, and the miners by following auriferous gravel in its bed, have proved conclusively, that the long mountain of basalt occupies the place of a stream.

Sonoma Valley.—The town of Sonoma in the beautiful valley of the same name, is interesting as one of the chief seats of grape culture in California, and also as the site of the first town laid off north of the Golden Gate. In 1835, the Mexican Government, fearing that the Russians intended to enlarge their settlement at Fort Ross, ordered M. G. Vallejo, commandant of the northern frontier, to select a site and establish a town north of San Pablo Bay—Sonoma was the result. The greater portion of the valley has a soil too poor for wheat, but it is well adapted to the vine, with which thousands of acres have been planted, so that there are more here, within an area 5 miles square, than in any other portion of the State. The first discovery of the phylloxera, on our Coast, was made here, and it has caused more loss here than anywhere else in California. The vineyard now owned by Mr. Johnson, and previously the property of the Buena Vista Vinicultural Society, which purchased from Col. Agaston Haraszthy, was at one time the largest in the State, and had 400 acres in vines, but many have been dug up on account of the phylloxera, and others are not productive. The wine cellars are tunnels, dug into the hill of volcanic sandstone. If the town and its vicinity were more conveniently accessible from San Francisco, they would have greater prominence as pleasure resorts.

The Mission at Sonoma was founded in 1822, and was called the Mission of San Francisco Solano. Having been established after Mexico threw off the Spanish dominion, under a government which never enjoyed the full sympathy of the ecclesiastics, and never supplying them liberally with funds, it never rose to much importance. The buildings were of adobe, and most of them are in ruins. Gen. Vallejo has a pleasant home on the outskirts of the town.

Russian River.—Russian River, though the largest Californian stream opening directly into the ocean, south of latitude 40°, is closed through most of the year by a bar, thrown up across its mouth by the sea. Over this bar travelers can walk dry-shod, while the waters of the river, standing somewhat higher than the sea, soak through the sand. Salmon in their spawning season, come up to the edge of the beach, as if they intended to jump across the bar into the river. They doubtless taste the fresh water and think they should be able to follow it up. The lower portion of the stream has dense forests of redwood on both sides, and Duncan's Mill, on the bank of the river, is the end of an excursion, which hundreds of people make every summer by railroad, 80 miles from San Francisco. The valley of Austin Creek, a tributary of Russian River, attracts many campers.

Guerneville.—At the end of a branch of the San Francisco and North Pacific Railroad, on the bank of Russian River, is a magnificent redwood grove, which is a favorite with camping parties. There are excellent bathing and fishing grounds in the vicinity.

Fort Ross.—There are pleasant camp grounds near Fort Ross, on the shore of the Pacific, in latitude 38° 30'. The place derives its name from a trading and fishing station, which the Russians established there, with the consent of Spain in 1814, and which they abandoned in 1841. The native California called the place "Coscoff Russo."

Sonoma Springs.—Sonoma Valley abounds with sulphur and soda springs, of which no analysis is obtainable. Mark West Spring, eight miles, and Taylor's Springs three from Santa Rosa, have many visitors. Skagg's Springs and Litton Springs are mentioned in Chapter IX.

Napa Valley.—Napa County, east of Sonoma, and fronting on San Pablo Bay, is one of the most interesting portions of our coast. Its chief valley, bearing the same name, and drained by a river of the same name, 40 miles long and 2 miles wide on the average, is noted for fertility and beauty. Lying north of San Francisco, and shut in on both sides, by steep mountains, which rise to a height of about 2,000 feet, it is moister than any valley, of equal size, further south. The fertility of its soil, the extensive vineyards at its northern end, the beauty of its landscape, the warmth of its summer climate, the number of health and pleasure resorts, and the possession of a railroad extending throughout the length of the valley, contributed to give to Napa Valley a density of population, a thoroughness of cultivation, and an appearance of rural comfort not elsewhere extending so far, except in the near vicinity of San Francisco. The Alameda plain, Santa Clara Valley, Los Angeles, San Gabriel, Monterey, Santa Cruz, San Mateo and San Rafael, are each unequaled in some features of their luxuriant gardens, extensive orchards, subtropical trees and shrubbery, elegant homes, or pleasant drives, but no one of them surpasses Napa in the variety and extent of its attractions. Nowhere else in California can the traveler go by rail for 30 miles through one unbroken stretch of enchanting landscape, combining fertility of soil, with relatively high tillage; comfortable country homes; indigenous and cultivated vegetation most pleasing to the eye in color and distribution, and in the distance a majestic framework of rugged mountains, ridge rising above ridge, with peaks, cliffs, grassy slopes, chaparral and deciduous timber, charming in their forms and rich in tints that range from grey, brown, green, blue and purple in the cool morning, to maroon, garnet, ochre and orange in the glowing sunset. On a clear day, from the volcanic cone of St. Helena, at the head of the valley to the tule swamps of Suscol at its foot, the eye is never out of sight of far-reaching landscapes, that combine fine artistic effects of foreground, middleground and distance. The towns are Napa City, Yountville, St. Helena and Calistoga. Napa, the county seat, 41 miles, by rail, from San Francisco, is a thriving town of 4,000 inhabitants, in the midst of the valley, there about 2 miles wide, and very fertile. It is the place to take a wagon for Napa Soda Springs or Atlas Peak. Most of the lowland near the town is cultivated in wheat; and the hills in the neighborhood have vineyards. At Yountville, 50 miles from San Francisco, by rail, we come to the grape region of the valley, which for the next twenty miles abounds with extensive vineyards.

St. Helena.—St. Helena rivals Sonoma and Los Angeles in the number of vines, and probably derives from them a larger net income than either. It is nearer to the market than Los Angeles, and has less phylloxera, and a larger proportion of the varieties most prized for wine than Sonoma. Among the most noted vineyards in the vicinity, are those of Krug, Pellet, Crane, Keyes and Schramm.

The valley being there about a mile wide, and not entirely straight, and the ridges on both sides being more than 2,000 feet high, the town is almost encircled by mountains which shut out the breezes, and give the place a high temperature at midday in the summer. Many wealthy San Franciscans have made their homes there on account of the climate and society, and the town is surrounded by elegant residences. The White Sulphur Springs, in a little canyon, 2 miles south-west from St. Helena, was for many years the most fashionable summer resort of California.

St. Helena is the station at which stages are taken for the White Sulphur Springs, the Etna Springs, in Pope Valley, and Howell

Mountain, the latter a summer resort and camping place. There are 2 roads to Pope Valley; both through interesting scenery, one over the summit of Howell Mountain, and the other round its eastern base, through several small valleys. Several wagon roads leading upon the mountain side of the west Napa ridge, have interesting views.

Calistoga.—Calistoga, the terminus of the Napa Valley branch of the California Pacific Railroad, and a favorite pleasure resort from 1866 to 1872, though now neglected, has a multitude of hot springs, scattered over several hundred acres. There are spots within this area, where the ground is warmed by subterranean heat, and borings have struck hot water, the temperature at 100 feet from the surface, being near the boiling point. Many of the springs give off sulphurous vapors so strong, that the wood of one bath house is corroded by them; and they may be the cause of the death of much of the ornamental shrubbery, planted out in 1868 and 1869, on the grounds.

Mt. St. Helena.—The County has one of its corners on the summit of Mt. St. Helena, 4,343 feet high, a notable feature in the topography and geology of the State. It is the most southern volcano in the Coast Range. So long a period has elapsed since its activity, that nothing of a crater shape remains, but the superior height, nature of its rocks, and abundance and position of eruptive material about it, indicate unmistakably that it was a great volcano. It was, probably, the source from which was derived the eruptive rock of the East Napa ridge—that is the ridge east of Napa Valley, 40 miles long and several miles wide, and perhaps 1000 feet deep. Other ridges to the eastward, and apparently derived from the same source, have much similar rock. A tunnel is cut through it on the line of the California Pacific Railroad near Cordelia. The West Napa ridge is made of the same material, which probably flowed from the same vent. The west Sonoma ridge has a deep covering of basalt, not traceable to any nearer source.

Mt. St. Helena is visible from San Francisco, presenting a coffin-like shape, with a flat top. The distance, by the traveled route from the city is 85 miles, including 73 by ferry boat and rail, to Calistoga; the remaining 12 on horseback. The tourist follows the stage road to Clear Lake, 7 miles to the summit of the pass, where he turns to the left, ascending on the south-western side of the mountain. There are four peaks almost on a level, and separated by slight depressions, the most northerly being the highest. The view is extensive. Knight's Valley to the north-west, various valleys in the basin of Putah Creek to the east, and Napa Valley to the south, comprise most of the lowland visible; but beyond them are numerous mountains, including Geyser Peak, Uncle Sam, Mt. St. John and Snow Mountain to the northward, and Diablo and Tamalpais southward in the Coast Range, while the summit of the Sierra is visible for 200 miles, from Mt. Lassen southward. It is said that on exceptionally clear days Mt. Shasta can be seen, but usually it is not visible. San Francisco Bay and much of its shore line, can be seen dimly in the distance.

East Napa Ridge.—Howell Mountain, the summit of which is 7 miles north-eastward from the town of St. Helena, has 5 square miles of nearly level land, at an elevation of 1,800 feet above the sea, the largest body of level land on a mountain in the Coast Range. This elevated plateau, possessing much good soil, a pleasant stream of water, numerous springs and abundant timber, is a favorite place for camping. The boarding-house of Mr. Anguin (whose post-office address is Anguin,) is full every summer. The soil, formed by the decomposition of a volcanic tufaceous rock, is, according to Prof. Hilgard, well-fitted for wine grapes, and many vines have been set out there recently. Frosts are severe on the mountain in the spring, but are very rare in the fall, and tomato vines have continued to thrive in the open air till February. The mountain has pleasant drives on its summit, and it is surrounded by attractive places. It is part of the East Napa Ridge, about 5 miles south of Blake's, and about 8 from Atlas Peak, on the same ridge. Those two places are the only elevated points on the Coast Mountains of California, where observations of relative humidity have been made regularly for a year, and as the figures, as explained in Chapter II, prove, that for persons suffering with plumonary diseases, the climate is better there than at any health resort elsewhere, so far as can be ascertained from published statistics. The Napa Soda Springs is on the same ridge. Atlas Peak has a summer boarding-house, kept by A. P. Evans, whose post-office is Napa City; and the drive from that place to his house is a pleasant one. Many places on the ridge between Anguins and Atlas Peak have been favorite resorts for campers.

The Napa Soda Springs are situated 1,200 feet above the sea, on the western side of the East Napa Mountain Ridge, in the midst of pleasant scenery, and in a climate unsurpassed for health or comfort. They are only 5 miles from Atlas Peak, which was recommended by the State Board of Health, in 1880, as the best site for a State Hospital for consumptives. For asthma, bronchitis and pulmonary complaints generally, the atmospheric conditions are excellent. A commodious hotel offers its accommodations to guests, and many pleasant people have adopted it as their favorite resort for summer rustication. Skaggs' Springs, the Pacific Congress Springs, the Summit Soda, the Etna, the Adams, and the Wilhoit have good hotels, and they are visited every year by many people for pleasure as well, by others, for health.

Solano.—Solano is a large and rich county, but has few pleasure resorts. The Vallejo White Sulphur Springs, 3 miles from Vallejo and five from Benicia, have a mild, tepid sulphur water, of which there is no obtainable analysis. The scenery in the vicinity is pleasant; the grounds are planted with numerous trees for shade, ornament and fruit; the hotel is commodious, and there are bathhouses. About 6 miles from Suisun, at the head of Green Valley, in a shady canyon, is a little waterfall, about 60 feet high. It is a beautiful place for a picnic. Five miles north-eastward from Vallejo is the St. John Quicksilver Mine, which has produced thousands of flasks of mercury, but reduced only 80 flasks in 1881. Pieces of the ore can be found lying on the surface of the adjacent hills, browned on the surface by long exposure to the atmosphere, but when broken showing rich red colors on the face of the fracture. The only National navy yard on our coast is at Vallejo.

Lake County.—Lake County, 100 miles north of San Francisco, most of its area 1,200 feet or more above the sea, on the eastern slope of the Coast Mountains, is, to the tourists, one of the most interesting portions of California. Its scenery is romantic; it has much game; and its climate and elevation are considered peculiarly favorable for persons suffering with pulmonary diseases. It is said that 10,000 persons go to the county every summer, for health and pleasure, the principal resorts being Clear Lake, Bartlett Springs, Blue Lakes and Harbin's Springs.

The greater part of the county is volcanic in geological character, and the evidences of volcanic action force themselves on the most inattentive observer. Mt. St. Helena, at the south-western corner of the county, and the Geysers 20 miles to the north-west, on the western line of the county, are dormant volcanoes; Mt. Uncle Sam, near the centre of the county, is the remnant of a crater; there was a crater at the Sulphur Bank; and there were many others. The craters in Lake and adjacent counties, are scattered over an area of 500 square miles, and the region of the lava rocks from these craters, has an area of more than 3,000 square miles. Hot springs, rich in sulphur and borax, minerals characteristic of volcanic influences, are abundant. At the Sulphur Bank there is a solfatara, through the hot earth of which steam and sulphurous gases are constantly escaping. Obsidian is found in small fragments and large masses.

Clear Lake.—Clear Lake is a remarkable body of water, 25 miles long, 6 miles wide, and 1,200 feet above the sea. The signs of volcanic action are to be found on all sides of it, and some writers have expressed the opinion that it occupies an ancient crater; but a crater of such vast size, would have raised a greater mass of volcanic material, than is to be found on the southern and south eastern shores of the lake. The lake has clear water, beautiful shores, and small steamers and sailing vessels, for the accommodation of pleasure seekers. The chief town on the shore of the lake, is Lakeport, 32 miles by stage from Cloverdale.

Borax Lake.—Half a mile south from the Sulphur Bank is Borax Lake, which occupies an area of ten acres, and has no outlet, occupying what was, apparently, a little crater. The water contains a large percentage of borax, and large crystals of crude borax are found in its mud. Borax was made here with profit in the dry year of 1863-4, but after the heavy rains of 1866-7 and 1867-8 the works were closed, and have been finally abandoned, in consequence of the discovery of the borax deposits in Nevada.

Thurston Lake.—Near the south-western corner of Clear Lake is Thurston Lake, a small body of saline water without an outlet. Its bed was probably a crater.

Cobb Valley.—Cobb Valley, about 25 miles northward from Calistoga, and 3,000 feet above the sea, is a favorite place for hunters and campers. Game is abundant, and the scenery beautiful.

Blue Lakes.—The Blue Lakes, near the northern end of Clear Lake, and 12 miles from Lakeport, a series of three lakes in a line, drained by one stream, have an aggregate length of $2\frac{1}{2}$ miles, with a width of half a mile. The greatest depth is 150 feet and the average 60 feet. Boating, bathing, fishing and hunting are among the common amusements. The scenery in the neighborhood is romantic. One of the lakes has a hotel on its shore, for the accommodation of pleasure-seekers, and the address of the proprietor is Theodore Deming, Bertha, Lake County, Cal.

Sulphur Bank.—Near the eastern shore of the lake, and 10 miles from its southern end is the Sulphur Bank, a solfatara, or mass of porous earth, through which, in numerous places, sulphurous vapors are continually rising, and near the surface they deposit their sulphur, which forms in beautiful crystals, but they are so delicate, that it is impossible to carry them away without shattering them, so that much of their natural beauty is destroyed. In some spots the fumes are acrid, like those of sulphurous acid, and elsewhere merely offensive, like those of rotten eggs. The fumes are warm, and one hole dug by the miners is so hot, that the hand cannot bear the heat more than a few seconds at a time. In another place, a subterranean roaring is heard, as if there were a great fire below, and not far off. In cold weather, birds and coyotes sometimes discover the warmth of the place and enter the excavations, where, if they remain long, they are killed by the poisonous gases. The earth contains so much sulphur, that at one time the place caught fire and burned to a depth of a foot, but the combustion could not go any deeper for the lack of fresh air. This deposit was worked as a sulphur mine from 1865 till 1870. The surface soil was dug in open excavations, and carried on wheelbarrows to a furnace, where the sulphur was driven off by heat into an iron receiver, in which it was melted, then run into a second pot, where it was purified, then into pine boxes ready for the market. Finally, the discovery was made that the earth was full of small particles of cinnabar, and was far more valuable for its quicksilver than its sulphur. In 1881, it yielded 11,000 flasks or 415 tons of quicksilver.

Bartlett Springs.—The Bartlett Springs, 24 miles in a direct line westward from the railroad station of Williams, in the Sacramento Valley, and 35 miles by the wagon road, is one of the most noted health resorts of California. There is a hotel with accommodations for 100 persons, besides 100 cabins which are occupied in the summer by campers. The situation is 2,300 feet above the sea. No analysis of the water has been published.

Adams Springs.—The Adams Springs, near Cobb Valley, at an elevation of nearly 3,000 feet above the sea, have a hotel with room for 100 guests. The water has been analyzed, and is of fine alkaline character.

Harbin's Springs.—Harbin's Springs have a hotel and a large patronage. They are 1,500 feet above the sea, and are 20 miles by stage from Calistoga. Richard Williams is the proprietor.

Highland Springs.—The Highland Springs are 30 miles from Cloverdale, 7 from Lakeport, and 1,700 feet above the sea. The hotel has accommodations for 100 guests. The scenery in the vicinity is varied and pleasing. The address is Dr. C. M. Bates, Highland Springs.

Other Lake County Springs.—Other mineral springs in Lake County are the Allen, (3 miles from the Bartlett), the Wetter, the Bradshaw, the Siblet, the Sulphur, the Siegler, (John Spaulding, proprietor), and the Howard, (Mrs. A. Heisch, proprietor), about which we have no further information. No analysis of the water of any of them is known to us.

Mendocino.—Mendocino County, extending from the main summit of the Coast Range to the Pacific, and from latitude 38° 48' to 40°, has a scanty population, much timber, and excellent hunting grounds and fishing streams. Among the favorite resorts of camping parties, are Mt. Sanhedrim and Leonard's Lake. The last is a beautiful sheet of water, a mile and a half long and half a mile wide, about 20 miles north-westward from Ukiah. Its water is fresh though it has no perceptible outlet. Sanhedrim is a high peak, with much game near its base. The rocks on the ocean shore have caves, which are supposed to extend inland a mile or more on a level with the sea; one of these cavities, 30 feet high at its mouth, near Big River, was followed for half a mile in a boat by some adventurous men, without finding its end. The beating of the surf at the mouth of these caves, called blowholes, is heard far inland. Near the south-eastern corner of the county is the Sanel Spring, the analysis of which is given in the Chapter on Mineral Springs.

Humboldt.—Humboldt County, north of Mendocino, has similar advantages for hunting and fishing, but has no noted mineral springs or resorts much in favor with pleasure-seekers, unless they are hunters or fishermen.

Sacramento.—Sacramento City on the eastern bank of the Sacramento River, the chief inland railroad centre of California, and the Capital of the State, is a city of 20,000 inhabitants. The State Capitol, erected at a cost of $3,000,000 is its most imposing structure, and, from the top of its dome, 220 feet high, an extensive view can be had of the Sierra Nevada and Coast Mountains, and also of adjacent portions of the Sacramento Valley. In the building are the

State Library and Mineralogical Museum, as well as the Halls of the Legislature, and the Chambers of the State Supreme Court. Eastward from the city is the site of Sutter's Fort, of which nothing is now left. The principal pleasure drive extends four miles southward along the eastern bank of the river to Riverside. East Park and the Capitol Park are other favorite resorts.

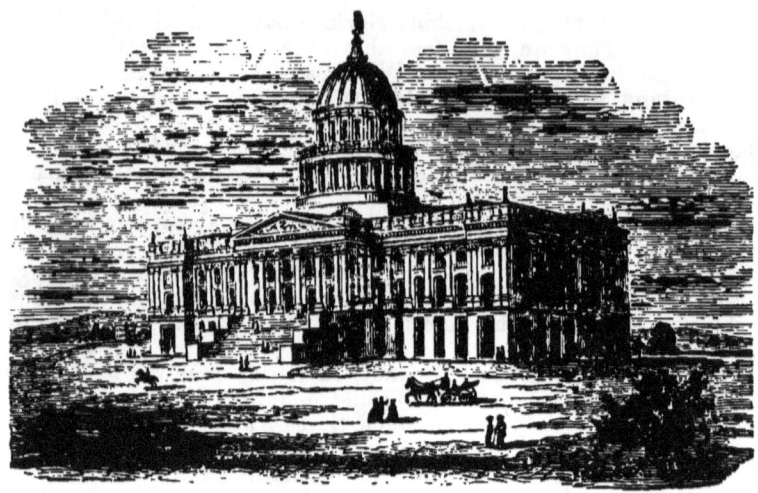

CALIFORNIA STATE CAPITOL.

Tehama.—Tehama, which extends across the Sacramento Valley, near its head, has numerous places of summer resort, near its western border. Among these are the Tuscan Springs, Hensley Springs, Sulphur Springs, and Toomes' Camp, which latter place is 5,000 feet above the sea, and 35 miles south-west from Red Bluff.

The Foot Hills.—The lower portion of the Sierra Nevada, within 2,000 feet of the level of the sea, generally designated as the Foot Hills, abounds with beautiful places, well adapted to orchards and vineyards, of which great numbers are found there. This region contained the richest of the shallow placers, which still produce several millions of gold annually. There are few places where the travelers can ascend the western slope of the Sierra, between the Tuolumne and Feather Rivers, without observing the miners, white men or Chinese, at work. Their ditches, flumes, sluices, pipes, wheels, derricks, and dumps, and the bare spots which they have left on the hill sides, and the piles of cobble stones along the streams, after washing away the lighter material, are prominent features in the landscape of the foot hills. Shallow placer mines usually reach the summit of their productiveness, within five years after their discovery, and then decline rapidly, so that within a generation, they are reduced to comparative insignificance. Labor in them gen-

SUTTER'S SAW-MILL, COLOMA.

erally receives very poor compensation, but there are chances of rich strikes, and the mode of life is independent, so that they continue to occupy the energies of thousands of white men as well as of Chinamen. The valuable hydraulic mines, generally, are from 2,000 to 5,000 feet above the level of the sea. Some of the rich auriferous quartz mines are in the foot hills, and there are places within 1,000 feet of the sea level, where the racket of the stamps can be heard by the traveler. Most of the mining towns present a very dilapidated appearance. Fireproof brick buildings are deserted, cabins are in ruins, orchards and vineyards are filled with weeds, and the streets have been washed away for the sake of the gold. One of the pleasantest of the mining towns is Coloma, where gold was discovered by James W. Marshall, January 19th, 1848, in the race of Sutter's Mill. An engraving of the building, as it was in 1849, appears on the preceding page. The place is now the centre of numerous orchards and vineyards.

Shasta.—Shasta County, at the head of the Sacramento Valley, has much interesting scenery. An area of 2,000 miles in the eastern and northern parts of the county is covered with lava, and the number of craters is large. Fall Lake, 2 miles long and half a mile wide, is formed by numerous springs in a region surrounded with lava. The McCloud River is noted for having a salmon hatching establishment, the most productive one on the globe. It turns out about 10,000,000 young salmon every year. The trout are abundant in the streams of Shasta.

CHAPTER IV.

SOUTHERN CALIFORNIA.

Territory Included.—The term Southern California—not to be confounded with Lower California in Mexico—is generally understood to mean the counties of Santa Barbara, Ventura, Los Angeles, San Bernardino, and San Diego, including an area of 50,000 square miles, with 39,000 in the desert of the Colorado and Mojave basins, and 11,000 in one of the most attractive portions of the globe, on the western slope of the Coast Range This slope, called also Subtropical or Semi-tropical California, shaped like a quarter-circle, 275 miles long and 40 wide, south of latitude 35°, is protected against the chill winds and ocean current of the San Francisco region, by the mountainous projection of Point Conception, which serves to divide sharply two different summer climates, that to the southward being relatively free from the cold breezes and fogs which abound to the northward. The average annual rainfall, about 15 inches, is not sufficient to secure regular crops of cereals without irrigation, except in those valleys which receive more than an equal share of moisture, and cultivation is generally limited to fields supplied with water from ditches or artesian wells. But on the irrigated lands the vegetation is so luxuriant, varied and beautiful, and the production of fruit so abundant, that the visitor is charmed, especially when arriving in the latter part of winter, fresh from the ice-bound north, he finds himself in the midst of extensive orange orchards, laden with ripe golden fruit, and covered at the same time with the fragrant blossoms in preparation for another crop. The lime, the lemon, the date palm, the olive, the fig, and a multitude of other sub-tropical trees, cultivated for fruit or ornament, contribute to fascinate the eye in the foreground, while mountains, grand in form and rich in color, supply a magnificent distance.

For years this region has enjoyed a great boom. Dwellings, hotels, street railroads, steam railroads, and towns have multiplied as if by magic. Los Angeles, San Diego, and Pasadena more than trebled their population between 1880 and 1887; Santa Barbara and San Bernardino have also made great advances. Monrovia had the credit of possessing eight millionaires among its residents within a year after work was commenced on its first house. The assessed value of the taxable property of Los Angeles County was $18,500,000 in 1880, and $92,000,000 in 1887. Notwithstanding the construction of numerous hotels and boarding and lodging houses —including such immense and magnificent establishments as the Raymond and Coronado Beach hotels—there has been much complaint in Los Angeles, San Diego, and Santa Barbara about the insufficiency of the accommodations for strangers. The throng has not been limited to a brief season in each year, but has continued through all the months, and has been accompanied by an increasing excitement in the real estate market.

Los Angeles.—Besides the precedence which Los Angeles has over the other counties of Southern California in population, wealth and agricultural production, as indicated by the preceding table, it is also superior in the amount of tillable soil, the supply of water available for irrigation, the length of iron track, the concentration of railroads within its limits, and the facilities for communication by rail with the Atlantic slope or with San Francisco. San Diego which has the only good natural harbor in California, south of San Francisco, is at a disadvantage in water supply, and in being at the outer limit of the State, with very little population or industry in the adjacent portion of Mexico.

The City of Los Angeles, styled by the Spaniards when they laid it out, *El Pueblo de la Reina de Los Angeles*—the Town of the Queen of the Angels—founded September 4th, 1781, is situated 14 miles east from the Pacific, at the mouth of a gorge in low hills, through which the Los Angeles River breaks to reach a wide plain, and near the western end of the San Gabriel, or Cucamonga, or Sierra Madre spur of the Coast Range. This spur has an average height of about 7,000 feet, and rises in the San Antonio Peak to an elevation of 10,142. These San Gabriel Mountains often show snow in the winter and early spring within 10 miles of the orange orchards at their feet, and are referred to in the following lines on the winter of Los Angeles Valley, by A. F. Kercheval.

> In restful, tender, rapt repose,
> Sweet Nature softly dreaming lies;
> Afar the slumb'ring Ocean glows,
> Above, the snowy heights disclose
> Their glittering banners in the skies.
> Soft at their everlasting feet,
> In green and gold, with incense sweet,
> Queen of the bright Hesperian lands—
> In royal splendor lovelier far
> Than man's vain glittering pageants are,—
> The gracious Orange proudly stands.
> * * * * * * *
> How soft the purple shadows sleep
> On every cloud-kissed solemn steep!
> Sweet fairy Vale! O, not more dear
> To tender thought and lover's dream,
> To muse's song and poet's theme,
> The dreamy vale of sweet Cachmere!

The site of Los Angeles was selected for its horticultural advantages of a large area of level land near a regular and conveniently manageable supply of water. The character given to the city by its first settlers, has not been lost. It is still, as it was in the last century, a place of gardens, vineyards and orchards, abounding in flowers and fruits, especially in oranges and grapes. Los Angeles (with its surroundings) is one of the most interesting places in the United States, and makes a vivid impression on travelers. In his book, *Aus Amerika*, Julius Froebel said: "I could wish no better home for myself and my friends than such a one as noble, sensible men could make here for themselves." Dr. J. W. Hough wrote: "The general view of Los Angeles, from the old fort, more nearly resembles that of Damascus, 'the Pearl of the Orient,' than any city I have elsewhere seen. * * * The vineyards have the same luxuriance, the pomegranates the same real blossom, and the orange groves the same ravishing beauty, while an occasional palm, stateliest of trees, gives an Oriental air to the scene."

Until 1849, Los Angeles was the largest town in California. The houses built before that year had adobe walls; the stores of recent construction are of brick, and the dwellings of wood or brick. If the city should grow much, it will probably expand over the plateau east of the river, where there is a handsomer and more healthful situation than in the moist bottom land of the valley. The best view is to be obtained from Fort Hill, in the northwest corner of the city. Street railroads run to the north, south and east, and in all those directions, charming gardens are to be seen from the streets. The places in Los Angeles County, most worthy of a visit after its chief city, are San Gabriel, Santa Monica, Anaheim, Pasadena, Westminster, Orange, the Sierra Madre Villa and Catalina Island.

San Gabriel Mission.—The Mission of San Gabriel, founded September 8th, 1771, the first white settlement in what is now Los Angeles County, the most prosperous of the Californian Missions, was originally established 4 miles southeastward from the site where the permanent mission church was erected. Though the official title was San Gabriel, so named after the senior archangel in the angelic hierarchy of the Catholic Church, who, like his associates, Michael and Rafael, has been promoted to Saintship, yet, in general speech, the establishment was called the Mission of the *Temblores*, or earthquakes, which were frequent there for 20 years or more. Nevertheless, the buildings there were never seriously injured by such shocks as they were at San Juan Capistrano, and Santa Inez, where the churches were thrown down in 1812, and at Santa Clara, where the church building, in 1818, was rendered unfit for further use. The church at San Gabriel, built of stone and adobe in the last century, is the best mission building in California, and the best of all erected in the State before the American conquest. There is no elegance in its design or finish.

San Gabriel Valley.—The valley of San Gabriel, lying at the southern base of the San Gabriel range, is fertile, well watered, and occupied by a wide expanse of orchards, vineyards and gardens. In 1880, the orchards covered 1800 and the vineyards 1770 acres, and a considerable area has been planted since. The orchard and vineyard of L. J. Rose cover 800 acres, making one of the finest horticultural estates to be found anywhere. The orange orchards of E. J. Baldwin and B. D. Wilson & Co., and the vineyards of E. J. Baldwin, J. de Barth Shorb, Gen. Stoneman, and J. F. Crank, are magnificent estates, and Rose, Shorb, Stoneman and Crank, resident owners (Wilson is dead and Baldwin resides in San Francisco), have studied the orange and grape, and are men of interesting character and career. There are numerous attractive drives, through vineyards and canyons, near San Gabriel.

Sierra Madre Villa.—Sierra Madre Villa, on the slope of San Gabriel Mountain, and 10 miles northward from the San Gabriel Railroad Station, at an elevation of 1,800 feet above the sea, is one of the leading pleasure resorts of Southern California. It has a spacious hotel, with a good table, a large orchard and vineyard, extensive grounds and a magnificent view across the San Gabriel Valley, with the Pacific and islands in the distance. The State Board of Health has recommended this as one of the best sites in Southern California for a State hospital for consumptives.

Santa Monica, 16 miles west from Los Angeles, by rail, is the principal place in Southern California, south of Santa Barbara, for sea-bathing. The beach is beautiful, the surf is slight, and the water warm. The situation is in the midst of a bend in the shore, which runs westward 12 miles to Pt. Duma, and south-southeastward an equal distance to Pt. Firmin. A canyon near by and the beach are occupied by numerous tents in the summer, and on holidays hundreds of people come down from Los Angeles.

Pasadena, Etc.—Along the southern base of the San Antonio mountain ridge, from the vicinity of Los Angeles to San Gorgonio Pass, a distance of 50 miles, extends a plateau about 4 miles wide and about 1,000 feet above the level of the sea. On this plateau, near its western end, and 7 miles from Los Angeles, is Pasadena, which, laid out in 1873 for a horticultural colony, has become one of the most beautiful and prosperous towns in California. The attractiveness of the town and of its surrounding scenery led to its selection as the place for the Raymond Hotel for the accommodation of tourists—an establishment of the first rank in size, management, public favor, and elegance of construction and equipment.

Anaheim, 20 miles southeast from Los Angeles by rail, a prosperous town, was laid off as a vineyard colony by a company of 50 Germans, who purchased 1,168 acres of land in 1858, laid off a town with 50 vineyards of 20 acres each round it, planted vines, and after three years divided the vineyards by lot among the members. The land is irrigated by a ditch from the Santa Ana River.

San Juan Capistrano, so designated in honor of a Spanish saint of the same name, 60 miles south-eastward from Los Angeles, is chiefly notable as the site of a mission founded November 1, 1776. The church building, completed in 1806, of stone, with a vaulted roof of the same material, was thrown down in 1812, killing 36 persons engaged in worship at the moment the shock came. Some hot springs, 12 miles north-east from San Juan (the hottest has a temperature of 135°), attract several hundred campers every summer, most of them the relatives and friends of invalids who want to bathe in the waters. There is no hotel, nor any bath-house, except such as each party of visitors provides for itself.

Santa Catalina Island, 20 miles long, 8 wide at the broadest place, and 30 miles south of the nearest mainland, has excellent fishing grounds in its vicinity, and on account of genial temperature in midsummer, is a favorite resort for pleasure seekers from the warmer valleys of Los Angeles and San Bernardino Counties.

The summit of San Antonio, or Old Baldy peak, 10,142 feet high, about 17 miles in a direct line northward from the Pomona Station on the Southern Pacific Railroad, on the boundary line between Los Angeles and San Bernardino Counties, may be reached on horseback over a steep and rocky trail. It is on the main divide of the Coast Range, and commands a very extensive view of the valleys of San Gabriel, Los Angeles and Santa Ana, including the richest portions of Los Angeles and San Bernardino Counties to the west and south, while to the eastward and northward are the Mojave Desert and Mt. San Bernardino, with its grand neighboring peaks.

Santa Barbara.—Santa Barbara County, between parallels 34° and 35° of latitude, has a southern frontage 80 miles and a western frontage 40 miles on the Pacific. Two mountain ridges run through the county from east to west, occupying much of its area. The San Rafael ridge is near the northern border; the Santa Inez ridge, about 3,000 feet high, is separated from the ocean by the Santa Barbara plain, which, with a length of 80 miles, and an average width of perhaps 4 miles, is one of the most attractive portions of California. The mountains give it a shelter against the cold winds which prevail to the northward and westward. The soil is fertile and moist. The sea is smooth and dotted with islands. The landscape is beautiful by nature, and has been made more attractive by art. The mean temperature of January is 53° in the air, and 60° on the ocean; and of July, 64° on the sea, and 68° in the atmosphere. The City of Santa Barbara, situated about midway in this plain, one of the favorite resorts for health and pleasure in the State, has numerous beautiful gardens and orchards within its limits and in its vicinity. The late Dr. Thomas Logan, first Secretary of the State Board of Health, thus spoke of Santa Barbara: "The trade winds which are so troublesome at San Francisco, during a considerable portion of the year, cannot strike this place at all. The close vicinity of the sea prevents the extreme heat to which inland places in this latitude are often exposed, while the overhanging mountains absorb dampness and tend to give a tonic, bracing character to the atmosphere. I know no place in the world so protected and bearing the same relation to the mountains and the ocean, unless it be the *Riviera* undercliff along the northern coast of the Mediterranean, at Hieres, in southeastern France, and at Nice and Mentone in western Italy. Between the Alps and the sea, there is a narrow strip of land, whose surroundings and advantages for invalids seem quite similar to those of Santa Barbara. Travelers who have tried both, however, give the preference to this place, because of the uncomfortable houses and un-American ways met with in those foreign places of resort."

A beautiful beach gives fine opportunities for bathing and driving. An intellectual population offers congenial companionship for refined people. A commodious hotel, kept in excellent style, makes a pleasant home for tourists. The records of the Mission, according to Dr. Logan, show that from 1784 to 1850, there were 2,047 births and 621 deaths, or more than 3 births for 1 death, more than twice as much as the average in healthy towns. There were in the same period 346 marriages, or about 1 for 6 children on an average. An extremely healthy record for a town. The late Dr. S. B. Brinkerhoff wrote thus: "Ten miles from Santa Barbara in a westerly direction, in the bed of the ocean, about 1½ miles from the shore, is an immense spring of petroleum, the product of which continually rises to the surface of the water, and floats upon it over an area of many miles. This mineral oil may be seen any day from the deck of the steamers plying between here and San Francisco, or from the high banks along the shore, its many changing hues dancing upon the shifting waves of the sea. * * * The prevailing westerly sea breezes, passing over this wide expanse of sea-laden petroleum, may * * * take up from it and bear along with them to the places whither they go, some subtle power which serves as a disinfecting agent, and which may account for the infrequency of some * * * diseases, * * * and possibly for the superior healthfulness of the climate of Santa Barbara."

No case of small-pox has ever been developed in Santa Barbara, and all who ever went there with the disease recovered.

Santa Barbara Mission.—The Mission, founded December 4, 1786, has one of the best buildings erected in California under the Spanish dominion. The main edifice is 200 feet long and 40 feet wide, with a wing 130 feet long. Two high towers of stone adorn its front. The property is in the possession of Franciscan monks, who use it for collegiate purposes.

Montecito.—Montecito (Little Forest), four miles north-eastward from Santa Barbara, has a number of luxuriant orchards and gardens. One of these has a camellia tree, the largest in the State; another has a famous grapevine of the Mission variety. It has a trunk 12 inches in diameter at the ground, and covers an arbor 60 feet square. It grew from a cutting from a larger vine on the same place. The latter having outlived its usefulness and shown signs of decay, was cut down in 1876, when 81 years old, and when its trunk had a diameter of 15 inches. It had produced more than 5 tons of grapes in a season—and the present vine bears about 4 tons in a good year.

A mile eastward from Montecito are the Santa Barbara Hot Springs, 1,400 feet above the sea. There are a dozen of these springs in a wild, rocky canyon, and the four largest have temperatures of 114°, 115°, 115°, and 118°.

Hollister's Rancho.—Twelve miles westward from Santa Barbara, are the ranchos of W. W. Hollister and Elwood Cooper, prominent citizens of California. Hollister introduced the Merino into California and was the first person to breed the sheep for wool, after the gold discovery. He made a fortune by his venture and his example was followed by many others. He has 350 acres in orchard, including 250 in almonds. The avenue in front of his house, lined with date palms, 10 years old, is very beautiful.

Cooper's Rancho.—Mr. Cooper's rancho is notable for having the largest olive orchard of the State, and the largest varieties of eucalyptus, in a plantation covering more than 100 acres. He is the leading producer of olive oil in the State.

Santa Inez Valley.—At the northern base of the Santa Barbara Mountains, and only 15 miles in a direct line from the county seat, is the Santa Inez Valley, drained by a stream 80 miles long, but small in the quantity of its waters. On the banks of the Santa Inez River, are the old missions of Santa Inez and Purisima. The buildings at both missions are of adobe; the latter in good condition; the former is in ruins.

Santa Barbara Islands Etc.—Twenty miles from the shore, and in a line nearly parallel with it, are the Islands of San Miguel, Santa Rosa, Santa Cruz and Anacapa. There are excellent fishing grounds near these islands, and the western side of Santa Cruz has a great number of abalones, which are taken for their shells, from the rocks, by Chinamen. Between the islands and the mainland lies the Santa Barbara Channel, which is noted for the calmness of its waters.

Ventura.—Ventura County lies east of Santa Barbara, and like it, has no railroad. All its freight and most of its travelers, entering or leaving the county go by sea. It has no harbor, but several roadsteads secure enough for ordinary shipping purposes, except, perhaps, during half a dozen days in the year. Its chief port, San Buenaventura (named after a saint of the Franciscan Order, Buonaventura, changed into Buenaventura to accommodate it to the Spanish tongue), is about 36 hours by steam from San Francisco, and first-class fare is $10 or $12. The town is at the mouth of the San Buenaventura river, on a narrow plain between barren hills and the beach. The place was the site of one of the Spanish missions founded March 24th, 1782. The church building, dedicated in 1809, is a substantial edifice, with walls 7 feet thick, brick outside and adobe inside. The parish priest, a native of Spain, has been a resident of California for many years and is an interesting gentleman. Date and olive trees, more than half a century old, are prominent features of the town. On the bank of the river, from 1 to 4 miles from town, there are some 30 orchards of oranges and other fruit.

Ojai.—The most attractive part of Ventura County for tourists is Ojai Valley, 15 miles north-westward from San Buenaventura, and from 600 to 1200 feet above the sea, the height near the centre, the town of Nordhoff, being 850 feet. The valley has a fertile soil, many inequalities of surface, a good supply of trees, grass and brush, a surrounding of grand and beautiful mountains, which rise on the east to a height of 6,000 feet, a dry atmosphere, and a pleasant class of inhabitants. There are two hotels, where the traveller will find a good table and clean rooms; riding horses can be hired at cheap rates, and there is neither lack of agreeable companionship nor danger of being crowded by a multitude of rude people. Although not so conveniently accessible as many other pleasure resorts, it is one of the most attractive for either a short or a long stay in California. As a winter resort for invalids and for persons who wish to live away from the throng, Ojai deserves special commendation. The indigenous plants are sycamore, alder, and cottonwood along the edges of the streams; walnut trees, evergreen and deciduous oaks, alfilerillo, bur, clover, malva and canegrass, in the moist lands of the open valley and the hills, and ceanothus and chamiso in the drier places.

Matilijá, Etc.—The Matilijá Canyon, which opens into the Ojai Valley from the northward, is a deep gorge through which the north fork of the San Buenaventura River flows, and is remarkable for its fine scenery, its numerous hot and cold mineral springs and the trout in the stream. There are good accommodations for a small number of visitors at the springs, which are 18 miles from San Buenaventura.

The oil region in Ventura County, situated in the hills near Santa Paula, have attracted much attention, and large sums of money have been spent in vain efforts to obtain a large flow of oil. The flowing oil springs are numerous, and occupy a tract of country 7 or 8 miles long, and nearly a mile wide. Two refineries have been built, and the purified oil is found to be of excellent quality, but the cost of refining and the distance from market render the enterprise unprofitable, about 30 barrels being the daily production.

Fifteen miles northward from San Buenaventura, and near the ocean, is a Solfatura, or place where the ground is hot, sulphurous gases are emitted, and sulphur is found, a sight well worth the visitor's attention.

San Bernardino.—San Bernardino, the largest county in California, has an area of 23,000 square miles, of which nearly one-fifteenth may be west of the main summit of the Coast Range, and two-thirds of that western division, valley land. The eastern portion is in the Utah Inclosed Basin, and in the Colorado Basin, and most of it desert. With relatively insignificant exceptions, the population and business of the county are limited to the San Bernardino Valley, which has an average diameter of 30 miles, and is the upper portion of the valley of the Santa Ana River, with an elevation varying from 500 to 1200 feet above the sea. On the north and east it is bordered by the main ridge of the Coast Range, with San Antonio Peak 10,142 feet high on the north, and Grayback 11,600, San Bernardino 10,800, and San Jacinto 10,000 on the east. To the southward are the Temescal and Santa Ana ridges. The enclosing mountains make a view 100 miles long, nearly enclosing the circle, and rising steeply from the plain, with summits not 20 miles distant from its centre, they give grandeur to the landscape, especially when covered with snow, as the higher peaks are for 8 months in the year. The cluster of Grayback, San Bernardino and San Jacinto, is especially beautiful. Nowhere else in the state are towering peaks found in such near proximity to orange groves and evergreen meadows. The scene is most impressive in February or March, when the ripe oranges, the orange blossoms, and the thick mantle of snow, extending nearly a mile down vertically from the top of the higher summits, may all be seen at the same time. By ascending the base of the mountains to a height of 1000 or 1,500 feet above the sea, comprehensive views of the valley as well as of the ridges beyond it can be obtained. The following lines of A. F. Kercheval about Riverside, may apply to the entire San Bernardino plain:

"Soft veiled in splendor, like some jeweled bride,
Far gazing down the future, dim and wide,
A glorious vision of enchantment gleams,
And lo, before us queenly Riverside.

What genius here hath waved his magic wand
Above the silence of a lonely land?
Lo! Spreading far beyond the vision's sweep,
The wealth of green and gold on every hand!

* * * * * *

Lone deserts made to blossom as the rose,
Hesperian fruits and bowers of soft repose,
Perpetual clothed in robes of emerald sheen—
These are the triumphs that thy years disclose.

* * * * * *

Queen ruler proud, beneath the burnished blaze
Of lordly, rapt San Bernardino's gaze,
Thou restest sweet beneath his sheltering love,
And dreamest of the fruits of coming days.

* * * * * *

Lo! more eternal than the boasts of Rome,
Her piles of marble or St. Peter's dome,
Thy everlasting watch towers looming o'er,
To guard the treasures of thy fairy home."

San Bernardino Town.—Near the eastern edge of the valley, and at an elevation of 1,100 feet above the sea, in a fertile district, watered by numerous artesian wells, 4 miles north from the railroad station of Colton, is San Bernardino, the oldest, largest, and commercially the most active town in the county. It was laid out by a colony of Mormons who came in wagons from Salt Lake in 1851, and after an examination of the place, they bought the San Bernardino rancho from the native Californian owners, agreeing to pay $77,500 for the 35,500 acres. They had brought only $700 in cash, but they were full of faith in one another, and as soon as the bargain was closed they began work as if every man considered his own interest to be in harmony with that of the colony. One of the first wants was lumber, and all turned out to build a road to the timber in the mountains. A few weeks of hard work finished that task, and then they were ready to build a town, which they laid off with square blocks of eight acres, separated by wide straight streets. They toiled for years before they completed their payments for the rancho, but they paid for it, and were beginning to beautify their town, when President Buchanan threatened to subject Utah to military rule, and Brigham Young called home all the Mormon colonists of Carson and San Bernardino Valleys, for the double purpose of leaving no helpless outposts and of concentrating all his forces at home. The San Bernardino Mormons had become very much attached to their new home, but bitter as was their regret at the necessity of returning to Salt Lake, they went promptly, with a few exceptions, selling their lands and houses for whatever could be got, whether a half, a fourth, or even only a tenth of the fair value. This was in the fall of 1857, and the Mormons never returned.

The first white settlement was made at old San Bernardino, 2 miles southeast of Colton, where Franciscan friars established a branch of the San Gabriel Mission, about 1820, and erected a large adobe building, now in ruins. The valley was not considered a safe place until after the Mormon settlement, as hostile Indians from the Mojave and Colorado Valleys took this route to steal horses and neat cattle in the neighborhood of Los Angeles, and often killed white men found near their line of travel.

Riverside, Etc.—The most beautiful town in San Bernardino is Riverside, 8 miles southwest from Colton. It was laid off in 1871, in what was then a desert, and having been supplied with water by a ditch, was planted with orchards and vineyards by settlers fresh from New England, bringing with them capital, enterprise, education and refinement. The climate seems peculiarly favorable for the orange tree, which there shows none of the red scale and black fungus that injure the orchards in many other parts of the State. The water supply is abundant, the soil fertile, and the plan of the colony judicious. The trees and vines are of good varieties and have been set out in large numbers. Within the last 10 years no horticultural town on our coast has made more rapid progress than

Riverside, or has drawn together a larger proportion of intellectual people. Its pecuniary prosperity, its horticultural skill and its social attractions make it a favorite resort for tourists.

Several other towns have been laid off to the south-west of Riverside, and all are connected by Magnolia Avenue, 130 feet wide and 12 miles long, lined with a double row of trees on each side, with magnolias at regular intervals. It is expected that all the land on both sides of the avenue will be occupied with orchards, vineyards, and gardens.

Colton, the chief railroad station of the county, has a central situation and good soil, but, until it has a larger water supply than at present, will probably not become important.

Lugonia, north-east of Colton, is a horticultural town so new that it has little of interest now, though it promises much for the future.

The slopes of the mountains abound to the height of 2,000 feet above the sea, with places more beautiful by nature than those in the lowland, and less troubled by frost, but they are more lonely, and few of them have, as yet, been improved.

Crafton, 10 miles eastward from Colton, 2,300 feet above the sea, in a beautiful situation, where a large brook issues from a canyon, is a well known pleasure resort, and a very attractive place.

San Bernardino Springs.—The Arrowhead Hot Springs, 2,035 feet above the sea, and 6 miles northward from San Bernardino have a hotel, bath-houses, and two basins walled in with stone, for bathing purposes. Some of the springs are hot and others cold, and the supply of water is abundant. They take their name from a natural formation. The steep mountain side near the springs and behind them is covered with chaparral, except a place perhaps half a mile high and a quarter wide, shaped like an arrowhead, or ace of spades, with the point down, and the figure thus made is visible at a distance of 15 or 20 miles.

Waterman's Hot Springs, 7 miles northward from San Bernardino, and 1,800 feet above the sea, number about 40, and have temperatures ranging from 173° to 200°. The waters contain carbonate of lime, soda and iron. A hotel and bathhouses offer their accomodations to tourists.

The San Jacinto tin mine, 10 miles south-westward from Riverside, had a shaft sunk in it for the purposes of exploration many years since, but very little metal has been reduced, and no work is in progress there, although report says the ore is rich and abundant.

The Temescal Hot Springs, six miles southward from the San Jacinto tin mines, are in a canyon, have a hotel, and fine scenery.

San Diego County.—San Diego County has an area of 14,600 square miles, three-fourths of which immense area may be set down as desert, east of the main summit of the Coast Range. West of that summit much of the land is mountainous, though the mountains afford excellent natural pasturage, and contain some valuable minerals. The western quarter of the county contains nearly all the inhabitants, and is much less broken, having fine table-lands, low hills, and many rich valleys, well adapted to the cultivation of the vine and sub-tropical fruits. A valley 12 miles east of San Diego, containing 40,000 acres, has extensive wheat fields, and several large orchards and vineyards produce fruits and grapes of superior quality. Of more than 10,000,000 acres in the county, only 35,000 are cultivated. The county is the most southern in the State; the dryest, though never hot; for the average of the year the warmest. The natural roads of the western side of the county, with but little dust in the summer or mud in the wet season; the fine climate, free from storms, harsh winds and chilly fogs, and never too hot or too cold for comfort, and the varied and pleasing scenery, render the drives most enjoyable and lend a rare charm to out-door life, making this county quite as attractive to sojourners and certain classes of invalids as any other portion of California.

San Diego City.—The chief resource of San Diego City is its bay, magnificent natural harbor, deep, commodious, secure, easy of entrance, with no dangerous rocks or currents, and almost free from fogs. San Diego had a population of 2,637 in 1880, and is rapidly growing under the impulse of the construction of the Southern California Railroad, which is completed to the Southern Pacific at Colton. The city having an excellent hotel, many beautiful gardens, a winter climate unsurpassed for mildness on our coast, and intelligent and enterprising inhabitants, has been a favorite place with tourists and invalids, who have contributed much to its prosperity. The first settlement by white men within the limits of what is now known as California, was made at the Mission of San Diego, April 11, 1769, when a small sailing vessel, the *San Antonio*, arrived with supplies for the projected missions.

The shores of the bay and the beach of the Pacific in the vicinity are nearly everywhere well adapted to bathing, but it is more prudent to bathe only at the frequented grounds, on account of stingrays, which sometimes inflict very painful wounds. They are rarely found at places where bathers are numerous.

The *San Diego Union* of December 16th, 1880, mentions the sudden disappearance of Andy Anderson while bathing in a quiet sea at San Dieguito, and adds "there is little doubt but that Anderson was devoured by one of these monsters"—a man-eating shark, which fish of large size are occasionally seen in the Pacific near the Southern Coast, though it is not known for certain that one has ever attacked a man in the California waters. Those of large size probably prefer to stay in the deep water. Some smaller species of sharks are numerous in the bays, and it is said that they have sometimes undertaken to bite bathers in San Francisco Bay, but have done no serious harm to any one.

Mud Volcanoes.—The most remarkable natural curiosity of San Diego County, is the group of mud volcanoes in the desert, five miles west from Volcano Station, on the Southern Pacific Railroad, a station not marked on the ordinary time-tables. These mud volcanoes, called also fumaroles or salses, are vents through which steam and gas escape through what seems to be a pond of thick, hot mud. A vent having been formed, the mud gradually rises until it forms a cone not more than 8 feet high and 8 feet wide at the base, though the sizes and shapes are very irregular, and, after a time the supply of gas gives out, the activity of that vent ceases, the mud sinks down to the common level, and a hard crust, looking like solid ground, forms over it; while the hard level crust in another place breaks and a little cone rises. Thus the site of the steaming mud, covering several square miles in area, is continually changing. It is dangerous to approach these vents as the crust may give way under a man's weight and let him down into the mud which has a temperature higher than that of boiling water. H. G. Hanks, State Mineralogist, while making a scientific examination of them, was badly burned on one foot in January, 1881, while examining one of these vents, and had a narrow escape with his life. The country in the neighborhood is barren and uninteresting, and the mud volcanoes will never become a pleasure resort. Some of the cones are curiously fringed with little crystals of sulphur and salts deposited from the fumes.

Below Sea Level.—Another natural curiosity of San Diego County is the deep desert, in its lowest point about 300 feet below the level of the sea. At Fink's Spring, on the Southern Pacific Railroad, the elevation is 260 feet below the ocean level. This was undoubtedly part of the Gulf of California, but the Colorado River deposited sand and mould along its banks, until they rose nearly to the level of its high floods, and extended the banks until an area of several hundred square miles in what is now California and Lower California, were cut off from the gulf and converted into a lake, which received less water from the rains than it lost by evaporation, and therefore dried out leaving its bed bare. Once in 20 or 30 years, on an average, the Colorado River rises high enough to overflow its eastern bank and send its waters out into this desert, below the level of the sea.

Mission of San Diego.—The Mission of San Diego, founded July 16th, 1769, on the bank of the San Diego River, eight miles from its mouth, and at the same distance from the present city, is in a dilapidated condition, the best preserved portion of it being the remains of its orchard, including olive trees, which bear good crops every year. The best pickled olives of California are made at San Diego.

Mission of San Luis Rey.—The Mission of San Luis Rey, on the bank of the San Luis Rey River, 6 miles from the ocean, and 45 miles northward from San Diego, founded June 13th, 1798, has well preserved buildings and a pleasant situation.

La Jolla, etc.—La Jolla, a place on the beach 15 miles north of the city, where the rocks have been worn into **fantastic caverns and**

openings by the sea, is the end of the favorite drives of San Diego.

Another drive, less interesting in its route and in its terminus, leads to the boundary monument marking the line between the United States and Mexico on the shore of the Pacific, 14 miles from San Diego.

Paradise Valley, 5 miles east of the city, has beautiful orchards and gardens, and attracts most of those who go out for a short drive.

Rose's Canyon is the favorite picnic ground

CHAPTER V.

THE SIERRA NEVADA.

The Chain. — The Sierra Nevada is a great mountain chain abounding in places and objects of interest to students, business men and pleasure seekers. As this book is written for the last of those three classes, we shall here speak only of those points specially attractive to them.

The name Sierra Nevada is usually restricted to the chain which forms the eastern and southern boundary of the Sacramento-San Joaquin Basin, extending from latitude 34° to 42°. Its average height is about 8,000 feet; its highest point, 15,000; its lowest pass about 4,000. Its rock generally is granite, with slate in the auriferous districts on its western slopes, and with large tracts of lava and basalt, covering extensive regions in the north of parallel 40°, and smaller tracts or streams of volcanic rock south of that latitude. The highest part of the chain is near 36° 30', and that portion of it between 36° and 38°, is known as the Californian Alps. Although the peaks are higher there than in any part of California, they are so far from the populous valleys, and as seen from either side, so near together and so little above the common level of the ridge, that they make far less impression on the beholder than do the more lonely peaks in the centre and north of the State, though with far inferior elevation. More than 100 peaks that exceed 10,000 feet in the Californian Alps have never been named, and most of those which have been named are not known by sight save to a few persons. According to John Muir, an excellent authority, Mount Ritter is "the noblest mountain of the range," and that as seen from Sentinel Dome or from any other point near to the Yosemite Valley, does not leave any such impression on the mind as does Mount Shasta, Mount Lassen, or even the Downieville Butte.

The western slope of the Sierra has a width of about 50 miles in a direct line, and in that distance it rises nearly 150 feet to the mile. This is not a steep ascent, but the slope is intersected transversely at short intervals of distance, by deep, steep and crooked canyons, so that the general character is marked by extreme roughness, and by extensive tracts of bare rock. There are also, especially in the foot hills, numerous tracts of fertile soil and thrifty timber. The oak and nut pine are found at an elevation of 2000 feet, the yellow pine begins to appear about 1,500 feet above the sea; at 3000 feet the oak and nut pine are rare and the sugar pine comes in; the large conifers have almost exclusive possession of the land suitable for the growth of timber from 3000 to 8000 feet; and above the latter elevation the greater part of the mountain is bare.

The objects of most interest to tourists in the Sierra Nevada, are the Yosemite Valley, the similar chasms of the Tuolumne, San Joaquin, Kings and Kern Rivers, the groves of big trees, the 65 glaciers found on the higher peaks of the chain, the scenery generally in the Californian Alps, between latitude 36° and 38°, Mount Shasta (which, though not belonging to the chain is connected with it, and is here treated with it for the convenience of arrangement), Mount Lassen, with its adjacent cluster of volcanic cones, Lake Tahoe, of which an account has been given in Chapter I, the hydraulic gold mines, and the gold quartz mines, which have also been mentioned briefly in the same chapter.

California has no club of mountain climbers; and few of her citizens have had the opportunity, as well as the inclination, to spend much time in the study of nature at high elevations. J. D. Whitney, Clarence King, Wm. H. Brewer, W. A. Goodyear and C. F. Hoffman, who examined extensive regions in the high Sierra while engaged in the geological survey, are not now residents of the State. The most noted mountain climber of the State is John Muir; and among the men who are known to have spent much time in the mountains for pleasure or study are J. G. Lemmon, botanist, George Bailey, Thomas Magee, Sydney Smith, Jr., James M. Hutchings, Galen Clark, George Davidson, A. F. Rodgers, Ebenezer Knowlton and John Swett.

The Swiss lakes, surrounded by thriving towns and highly cultivated fields, have beauties for which there is no parallel in the Sierra lakes, and yet there is nothing in the lakes of Geneva and Zurich to approach some of the notable features of Lake Tahoe.

The Californian Alps have no inhabitants, no roads, no hotels, few trails, and those very rugged, and few visitors. The general level of the country is higher and the peaks relatively lower than in Switzerland. The glaciers are smaller; there are no lakes; and, while the scenery has many grand features, it has generally less majesty and beauty than that of the European Alps.

In many respects the Sierra Nevada is one of the most interesting chains of mountains. Though inferior in elevation to the Himalayas or Andes, it has great advantage over them of being more conveniently accessible from the leading centres of civilized population. If not so well provided with horses and guides for the accommodation of tourists as Switzerland, it has, on the other hand, greater length and variety, a peculiarly attractive mining industry, a grander forest, greater cliffs and wilder gorges, and an interest in its volcanic phenomena which are lacking in the Swiss Alps.

Yosemite.—In the opinion of travelers familiar with the places most noted for their natural scenery in other countries, there is nothing elsewhere to equal the Yosemite Valley and its surroundings in the variety and interest of the views to be found within a space 15 miles long by 5 wide. This wonderful combination of great cliffs, great waterfalls, dome-shaped mountain peaks, park-like meadows, deep umbrageous canyons and charming nooks, is unlike anything to be found out of California, and its general character is almost as different from the Niagara Cataract, from the Chamouni View of Mt. Blanc, from the boiling lava lake of Hawaii, from the Yellowstone Park, from a grove of *Sequoia Gigantea*, or from the Mt. Diablo birdseye view over Central California, as a picture is from a piece of music. Yet people will make comparisons in the general interest of things that have no other quality in common; and on the basis of attractiveness that does not diminish with prolonged acquaintance, the predominant judgment of distinguished tourists who have visited Yosemite is that it has an unequaled wealth of grand and romantic features within a radius of 10 miles from its centre; Switzerland within a radius of 50 miles has more noteworthy sights than are to be found in the Sierra Nevada, but any one of its mountains or valleys, taken separately, is decidedly inferior to the remarkable chasm of the Merced,

A dozen natural wonders of stupendous proportions and remarkable forms are so situated, that they can be seen to the best advantage at short distances, visible from below and from above, in many directions and in many lights, and from every new elevation, direction and light, there assume new and interesting phases, so that the landscape never grows stale, and the eye never tires. If the valley and its sides, to an elevation of 200 feet above the Merced River, were transferred, with its magnificent trees, its shrubs, its ferns, its meadows, its rocks, its streams, its shady nooks and its drives, to some place within 10 miles of New York City, and converted into a public park, the world would go wild over the incomparable beauty of such a popular pleasure ground near a great metropolis; and myriads, perhaps millions, of people would visit it every year from distant States. And yet the valley proper is scarcely accounted among the attractions of the Yosemite.

One of these waterfalls, one of these vertical cliffs, half a mile high; one of these dome-shaped mountains, or the chasm itself, as a geological curiosity, would be worthy of world-wide fame; but at Yosemite there are a dozen cliffs, nearly as many cataracts, half as many domes, several lakes and caverns, and numberless minor wonders in and near the valley, besides a multitude of grand snow-peaks not far distant. The cataract of the Staubbach, of Switzerland, reputed to be the highest waterfall of the Old World, is only 900 feet high, and that of Tequendama, in New Granada, which had the first place in the New World before the discovery of the Yosemite, is only 650. The largest and highest works of human art dwindle into insignificance when compared in bulk or elevation with the tremendous precipices of Yosemite. The Cheops pyramid, 498 feet, and the cathedral spire of Strasburg, 466 feet, would be lost in the unnoticed talus of the Capitan, which rises to 3,300 feet, or of Sentinel Rock, which ascends to 3,000.

General Effect.—Prof. Whitney says: "The peculiar features of the Yosemite are: first, the near approach to verticality of its walls; next, their great height, not only absolutely, but as compared with the valley itself; and finally, the very small amount of debris or talus, at the bottom of these gigantic cliffs. These are the great characteristics of the valley throughout its whole length; but besides these, there are many other striking peculiarities and features, both of sublimity and beauty, which can hardly be surpassed, if equalled, by those of any other mountain scenery in the world."

Horace Greeley, says: "The Yosemite Valley (or gorge) is the most unique and majestic of nature's marvels. * * * Of the grand sights I have enjoyed—Rome from the dome of St. Peter's, the Alps from the valley of Lake Como, Mount Blanc and her glaciers from Chamouni, Niagara—and the Yosemite—I judge the last named the most unique and stupendous. It is a partially wooded gorge, 100 to 300 rods wide, and 3,000 to 4,000 feet deep, between almost perpendicular walls of gray granite, and here and there a dark yellow pine rooted in a crevice of either wall, and clinging with desperate tenacity to its dizzy elevation. The isolation of the Yosemite—the absolute wilderness of its sylvan solitudes, many miles from human settlement or cultivation—its cascade 2,000 feet high, though the stream which makes this leap has worn a channel in the hard bedrock to a depth of 1,000 feet—renders it the grandest marvel that ever met my gaze. Next to Yosemite, I judge that Niagara has more distinct and diverse attributes of sublimity than any other."

The following is an extract from Samuel Bowles : "Indeed, it is not too much to say, that no so limited space in all the known world offers such majestic and impressive beauty. Niagara, alone, divides honors with it in America. Only the whole of Switzerland can surpass it; no one scene in all the Alps can match this, before me now, in the things that mark the memory and impress all the senses for beauty and for sublimity."

Yosemite Falls.

The opinion of Starr King was, that "Nowhere among the Alps, in no pass of the Andes, and in no canyon of the mighty Oregon range, is there such stupendous rock scenery as the traveler now lifts his eyes to."

A State Park.—The Yosemite, with adjacent territory, averaging about 2 miles in width on each side and at each end of the valley proper, is the property of the State, given by an act of Congress passed June 30th, 1864. The Statute provides that the gift is subject to the conditions "that the premises shall be held for public use, resort, and recreation, [and] shall be inalienable for all time, but leases not exceeding 10 years may be granted for portions of said premises. All incomes derived from leases of privileges to be expended in the preservation and improvement of the property, or the roads leading thereto; * * * the premises to be managed by the Governor and 8 other Commissioners to be appointed by the Executive of California, and who shall receive no compensation for their services."

The summits of Mt. Watkins, Cloud's Rest, and Mt. Starr King are the eastern corners of the Yosemite Grant; the western corners are not distinguished by prominent landmarks. The level part of the valley is 5 miles long and less than half a mile wide, its area being 1,141 acres, including 745 of meadow, and 396 of sparse timber, the soil in places being bare granite sand.

Routes.—The Yosemite is a little south of east from San Francisco, distant 165 miles in a straight line, and 279 by the most traveled route.

There are five **stage roads leading** to the Yosemite from the San Joaquin Valley, but three of them unite at Clark's—called also the Big Tree Sta ion. The Raymond or Berenda road takes most of the patronage; next to it in public favor is the Big Oak Flat road. Raymond, 200 miles by rail from San Francisco, is the terminus of the Yosemite branch railway, which turns off from the main road in the San Joaquin valley at Berenda. The distances in miles and tenths of miles from Raymond to various points on the way, are thus given by the Yosemite Commissioners: To Grant's, 25; Clark's, 37; Eleven Mile Station, 47.76; Inspiration Point, 56.71; El Capitan Bridge, Yosemite Valley, 60.27; Leidig's Hotel, 62.83; Cook's Hotel, 63.13; Barnard's Hotel, 63.90.

This route has less staging, less dust, pleasanter scenery, and better hotel accommodation than any other. Raymond is in the timbered foot-hills and the road to the valley is almost continuously beautiful.

The Yosemite tourist, going by the Raymond route, leaves San Francisco at 3:30 P. M., arrives at Berenda at 11.22. P. M., remains there in his sleeping car till 5:15 A. M.; arrives at Raymond for breakfast at 6:30 A. M., takes stage at 7 A. M.; lunches at Grant's, where he spends an hour and a half; arrives at Clark's at 5:30, where he dines, sleeps and breakfasts, and leaves at 7 A. M. for the valley where he arrives at 1 P. M. He travels a day and a half by stage, making 37 miles in the full day and 27 in the half day. Returning, he leaves the valley at 6 A. M., reaches Clark's at 2 P. M.; spends the remainder of the day after lunch visiting the Mariposa Big Tree grove (a round drive of 17 miles); leaves Clark's at 8 A. M. the second day; reaches Raymond at 5 P. M. and arrives in San Francisco at 10:40 the next morning.

The route, which, next to that by Raymond has the most patronage, is that by Big Oak Flat. The tourist goes to Milton, by rail, 133 miles; and thence he has 91 miles of staging making the entire distance 224 miles.

The main intermediate stations, by rail, on this route, are Lathrop 94, and Stockton 103 miles from San Francisco. The stations on the stage road, and their distances from Milton are these; Viz.: To reservoir House, 6.13; Copperopolis, 14.83; Stanislaus river, 21.83; Table Mountain Pass, 25.33; Chinese Camp, 28.83; Jacksonville, 33.01; Stevens' Ferry, 35.28; Priest's Hotel, 40.94; Big Oak Flat, 42.01; Second Garrote, 46.40; South Fork Tuolumne, Lower Bridge, 58.83; South Fork Tuolumne river, Upper Bridge, 64.59; Tuolumne Big Tree Grove, 74.37; Crane Flat, 75.37; Tamarack Flat, 80.44; Junction of Coulterville road, 87.62; Barnard's Hotel, Valley, 91.28.

The tourist going by Big Oak Flat leaves San Francisco at 3:30 P. M. for Stockton, (distant, by rail, 92 miles,) arrives there at 8 P. M.; leaves Stockton at 10 o'clock, by rail, the next morning for Milton, distant 30 miles; takes stage at Milton at 1 P. M., drives 42 miles to Priest's Hotel arriving at 7 P. M.; the next morning drives 50 miles to the valley arriving about 7 P. M. Returning, he leaves the valley at 7:30 A. M., drives 64 miles to Chinese Camp where he spends the night; the next morning leaves at 6 A. M. and drives 28 miles to Milton where he takes the cars for Stockton, arriving there at 12:35 P. M., and thence to San Francisco, arriving at 5:40 P. M.

The fare for rail and stage is $50 by Raymond and $40 by Big Oak Flat; and from $12 to $16 should be allowed for meals and lodgings on the way. The expense in the valley will depend on the tourist's length of stay and his use of horses and guides.

Tourists can go to Yosemite by way of the Calaveras Big Tree Grove. The distances on that route are from Milton to the Grove 45 miles, thence to Murphy's 16, Stanislaus river 26, Columbia 30, Sonora 34, Chinese Camp 45, and to Berenda Hotel 105 miles.

The stages run daily from the first of April to the last of August, and until November if the travel justifies, unless the winter begins unusually early or lingers unusually late, blocking the road with snow. The elevation to be crossed is about 6,500 feet, and snow in mid-winter falls to a depth of 20 feet on the higher parts of the route. When the regular stages do not run, the tourist must hire a special conveyance at greater expense, and may have to spend more time on the trip. In the midst of the tourist season the stages do not run by fixed time-tables, but will start and stop in accordance with the wishes of any party numerous enough to make a load. Toll is charged on every traveler going into the valley, but this is included in the price of the tourist's ticket if he goes by stage, so that, usually the matter is not mentioned to him. The tolls for horses and riders will be mentioned in the chapter on camping.

The Coulterville wagon road to Yosemite is 88 miles long from the railroad station of Merced to the valley. The distances from Merced and elevations above the sea for the leading stations on the road are: Snelling, 16 miles and 120 feet; Coulterville, 42 miles and 1,800 feet; Greeley Hill, 48 miles and 3,350 feet; Dudley's, 50 miles and 3,000 feet; Bower Cave, 54 miles and 2,450 feet; Brown's Ranch, 57 miles and 3,350 feet; Pilot Peak Branch Road, 64 miles and 5,350 feet; Hazel Green, 68 miles and 5,600 feet; Highest Point, 169½ miles and 5,800 feet; Merced Grove, 71 miles and 5,400 feet; Buena Vista Gap, 75 miles and 5,150 feet; Big Meadows, 78 miles and 4,325 feet.

The tourist starting from San Francisco on Monday afternoon by this route can be in the city on the forenoon of the following Saturday, thus making the round trip in less than 5 days, with half a day in the valley. Returning from the valley he may take the stage at Glacier's Point where the distance to Clark's is 25 miles; but a new road, to be finished, perhaps, in 1888, will reduce this distance to 14 miles and give access to much interesting scenery. It is expected that a horse-trail along this line will be open next spring. The tourist can then leave the valley by way of the Nevada Fall, go thence to Glacier Point, and thence to Clark's.

The Raymond and Big Oak Flat roads reach an elevation of about 6,500 at their highest points. Clark's is 3,923 feet above the sea; Chinese Camp, 1,300; Priest's, 2,823; and the Tuolumne Big Tree Grove, 5,794 feet.

The Calaveras Grove route has 133 miles of rail and 153 of stage—286 in all.

The Big Oak Flat route has 133 of rail and 91 of stage—224 in all.

The Coulterville route has 114 of rail and 99 of stage—212 in all.
The Raymond route has 200 of rail and 64 of stage—264 in all.

Programme.—Those tourists who have a definite programme before reaching the Valley, and are with a party prepared to stay the same length of time and make the same excursions, obtain the most satisfaction from their trip. If only four days are to be spent in the valley the following programme may be adopted: The first day go to Sentinel Dome, stopping at Union Point and Glacier Point, and making a longer stay at Glacier Point than on the Dome. The second day, the Nevada Fall; on the third, Eagle Point, and on

YOSEMITE VALLEY FROM THE WEST.

the fourth, Mirror Lake in the early morning, and the Bridal Veil in the afternoon.

If more than four days are to be spent in the valley, then stay over night at the Nevada Fall, and from there go to the summit of Cloud's Rest. One day may be given to the Tooloolweack Fall. A day may be devoted to a trip from the village by way of Glacier Point to the Nevada Fall, crossing the Tooloolweack Creek above its fall. Those who can give two weeks to the valley and its surroundings should consider the Tuolumne Meadows and the Tuolumne Glacier, to be mentioned hereafter.

Trails.—Several points mentioned in the last two sentences are accessible by trails, or bridle-paths, some of which have been made with much labor, and were private property, the owners of which charged tolls; but in 1882 all the trails were purchased by the State, and are now free. They are injured by the rains and snowslides of every winter, and are repaired by order of the commissioners every spring. For portions of the distance from Glacier Point to the top of Sentinel Dome, and from the Nevada Fall to the top of Cloud's Rest, there is no distinctly marked trail.

Out of 100 tourists who visit the Yosemite, 80 go to Glacier Point, as many to the Nevada Fall, 20 to Eagle Point, 10 to Cloud's Rest, and 3 to the top of the Half Dome. The average period in the valley is about 4 days, some remaining only a single day, and others months.

The Walls.—The walls enclosing the valley are of granite, varying in height from 1,200 to 4,700 feet, in many points vertical, and in all very steep, so that until roads were made at great expense, there was no place where a wagon could enter it, and only two where horses could get in, and then with much difficulty. The sides of the valley are nearly parallel to each other, suggesting the idea that they were torn apart, and have not changed much in outline since. At the base of the walls on each side is a talus, or slope of rocks and dirt which have fallen from above. The angle of this talus is from 25 to 40 degrees; the height from 100 to 500 feet, the main material is rock, covered in most places with a stony soil, and elsewhere bare, showing here small fragments of rock, and there immense masses with great passages under their projecting edges. The bare rocks of the talus are largest in the Tooloolweack Canyon. The color of the walls is yellowish on the north side of the valley, and blue or gray on the south.

The River.—The Merced, running nearly in the middle of the valley, is 60 feet wide; from 3 to 8 feet deep in July, and the water is generally from 5 to 10 feet below the level of the valley. The river is clear and the current lively; the descent in the 8 miles of valley being about 50 feet. The water is never warm enough for comfortable bathing, but there are ponds which get warm in the summer.

First View of the Valley.—The tourist gets some fine views of the valley while descending into it by the wagon roads from Big Oak Flat, and the Big Tree Station; those near Inspiration Point, on the latter road, being by far the most pleasing. The best view from the west, however, is obtained at Old Inspiration Point, near the horse trail, and perhaps half a mile from the wagon road—a place from which many photographs and some oil pictures have been taken. The Capitan, the Bridal Veil, the Virgin's Tears or Ribbon Fall, the North Dome, Mt. Watkins, the Half Dome, and the lower part of the valley are seen distinctly, and with the best effect in the afternoon.

Ribbon Fall.—Of the Fall of the Ribbon or Virgin's Tears Creek, the first cascade in the valley visible to the tourist who goes by the Madera or Mariposa route, Prof. Whitney says: "The Virgin's Tears Creek, on the other side of the valley, and directly opposite the Bridal Veil, makes also a fine fall, over 1,000 feet high, included in a deep recess of the rocks near the lower corner of El Capitan. This is a beautiful fall as long as it lasts, but the stream which produces it dries up early in the season. In quantity of water, elevation and general effect, this fall, hardly spoken of at the Yosemite among so many grander ones, is far superior to the celebrated Staubbach of Switzerland."

The Capitan.—The first object of interest to attract the attention of the visitor when entering the valley from the west, is the Capitan, or Tutucanula, rising perpendicularly from the valley to a height of 3,300 feet. It has 2 fronts, one facing to the west, and the other to the south, the 2 meeting nearly at a right angle, and together about a mile long. This cliff is considered by many the most stupendous and sublime feature in Yosemite scenery. The immensity of its bulk, the elevation, verticality and relative smoothness of its surfaces, and its prominent position (being visible from nearly all the principal points of view), fix the attention of the beholder. Its height exceeds the width of the valley in front of it, so that if it should topple over, it would rest on the opposite cliff. The Indian name means the Great Spirit, and Capitan is Spanish for Captain. Prof. Whitney says: "It would be difficult to find, anywhere in the world, a mass of rock presenting a perpendicular face so imposing." Starr King declared: "A more majestic object than this rock, I never expect to see on this planet." Horace Greeley, who entered the valley at night, thus speaks of his first impressions of the great cliff: "That first, full, deliberate gaze up the opposite height! Can I ever forget it? The valley is here scarcely half a mile wide, while its northern wall of mainly naked perpendicular granite is at least 4,000 feet high—probably more. But the modicum of moonlight that fell into this awful gorge gave to that precipice a vagueness of outline, an indefinite vastness, a ghostly and weird spirituality. Had the mountain spoke to me in an audible voice, or began to lean over with the purpose of burying me, I should hardly have been surprised. Its whiteness, thrown into bold relief by the patches of trees or shrubs which fringed or flecked it, wherever a few handfuls of its moss, slowly decomposed to earth, could contrive to hold on, continually suggested the presence of snow, which suggestion, with difficulty refuted, was at once renewed."

The Bridal Veil.—The largest fall to attract the tourist when descending into the valley, and a prominent feature in the best general view, is the Bridal Veil, formed by the creek of the same name, which there makes a descent of 1,000 feet, of which about 850 consist of vertical fall, the remainder being rapids, below the main cascade. The creek is about 70 feet wide in June. In consequence of its great height, and its position where the valley is wide and the wall nearly straight for a considerable distance, the fall influences, and is influenced by the winds greatly, and strong gusts blow about it, carrying the stream from one side to another, "making it flutter like a white veil; hence [says Whitney] the name, which is both beautiful and appropriate." The stream falls upon the talus, which is there 200 feet high or more, and a heavy mist surrounds its foot. Beautiful rainbows can be seen here every clear afternoon. The stream, after striking the talus, divides into 3 branches before reaching the Merced. Travelers not unfrequently go far up into the gusts and mist, but do not report very favorably of the adventure. The best distant view of the fall is obtained from a point half a mile to the northwest. The best near view from the talus on the west side of the stream, about 200 yards from the fall, in the middle of the afternoon. The situation varies with the course and force of the winds. Starr King gives his impressions of the Bridal Veil, thus: "As I think of it, I lose quickly the impression of the widening of its watery trail before it struck the rocks to thunder from them; I do not dwell either on the fascinations of its ever-melting and renewing tracery, nor on the brilliance of its iris banners that are dyed into its leaping mists and flying shreds; I can recall for my supreme delight only the curve of the tide more than 800 feet aloft, where it starts off from the precipice, and the transparency of its vitreous brink, with the edge now and then veiled with a little curling misty vapor, when the wind blew hard against it, but generally tinged with a faint apple-green lustre."

The Bridal Veil Creek, like the Yosemite Creek, goes dry in September, if not in August.

Cathedral Rocks.—On the south side of the valley, immediately opposite to the Capitan, are the Cathedral Rocks, which rise to a height of 3,000 feet. Near them, and at the top of the cliff, are the Cathedral Spires, 2 "slender and beautiful columns of granite," each about 800 feet and 300 feet in diameter. Cathedral Rocks, as they are generally called, are seen to the best advantage from a point about a mile distant to the northeastward. Prof. Whitney calls them Cathedral Peak, and says: "This is one of the grandest landmarks in the whole region, and has been most appropriately named. As seen from the west and south-west it presents the appearance of a lofty mass of rock, cut squarely down on all sides for more than 1,000 feet, and having at its southern end a beautiful cluster of slender pinnacles, which are several hundred feet above the main body. It requires no effort of the imagination to see the resemblance of the whole to a gothic cathedral; but the majesty of its form, and its vast dimensions are such that any work by human hands would sink into insignificance beside it."

The Three Brothers.—A mile and a half east of the Capitan are the Three Brothers, 3 peaks in close proximity, jutting out into the valley on its north side. The highest of these summits, 4,000 feet above the hotels, and known as Eagle Point, is accessible by a horse trail, which ascends the wall of the valley between the Yosemite Creek and the Three Brothers.

The Yosemite Fall.—Nearly midway in the valley, on the north side, is the Yosemite Fall, where the creek of the same name, in three cataracts, jumps down 2,550 feet. The upper Fall is 1,500 feet high, and is a third of a mile back from the valley, in a gorge; the second fall is rather a succession of cascades, measuring in all 626 feet, after which comes the third fall, 400 feet high, below which is a talus, 200 feet high. Below the lower fall the stream divides into three branches, and one of these straight for half a mile, and lined with tall trees, so as to present a beautiful vista, is called Cascade Avenue, because of numerous little cascades in its course. In the canyon between the Upper and Lower Falls there are very fierce gusts of wind, so strong that visitors frequently find difficulty in catching breath, and the spray sweeps down almost in showers. Most of the water of the upper Fall breaks into mist and spreads out gradually, from 30 yards at the top of the cliff to 100 yards at the bottom. The creek goes nearly dry in September, and it is not more than 40 yards wide and 4 feet deep at its best, so the bulk of water is small. The general impression is, that the fall is not an important part of the attractions of the valley, and the time for a visit should be selected without special reference to the fullness of the streams.

At the base of the Upper Fall, on the west side of it, is a cavern 8 feet high, 300 feet wide across the mouth, and 30 feet deep horizontally. It can only be reached in the dry season, and then by walking across from the east on a ledge of rocks about 20 feet wide, upon which the water strikes with great force when the stream is full.

Horace Greeley, who saw the fall in August, says: "The fall of the Yosemite, so called, is a humbug. It is not the Merced River that makes this fall, but a mere tributary trout brook, which pitches in from the north by a barely once-broken descent of 2,600 feet, while the Merced enters the valley at its eastern extremity, over falls of 600 and 250 feet. But a river thrice as large as the Merced at this season would be utterly dwarfed by all the other accessories of this prodigious chasm. Only a Mississippi or a Niagara could be adequate to their exactions. I readily concede that a hundred times the present amount of water may roll down the Yosemite Fall in the months of May and June, when the snows are melting from the central ranges of the Sierra Nevada, which bound this abyss to the east; but this would not add a fraction to the wonder of this vivid exemplification of the Divine power and majesty. At present, the little stream that leaps down the Yosemite, and is all but shattered to mist by the amazing descent, looks like a tape line let down from the cloud-capped height to measure the depth of the abyss."

On the other hand, Professor Whitney says: "The traveler who has not seen the Yosemite when its streams are full of water, has lost if not the greater part, at least a large portion of the attractions of the region, for so great a variety of cascades and falls as those which leap into this valley from all sides has, as we may confidently assert, never been seen elsewhere; both the Bridal Veil and the Nevada Fall being unsurpassed in some respects, while the Yosemite Fall is beyond anything known to exist, whether we consider its height, or the stupendous character of the surrounding scenery."

The same writer remarks that "The first and most impressive of these elements (of grandeur and beauty) is, as in all other objects, about the Yosemite, vertical height. In this it surpasses, it is believed, any waterfall in the world with anything like an equal body of water. And all the accessories of this fall are of a character worthy of and commensurate with its height. * * * One of the most striking features of the Yosemite Fall is the vibration of the upper portion from one side to the other, under the varying pressure of the wind, which acts with immense force on so long a column. The descending mass of water is too great to allow of its being broken entirely into spray, but it widens out very much towards the bottom—probably to as much as 300 feet at high water, the space through which it moves being fully three times as wide. This vibratory motion of the Yosemite and Bridal Veil Falls is something peculiar, and not observed in any others, so far as we know. The effect of it is indescribably grand under the magical illumination of the full moon."

The Yosemite Creek, at the foot of the Fall, becomes dry in September, and sometimes in August, and contains, when at its best, but a small bulk of water, never exceeding 40 yards in width and 4 feet in depth, In the middle of June, 1865, after a winter of average rainfall, it was measured by J. F. Houghton, then Surveyor-General for the State of California, and found to have a width of 37 feet, a depth of 25 inches, and a current of 1 mile an hour, showing a flow of water equal to 400,000 cubic feet per hour.

SENTINEL ROCK.

Sentinel Rock.—One of the most prominent and remarkable features of the rock scenery of the Yosemite is Sentinel Rock, a natural obelisk, about 1,000 feet high, and 300 feet thick at the summit, which is 3,000 feet above the valley. The sides show the vertical cleavages of the granite. The Sentinel Rock is seen to the best advantage from the west.

Sentinel Dome.— A mile southwestward from Glacier Point, hemispherical in shape, and 4,150 feet above the valley is the Sentinel Dome, next to Mt. Starr King, the most regularly shaped of all the dome-like peaks of the Yosemite. The summit, accessible on horseback in 4 hours from the hotels, is the highest point visited by the Yosemite tourists, as a class. It is not only easier of access than Cloud's Rest, but it is nearer the valley, is in the midst of the objects of greatest interest, and commands a good view of the Yosemite and Nevada Falls which are not visible from Cloud's Rest. The Sentinel Dome commands a good view of the high Sierra, but the valley with its falls and cliffs generally is seen more satisfactorily from Glacier Point. Every addition to the height and distance renders the landscape more dim.

Glacier Point.—Glacier Point, one mile east of Sentinel Rock, and 3,705 feet above the valley, should be the first place for the tourist to visit. The trail leading to it, one of the most interesting in the valley, starts near the base of Sentinel Rock, and with an eastward zigzag, ascends the steep mountain side, presenting a succession of interesting views. The visitor should not, however, stop a longer time than is needed for rest, until he reaches Glacier Point, where the cliff juts out into the valley, and commands a series of extensive views, reaching from the southeast almost to the southwest, and including the Nevada Fall, Cap of Liberty, Half Dome, North Dome, Royal Arches, Yosemite Fall, and the Capitan. All these are within a radius of about 2 miles, and the situation is excellent for seeing their beauties; nor can they be seen so well from any other point, not even from Sentinel Dome, which is too far from many of them, as well as too far above them, to give a distinct view. Numerous peaks of the high Sierra appear in the distance.

Those who wish to obtain a distinct idea of the position of the peaks visible from Glacier Point, with reference to the main ridge of the chain and the streams flowing westward from the summit of the Sierra, will find something upon that point under the head California Alps.

Elevations.—The following table shows the elevations in feet above the valley and above the sea, and the approximate distance in miles, and directions, from the Sentinel Dome, of various points in and near the Yosemite Valley, and also of some other notable points. Sentinel Dome is a mile and a half south-southeast from the village, and half a mile southwest from Glacier Point.

NAMES.	ELEVATIONS.		Direction.	Distance.
	Above Valley.	Above Sea.		
Yosemite Village	......	4,000	N. of N. N. W.	1½
Mt. Hoffmann	6,872	10,872	N. N. E.	9
Mt. Watkins	7,568	3,568	N. N. E.	4½
North Dome	......	......	N. N. E.	3
Washington Column	......	......	N. E.	2½
Mt. Conness	......	......	N. E.	22½
Cathedral Peak	7,000	11,000	N. E.	13½
Mono Lake	2,400	6,400	N. E.	31
Soda Springs	4,680	8,680	N. E.	16½
Unicorn Peak	......	......	N. E.	13½
Half Dome	4,737	8,737	E. N. E.	3½
Cloud's Rest	6,150	10,150	E. N. E.	6
Mt. Dana	9,227	13,227	N. E.	23
Glacier Point	3,705	7,705	N. E.	½
Cap of Liberty	......	......	E. of E. N. E.	2¾
Nevada Fall	......	......	E. of E. N. E.	2¾
Vernal Fall	......	......	E. of E. N. E.	1¾
Mt. McClure	......	......	E. of E. N. E.	16¾
Mt. Lyell	......	13,217	E. of E. N. E.	17
Mt. Ritter	......	13,520	E. of E. S. E.	21
Minarets	......	......	E. of E. S. E.	22½
Mt. Clark	......	......	E. S. E.	9
Tooloolweack Fall	......	......	E. S. E.	1¼
Mt. Starr King	......	......	E. S. E.	4
Black Mountain	......	......	S. E.	15
Buena Vista Peak	......	......	S. S. E.	9
Iron Mountain	......	......	S. S. E.	16½
Mariposa Big Trees	......	......	S.	13½
Big Tree Station	......	4,000	S. S. W.	13½
Devil's Mountain	......	......	S. S. W.	15
Cathedral Rocks	2,660	6,660	W.	3
Mt. Bullion	......	5,000	W.	20
Pilot Peak	......	......	W. of W. N. W.	19
Capitan	3,300	7,300	W. of W. N. W.	3
Hetchhetchy Valley	......	......	N. W.	18
Three Brothers	3,400	7,400	N. W.	2
Sentinel Rock	3,043	7,043	N. W.	½
Top Upper Yosemite Fall	2,640	6,640	N. N. W.	2½
Mt. Whitney	10,887	14,887	S. E.	100
Mt. Brewer	9,386	13,386	S. E.	80
Mt. Hamilton	......	4,449	W.	100
Mt. Diablo	......	3,848	W. N. W.	130

The Half Dome.—The Half Dome—one of the most prominent features in the scenery of Yosemite, in general shape, suggests half an egg which has been cut in two lengthwise, and set up on the blunt end. The summit is 4,737 feet above the valley, and for 2.000 feet down from the top, the face fronting the northwest is straight and plumb, and below that point the mountain, or the talus, slopes down at an angle of 40° to the horizon. The peak is in no place more than 1,500 feet through horizontally, from northwest to southeast, the height being considerably greater than the width in that direction. A horse trail ascends high up on the eastern side of the dome, and the tourist after dismounting, must walk half a mile over the talus, and climb several hundred yards on a rocky slope that rises at an angle of 38° to the horizon. The ascent is made with the help of a rope, and at intervals of 10 feet there are resting places. There is no charge for the use of the trail or rope. About one in 30 of the Yosemite tourists goes to the top of the South Dome.

Professor Whitney speaks thus of this "truly marvelous crest of rock:" "From all the upper part of the valley, and from the heights about it, the Half Dome presents an aspect of the most imposing grandeur; it strikes even the most casual observer as a new revelation in mountain forms; its existence would be considered an impossibility if it were not there before us in all its reality; it is an unique thing in mountain scenery, and nothing even approaching it can be found except in the Sierra Nevada."

Royal Arches.—On the north side of the valley, directly opposite to Glacier Point are the "Royal Arches," a wall of nearly vertical rock, from the sides of which huge masses have fallen, leaving arches 300 to 400 feet in length, and projecting, like eyebrows, 70 or 80 feet beyond the hollow part of the wall beneath them.

Washington Column.—East of the Royal Arches, at a bend in the northern wall of the valley, is the Washington column, rising vertically to a height of 2,400 feet. As seen from the southwest it suggests a round tower at the corner of an immense castle.

North Dome.—Half a mile northward from the Washington Column is the North Dome, the summit of which, 3,568 feet above the valley, can be reached on horseback from the north. The view is considered inferior to that from many other points in the vicinity.

Mirror Lake.—About half a mile eastward from the Washington Column is Mirror Lake, an enlargement of Tenaya Creek, with an area of 8 acres and a depth at the deepest place of 20 feet. The water is remarkably clear, and before the winds rise in the morning, so placid, that reflections of the Half Dome and the Washington Column are wonderfully like the direct view of those objects.

Vernal Fall.—The Merced River enters the Yosemite Valley from the southeastward, and shortly before reaching it, makes the Nevada and Vernal Falls, the latter the lower of the two. The Vernal Fall, 2½ miles in a direct line from the village, is 475 feet high, and because less in height than the other falls, while the quan-

VERNAL FALL.

tity of water is greater than in any save the Nevada, it is distinguished by the greenness of its color, and from that circumstance obtained its name. A natural battlement of rock at the top, just high enough to lean upon and look over, offers a convenient place for seeing the cataract from above. The narrowness and roughness of the canyon below, limits the views from that direction. In the distance of a mile, between the Nevada and Vernal Falls, the river makes a descent of 275 feet, with numerous beautiful rapids, and little cascades, the largest of which, the Wild Cat Fall, is 30 feet high.

The Nevada Fall.—The Nevada Fall is 639 feet high, and it is rather a slide or chute than a fall, for the water runs down a rock which has a slope of 85° for about half its height, and 75° the other half. The friction of the rock breaks the stream into a white froth, and hence the name of Nevada or snowy. For ages and until sometime in this century, the river made its descent a few hundred yards east of the Nevada Fall, where it cut a canyon nearly 100 yards deep, so that the fall was not more than 400 feet. That old channel, which can be seen in most photographs of the Fall, was choked up by a raft or accumulation of trees and dirt, and so the river was turned into its present course. Mr. Bowles says of the Nevada: "This is the fall of falls; there is no rival to it here in exquisite, various, and fascinating beauty; and Switzerland, which abounds in waterfalls of like type, holds none of such peculiar charms. Not a drop of the rich stream of water but is white in its whole passage; it is one sheet—rather one grand lace-work of spray—from beginning to end. As it sweeps down its plane of rock, every drop all distinct, all alive, there is nothing of human art that you can compare it with but innumerable and snow-white point-lace collars and capes; as much more delicate, and beautiful, and perfect, however, as nature ever is than art."

The opinion of Whitney is thus expressed: "The Nevada Fall is, in every respect, one of the grandest waterfalls in the world, whether we consider its vertical height, the purity and volume of the river which forms it, or the stupendous scenery by which it is environed."

Little Yosemite Valley, half a mile above the Nevada Fall, is a mile and a half long and half a mile wide, and has some beautiful timber and meadow land, but lacks the cliffs and waterfalls that give majesty to the main valley.

Cap of Liberty.—Cap of Liberty, north of the Nevada Fall and very near it, rises steeply to a height of 4,600 feet above the valley, a magnificent dome, which in its general shape bears some resemblance to a Phrygian cap. Half a mile further north is Wild Cat Rock, the summit of which is about 4,200 feet above the valley. Its southern face is a cliff 1,600 feet high and nearly vertical.

Mt. Starr King.—Five miles southeastward from the village and half that distance in the same direction from the Vernal Fall, is Mt. Starr King, the summit of which, 5,000 feet above the valley, has never been reached by civilized men, the slopes being too steep for ascent. Professor Whitney says of it: "This is the most symmetrical and beautiful of all the dome shaped masses around the Yosemite; but it is not visible from the valley itself. It exhibits the concentric structure of the granite on a grand scale, although its surface is generally smooth and unbroken. Its summit is absolutely inaccessible." Mt. Starr King is visible from the valley near the base of the Yosemite Fall.

Cloud's Rest.—The summit of Cloud's Rest, 10,150 feet above the sea, and 6 miles east, northeast from the village, the highest point within the limits of the Yosemite grant, can be reached on horseback without difficulty. Tourists making this trip, spend the night at Snow's, near the foot of the Nevada Fall, start early in the morning, reach the summit before noon, spend several hours there, and return either to Snow's or to the valley. The view from Cloud's Rest is very comprehensive, and for the high Sierra is excellent, but the most interesting points are so distant, and so bedimmed with haze that the trip is not to be recommended for any, save those who feel a special interest in the higher mountains. For seeing the valley, the position and distance are equally unfavorable. The best way to reach Cloud's Rest is to go to the Nevada Fall in the morning and spend the day there, seeing everything within convenient distance of the hotel, where the night is to be spent, mount at 6 o'clock the next morning, reach the summit (distance 9 miles) at 10 or 11; stay till 1 o'clock; and reach the fall at 4 and the village at 6.30.

Tooloolweack Fall.—A mile southeastward from the Vernal Fall is a cascade 800 feet high, formed by the Tooloolweack Creek, as the stream is generally styled in the valley, though Whitney, by a strange misunderstanding of the Indian name, calls it the Illilouette. As the Merced River and Yosemite Creek have abandoned old channels to make the Yosemite and Nevada Falls, so the Tooloolweack has changed its course, and the cascade comes down into the canyon, not at its head, but at its side. The canyon abounds with pleasant vegetation, beautiful rocks and wild scenes, amidst immense blocks of granite, leaving large cavern-like spaces between and under them. The foot of the fall would have many visitors if accessible on horseback, but it cannot be reached without 2 miles of walking and climbing. In the canyon beyond the fall, and nearly on a level with its top, is a cavern 250 feet high, 100 feet wide across its mouth, and running 150 feet back into the rock.

Snow and Hail.—In the average winter the valley is covered for several months with snow, which occasionally reaches a depth of 8 feet, but besides the snow from the clouds, there is a formation of snow, or fine hail, about the falls from the freezing of the spray. This spray-hail collects in large quantities about the higher falls, and at the foot of the Upper Yosemite Cascade forms an arch, or ice-bridge, sometimes 100 yards high over the stream. The process of freezing does not end with the winter months, but continues when the thermometer marks a temperature of 50° in the valley. The tourist is not secure against snow or rain in May, and brief showers sometimes occur in June. The general condition of the sky, however, from April 15th to October 15th in the Sierra Nevada, as compared with that in the Alps or White Mountains in the same season, is remarkably clear. Yosemite visitors run little risk from clouds, such as often hide Mt. Blanc, the Jungfrau, and Mt. Washington for many midsummer days in succession.

Saddle-horse Charges.—The Board of Yosemite Commissioners has published a schedule of "maximum rates," a term suggestive of the possibility of getting lower rates by bargaining. These rates are $3 for a round trip in a day from the valley to Glacier Point and Sentinel Dome; or to Summits, Vernal, and Nevada Falls; or to upper Yosemite Falls and Eagle Peak; or for a trip from the valley to Glacier Point, Sentinel Dome, and Fissures, passing the night at Casa Nevada (Snow's); or to Vernal, Nevada Falls, and Glacier Point, passing the night at the last-named place; or to Cloud's Rest, passing the night at Casa Nevada; or from Casa Nevada to Cloud's Rest, returning same day to Casa Nevada or valley; or from Casa Nevada to Sentinel Dome, Glacier Point, and valley same day. The rate for the trip from Casa Nevada or Glacier Point to the valley is $2; for the round trip in one day from the valley to Glacier Point, Sentinel Dome, and Fissures, $3.75; for the round trip in one day from the valley to Glacier Point, Sentinel Dome, Nevada and Vernal Falls, $4; and for the round trip in one day from the valley to Cloud's Rest, $5. For horse on the level of the valley, per day, $2.50.

Carriage Charges.—The maximum rates for carriage charges for round trips for each person are $1 to Mirror Lake or to Bridal Veil Falls; $1.25 to Mirror Lake, returning by Tissayack avenue; $1.50 to Pohono Bridge, stopping at Yosemite and Bridal Veil Falls; $2 to Artist's Point, stopping at Bridal Veil; $2.25 to Cascade Falls, stopping at Yosemite and Bridal Veil Falls; $2.50 to New Inspiration Point, stopping at Bridal Veil; $3.50 for the Grand Round, including Lake and Cascades, Yosemite and Bridal Veil Falls. Not more than $15 for a two-horse team, or $25 for a four-house team for any trip. For a saddle-horse the charge shall not exceed that in a carriage.

Guide Charges.—The Commissioners say: "The charge for guide (including horse), when furnished, will be $3.00 per day. The above charges do not cover feed for the horse at Snow's or McCauley's."

Guides.—In the hotels the charge per day is $4.00 One guide will suffice for 12 tourists. The horse may often be obtained for less than $3.00, if there is a party. It is the duty of the guide to see that the saddles are all right before mounting, to assist the party in mounting, to carry the lunch, to see that the saddles do not slip too far back while going up hill, nor too far forward while going down, to take charge of the horses at the stopping places, to assist in preparing the lunch, and to point out the places of interest. The Yosemite guides, generally are affable, trustworthy men, with little education, and a very limited knowledge of the country, beyond the common trails. It is their general policy to start as late, stop as often, stay as long, and make the work as easy as possible for themselves and horses.

Horses.—The Yosemite horses are generally old nags of little use for other purposes, and they pay for themselves three or four times over in a season. They are much safer for the average tourist than spirited young horses would be. There are wagon roads from end to end of the valley, but the tourist who visits Glacier Point, Sentinel Dome, the Nevada Fall, Cloud's Rest, the top of the half Dome, the foot of the Upper Yosemite Fall, or Eagle Point, and these include the chief attractions, must go afoot or on horseback; and the latter is the easier and more satisfactory, and for ladies and men not of robust health is the only possible conveyance.

Guardian of the Valley.—The Yosemite Commissioners appoint a guardian, who is to reside in the valley through the tourist season, to protect the interests of the State, to superintend the improvements made, and to see that the hotel keepers, trail owners, guides, and owners of horses and carriages do not exceed the legal charges. His duties have not been defined in precise language, and much is necessarily left to his discretion. The present guardian is Mark L. McCord, who during a long residence in the valley has become familiar with it and with the surrounding country. In case of any controversy about the prices of horses or guides, application should be made to him. He also assigns places to campers. Tourists who want information about the valley, the routes to it, the places of interest, and the charges, can go to him without hesitation. He may perhaps also give the tolls on the roads leading into the valley, though as tolls are collected only on roads outside of the limits of his jurisdiction he is not required officially to be familiar with them. In response to a private letter, Mr. Hutchings, at one time guardian, wrote thus: "In answer to your last question, I am somewhat at a loss. I scarcely know the scope of my authority myself. I think it means that I must protect all the best interests of the valley—not only in seeing that its natural beauties of forest, etc., are preserved, but also that courtesy and right should be assured the tourist, so as to enable him to see our wonders in a good frame of mind—not chafed by impertinent conduct, or pained by extortionate charges. That at any and all times I should be ready to give information on every subject required; show every attention in my power—in short, make the visit a pleasure and its memory a delight, so that every person leaving Yosemite shall feel that he has been well and kindly treated, has had a good time, and wherever he goes can say a good word for both the valley and the people of California. I think that is about the scope of my duties in that particular. Perhaps I ought to have said above, that I have positive orders from the Board to order out every unsuitable or untrustworthy horse from any saddle train or carriage."

Yosemite Valley.—The collection of houses near the Yosemite hotel constitutes a village with perhaps 50 inhabitants in the summer and not half so many in winter. It has a post-office and receives its mail daily from April 1st to August 30th, three times a week in September and October, and once a week in the other four months. The three hotels can accommodate about 500 persons, and are ready to receive visitors in the winter, though very few make their appearance from November 1st to March 30th. There are also, in the summer, about 25 Indians who have wigwams near the base of the Capitan and gain a living by washing and fishing.

Method of Formation.—It is evident that most of the great canyons of the Sierra Nevada have been formed by erosion—that is, by the wearing influence of streams of water, and of the matter which they have carried down. But the Yosemite Valley is an exception. These vertical walls, half a mile deep, with numerous sharp angles, could scarcely have been formed by water, and the narrowness of the canyon below shows that there never has been any sufficient outlet for a large stream. Besides, it is evident that, since the main chasm was formed, great masses of rock have been split off, in many places, from the sides, and if the valley had been the result of erosion, these masses would have made mountains in it. The most probable explanation of its origin is the theory that it was formed by a great convulsion which tore apart the mountain to a depth very much greater than that now perceptible, that vast masses of rock fell down into the chasm, and that after a time they were covered up by the washing of the waters, leaving a level valley over them. Professor Whitney says: "It appears to us probable that this mighty chasm has been roughly hewn into the present form by the same kind of forces which have raised the crest of the Sierra and moulded the surface of the mountains into something like their present shape. The Domes and such masses as that of Mount Broderick, we conceive to have been formed by the process of upheaval itself, for we can discover nothing about them that looks like the result of ordinary denudation. The Half Dome seems, beyond a doubt, to have been split asunder in the middle, the lost half having gone down in what may truly be said to have been 'the wreck of matter and the crash of worlds.' * * * If the bottom of the Yosemite did 'drop out,' to use a homely, but expressive phrase, it was not all done in one piece or with one movement, there are evidences in the valley of fractures and cross-fractures at right angles to these, and the different segments of the mass must have been of quite different sizes, and may have descended to unequal depths."

Again, Prof. Whitney says: "The eroded canyons of the Sierra, however, whose formation is due to the action of water, never have vertical walls, nor do their sides present the peculiar angular forms which are seen in the Yosemite, as, for instance, on El Capitan, where two perpendicular surfaces of smooth granite, more than 3,000 feet high, meet each other at right-angles. It is sufficient to look for a moment at the vertical faces of El Capitan and the Bridal Veil Rock, turned down the valley, or away from the direction in which the eroding forces must have acted, to be able to say that aqueous erosion could not have been the agent employed to do any such work. The squarely cut re-entering angles, like those below El Capitan, and between Cathedral Rock and the Sentinel, or in the Illilouette Canyon, were never produced by ordinary erosion. Much less could any such cause be called into account for the peculiar formation of the Half Dome, the vertical portion of which is all above the ordinary level of the walls of the valley, rising 2,000 feet in sublime isolation, above any point that could have been reached by denuding agencies, even supposing the current of water to have felled the whole valley."

John Muir published a series of articles in the *Overland Monthly*, taking the ground that the Yosemite Valley was formed by glaciers, which were undoubtedly numerous in the vicinity during the glacial era of this coast, but the valley has features not to be found in any valley or deep gorge unquestionably scooped out by glaciers. Such valleys have neither vertical sides, sharp angles nor narrow canyons at their lower ends. The glacial polish and groovings are found in all the canyons leading into Yosemite Valley, and especially in the Little Yosemite Canyon, at the lowest place where it can be crossed, and also on the rocks at the Nevada Fall. A moraine runs from the base of the Half Dome to the Washington Column, extending from each side in a curve down the valley. Another begins at the western end of the South Dome, and runs down the valley. Another marks the line on which the glaciers from the Little Yosemite and Illilouette met. A fourth starts just below the Bridal Veil Fall on one side and a quarter of a mile below the Capitan at the other, and runs down to a point in the middle of the valley.

Professor Whitney thus expresses his opinion on the glacial theory: "A more absurd theory was never advanced than that, by which it was sought to ascribe to glaciers the sawing out of these vertical walls and the rounding of the domes. Nothing more unlike the real work of ice, as exhibited in the Alps, could be found."

Other Yosemites.—The Sierra Nevada has 4 other great chasms bearing some general resemblance to the Yosemite Valley. The most distant of these, and the most difficult of access, the Kern River Chasm, 150 miles southeast of Yosemite, is larger than the latter, and has higher walls, but they are less steep, and the waterfalls are decidedly inferior. The Kings' River Canyon, 75 miles southeast from the Yosemite, is grand, but that, too, lacks the waterfalls. The San Joaquin, 25 miles southeastward from the Yosemite, is the least interesting of the series. The Hetchhetchy, on the Tuolumne, 14 miles in a direct line northwest from Yosemite, bears the closest resemblance to it, in its construction of cliffs, cascades and domes, but is on a smaller scale. This minor Yosemite is 3,800 feet above the sea, 3 miles long and is cut in two near the middle by a hill, which comes down to the edge of the stream. The direction of the valley is east and west; its width, at the widest, half a mile. Near the middle on the northern side, is a perpendicular cliff, 1,300 feet high above a talus, 500 feet high; and in the spring, while the snow is melting, a large creek makes a splendid cataract over the precipice. Before the end of summer, the stream ceases to flow. Half a mile further east, on the same side, is the Hetchhetchy Fall, 1,700 feet high, but not vertical. The stream is constant, and when large, the roaring of its cascades can be heard a long distance. There is very little talus in the valley except under the falls. There are numerous marks of glacier action in the valley, through which, according to Prof. Whitney, the big glacier that headed at Mt. Dana and Mt. Lyell made its way. The valley can be reached from Big Oak Flat, by going 18 miles on the Yosemite trail to Hardin's fence; then turning to the left 7 miles to Reservoir or Wade's Meadows; crossing the Middle Fork of the Tuolumne to the Hog Ranch, 5 miles; thence up a divide between the middle fork and the main river, 2 miles to the Canyon Ranch, and 6 miles down through the rocks to Hetchhetchy Valley. The total distance from Big Oak Flat is 38 miles.

Mountain Topography.—Mt. Lyell, 13,217 feet high, the nearest part of the main ridge of the Sierra Nevada to the Yosemite Valley, only 17 miles from Sentinel Dome, and in plain view, though it does not tower much above the level of other peaks in the vicinity, is remarkable, because three of the leading rivers of the State rise on its slopes. The Tuolumne rises in a glacier or bank of snow that never fully disappears, in a deep canyon 2 miles long and a mile wide, running due north from the peak. The Merced flows down its western flank. A mile and a half south of the Summit, the San Joaquin heads and takes a southward direction. The snows melting on the eastern flank of the mountain send their waters into Mono Lake.

Mt. Conness, Mt. Dana and Mt. Gibbs, north of Mt. Lyell, and Mt. Ritter and the Minarets to the southward, are all on the main ridge of the Sierra. The waters on the western side flow to the San Joaquin Valley, and on the eastern, to the Utah Basin.

A secondary ridge of the Sierra Nevada running northwestward from Mt. Lyell, and serving to separate the headwaters of the Tuolumne from those of the Merced River, reaches its most notable elevations in Unicorn Peak and Cathedral Peak. A spur running northwestward connects this ridge with Mt. Hoffman, which separates the Tenaya Fork of the Merced from the Yosemite Creek. Mt. Watkins is lower down on the same spur.

Cloud's Rest and the Half Dome are on the spur or tertiary ridge which separates the Tenaya Fork from the main Merced, which has its head in Mt. Lyell, and passes from the Little Yosemite Valley to the Yosemite Valley by the Nevada and Vernal Falls.

Starting from the main ridge, a mile south of the summit of Mt. Lyell, the secondary ridge dividing the headwaters of the Merced from those of the San Joaquin, runs southwestward. Its most notable points are Red Peak, 9; and Black and Iron Peaks, each 14 miles from Mt. Lyell. At Red Peak a tertiary ridge, running out 7 miles to the northeastward, and separating the waters of the main Merced from those of the Tooloolweack Creek, has Grey Peak midway in its length, and Obelisk Peak, or Clark Mountain, at its end. The last named peak is only 15 miles from Sentinel Dome, whence the tourist can look into the canyons opening to the northwest and see snow, when southward slopes at higher elevations are bare or green. Clark, Grey, Red and Black Peaks are all about 11,600 feet high. Buena Vista Peak is on a tertiary ridge that starts out to the westward from Red Peak, and separates Tooloolweack Creek from the South Fork of the Merced.

The Devil's Peak is on a ridge that separates the waters of the Merced from those of the Chowchilla River.

The Californian Alps.—When we reach the Yosemite we are near the northern end of a mountain region known as the Californian Alps, which extend from the 35th to the 38th parallel of latitude, and have an area of 300 square miles more than 8,000 feet high, with 100 peaks that rise to an elevation of 13,000 feet or more. No one of these peaks rises, however, very much above the level of adjacent peaks and, therefore, the spectator looking from Sentinel Dome or Cloud's Rest sees no one mountain obviously predominant over all the others. Mt. Whitney, the highest peak in the State, is not known by sight to the people generally in Owen Valley, 20 miles eastward, nor to those in the San Joaquin Valley, 30 miles westward.

The most interesting excursion to be made from the Yosemite within a period of 4 or 5 days, is to visit the Tuolumne Meadows, 16½ miles to the northeast. The tourist can ascend Mt. Hoffman, see the Mt. Lyell glacier, and find himself among the very high points of the Sierra during this trip, with comparatively little effort. If he sees fit to prolong his stay, he can go to the top of Mt. Dana, 13,227 feet above the sea, and then he can go to the glacier at the headwaters of the Tuolumne River, on the northern slope of Mt. Lyell. Mt. Dana is on the main ridge of the Sierra, and commands a view of Owen Valley on the east, and of the San Joaquin Valley on the west. The tourist should leave the Yosemite by the Eagle Point Trail, and if he intends to ascend Mt. Hoffman, should camp the first night at Porcupine Flat, 8,173 feet above the sea.

miles by the trail from his starting point, and 4 miles southwest of the summit. Prof. Whitney says: "The view from the summit of Mt. Hoffman is remarkably fine, and those who have not time or inclination to visit the higher peaks of the main ridge of the Sierra, are strongly advised to ascend this, as the trip from the Yosemite and back, need only occupy 2 or 3 days. * * * This is a particularly good point for getting an idea of the almost inaccessible region of volcanic masses lying between the Tuolumne River and the Sonora Pass road, and forming great tables, in places 700 feet thick, resting on the granite, at an elevation of 3,000 feet above the adjacent valleys, the dark lava contrasting finely in color with the almost white granite masses. The number of distinct peaks, ridges and tables visible in that direction, crowded together, is too great to be counted." The next camp should be at the Soda Springs, on the bank of the Tuolumne River, 8,680 feet above the sea, near the Tuolumne Meadows, and in the grandest scenery of the high Sierra. "The vicinity of Soda Springs and, indeed, the whole region about the head of the Upper Tuolumne," as Prof. Whitney remarks, "is one of the finest in the State for studying the traces of the ancient glacier system of the Sierra Nevada. The valleys of both the Mt. Lyell and Mt. Dana forks exhibit abundant evidence of having been filled, at no very remote period, with an immense body of moving ice, which has everywhere rounded and polished the surface of the rocks, up to 1,000 feet above the level of the river. This polish extends over a vast area, and is so perfect that the surface is often seen from a distance to glitter with the light reflected from it as from a mirror. Not only have we these evidences of the former existence of glaciers, but all the phenomena of the moraines—lateral, medial and terminal—are here displayed on the grandest scale." At the Soda Springs the tourist is in the midst of high peaks, which wall him in. Mt. Hoffman is 10 miles westward, Mt. Conness 8 miles northward, Mt. Dana and Mt. Gibbs are 8 miles eastward, Mt. Maclure and Mt. Lyell are 10 miles south-eastward, and Cathedral Peak and Unicorn Peak are 4 miles southward. The water of the springs is mildly chalybeate and sparkling with carbonic acid gas. "Of all the excursions," in the opinion of Prof. Whitney, "that can be made from the Soda Springs, the one most to be recommended, is the ascent of Mt. Dana, as being entirely without difficulty or danger, and as offering one of the grandest panoramic views which can be had in the Sierra Nevada. * * * Several parties have ascended, riding nearly to the summit on horseback, and there can be no doubt that the ascent will, in time, become well known and popular among tourists."

Big Tree Station.—Big Tree Station, 25 miles from the Valley, and about on the same level, 4000 feet above the sea, is near the South Fork of the Merced River, in the midst of a pleasant meadow. The hotel large, well furnished, and well kept. The mountains in the neighborhood have deer, bear and other game, and the streams have trout. A fall about 400 feet high of the Chilnoialny Creek, distant 4 miles to the east-northeastward, is visible from the hotel. Devil's Mountain is 4½ miles distant to the westward. Mt. Raymond is 7 miles and Iron Mountain Peak 10 miles away to the east-south-eastward; and Buena Vista Peak 9 miles to the east-southeast. Most of these points, however, are not visible from the hotel.

Mariposa Big Trees.—Seven miles by the wagon road from the Big Tree Hotel Station is the Mariposa Big Tree Grove, which, for persons going to Yosemite, is the most conveniently accessible of all the groves of the *sequoia gigantea*, and although in some respects inferior to other groves, is large enough in the number, diameter and height of its trees to satisfy the beholder. It has 427 trees, the largest 34 feet through; 2, each of 33 feet; 13 between 25 and 32 feet; 36 between 20 and 25 feet; and 82 between 15 and 20 feet. The total number exceeding 15 feet in diameter is 134; and 293 are of smaller sizes, some not more than 2 feet through. The highest tree is 272 feet; and others have heights of 270, 268, 260, 256, 255, 250, 249, 244, 243 and 235, making 11 more than 230 feet high. The largest tree in circumference at the ground was 92½ feet; and others 91½, 89½, 87½, 86½, 82½, 82¼, 81½ and 81½, making 9 trees, each more than 80 feet in circumference at the ground, according to J. D. Whitney. Of the tree 91½ feet in circumference, he says it is "a splendid tree, over 100 feet in circumference originally, but much burned at the base." Several of these trees have been cut through, leaving part of the trunk on each side, so that the stage, with its passengers, can go under as if they were driving through a tunnel.

Everybody who approaches these trees, can see that they are large, but few without experience, imagine them to be so tall or thick in the trunk as they really are.

Prof. Whitney, says: "The more time one spends among these trees, the more their grand proportions and colossal size become impressed on the mind. The extraordinary dimensions of the other species, which are associated with the Big Trees, especially of the Sugar Pine—a tree of which the beauty and majesty can hardly be exaggerated—make it difficult to realize that these are really so large, as exact measurements prove them to be."

The same authority wrote thus, in reference to the matter of age: "The age of the tree which was cut down in the Calaveras Grove, and which at 6 feet above the ground, has a diameter of 23 feet inside the bark, [sometimes 3 feet thick, so that the diameter of the tree may have been 29 feet], was found to be about 1300 years. It was easy to count the annual rings—and they amounted to 1255 in number—but there being a small space, about a foot in diameter at the centre of the tree, from which the wood was decayed away, it would be a reasonable estimate to call the age of this particular tree about 1300 years. The difference in the rapidity of its growth at different ages may be inferred from the fact that the width occupied by 100 rings at the centre of the tree was 13 inches, and next to the bark only 3."

The Sierra Forest.—A full appreciation of the attractive features of a magnificent forest, requires besides a poetic taste, also that closeness of observation which comes with botanical knowledge and familiarity with lumbering. Perhaps no one has written better about the timber of the Sierra Nevada than Horace Greeley, who had learned something of trees while working on a farm. He said: "And here let me renew my tribute to the marvelous bounty and beauty of the forests of this whole mountain region. The Sierra Nevada lack the glorious glaciers, the frequent rains, the rich verdure, the abundant cataracts of the Alps; but they far surpass them—they surpass any other mountains I ever saw—in the wealth and grace of their trees. Look down from almost any of their peaks and your range of vision is filled, bounded, satisfied, by what might be termed a tempest-tossed sea of evergreens, filling every upland valley, covering every hillside, crowning every peak but the highest, with their unfading luxuriance. That I saw, during this day's travel, many hundreds of pines 8 feet in diameter, with cedars at least 6 feet, I am confident; and there were miles after miles of such and smaller trees of like genus, standing as thick as they could grow. Steep mountain sides allowing them to grow, rank above rank, without obstructing each others sunshine, seem peculiarly favorable to the production of these serviceable giants. But the summit meadows are peculiar in their heavy fringe of balsam fir of all sizes, from those barely 1 foot high to those hardly less than 200, their branches surrounding them in collars, their extremities gracefully bent down by the weight of winter snows, making them here, I am confident, the most beautiful trees on earth. The dry promontories which separate these meadows, are also covered with a species of spruce which is only less graceful than the fir."

Calaveras Big Trees.—There are 9 groves of the Big Trees in California. The most northern is the Calaveras grove, in latitude 38° 15′, at an elevation of 4,750 feet above the sea. The trees are scattered over an area 3,200 feet long by 700 wide, and there are 100 of large size besides many smaller ones. One tree is 325 feet high, another 319, a third 315, a fourth 307, and 20 others are more than 250 feet high. The largest in diameter has a circumference of 61 feet, 6 feet above the ground; the next has 53; three have each 51; 2 have 50; and many have between 40 and 50. This grove, the nearest to San Francisco, is the only one that has a hotel, and has higher trees than any other visited by many tourists, but has the great disadvantage of being distant from the main roads to Yosemite, while three others are near those roads.

The engraving on the next page represents a Calaveras Sequoia, 300 feet high and 30 feet in diameter after the bark had been taken off to a height of more than 100 feet. The tree did not die until 3 years after it had been thus denuded.

MOTHER OF THE FOREST, CALAVERAS GROVE.

Other Groves.—The Stanislaus Grove, about 5 miles south of the Calaveras Grove is about as large, but is not accessible by wagon road and has no peculiar attractiveness. Its trees are about 600 in number but are not remarkable for size.

The Tuolumne Grove is on the line of the Big Oak Flat road to the Yosemite, at an elevation of 5,600 feet above the sea. The trees are few and relatively small, though one has a circumference of 57 feet, 3 feet above the ground.

The fourth grove on our southward course, known as the Merced Grove, is a small collection of trees on the line of the wagon road from Coulterville into the Yosemite Valley.

The fifth is the Mariposa Grove, which has been described. The Fresno Grove, 10 miles southeast from the Mariposa Grove, is the sixth. It is scattered over an area 3 miles long, and 2 miles wide, and has 600 trees. Fifty miles beyond, to the southward, is the Kings River Grove, or belt, 10 miles long and 5 wide, with thousands of *sequoias*, most of them small, and some of them large. The eighth grove is in the basin of the North Fork of the Tule River, and the ninth, in the basin of the South Fork of the Tule River, in latitude 36°, is the last.

Shasta.—Shasta is one of the grandest of mountains. Rising to a height of 14,440 feet in a plain, the general level of which is about 3,500 feet above the sea, with some spurs above which it towers more than a mile and a half, it occupies a position of majestic solitude, and commands a view which, for extent, has few superiors. Covered with snow through most of the year, for 7,000 or 8,000 feet down from its summit, it is a beautiful and sublime feature in the landscape, as seen from a great portion of the area, within a circuit of 100 miles. On the northern and northeastern slopes the snow always supplies the predominant color of the mountain; on the southern slopes, after a wet winter, the brilliant white mantle remains till the beginning of autumn. In the canyons, on the northern slopes, there are 5 glaciers, the largest of which is 3½ miles long and a mile wide, with a slope near its head of nearly 35° of the mountain as a whole. Prof. Whitney says of the peak: "The surprising regularity of its outline, and its beautiful conical form, have again and again excited our admiration."

The mountain is volcanic, and owes its predominance over the adjacent hills, and perhaps all its elevation above the neighboring plain, to the accumulation of igneous rock, thrown up through the numerous craters associated with it. There are two summits, about a mile apart, with a gap several thousand feet deep between them. The lower summit 13,242 feet high, called the crater summit, had a crater nearly a mile in diameter, with an encircling wall 1000 feet high, but the western half of the wall has disappeared. The main summit had one main crater about half a mile in diameter, and four or five smaller ones. On the main peak, and only 450 feet above its extreme summit, there is a bench that formed part of a crater, and there, in the midst of a soil smoking with sulphurous vapors, and elastic under the weight of a man, is a boiling spring of sulphur water. This spring is notable from the fact, that in 1875, when John Muir and his companion, Jerome Fay, were on the mountain, a snow storm caught them without fire, and they would have frozen to death if they had not been warmed or scalded by the hot mud, first on one side and then on the other, half the body subject to intense cold while the other suffered scalding heat.

The lava from Shasta has flowed out in immense streams, covering an area of 5,000 square miles or more, and on its slopes there are 100 craters. The rock is a chocolate-colored lava.

Ascent of Shasta.—Clarence King says of his ascent of Shasta: "I have never reached so high an altitude with so little labor." But he is a professional mountain climber, and it is not an easy matter to climb to an elevation of 14,000 feet on any peak. Tourists usually start from Sisson's Hotel, near Berryvale post-office, 3,567 feet above the sea, in Strawberry Valley, on the California and Oregon railroad. The distance to the summit is 12 miles in a direct line, and 18 miles by the trail. At Sisson's the tourists take horses and a guide, and ride to the upper edge of the timbers on the southern slope, at an elevation of 8,000 feet. The nights there are very cold in the late summer or early fall, the best time for the ascent, and a large fire is kept up until 3 A. M., when they must rise, get breakfast, and start afoot. The summit may be reached by good climbers in from 5 to 10 hours, according to the condition of the mountain and the weather. It frequently happens that steep slopes of hard snow are to be crossed, not without danger; and these and mountain sickness induce many of those who start on the trip to turn back.

View from Mount Shasta.—The best month to climb the mountain is in September; the best to get a good view after the ascent becomes practicable is July. The view from the summit is very extensive, but nothing save rugged mountain is near enough to have its features distinctly visible. Yreka, the nearest town of note, has 1,000 inhabitants and is 30 miles from the mountain, so that it is with difficulty distinguishable by the naked eye on a clear day. The peaks of the Cascade Mountains, 200 miles to the northward, and those of the Sierra Nevada and Coast Mountains of California, further to the south are seen. Signals have been exchanged by observers of the Coast Survey with mirrors, between the summits of Shasta and St. Helena, but the points of both are so near the edge of the horizon that they cannot be distinguished even in the clearest weather without careful observation of the directions by the compass, and they are entirely hidden when there is a little haze in the atmosphere. One of the most beautiful parts of the scenery from Shasta is Mount Lassen, 70 miles distant, the only high peak distinctly visible from its foot to its summit.

Another prominent mountain, nearer but relatively low, is Sheep Rock, near which is a remarkable cave, consisting of an archway of black lava 60 feet wide, 80 feet high, and half a mile long, under a roof 20 or 30 feet thick. Clarence King, quoting Whitney as his authority, thus explains the manner in which this singular cave had its origin : "A basalt stream flowing down from Shasta, cooled and hardened upon the surface, while within the mass remained molten and fluid. From simple pressure, the lava burst out at the lower end, and, flowing forth, left an empty tube."

Descent from Shasta.—J. G. Lemmon, the botanist who ascended Shasta in 1879 wrote, that "The descent of Shasta is a speedy, and, in our case, was a most enjoyable experience. Arriving at the top of the precipitous canyon, *   *   *   * we prepared to slide down on the now softened snow, by passing a loop of baling-rope attached to a barley sack over our necks, allowing the sack to drop down in front, then sitting down upon the sack for protection against injury to clothes—aye, and flesh, too, perhaps, if certain rocks known to be near the surface around yonder bend should be exposed by this warm afternoon sun. Sitting down on the edge of the precipice, then removing the pike from the snow, away we dropped one after the other, skurrying along and swaying from side to side, swiftly down the long canyon. At once, as soon as the leader plunged off the precipice, he set up a shout of joy, which was taken up by each follower in turn, and soon a grand chorus of yells and cheers resounded all along the line. There were several collisions and upsets, which were instantly rectified, and one sharply-contested race. Friends at the hotel, 10 miles away, happened at the moment to be looking for us with the aid of opera glasses, and they declare that we shot down the whole mile and a half in less than half a minute. It was noon next day before all the Shasta pilgrims became visible around Mrs. Sisson's dining table, exhibiting nearly every degree of exhaustion, blindness and suffering. Each had a story of special adventure to relate, and of peculiarly ecstatic enjoyment experienced, but the expression most often heard—the one that met with unanimous concurrence—was : 'I'll never be so foolish again.'"

People frequently return from the top of the mountain to Sisson's in the afternoon, but many are too tired when they get back to the camp where the horses are, or the evening has advanced too far, and they stay there till morning.

Berryvale.—Berryvale, about 13 hours by rail from San Francisco, is a favorite summer resort on account of its climate, scenery, and central situation for excursions to Mount Shasta, Black Butte, Big Spring, Castle Lake, McCloud River, and Soda Springs. Riding-horses are abundant, and fishing excellent. Fourteen miles south of Berryvale are the Upper Shasta Soda Springs, 2,363 feet above the sea. Their water is chalybeate, and it sparkles with carbonic-acid gas. The Lower Soda Springs, the water of which is less palatable, are $3\frac{1}{2}$ miles to the southward. Twelve miles from the Soda Springs, and $2\frac{1}{2}$ miles west from the road, are the Castle Rocks, a remarkable collection of granite pinnacles rising high above the adjacent country.

Scenery near Shasta.—There are a great number of volcanic cones northwest from Mt. Shasta. One of these, west of Shasta, and conspicuous in the landscape seen from Strawberry Valley, is Cone Mountain, a beautiful peak rising to a height of 3,000 feet above the adjacent country, with sides that have an angle of about 30°. Of Strawberry Valley, Prof. Whitney says: "The time will undoubtedly come, when the travel to this beautiful spot [Strawberry Valley] will be sufficient to justify more ample preparations than have yet been made to accommodate those who seek to climb Mt. Shasta. It is hardly possible to exaggerate the beauty and grandeur of the views from this point, so that those who do not feel equal to the task of ascending to the summit, will find themselves amply repaid for visiting Strawberry Valley, by the nearer view of the mountain itself from that place, as well as the clear water, cool air, and magnificent forest vegetation."

Mt. Lassen.—Mt. Lassen, called also Lassen Butte, an extinct volcano, in latitude 40° 30', 10,577 feet high, is near the edge of the Sacramento Valley and is one of the most prominent peaks in California. Its summit, accessible on horseback, commands an extensive view over the northern part of the great interior valley and looks down on all the higher points in the Coast Range from latitude 41° to Mt. Diablo in 37° 50'. Shasta, 70 miles to the northwest, is a grand feature in the landscape, but more attractive is the district to the northward, northeastward, eastward and southeastward, in which directions, 35 extinct volcanic craters can be distinguished. This was, apparently, the scene of the most recent volcanic action in California; and there is reason to believe that there was an eruption since 1850 at Cinder Cone, 2 miles northeast from Mt. Lassen. Besides the 35 craters visible from the chief summit, there are scores of others in the vicinity.

Snag Lake—One of the most interesting points in the neighborhood is Snag Lake, situated 12 miles northeast from the mountain, at an elevation of 6,000 feet. Directly across the northern end of the lake is a lava bed, bearing traces of an upheaval which occurred about the winter of 1850–'51.

According to Dr. W. H. Harkness, the lava bank rises from the water to a height of 80 or 90 feet, and extends across the whole breadth of the lake for a mile or more, with a gradient as regular as that of a railroad embankment. At the eastern end, the lava bed as it strikes the shore of the lake, turns abruptly to the north and extends in a northerly direction for a distance of at least a mile and a half, when it strikes another lake, or more probably what was once the lower end of Snag Lake. From this point the line turns sharply to the west, the lava dike crossing the lower lake to its western shore, when it deviates to the southwest.

In Snag Lake, across which the dike of lava extends, there were, in 1874, several dead trees still standing, and on the shore, especially on the eastern border, were many trunks and stumps, battered and torn by ice, which had been driven upon the beach by the wind. These facts indicate, that what is now the bed of the lake was but recently a forest, and that the presence of the lava has caused the change in the level of the lake. Along the borders of the lava bed, were numbers of trees still standing, with lava nearly or quite encircling them, their dead and blackened trunks furnishing evidence that the eruption occurred while they occupied their present position.

West and northwest of the Cinder Cone was a tract of 100 or more acres in extent, where the trees had nearly all disappeared. There was but one living tree remaining amid the field of ashes, and that one had lost all its green branches, while its scarred trunk indicated a desperate struggle for life. The dead trees, still standing, were burnt on all sides, precisely as a green tree burns, a thin stratum of charcoal still adhering to the surface of the remaining wood.

In the forest beyond this tract, the trees were invariably surrounded by a zone of ashes, and many of them showed scars, the new wood formed by the reparative process being apparently of but a few years' growth.

Cinder Cone.—From the border of the lava bed, nearly midway on its western face, rises the Cinder Cone, one side of it resting on the lava, and the other on the plain. This is usually believed to have been the central point of the disturbance. Barometrical measurement shows the summit of the Cone to be 600 feet above the plain at its base—the exact height of the Cone of Vesuvius. The outer rim of the Cone is about 600 feet in diameter, and the inner crater, which is funnel-shaped, has a depth of nearly 100 feet. After descending the crater to a depth of 60 feet, a level bench is reached on which one may walk entirely around the inner rim. The ashes and pumice discharged from this volcano cover an area of 80 to 100 square miles. In the neighborhood of the Cone the deposit is 12 to 20 inches in thickness, and, at a distance of two miles, it is 5 or 6 inches. Bits of pumice about the size of a bean are plentifully mixed with the deposit.

Recent Volcanic Action.—Judging from the appearance of the lava bed, Dr. Harkness is of opinion, that the Cinder Cone threw out but a small portion, if any, of the lava, but rather, that it was elevated by forces acting directly beneath the site which it now occupies. He also states that throughout the entire circumference of the lava bed, there is no indication that it was in a molten state when thrown out.

Additional testimony as to the existence of an active volcano in 1850–51 is furnished by Dr. Wozencraft, who, when residing near Red Bluffs, during that winter, observed a great body of flame to the eastward of Lassen's Butte, which continued for many nights without change of position. Dr. J. B. Trask who was, about the same time, near Rich Bar, on the North Fork of the Feather River, a distance of 40 miles from the Cone, saw the same display for many nights in succession. Mr. Charles Gibbs, with a party of miners, observed the same phenomenon while at Angel's Camp, a distance of 160 miles. Two men prospecting for gold, who arrived at a wayside hotel near Georgetown, El Dorado County, in the summer of 1851, stated that they had discovered a boiling lake and a volcanic mountain, which "threw up fire to a terrible height" and that a large breadth of country was still on fire, as the result of the eruption. They stated, that for a distance of ten miles, they traveled across a strip of country, where the rocks were so hot as entirely to destroy their boots, and that they lost a horse and a mule in the transit.

Boiling Lake.—The boiling lake referred to, is beyond doubt, the one at present known by the name of Lake Solfatara, and is situated about 8 miles south of the Cinder Cone, and about 6 miles in an easterly direction from Lassen's Peak, at an elevation of 5,976 feet. It is oval in shape, contains an area of a little more than 4 acres, and is surrounded by hills about 100 feet in height, broken only at one point by a small fissure which allows the escape of surplus water. The water of the lake is hot, and of a creamy color. The surface is from time to time disturbed by the escape of gases from the earth beneath. Around its border are numerous mud cones, from 1 to 4 feet high, and formed of finely pulverized volcanic rock. In former years, these miniature craters were in a state of ceaseless activity, ejecting mud and sulphurous vapor.

Lassen Basaltic Columns.—One mile east of the boiling lake is a large dike of columnar basalt, resembling those seen in Fingal's Cave, on the west coast of Ireland.

Lassen Geysers.—About a mile to the south of it, is a geyser called Steamboat Spring, ejecting hot water to a height of 3 or 4 feet, when in a state of activity. In former years the water was elevated to a height of 20 or 25 feet, and the spray to a height of at least 40 feet.

Three or four miles west of the lake, at an elevation of 6,000 feet, there is a huge geyser canyon with hundreds of springs still in action. The whole canyon, comprising a space of 30 acres, is underlaid with a stratum of boiling mud. Here may be seen numerous cavities or depressions through which boiling water and gas escape from below. There are also many smaller basins, through which steam jets find their way to the surface. There are, besides, many large cauldrons which are now inactive. Perhaps the most curious feature of this geyser canyon is that through its centre runs a large stream of cool water, in close proximity to numerous hot water streams.

A mile or two to the south-west of the canyon is Bumpus' Hell, an opening in the rock through which issues a stream of sulphurous acid which crystalizes and leaves on the rock a deposit of solid sulphur.

Ascent of Lassen.—All the mountains in the vicinity, even Mt. Lassen itself, can be ascended on horseback, without difficulty. The summit of main peak is 18 miles from Prattville, which is 40 from Chico.

Cottonwood Cave.—Near the western base of Mt. Lassen and 20 miles eastward from Cottonwood railroad station, is a large cave, one chamber of which is 300 feet long, 60 wide, and 40 high.

Redding Cones.—About 15 miles east of Redding there are some volcanic cones, the highest of which has an elevation of 2,633 feet above the sea and 800 feet above the adjacent land. Its crater is 300 yards across and 75 yards deep. Two other cones are within a few miles.

Cedar Petrified Forest.—In the Cedar mountains, near the northeastern corner of California, and 20 miles from Camp Bidwell, pieces and trunks of petrified trees are found over a considerable area, called the Cedar Petrified Forest, said to be in many respects, more interesting than the Calistoga Petrfied Forest.

Sierra Lava Beds.—Mt. Lassen is at the edge of California's largest volcanic region, which has an area of about 9,000 square miles, of which nearly half may be covered with lava, in the higher part of the Sierra Nevada, in the northeastern corner of the State. It is triangular in shape, its sharp southern end being at Mt. Stanford, in latitude 39° 30', near and north of the Central Pacific Railroad. The most notable volcanic peaks in this region are Mt. Stanford, Downieville Peak (called also Downieville Buttes), Pilot Peak (7,605 feet), Mt. Lassen (10,577 feet high), and Mt. Shasta. Near Mt. Lassen there are hot and steaming springs. A stream of basalt, left as an elevation by the erosion of the softer country rock near it, and called Table Mountain, is a prominent feature in the landscape near Oroville.

The Southern Sierra Volcano Region extends from 36° to 38° 40', and most of its lava flow was on the eastern slope, the summit of the ridge and nearly all high points being granitic. In Calaveras and Tuolumne Counties, however, there are several places where the lava flowed westward, covering auriferous streams. The most recent volcanic action in this region was near Mono Lake, which has a multitude of craters in its vicinity.

Mono Lake.—Mono Lake has been called the Dead Sea of California, and is, in some respects, the most remarkable body of water on the continent. It is so strong with caustic alkalies, that after 5 minutes it causes the skin to shrivel up, and after half an hour to crack with acute pains. The lake has no fish, nor are trout found in its tributary streams, though they abound in neighboring streams that flow to other lakes. Small worms seem to be the only living tenants of the lake, and after storms they are found in ridges 2 or 3 feet high, on the beach, where they taint the air. Near the

THE SIERRA.

southern end of the lake there are 3 volcanic cones, which look as if they were of very recent origin, their craters being apparently altered but little since the last eruption, and the ashes and pumice in their vicinity having a fresh look. These cones are about 1,500 feet above the general level of the surrounding land. There are many older craters within a radius of 20 miles, including 3 on islands in the lake. The larger island has 2 craters, and a tract of 30 acres covered by hot springs, and by openings from which steam and sulphurous gases escape. The smaller island has a crater which seems to be more recent than any in California, save one near Mt. Lassen.

Snow-Shoes.—With snow-shoes, tourists can go into the high Sierra in midwinter. Horses are also provided with snowshoes, consisting of boards, 13 inches long and 9 wide. With such shoes some riders reached Yosemite Valley on the 15th April, 1882, traveling over snow 12 feet deep, and so soft that men afoot sank to their knees in it. The horses with their shoes sank only four inches.

Glaciers.—Most of the Glaciers in California were discovered by John Muir, according to whom, the Sierra Nevada between latitudes 36° 30' and 39° has 65, and of these, two-thirds are between 37° and 38°. Switzerland has 1,100, with an average area of about a square mile to each; the average is less in California, probably not more than half so much. The average elevation of the lower ends of the Swiss glaciers is about 7,000 feet above the sea, and of the Californian 11,000; the lowest on Mt. Shasta having an elevation of 9,500. The largest glacier in California is on Mt. Shasta. Mt. Ritter 13,300 feet high, 21 miles eastward from Sentinel Dome, has 5 glaciers. The Kern, Kings, Owens, Tuolumne, and Walker Rivers, and Rush Creek (the last a tributary of Mono Lake), all have their heads in glaciers. Mt. Whitney, the highest peak in California has no glacier. All the Californian glaciers are in gorges on the northern slopes of mountains, and are thus protected against the sun. Their speed varies from a mile to 5 miles in 500 years. The signs of glacial action at levels much lower than any of the glaciers now existing in California are abundant, and many of them very interesting in the Sierra Nevada. The State Mineralogical Museum in San Francisco, has a beautiful sample of granite polished by a glacier. Donner Lake was formed by a moraine deposited across the valley by a glacier.

Other Lakes.—Besides the lakes already mentioned, the Sierra Nevada has hundreds of others, most of them with less than a square mile of area, and many very attractive to the tourist, fisherman and artist. Generally they are at elevations of 4,000 feet or more above the sea, and owe their existence to glaciers, which have either scooped hollows in the rocks or deposited moraines across the valleys. From Tahoe northward to the Oregon line, the mountain lakes are most abundant. Some of them such as Goose Lake, Honey Lake and Eagle Lake are saline, having either no outlet or none at their ordinary levels. Generally, however, their waters are pure and remarkably clear, abounding with fish, and surrounded by beautiful shores. Webber Lake, north of the Central Pacific Railroad, is a favorite resort for pleasure seekers; and Gold, Truckee, Independence, Eureka, Meadow, Medley, Glacier, Echo, Twin, Silver and Blue Lakes, though far inferior to Tahoe in size, variety of attraction, and convenience of access, are all worthy of the attention of tourists.

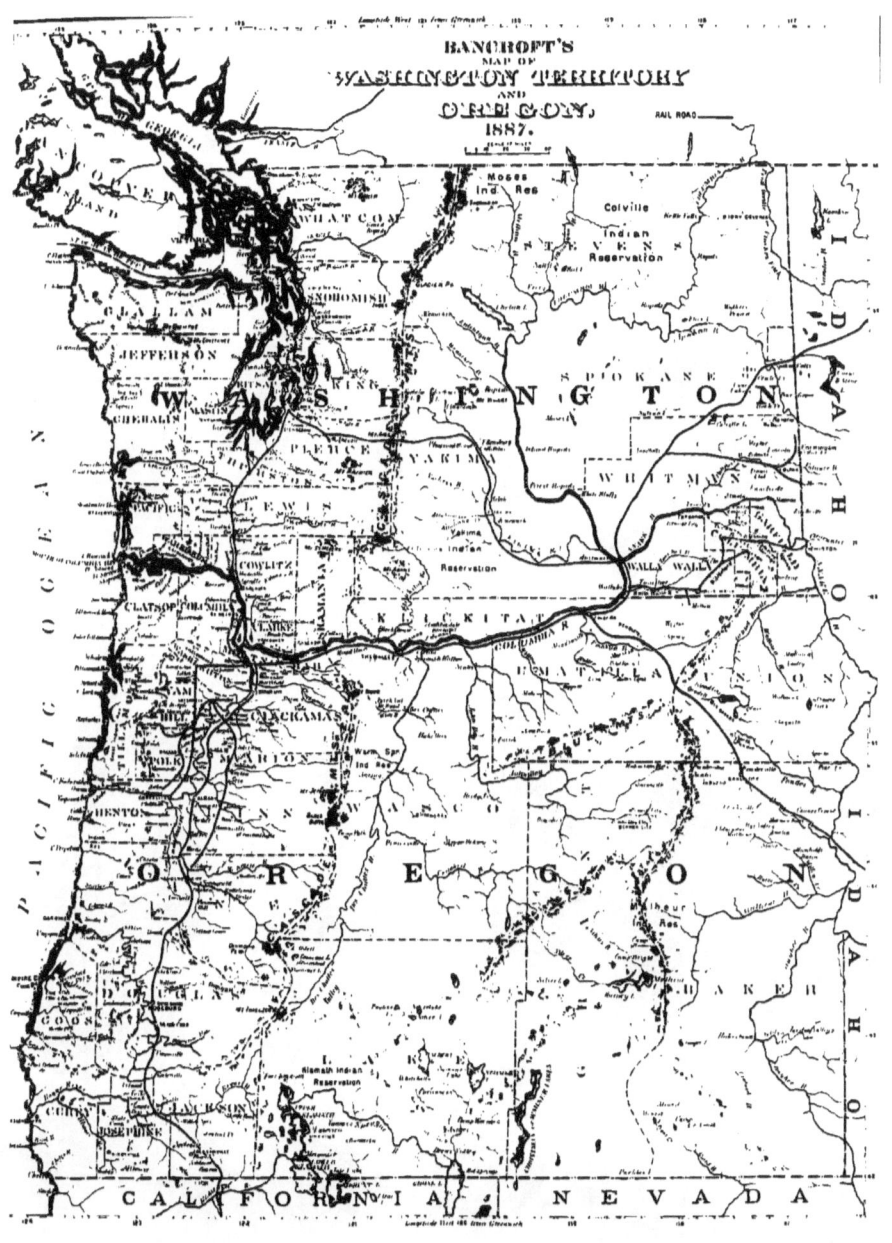

CHAPTER VI.

OREGON, WASHINGTON, ETC.

Scope of Chapter.—In preceding chapters, some account has been given of the leading points of interest to tourists and California, Nevada and Utah; and this chapter is to treat of similar points in Oregon and other portions of our slope, including Washington, Oregon, British Columbia, Alaska and Mexico.

Columbia River.—No navigable river on our continent, and probably, none anywhere, presents to the traveler who views its banks from a boat, a finer combination of grandeur, with beauty in its scenery, than the Columbia. The Hudson, Mississippi, St. Lawrence and Ohio, are each inferior to it in many important respects. The palisades of the Hudson and the hills of the Ohio sink into insignificance when compared with the cliffs and mountains of the great river of Oregon. Mt. Hood, Mt. Adams, Mt. St. Helens, and Mt. Rainier, all visible from the Columbia, are majestic features in the landscape. The average width of the stream below the Cascades is about a mile, and the lands on both sides rise to an elevation sufficient to give extensive views, and these change rapidly when passing up or down the river on the swift and comfortable steamers of the Oregon Railway and Navigation Company. At the Dalles the stream is compressed into a very narrow channel, and there, as well as the Cascades, makes a considerable descent over rapids, the banks as well as the waters, take new and wild forms.

Cascade Range.—The chain of mountains called the Sierra Nevada in California, is known as the Cascade Range in Oregon, Washington, British Columbia and Alaska; and while the general level is lower north of latitude 40° than in the Californian Alps, the grand and solitary peaks are more numerous. The most noted peaks of Oregon are Mt. Hood, 30 miles south of the Columbia River, and Mt. Jefferson, 40 miles south of Hood, both on the summit of the chain, and both rising to a height of about 12,000 feet, and nearly a mile above the level of the adjacent mountain ridges. They are covered with snow through the greater part of the year, and are visible from large areas in the Willamette Valley, in the scenery of which they are prominent and attractive features. Erroneous reports that Hood is 17,500 feet, and Jefferson 15,000 feet high, have been published. Both have glaciers on their northern slopes, and both are dormant volcanoes. It is said that steam rises occasionally in large quantities from Mt. Hood, as if the water from the melting snows ran down to the region of internal heat. A cluster of peaks, about 11,000 feet high, known as the Three Sisters, is 35 miles south of Mt. Jefferson, and 120 miles further south is Mt. Pitt, which has an elevation of 11,000 feet.

Hood River.—On the bank of Hood River, about 30 miles from Portland, in a region rich in romantic scenery, is the Hood River House, which has accommodation for 50 guests. Situated only 10 miles from the summit of Mt. Hood, with that peak and Mt. Adams in full view, it is a favorite resort.

Tillamook Bay.—Tillamook Bay, 70 miles west from Portland, and 45 miles south of Astoria, is considered the most attractive place in Oregon, for sportsmen generally, combining as it does a variety of attractions. When made accessible from the Willamette Valley, by rail, it will probably become the leading pleasure resort of the State. It has fine sand beaches and a surf well suited for bathing, though the water is never warm. Clams, crabs, oysters, and marine fish of many kinds are found in its salt waters; trout abound in its tributary streams; and deer, grouse, and wild geese and ducks, are numerous in the vicinity. The bay is large enough to give opportunities for pleasant sailing; palatable wild berries cover the adjacent hills in summer; and the scenery is romantic.

Clatsop Beach.—Every summer, many Portlanders go to the Clatsop Beach, on the Pacific, south of the mouth of the Columbia, where the Seaside House has excellent accommodations for 150 guests at a time. The place had 800 visitors in 1881. Elk, deer, bear and duck are abundant in the vicinity.

Wilhoit Springs.—The most noted health resort of Oregon is the Wilhoit Springs, 37 miles south from Portland. A hotel offers its accommodations to visitors, and many campers go to the place every season.

Mystic Lake.—Mystic Lake about 7000 feet above the sea, near the summit of the Cascade Range, and 20 miles north from Fort Klamath, is a remarkable sheet of water. It is 12 miles long and 7 wide, enclosed walls which rise 2000 feet, almost vertically, from the water's edge. There is no outlet nor is there any tributary stream worthy of mention. The lake evidently occupies the crater of a great volcano, in which rose a small crater, which now forms an island. Fort Klamath, on the northern shore of Klamath Lake, is 185 miles by the stage road northeastward from Delta.

Washington.— The most striking features in the scenery of Washington are the great snow peaks of Mt. Baker, 10,720 feet high; Mt. Rainier, 14,444 feet; Mt. St. Helens, 10,000 feet; and Mt. Adams, 13,250 feet, all dormant volcanoes, which are scattered along the line of the Cascade Range. Adams, St. Helens and Rainier are visible from the Columbia River, and also from the coun-

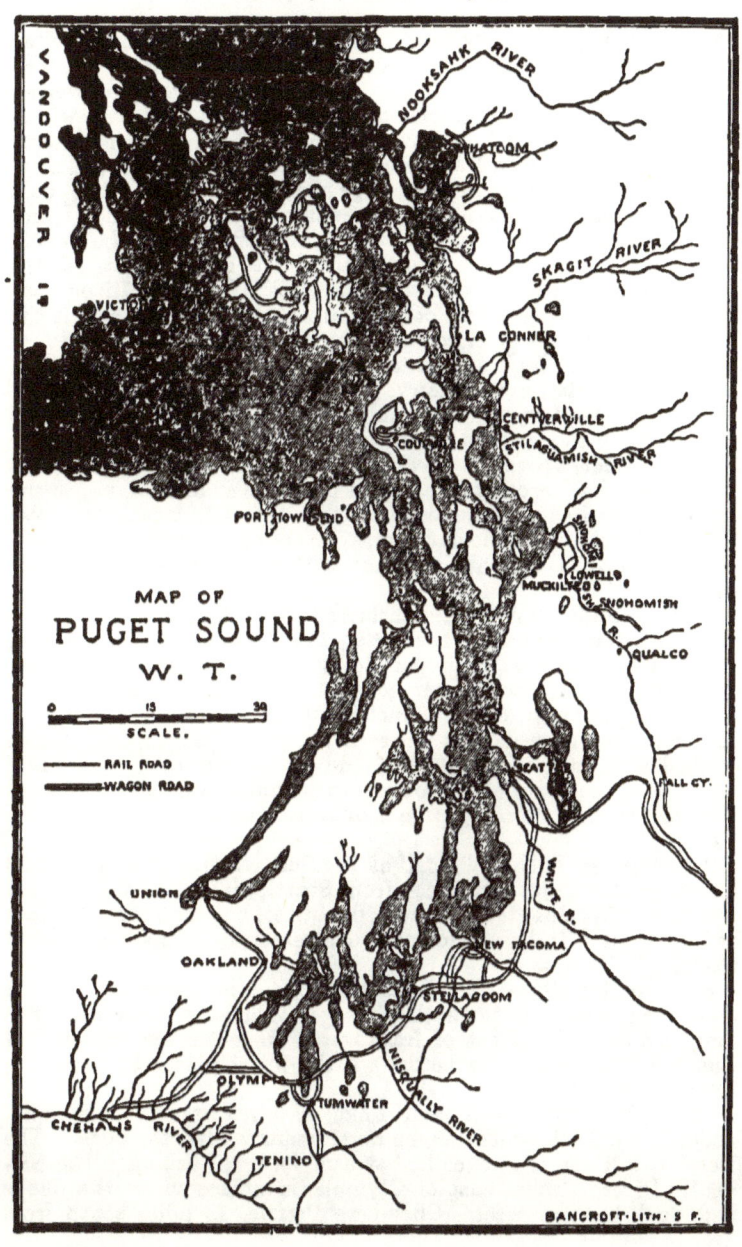

try near the southern portion of Puget Sound; and Mt. Baker from the northern end of the Sound. It is said that lights have been seen on the clouds over Mt. Baker, as if there were molten lava in its crater; and St. Helens sometimes emits steam, which forms in a cloud around or above the summit. All these mountains have glaciers, those on Rainier being the largest. Rainier, like St. Helens, occasionally sends up large masses of steam. The best view of the mountain obtainable on the shore at Puget Sound, is found at Steilacoom. The *Atlantic Monthly* and the *Overland Monthly* have published accounts of the ascent of Mt. Rainier. St. Helens is seen directly in front of vessels entering the Columbia River, and, as seen from the lower part of that stream, or from the sea, is the most imposing snow peak on the coast south of Alaska.

Though not so high as Shasta, Rainier, Adams or Hood, Mt. St. Helens is at least, in symmetry, the most beautiful of all. It has apparently been formed from a single crater, round which its lavas have built up an exact cone, which, as seen from the mouth of the Columbia river, above the level of the intervening hills, has a base about two miles across, and a height of a mile and a half, all, in the spring and early summer, covered with a complete mantle of snow. No bare slopes of rock, no dark forest, no double summit, subordinate crater, or near rival peak interferes with the completeness of this white cone.

Puget Sound.—Whether considered from the standpoint of the merchant, the mariner or the artist, Puget Sound is a wonderful, and, in many respects, an unparalleled arm of the sea. Extending inland 100 miles, with an average width of 2 miles, a depth sufficient for the largest ships, coves, branches and islands so extensive that the shore line exceeds 800 miles in aggregate length, bold banks clothed with magnificent forests, and grand volcanic peaks rising high above the horizon, it abounds with grand and varied scenery. The map on the preceding page is on a scale of about 33 miles to an inch.

Snoqualmie Fall.—The fall of the Snoqualmie River, about 200 feet high, 200 miles northeast from Seattle, is one of the natural wonders of Washington, and will, doubtless, become a favorite place of resort after it has been made conveniently accessible by good roads.

Seattle Resorts.—Lake Washington, 4 miles from Seattle, 28 miles long, 4 miles wide on the average, with a shore line 100 miles long, is a beautiful sheet of fresh water, 15 feet above the level of Puget Sound, and on its banks are the finest places for picnicing in the territory.

Olympia Resorts.—Summit Lake, 17 miles west from Olympia, abounds with fish which can be taken readily with the hook. The Deschutes River is an excellent stream for trout fishing. The Nisqually River, 8 miles east of Olympia, is a place where the ducks and duck-hunters meet. Chambers' Prairie, 15 miles south from

Olympia, is noted for its fine views of Mts. Rainier, St. Helens, and Adams.

Gray's Harbor.—When Oregon and Washington become populus, and perhaps before, Gray's Harbor and Shoalwater Bay will be favorite summer resorts for the hunter and fisherman; they have great attractions; wild fowl, fish of large size and many species, oysters, clams, and crabs are abundant. There are agreeable drives on long and level sandy beaches; and the combination of breeze and shelter are about right for pleasant sailing.

Ilwaco.—The town of Ilwaco, on the shore of Baker's Bay, 15 miles from Astoria, is a favorite resort for people from Portland. A comfortable hotel offers accommodations to 70 guests at a time. There is a beautiful beach, suitable for those who wish to walk, ride, or drive. Game is abundant on the land, and fish, clams, crabs, and oysters in the near waters.

Oysterville.—Oysterville, on the shore of Shoalwater Bay, 35 miles from Astoria (15 by steamboat and 20 by stage), is another pleasure resort, patronized by visitors from Oregon as well as from Washington.

British Columbia.—British Columbia has no solitary snow peaks approaching Rainier, St. Helen's, or Adams, for prominence in the landscape, but the scenery is very mountainous, and in many places inland and along the shores very attractive. Mt. Brown, in latitude 54° 45', 16,000 feet high; Mt. Murcheson, in 51° 51'; 15,800 feet, and Mt. Hooker, 15,700 feet, are in the Rocky Mountains, and are not visible from any populous valley or navigable water. The natural scenery of Vancouver's Island is marked by quiet beauty, many of the views having a park-like appearance.

Alaska.—A favorite summer excursion from San Francisco is a trip to Alaska. Nearly the whole distance from Victoria to Harrisburg, about 1,000 miles, is made in the crooked and usually narrow channels of the Alaskan Archipelago, between steep timber-covered mountains, with occasional water-falls, glaciers, and high snow peaks, to give variety to the landscape. Several of the glaciers come down to the water's edge. The loftiest mountains in the United States are in Alaska. Mt. St. Elias, according to various trustworthy observers, is at least 17,000 feet high, and according to several, 19,000; Mt. Cook is credited with 16,000, Mt. Crillon with 15,900, and Mt. Fairweather with 15,500 by Dall. All are near the coast, and visible far out at sea.

New Mexico.—New Mexico is crossed from north to south by the Atchison, Topeka, and Santa Fé Railroad; from east to west by the Southern Pacific; and from the Rio Grande westward by the Atlantic and Pacific. The greater portion of the territory is barren mountain, under an arid sky, but the most interesting region is that occupied by the Zuñi Indians near the Atlantic and Pacific line. These people, to escape persecution when under the dominion of Spain and Mexico, pretended to be Catholics, but maintained in secret the sun worship of their ancestors, and still adhere to it. Their dwellings, and many of their usages, indicate a pecular condition of culture. Albuquerque 5,010 feet above the sea, with a population of about 2,500, is situated on the upper waters of the Rio Grande, east of the summit of the Rocky Mountains.

Laguna Station, 66 miles from Albuquerque, named from the pueblo or village of Laguna, one of the oldest in New Mexico is situated on a high limestone bluff, on the bank of a small stream called the Rio San José. The houses, built of stone and plastered with mud, are fortifications as well as dwellings, according to the custom of the region. Buildings are several stories high, each succeeding story being smaller than the one below it, thus leaving a flight of terraces. The ground story is a continuous dead wall, without external openings of any kind, entrance being had by means of a ladder reaching the story terrace, and each succeeding floor being reached in the same manner. At night the ladders are drawn up, and the sleepers of the several terraces rest secure from attack. Mt. Taylor, 11,200 feet high, is near by, and other peaks are visible to the northward.

Acoma is named after a neighboring pueblo which stands on a rock 350 feet above the surrounding plain, and is reached only by ascending 375 steps cut in the rock, and then climbing 18 feet up a ladder, made by cutting notches in a tree trunk. The pueblo is supplied with water from large stone cisterns.

At the Continental Divide, 130 miles from Albuquerque, 7,295 feet above the sea, we come to a region, the streams of which flow to the Gulf of California.

Our grade gently descends for at least 150 miles, at an average of 16 feet to the mile.

Arizona.—At the distance of 180 miles from Albuquerque we cross the line dividing New Mexico and Arizona, across which latter territory the route runs in a general direction along the 35th parallel for a distance of 386½ miles.

Near Navajo Spring Station is Jacob's Well, a remarkable funnel-shaped opening 600 feet in diameter at the surface and 160 feet deep, at the bottom of which is a spring of pure cold water. The water is reached by winding steps cut in the wall.

At Winslow Station, 4,900 feet above the sea, we begin the ascent of the Arizona Divide, reaching the summit 350 miles from Albuquerque, at an elevation of 7,286 feet above the sea, the grade averaging about 35 feet to the mile. From the divide the grade descends to the Colorado River, with an average of 31½ feet to the mile, the elevation at the river being 485 feet above the sea.

Peach Springs, 240 miles east from the Colorado River and 4,890 feet above the sea, is the station from which we drive in a stage 18 miles to the Cañon of the Colorado; one of the natural wonders of the world; 300 miles long, 6,000 feet deep, and half a mile wide, with nearly vertical walls of rock.

MISSION OF SAN XAVIER DEL BAC.

The Southern Pacific Railroad passes through much of the most unattractive land in Arizona, and the traveler should not estimate the value of the whole territory by the country visible from the cars on that line.

Ruins.—Arizona abounds with the remains of buildings and irrigation ditches constructed by the red men centuries since, probably before the time of Columbus. These ruins have not been carefully studied and the information about them is fragmentary. Twelve miles from Florence is the Casa Grande (big house), 65 feet long, 45 wide, and 40 high, with $4\frac{1}{2}$ stories. The material is a concrete of gravel with mud or mortar to give cohesion. The floors, roof, and doors have entirely disappeared, and there is nothing to indicate what their material was. This building has higher walls than any other prehistoric structure in Arizona.

Six miles east of Phœnix are the ruins of a large town. One building, that was about 275 feet long and 130 wide, now makes a mound 30 feet high. Other ruins are found 18 miles east, 40 miles east, 8 miles south, 20 miles south, and 20 miles north from Prescott.

The best of the buildings erected in Arizona by the Spaniards is the mission at San Xavier del Bac, commenced in 1768 and finished in 1798. The engraving on the preceding page shows the building in its present condition.

CHAPTER VII.

CAMPING.

Outdoor Life.—Camping is, and will, probably, long continue to be, a common amusement in California—more common here than in any other civilized land. A multitude of circumstances, not found elsewhere in combination, concur to make it attractive. Among these, are the lack or great rarity of rain, dew or severe cold, the dryness of the soil and clearness of the sky in the camping season, from May to October inclusive; the number of umbrageous and romantic sites in many parts of the State, even near the cities, convenient for campers and open to them without charge; the multitude of interesting places accessible to none, save campers; the quantity and variety of game, and the opportunities to change climate by moving short distances; and the facility of getting camping supplies and experienced camper companions, and of mingling business with pleasure while camping. A large proportion of Californians have spent weeks without sleeping in a house while prospecting, exploring, mining, hunting, lumbering, emigrating, taking their cows, sheep or bees to new pastures, or seeking health, or pleasure at the sea-side, at medicinal springs, in the mountains or canyons. Probably the average number of those who go into camp every spring or summer in California is 10,000; perhaps, twice as many. Napa, Lake, Marin, Santa Cruz, Monterey and Los Angeles counties have each at least 1,000 campers for health or pleasure annually.

Among the places in special favor with campers—it is not to be supposed that any complete list can be made of them—are the Yosemite Valley and the State Big Tree Grove in Mariposa County; Bartlett Springs, the shores of Clear Lake and Cobb Valley in Lake; Pope Valley and Howell Mountain in Napa; the banks of Paper Mill Creek, the Willows east of Bolinas Bay, Bear Valley, and the grove near Olema in Marin; the banks of Russian River and the vicinity of Fort Ross in Sonoma; the valley of Russian River in Mendocino; the valley of Eel River in Humboldt; the beach and the mountains in Santa Cruz; the cypress grove in Monterey; the beach and canyon of Santa Monica, the San Juan Capistrano Spring, and Santa Catalina Island in Los Angeles. The basin of San Gregorio Creek, in San Mateo County, abounds with numerous good camping sites, varying in their attractions and offering facilities for frequent and convenient changes. It is a favorite resort for campers from San Francisco, who usually leave the railroad at Redwood City. The vicinity of Pescadero may be said to belong to the San Gregorio camping district. The most noted elevated camping grounds in the Coast Range are the vicinity of Skyland, in the Santa Cruz Mountains, Cobb Valley, Howell Mountain, (all those are about 2,000 feet above the sea), and Clear Lake Valley, about 1,500 feet up. The best hunting grounds are in the Eel River Valley and the upper part of the Russian Valley; the best fishing streams in the redwoods, and in the northeastern part of Shasta.

Camping Tours.—It is a common custom for campers to move at short intervals, staying in one place not more than 2 or 3 days, and then not traveling more than a day's journey to new scenery, new hunting and fishing grounds, and perhaps, to a place where they will make new acquaintances, for it not unfrequently happens that they will find a dozen tents in a desirable camping place of which they never heard before and miles from any house. In this way they can become familiar with a considerable scope of country in a month or two, and find something new at every stopping place. Some parties and families that go camping every summer, take a different direction every year, so as to see the Sierra, the redwood, and the beach in all their most attractive phases.

Time for Camping.—The time for camping depends on the place, and the amount of rain in the preceding winter. The best is that immediately after the ground has become dry and the weather warm enough, and before the heat and dust of the midsummer have arrived. When the rains have been abundant through the winter and have continued until April, the muddy roads and moist ground warn pleasure seekers to stay at home till May. On the other hand, if the rains of February and March have been light, the first week of April may be a good time to start, especially for the region south of Santa Barbara. In the Sierra Nevada, at an elevation of 4000 feet or more, snow storms, freezing nights and soaked soil, are not uncommon in the early part of June. At a distance of 10 miles from the ocean, or further inland, the best time is from May to July; but near the beach, from Monterey northward, the canyons remain green through the year and camping may be pleasant till the end of October.

Saddles.—The best of all saddles for men, and for all who ride astride, is the Californian. The cinch or girth holds better, and can be drawn tighter with less effort, the stirrup is easier and the seat more comfortable than in the English saddle. The last is so flat that it has no fit, and does not require so much attention to its size as does a Californian saddle, which, with its high pommel or cantle, may be too small for a large rider. It would be well for inexperienced riders that the saddle blanket should be tied to the front of the saddle so that it cannot be lost; and, if steep mountains are to be climbed, there should be a crupper to prevent the saddle from slipping forward, and a breast-strap to keep the cinch from slipping back. The breast-strap can be connected with a neck-band like that used in a martingale. So long as the cinch does not slip back, the saddle cannot go back; and when the cinch gets past the ribs, it tickles the animal intolerably, so that unless remarkably tame, he will turn his head down hill, buck, and throw off his rider, for the saddle gets loose and swings round under his belly. The breast-strap is a protection against that danger. Livery stable-men do not adopt the fixed blanket, the crupper, and the breast-strap, for the reasons that they generally prefer to let horses with buggies; and in the mountains, where they let riding horses, they want the riders to feel dependent on the guides for the management of the saddles.

If a saddle is to be used sometimes for riding and for packing occasionally, then the Californian, or the McClellan army saddle may be selected, the latter being better if there is much packing. The Californian saddle, by attaching rings to it may be easily converted into a pack-saddle.

Persons not accustomed to the saddle, may ride almost continuously for a week without being chafed by getting a cushion two inches thick, packed with the best horsehair and filled in two equal halves on a Californian saddle. A lady who had never been astride on a horse, and had not ridden for years, rode 27 miles the first day without chafing on such a cushion, to reach the Yosemite Valley, and took long rides every day during her stay there, though the other ladies in the same party, riding in the same way, were extremely sore after riding 18 miles without a cushion, and could not make their appearance the next day, nor ride with comfort while in the valley.

When four or five ladies are together in a camping party, well supplied with horses, there is a great saving in baggage, as well as in other respects, if they ride astride. The side saddle has many objectionable features, without anything to recommend it save its conventional authority. It is hard on the horse, and tiresome and dangerous to the rider. No women make a more graceful appearance on horseback than the Hawaiians, all of whom ride astride. Miss Isabella Bird, the noted traveler and authoress, after becoming accustomed to a man's saddle would not have any other; and Californian ladies who have had a similar experience, entertain a similar feeling in reference to their comfort on horseback, though many of them will not ride astride where "society" can observe and criticise them. Ladies riding astride, should have 3 cotton batting pads, each about 8 inches long, 5 wide, and 2 or 3 inches thick, with strings. One pad to protect the calf of each leg, and one to be fastened on the pommel of the saddle.

Tents.—The simplest tent and the one best adapted for the use of small parties, is that known as the "A" pattern, called also the "gable-end," or "dog-kennel" tent. It is supported by two upright poles, six feet in height, with a ridge pole to connect their tops. Poles to serve as supports can be cut in the woods, but it is more convenient to take them along, and to have them bound at each end with an iron ferrule, and fitted with iron pegs, half an inch in diameter, projecting from each end of the upright with holes to correspond in the ferrules on the ridge-pole. The tent should be strengthened at the seams and edges with rope, and when carefully staked, possesses great strength, which, however, is seldom needed, when in use for pleasure parties, as, a short distance from the coast, high winds are almost as rare as rains, from May to October. A tent 7 feet long and 8 feet wide on the ground will accommodate 3 persons. As a general rule it is more convenient to have several small tents than one large one.

Prospectors and miners and bachelor parties, when camping only for a few days, seldom put themselves to the trouble of carrying a tent.

The proprietors of the camping grounds at Taylorville, at Cypress Point, and at Soquel, have tents to let for the accommodation of campers, and board can be obtained in the vicinity by those who wish to avoid the trouble of cooking. Elsewhere, parties must provide their own tents, and carry with them cooking utensils and a stock of provisions.

Personal Outfit.—Of primary use during even a short stay from home, are a change of outer and underclothing, handkerchiefs, towels, soap, cup, tooth-brush, clothes-brush, whisk-broom, slippers, paper, ink, pens, pencils, envelopes, postal cards, postage stamps, pins, needles, thread, thimble, tape, scissors, buttons, watch key, large sheath knife, matches and money. The personal outfit should also include rubber shoes, an overcoat or cloak with cloak strap, and for ladies, an umbrella for protection against the sun. A bottle of ammonia, as a cure for the stings and bites of insects, and a box of carbolic salve for bruises may also be of service.

For lights, candles are preferable to coal oil and oil lamps, on account of their smaller bulk and for other obvious reasons. If the camp is to be without facilities for laundry-work, the clothing should be selected with reference to that fact. Fine white cotton or linen, which cannot be worn satisfactorily without frequent washing and ironing, should make way for coarse, dark-colored cotton, or a mixture of cotton and wool, which are better adapted for rough wear, easier to wash, and not apt to show a little dirt.

Provisions.—The stock of provisions may be selected from such articles as dried and canned meats, fruit and fish, bacon, beans, vegetables, eggs, butter, cheese, salt, pepper, vinegar, sugar, tea and coffee. Bowen's condensed coffee in cans is convenient and passably good. The canned goods should be tested, before starting, to make certain that they are of proper quality. Baking powder or leaven should be taken if bread is to be made. Butter should be kept in strong brine. If lunch is to be eaten on the road, before reaching the camping ground, a separate package should be prepared.

Cooking Utensils.—The cooking utensils best suited for camping parties are the coffee-pot, stew-pan, frying-pan, gridiron, soup-pot, Dutch-oven and cooking-stove. The pots and pans that are to be exposed to the action of fire, should be provided with sacks or coverings, to keep them from contact with other articles. The Dutch-oven, a skillet of cast-iron, about a foot in width and 4 inches deep, with a cover to hold burning coals, is useful for baking meat, bread or beans. If a sheet-iron stove is to be purchased, it may be well to order one after the pattern recommended by John M. Gould.

Tableware.—The quantity and description of tableware needed, depends on circumstances; but thought should be given to plates, cups, knives, forks, spoons, napkins and tablecloths. If crockery or glassware be included, they should be taken in sufficient quantity to make a liberal allowance for breakage.

Bedding.—For bedding purposes, it is usual to carry blankets and sometimes sheets and pillows, or pillowcases. Comforters, made of cotton batting, quilted in chintz, are better than blankets because they are smoother and less liable to absorb dust and dirt, or harbor fleas. If, however, there be any apprehension of wet weather, comforters will not answer for camping. For a mattress, it is usually sufficient to take along an empty sack and fill it with hay, straw or dry grass, at or near the camping ground. A pillowcase may be filled in the same way. It is often desirable to place a rubber or oilcloth under the mattress, to keep out moisture, and if no mattress can be obtained, and the bed must be made on the ground, this precaution becomes necessary.

Tools.—The tools most useful for a camping expedition, are an axe, hatchet, saw, spade, auger, gimlet, nails, screw-driver and screws. A sail-needle, twine and rope may also be needed. Fishing lines, hooks, sinkers, floats, flies, guns, pistols, and cartridges will usually form part of the outfit. As a general rule, it is best to take only such articles as have been found serviceable by others, and to avoid new inventions, such as bedsteads convertible into camp-stools, etc. Simplicity of pattern and the approval given by experience, are more to be considered, than the advice of inventors and of drummers interested in selling their patents.

Books on Camping.—Those who expect to travel long distances, and to transport heavy loads, on pack-animals, may obtain some valuable hints from the books of Lord, Galton, Marcy and Gould. John K. Lord was in charge of the packing department of the British Boundary Commission, when the line between the United States and Canada was run eastward from the Pacific, and he gives advice about packing, based on that experience, in a book published in London, by J. R. Hardwicke, entitled, *At Home in the*

Wilderness. Francis Galton has traveled much in the wilder parts of South Africa. His *Art of Travel,* the sixth edition of which was published in London, by John Murray, in 1876, contains many passages that are of interest to persons about to undertake long expeditions, though most of it is, of course, not adapted to camping parties in California. Many hints about fitting out emigrant, hunting and military expeditions, guarding against Indian attacks, packing and hunting, are given in *The Prairie Traveler,* by R. B. Marcy, U. S. A., published by Harper & Brothers in 1859, *How to Camp Out,* by John M. Gould, published by Scribner, Armstrong & Co., though designed for campers on the Atlantic Slope, contains much that may be of service to camping parties in California.

The Camping Party.—The experience, tastes, habits and purposes of campers differ so much, that it is impossible to give a brief summary of advice that would be suitable to every case. Nevertheless the following are good general rules.

First.—See that the company includes persons competent to do the work that may have to be done. If you go with a wagon, there should be a man who knows how to attend a horse, mend harness, and take care of a wagon. If you go with pack animals there should be an experienced packer.

Second.—It is well to understand, before hand, how the work is to be distributed, so that there will be no room for controversy, or excuse for shirking, and no unfair burden on the generous. If there are ladies in the party, it may be better to have a hired cook.

Third.—It is well to see that no morose or quarrelsome person be admitted into the party; for one such will destroy the pleasure of all others.

Fourth.—Prefer the companionship of old friends, or of those who have strong motives for keeping up kindly relations with you.

Fifth.—Be careful, before starting, to see that the supplies are sufficient in quantity and good in quality.

Santa Cruz Camping Tour.—Of the many camping grounds within easy reach of San Francisco, those in the Santa Cruz Mountains deserve special mention. They are so numerous that parties often spend several weeks there, changing their camp every few days from one location to another. Many of the most attractive spots are but a short distance off the public road and quite easy of access. Approaching the mountains by way of San Mateo, Half Moon Bay and Pescadero, one meets with very fine scenery, and every few miles a stream of clear, sweet water is encountered. After leaving the village of San Mateo, the road skirts the San Mateo Creek for some distance, and then curves among the hills until it reaches an altitude of 2000 feet above the bay. Thence it descends through a narrow pass towards the Pacific, striking the coast at Half Moon Bay. From that point the road turns southward to the village of Pescadero, near which there are excellent camping and fishing grounds. At the foot of a bluff, two miles from Pescadero, is a beach composed of pebbles worn smooth by the action of the surf. Among them are found agates, carnelians and jasper, too small to be of value, but often beautiful specimens. On the neighboring sands, may be found abalone shells and some beautiful varieties of algæ. The streams in the vicinity of Pescadero are well stocked with fish when the tides come up from the sea, and the surf along the shore affords excellent sport with hook and line.

From Pescadero to Santa Cruz is an easy day's journey, and on the road one passes some excellent camping grounds. A drive of a few miles from Pescadero, brings the traveler into the very heart of the redwood forests, that cover the western slopes of the Santa Cruz Mountains. Some of the trees exceed 15 feet in diameter, and are nearly 300 feet in height, the distance from the ground to the nearest branch, being often 150 feet. In places they are thickly grouped and their dense foliage forms a canopy that shuts out all sunlight, and excludes all sound except that of the surf. The wagon road leads along the coast hills, or across the beach, passing sometimes over narrow terraces between the mountains and the Pacific, which mark the gradual retrogression of the ocean during past ages. The drive is extremely picturesque, and affords some rare glimpses of scenery.

The journey back to San Francisco can be made by way of the Santa Clara Valley. The mountains in that direction rise to a height of 3000 feet. On portions of the road the forests completely shut out the scenery. Some very deep gorges come in view, and there are several well watered undulating valleys suitable for camping. On reaching the summit of the range, the Santa Clara Valley comes in sight, and the party may return by way of San Jose.

Marin County Camping Tour.—Another pleasant camping excursion, which need not occupy more than a week, nor take the excursionist far from San Francisco, can be made in Marin County. The road from Sancelito to Bolinas works up by easy grades to the summit of a high ridge, and then crosses a deep ravine close to the ocean. From that point it leads, for several miles, along the sides of very steep hills, whose base is washed by the sea. In clear weather, the Farallones, the Cliff House, and the various lighthouses are plainly in view. The off wheel of the carriage will sometimes be within a foot or two of the edge of the road, but with steady, sure-footed horses there is not the least danger. This portion of the route is almost level, and vehicles, approaching from the opposite direction, can be seen at a distance. At intervals there are spaces wide enough for carriages to pass. The distance to Bolinas is less than 20 miles, and for the last few miles the path skirts the margin of Bolinas Bay, leading to a village of the same name, from which was shipped, in early days, the greater portion of the lumber supply of San Francisco. Olema, about ten miles distant from Bolinas, is reached by a road almost perfectly level, and about a mile from Olema is an excellent camping ground. A mile or two further on is a range of hills nearly 2000 feet high, the ascent of which is steep in places; it may, therefore, be as well to leave some of the heavier baggage at the village of Olema. Descending their western slope, you come to Bear Valley, another excellent camping ground, with a mountain stream of clear, cold water, near which hare and rabbit are plentiful. From Bear Valley the road leads over a second range of hills, but only a few hundred feet high, and of easy grade. A short distance from their summit you come to the peninsula of Point Reyes, a narrow plateau, from most points of which the ocean is in view on both sides. Here are some of the best dairy ranches in California; the moisture from the fogs causing the grass to grow until late in the summer. On the southern slope of the plateau is Drake's Bay, named after the famous navigator, who is said to have visited it in 1577. Here is a beautiful camping ground, good fishing, and abundance of timber. Water sometimes fails but a supply can be obtained at any of the ranch-houses near by. The vicinity of Drake's Bay is a favorite resort for Italian fishermen, who supply the San Francisco market. The light-house and fog-whistle at the extreme point of the peninsula are well worth a visit. The keeper's residence is high above the sea and commands one of the finest sea views on the coast of California. Flights of wooden steps lead down to the light-house, which is on a ledge of rock several hundred feet below. The distance from Olema to Point Reyes is about 15 miles.

From Olema the party may return by the road leading to Ross Landing, over White's Hill, at the foot of which is a fine grove of redwoods. At the junction station, a mile and a half from Fairfax, on the line of the North Pacific Coast Railway, the road to Ross Landing turns off at right angles. Less than half a mile from this point it skirts the foot of a hill thickly covered with redwoods; and here is a road leading off to the right towards Lagunitas Reservoir, near which is a favorite camping ground. From Olema to Ross Valley is about twenty miles, and from the valley to the camping ground about 5 miles. The last 2 or 3 miles have several steep grades, and time should be allowed to reach the halting place before dark. Lagunitas (Little Lakes) Reservoir is at the foot of Mt. Tamalpais, and the camping ground is reached on the banks of a small stream, about a mile before coming to the reservoir. In the vicinity is some beautiful park-like scenery, plenty of timber, and an abundant supply of water.

Hunting.—The best hunting ground of California is in the Coast Mountains and valleys from Mendocino to Del Norte County inclusive; in Oregon, its southwestern quarter; in Washington, a strip about 30 miles wide in the foot-hills, along the western slope of the Cascades; in British Columbia, the southwestern corner of the mainland; in Idaho, an extensive district near its centre, and in Arizona, the White Mountains.

Bear.—The grizzly lives in timber or chaparral, and is found in all the American portions of the Pacific Slope, and has been especially abundant in the Coast Mountains of California, in the remoter portions of which it may be found with little difficulty. In consequence of the hilly and bushy character of this favorite resort, it is often not seen by the hunter until the two are very near together, and usually the bear even of the largest size moves away at a brisk pace, but sometimes, especially if wounded or if a dam with young, will attack the man, who is extremely lucky if he escapes without serious injury. The grizzly is so large, strong, quick in movement, hard to kill, and fierce when provoked, that it is one of the most dangerous of all the brutes to attack. Sonoma, Mendocino and Humboldt Counties are the best places to hunt the grizzly.

Buffalo.—Buffaloes are so rare, and will so soon disappear entirely from the valleys of Idaho and Western Montana—the only portions of the Pacific Slope visited by them in the last 30 years—that they scarcely deserve to be considered as belonging to our game quadrupeds.

Deer.—Animals of the deer kind occupy a prominent place on our coast. First of these in size, flavor of meat and excitement of the hunt, is the elk, which is still abundant in portions of Humboldt, Trinity, Del Norte and Siskiyou Counties, and in Southern Oregon. Indeed, it is found in nearly all the forest districts of the Pacific Slope, except the Sierra Nevada. Coos County, Oregon, and Yavapai, Arizona, have some good elk grounds.

Idaho, Washington and British Columbia have the moose in small numbers, but it is very shy.

The mule deer, found in the timber regions from Mexico to British Columbia, west of the Rocky Mountains, except in California, is larger than the Virginian deer, and better for the table. The best hunting grounds for it are in the Blue Mountains of Eastern Oregon and Idaho.

The black tail deer has its home in the timber and chaparral, west of the summit of the Cascade Range and Sierra Nevada. Its meat is inferior to that of the mule deer and elk in flavor. It is abundant in the mountains of Sonora, Mendocino, and Marin Counties, many being killed every season within 20 miles of San Francisco.

The antelope avoids the timber and moist regions, and finds a congenial home in the dry valleys of California, Nevada, Utah, New Mexico and Arizona. One of the best places for hunting it is the Mojave Desert.

The mountain sheep are found in nearly all the high mountain sides of the Pacific Slope, between latitudes 32° and 54°, and are perhaps more numerous on the Sierra Nevada, between 35° and 38°, and about Mt. Shasta, than elsewhere, but they are very shy and usually limiting themselves to the high, very rugged peaks, the chase requires unusual strength and enthusiasm.

The mountain goat is a still rarer animal and even more shy.

Rabbits, Etc.—There is no large valley between the Arctic and the Torrid Zone, west of the Rocky Mountains, without its hares and rabbits, so that the hunter, in search of such game, needs seldom go far to find its signs. The best known of the hares, on account of its very long ears, is generally called the jack rabbit.

The tree squirrels are comparatively rare animals on our slope, though a few are found in Northern California, in Oregon and Washington. The ground squirrel so abundant in the Californian valleys, that it does great damage to the farmers, but is often poisoned, and rarely killed for the table.

Wild Hogs, Etc.—Wild hogs, numerous in the swamps about Tulare Lake and in some other portions of the tule lands of California, offer much material for sport. They are seldom large enough to be dangerous to the hunter, and are not fierce in disposition, but shy, and living amidst a dense vegetation, are not easily found.

The raccoon of California, smaller than that of Virginia, is not abundant, and is not hunted at night like the latter animal; indeed it is seldom hunted, though often killed by hunters, out looking for other game.

The Californian opossum is not abundant enough to become a special object of the chase.

The badger is abundant, but nocturnal in its habits, and, therefore, seldom seen. The animal can be obtained by digging him out, but the process requires tedious toil, and when reached, must be quickly despatched to save dogs from injury.

Carnivorous Animals.—In a wild region abounding with luxuriant vegetation, and with herbivorous animals, as does a considerable part of our slope, there are, of course, many carnivorous animals classed as game.

First among these is the puma, cougar, or, as it is often called, the Californian lion, which inhabits the timber districts from latitude 55° southward, and is more abundant in the Coast Range between 39° and 42°, than in any other part of the continent. When full grown, its body is usually about as large and long as that of a sheep, making a powerful animal, though decidedly inferior to the tiger and lion in size and strength. It is cowardly, and unless wounded or desperate, flees at the sight of man. With hounds accustomed to the puma, the chase is interesting.

Wild cats and lynxes are found, like the pumas, in all the timbered districts. The gray wolf is found in most of the sparsely settled districts, in or near timber, but is not abundant anywhere. The coyote is abundant in many parts of California, and is sometimes hunted with hounds. Like the fox, it lives in burrows. Foxes are also abundant.

Turkey.—Among the game birds belonging to the order of scratchers, the largest is the wild turkey, which is not found anywhere on our slope save in the Pacific portions of New Mexico and Colorado, and the higher lands of Arizona. The large size and excellent flavor of the wild turkey make it one of the most attractive kinds of feathered game, and will, doubtless, draw many sportsmen to the mountains of Arizona as soon as the advance of civilization shall have done a little more to provide for the comfort of travelers and the quietude of the redmen there.

Grouse.—Grouse of various kinds are found over a large part of the Pacific Slope. The sage hen occupies the deserts, and several species of mountain grouse inhabit the Sierra Nevada, Cascade and Blue Mountains, and part of the Coast Range. They are most numerous in places where the timber is not dense, and offer attractive sport to the skillful hunter. The Pit river basin near its head is an excellent place for them.

Quail.—The Californian quail, an inhabitant of all the valleys of California and Oregon, makes its home usually in the brush or chaparral, and is, therefore, not found so readily by hunters as the Virginian quail, though the greater abundance is a partial compensation. It has increased in numbers within the last 30 years; the shotgun being less destructive to it than were the coyotes, hawks and owls, while the country was in the possession of the savages. Wild quail are often seen in the San Francisco Park and in the gardens and fields of Oakland and Alameda, and large flocks are to be found a few miles out in the hills. The mountain quail of California is comparatively rare, and is seldom made the special object of a hunt.

Pigeons.—The wild pigeon is found in most of the timber districts of our slope, and many of them spend the summer in Washington and British Columbia, and the winter in Arizona, New Mexico and Southern California, though they are more abundant in the spring and fall, while migrating, than in midsummer or midwinter. The best places for hunting them, according to report, are the White Mountains, of Arizona, in the spring; and northwestern California and southwestern Oregon in the autumn.

Water Fowl.—Two species of swan visit the waters of our coast, but being rare and shy are seldom shot.

The numerous inlets of Washington, British Columbia and Alaska, are favorite summer resorts for half a dozen species of wild geese, which pass through Oregon and California in their spring and fall migrations, some of them spending their winters in the latter State. There are excellent hunting grounds for them in the tule swamps about Suisun Bay, Tulare Lake, Humboldt Bay, and along the Sacramento and San Joaquin Rivers. The geese pasture on the young grain fields, and are so numerous that they do much damage. They are shot in all the lakes and streams of the coast.

The ducks are more numerous than the geese, and found in the same resorts, but are shot with greater ease near the towns.

Snipe and curlew are found in the lowlands along the streams within 100 miles of the ocean; and the sandhill crane, found in the dry as well as the moist valleys, is fit for the table, and a good game bird.

The wide belts of tule swamp along the borders of San Francisco, San Pablo, Suisun and Humboldt Bays, and the lower portions of the Sacramento and San Joaquin Rivers abound with geese and ducks in their season.

Fish.—Among game fish the first place belongs to the trout, which is found in nearly all the smaller streams of the coast. There are half a dozen species indigenous and peculiar to this Coast, and besides these the Atlantic trout has been transplanted into many of our streams.

The Dolly Varden trout, inhabiting cold streams, formed by melting snows, in the Sierra Nevada and Cascade Range, from latitude 40° to Alaska, offers the best sport to fishermen, and is unsurpassed for the table.

The Pacific brook trout is found in the streams of the Sierra Nevada, Cascade and Coast Mountains. It reaches a weight of 6 lbs., and is good from May till December inclusive. The fish is not so vigorous in its motions as its Atlantic relative, nor is its appetite so sharp, and will often refuse to bite, especially after midsummer, when it has become shy.

The Utah trout is caught with seine in Utah Lake, and with the hook in the tributary streams, especially in the Provo River.

Salmon trout are caught in various ways in Lake Tahoe, one of the favorite being trolling.

Lake Merced, within the corporate limits of San Francisco is stocked with trout, and is under the control of the Sportsman's Club.

Pilarcitos Reservoir, 17 miles south of San Francisco, has trout, which may be taken under a permit from the Spring Valley Water Company. Stockholders can obtain the paper for themselves or friends without charge; strangers must pay $2.50.

Lake Chabot, 10 miles from Oakland, has trout, and they can be taken under a permit from the Oakland Water Company.

The Salmon takes the hook in salt water, and is one of the most attractive of the game fish, but few are caught save with the net or seine.

The Whitefish or Mountain Herring *(Coregenus Williamsonii)*, found in the streams of Utah, Idaho, Oregon, Washington and British Columbia, reach a length of 18 inches, take the hook readily, and are favorites with sportsmen.

Several lakes in Southern Idaho and Eastern Oregon have the redfish, deep scarlet in color, 20 inches long, and very palatable. They are caught with nets in the rivers during their spawning expeditions.

The catfish, introduced by the Fish Commissioners into the waters of California, is caught with the hook.

CHAPTER VIII.

THE HAWAIIAN ISLANDS.

The Group.—The islands that form the Hawaiian group lie between the 19th and 22d parallels of north latitude. Their entire area is about 6,750 square miles. Hawaii, the largest, has 4,210; Maui, 760; Lanai, 150; Molokai, 270; Oahu, 600; and Kauai, 590; The entire population was reported, in the census of 1878, at 57,985; of whom 44,088 were natives, 3,420 half-castes, 5,916 Chinese, 1,276 Americans, and 3,285 foreigners of other nationalities. The native population is decreasing so rapidly as to threaten extinction at no very distant day, the decrease during the past 30 years being no less than 35 per cent. The cause is attributed to diseases introduced by foreigners, and to the use of tobacco and alcoholic liquor. It is not uncommon to see native children smoking at 3 or 4 years of age, the pipe being passed around the family circle, as is the custom in a group of American Indians. The foreign population is gaining rapidly. In 1872 the number of foreigners was reported at 5,366; in 1878 at 10,477; a gain of 95 per cent. in 6 years.

American money is the legal currency.

Honolulu.—The trip from San Francisco to Honolulu is made in about 6½ days by the steamers *Mariposa* and *Alameda*, each of 3000 tons, leaving San Francisco on the 1st and 15th of every month. First-cabin passage $75; (round trip $125); steerage $25. By sailing vessel, the time may be 18 days, and first-cabin passage $40.

The promontory of Diamond Head, on the southern coast of Oahu, is the landmark that indicates a near approach to Honolulu. After sailing through the Molokai Channel, and past Waikiki, (a favorite holiday resort), the steamer makes a sharp turn and sails through a narrow channel, between the coral reefs. You enter the small landlocked harbor, and come in sight of Honolulu almost before you are aware of its proximity.

The Hawaiian Hotel, a large two story structure of concrete, built by the government at an expense of $120,000, affords excellent accommodation. The charge is $3.00 a day, or $15.00 a week. The house is provided with deep piazzas and balconies, and faces, in one direction, the beautiful Nuuanu Valley. In front of it is a rotunda, where promenade concerts are frequently given by the Royal Band.

There are also numerous private boarding-houses; and furnished cottages can be hired by the week or month.

In the summer the thermometer ranges, in Honolulu, between 75° and 85°, and in winter from 65° to 80°. The forenoon is the hottest part of the day. During most of the year the trade wind sets in about 10 or 11 A. M. When it ceases, the weather becomes sultry, but the nights are nearly always cool enough for rest, though there are people in Oahu who make a boast that they have never had a blanket in their house.

Among the different objects of interest in Honolulu is the King's Palace, a four-story building, occupying an area of about 17,000 square feet, with a central tower 80 feet in height. The Palace contains, in addition to the apartments devoted to the private use of the royal family, a fine reception-room, a ball-room, a library, a crown room, and a plate-room. Here are to be seen some fine portraits and steel engravings, and in the plate-room are some beautiful specimens of plate and crystal presented by various monarchs and potentates. Near the Palace are the Government buildings, containing the Hawaiian Parliament house, the public offices, etc.

On Saturday afternoon, the great resort, for both visitors and residents in Honolulu, is the fish market, on Queen Street. Besides fish, butchers' meat, fruit and vegetables are for sale. On this day, all the people from the surrounding country, who can spare the time, come to the market to make their purchases and to exchange gossip. The Kanaka women with their quaint dresses, and necklaces of flowers, form the most striking feature of the scene.

Tour of Oahu.—A trip through the most interesting portions of Oahu, can be made, on horseback, in 4 days, though a complete circuit of the island would occupy 10 days. Outside of Honolulu, there are few places built specially for the accommodation of tourists, though in Oahu, as in the other islands, room and board can be obtained at the houses of natives, for about $2.50 a day. The board consists mainly of poi, (a fermented paste made of the taro root, and the national dish of the Hawaiians), fish, beef or chickens, and cocoanut milk. Whatever else the tourist may want, he should take with him as part of the outfit. The best mode of travel is to hire pack-horses, with a tent and camp equipage. The cost of saddle-horses is about $2.00 a day; of a guide, furnishing his own horse, $2.50 a day.

The most attractive sights in Oahu are the Nuuanu Valley, the entrance to which is close to Honolulu, and the palis, or wall-like precipices of black ferruginous rock that enclose its upper portion. Here was enacted one of those historic tragedies that sometimes occurred in the Islands, before they were inhabited by white men. The forces of the King of Oahu were driven by Kamehameha, the conquerer, to the edge of the precipice, from which hundreds leaped in despair, and to this day their bones lie bleaching 800 feet below.

Ten miles from the city, and 4 from the palis, at a short distance from the main road, is the Waimanalo Valley, fronting the sea, and backed by mountain ranges. Here is the nearest large sugar plantation to Honolulu—that of the Waimanalo Sugar Company, which has leased a tract of 8,000 acres, and has already over 1,000 under cultivation.

Four miles from this valley, and 12 from Honolulu, is the Kaelepulu Lake, the resort of large flocks of wild fowl, and containing plenty of fresh-water fish. From this point one may regain the main road by a short circuit, and ride along the northern coast of the island, returning by the inland track, the roads, after crossing the palis, being easily traversed by horse or buggy.

A short drive from Laie (which is 32 miles from Honolulu) brings the tourist to the Waimea Beach, where there is a great variety of shells, but where no traveler should venture without a guide, on account of the dangerous quicksands. Hence the road leads through the Waimea and Lauhulu valleys to Waialua. From this point there is a choice of two routes; one, the inland track, leading through the Ewa district, back to Honolulu, a distance of 27 miles; the other around the western coast, by way of Keaua Point, making a circuit of more than 50 miles. The latter road is, in some parts, difficult of travel, but brings the traveler in sight of some fine scenery. A few miles from Keaua Point is the Kaala Mountain, the highest in Oahu, rising 4,060 feet above the sea level. High up on the mountain are perennial springs, which unite in a single stream and form a cascade, with a fall of 1,000 feet down the mountain side. On a plateau, easy of access, and at no great elevation, is a small house, from which a good view can be obtained.

Maui.—The trip from Honolulu to Kahului, the principal harbor of Maui, occupies 15 hours by steamer. The fare is $6. The packet ships of the Spreckel's Line keep up direct communication between San Francisco and Kahului. At Wailuku, the chief town of the island, there are several lodging-houses and restaurants. At Kahului there is also public accommodation, with excellent bathing, fishing and hunting.

The island of Maui, which lies between Oahu and Hawaii, contains a large number of sugar plantations. Four tons to the acre is no uncommon yield, and the average is about $2\frac{1}{2}$ tons. Cane is being planted nearly all the year round, on some portion of the island. In 1860, the export of sugar from all the Islands was but 722 tons; in 1871, it had increased to 10,880 tons, and in 1881 it exceeded 44,000 tons. A few miles from Wailuku are the plantations of CLAUS SPRECKELS, who holds a lease of 15,000 acres of crown lands in the neighborhood, besides owning a large adjoining tract acquired by purchase. Irrigation is an absolute necessity in this district, and Mr. Spreckels obtains his supply by means of a water-race and pipe line connecting his plantations with the northern coast of the island. In constructing these works, over 20,000 feet of heavy piping were used, and 30 gulches were crossed, with a width varying from 200 to 2,000 feet, and some of them having a depth of 400 feet. The delivering capacity of the race is nearly 60,000,000 gallons a day. The furrows, in which the cane is planted, can be filled with water in 20 minutes, and one man can irrigate 25 acres a day. It is anticipated that the yield of this plantation for 1882 will amount to 10,000 tons.

The greatest attraction in Maui is the extinct volcano of Haleakala (House of the Sun), 10,000 feet in height, with a crater 30 miles in circumference, and a floor 2,000 feet below the top of the surrounding wall. The ascent, which is made from Makawao, 12 miles distant from Wailuku, involves a ride of a few miles over lava beds, but presents no great difficulty. It is usual to ride up in the afternoon and camp near the summit, where there are wood and water, and lava caves roomy enough for parties of 4 or 5 persons; but the nights are very cold, and the better plan is to start by moonlight, with a competent guide, at 2 or 3 A. M., arriving at the summit in time for sunrise, and returning the same day. The crater of Haleakala is the largest in the world.

Wailuku is built on the banks of a stream, which issues from the Iao Valley, a short distance from the town, and a few hours will suffice to explore the beauties of this region, which is sometimes called the Hawaiian Yosemite. Beyond the Iao Valley is the Wailuku Pass, and beyond the pass is a mountain, at the base of which is situated the town of Lahaina, at one time the most important commercial place in the Hawaiian Kingdom. In returning from Lahaina to Wailuku the road through the pass, though difficult, is often selected by male tourists on account of the fine opportunity it affords of viewing the great gorge of the Iao. The more usual route leads over a spur of the mountain. At Lahaina there are several lodging-houses and restaurants. Horses can be obtained at Wailuku and Lahaina for $2 to $3 a day, and at the latter town express wagons can be hired at $1.25 an hour, for each passenger, to visit points of interest in the neighborhood.

Molokai.—The island of Molokai lies about 15 miles to leeward of Maui, and whale-boats can be hired at Lahaina for a visit. The charge for a boat pulled by 6 men, and with accommodation for 4 passengers, is $10. Molokai can also be reached by steamer from Honolulu in a few hours, at an expense of $5 for each passenger. In this island, at the foot of a precipice 2,000 feet high, and bounded seaward by a pali 1,000 to 2,000 feet in depth, is the leper asylum of the Hawaiian Kingdom, occupying a plain of about 20,000 acres. He who is sent to Molokai is dead to the world; his wife may obtain a divorce, and his estate be administered as though he were actually deceased.

The lepers number about 700, and are provided by the Government with house-room, clothing and sufficient rations of poi and beef, or salmon. There is a hospital for the treatment of persons in advanced stages of the disease, and a store, where goods are sold at cost. The patients are allowed to cultivate the land, and the products are purchased by the Board of Health.

Lanai.—This island lies about 5 miles to the south of Molokai, and can also be reached by fishing and whale-boats from Lahaina, but not by steamer direct from Honolulu. Lanai is the favorite resort of botanists, and contains many rare varieties of mosses and ferns. It also offers to the antiquary a choice field for his research. Before the spread of Christianity in the Hawaiian Kingdom, it was believed to be the abode of the Hawaiian gods; and there are yet in existence many ruins of their heiaus, or places of worship. One of them is still in as perfect a state of preservation, as when human victims were sacrificed on its altars, less than a century ago. Near another, at a place called Kaunolu, was a favorite fishing ground of Kamehameha, the conqueror of Oahu; and traces of his residence are still to be seen in the neighborhood.

Hawaii.—Hilo, the principal town in this island, and the rainiest town in the group. The steamers *Likelike*, *Lehua* and *Mokolii* sail every week from Honolulu for Maui, Hawaii, Molokai, and the windward ports of Oahu. The trip from Honolulu to Hilo occupies about 40 hours, and the fare is $12.50. On the return trip, the steamer makes the circuit of the island each alternate week, calling at several points of interest on the way. For this there is an additional charge of $12.50. Kaawaloa, in Kealakakua Bay, is one of the calling places most frequented. It is but a collection of native huts, but a stone obelisk, 30 feet in height, and shaded with cocoa palms, marks the place where Cook was killed. The inscription on the monument reads: "In memory of the great circumnavigator, Captain Cook, R. N., who discovered these islands on the 18th of January, A. D. 1778, and fell near this spot, on the 14th day of February, A. D. 1779. This monument was erected in November, A. D. 1874, by some of his fellow-countrymen."

Surf-board is one of the favorite sports at Hilo. On a rough day, when a heavy sea is rolling, a party of natives, each with his *papehe-nala* (a tough plank, 6 to 10 feet long, and 2 feet wide), swim out to the first line of breakers, and watching their chance, dive underneath, and are carried by the undertow into the smooth water beyond. Here they remain until some huge roller gives them the chance they seek, when they place themselves in front of it, lying face downwards on the board. The wave speeds on, and its base soon strikes the ground, while the top curls over, and propels the swimmer before it with the speed of an express train, until he is landed high and dry on the shore.

A short distance from the town is a small lagoon, where beautiful specimens of coral may be obtained, and on the rocks, near by, are cowrie shells. Opposite the lagoon is Cocoanut Island. There is no pleasanter spot for a picnic in all Hawaii.

The bay is deep enough for ships of heavy tonnage, and roomy enough to accommodate a large fleet of vessels. If a breakwater were built out from the shore to Cocoanut Island, it would make the harbor secure in stormy weather. Within half an hour's ride of the island is Keokea Point, from which there is a fine view of the town, the sea, the coast line, and the neighboring sugar plantations, beyond which are forests, covering the mountain slopes up to the point where vegetation ceases. Beyond the forests is the huge snow-covered tufa cone of Maunakea (white mountain), 14,500 feet above the sea level. Two miles further is Lelciwi Point, commanding a view of the south-eastern coast of Hawaii.

The "Rainbow Falls," in the Wailuku gorge, a few miles north of Hilo, are well worthy of a visit. A good view of them may be obtained from a bridge that spans the Wailuku River, near its mouth.

Thirty miles from Hilo is the active volcano of Kilauea, 4,400 feet in height, and easy of access. The journey requires 8 to 10 hours. The charge for horses and guide is $10 each for the trip. The guides understand English imperfectly, and should be carefully instructed before starting. The equipments for the journey should include waterproof clothing, plenty of shawls or cloaks, as it seldom fails to rain either part of the day or all day, and the evenings are chilly on the mountain summit.

After a ride of 3 or 4 miles, the road passes through a forest dense with undergrowth. Then comes swampy ground, covered with the ti tree, and sometimes impassable in very wet weather. Beyond this are beds of lava, or *pahoehoe*, in native parlance. The Half-Way House, kept by a native Hawaiian, is 13 miles from Hilo, and 17 from the summit. Here food and fodder can be obtained, and 2 or 3 hours' rest may be taken, if the party have started early enough. The remainder of the road is rough, though not very steep, and much of it still leads over lava beds. At the summit is the Volcano House, which has good fare and excellent accommodation.

Facing the sleeping apartments of the hotel are the burning lakes, called in the Hawaiian tongue Hale-mau-mau, or "the house of everlasting fire." The crater is 9 miles in circumference, and about 1,000 feet deep. From the Volcano House to the edge of Hale-mau-mau is a distance of 3 miles, by a steep but not difficult path. There are two burning caldrons or lakes, separated by a bank of lava 80 feet high, and having an extreme diameter of about a furlong. Here the visitor may stand and listen to the rumblings, detonations and hissings of the molten sea as it dashes its waves against the shore, only 80 feet below. During the eruptions, fire-fountains play to a height of several hundred feet, from which lava threads are spun out by the wind, and adhere to the neighboring rocks. These are called "Pele's hair," from the name of the goddess who is supposed to preside over Hilauea.

Many visitors prefer to return by way of the Puna coast. By this route the journey back to Hilo is 70 miles from the Volcano House. At Kaimu, 25 miles distant, sweet potatoes, bananas, cocoanuts, and chickens may be obtained, but no other eatables, and the water is very bad. Fifteen miles further on, good water and comfortable quarters may be obtained, at the house of Captain Eldart. Thence a ride of 23 miles brings the visitor back to Hilo.

In the interior of Hawaii is a desert plateau, 5,000 to 6,000 feet in height, lying between the volcanic mountains Maunaloa, Maunakea and Hualalai. This plateau is entirely destitute of water, and does not contain a single inhabitant, or even a trail. The forests which skirt the base of Maunakea are the resorts of large droves of wild cattle and hogs, which are hunted for their skins, the carcass being worthless. The ascent of this mountain is made from Waimea, in the northern portion of the island. The path leads through the sheep station of Kalaicha. From Waimea the ascent occupies about 11 hours; from Kalaicha 6 hours. Persons wishing to make the ascent should arrange to camp at the station, high up on the mountain, near a lake, which usually forms the goal of the journey. The lake can be reached within 5 hours from Waimea, and a road to it has been built through the sheep ranch. Soundings have been taken to a depth of more than 300 feet without finding bottom. From the neighborhood of the lake a view can be obtained of Haleakala in the island of Maui. On the southern slope of the mountain grows, in its greatest perfection, the sword plant, with leaves resembling a silver fan, and branches that bear flowers of a delicate dove color. The plant flowers in November, and is found elsewhere on the islands, but nowhere in such perfect development as on Maunakea. The ascent of the mountain presents no great difficulty to persons not liable to mountain sickness, and on its summit one may dismount at an elevation of 14,500 feet above the sea level, on the crest of the highest mountain in the Pacific.

The ascent of Maunaloa is a more ardurous task, and one less frequently attempted. The height is 13,603 feet. The mountain sides have deep ravines and slopes of loose scoriæ, difficult to cross. Mountain sickness, attended with severe headache and prostration, is apt to ensue, but can be partially relieved by rubbing the head with snow. The crater of Mokuaweoweo, at the summit, is 6 miles in circumference, and contains probably the largest volcano in the world. The center of activity is an incandescent lake, about 800 feet below, and nearly a mile distant from the nearest accessible point. When the volcano is active, the center of the lake shows waves of white-hot lava, and from it rises to a height of about 400 feet a fountain 150 feet in diameter at the base, with cross fountains, like wheat-sheaves, at the lower part, twining as it rises into the air, and returning in a fiery spray to the surface. Occasionally almost the whole surface of the lake rises in one burning mass to a height of 1,500 feet, under the influence of some violent internal action. Since Hawaii was inhabited by white men, there have been 10 volcanic eruptions from the crater of Maunaloa. The eruptions do not proceed from the crater's filling up and running over, but from the sides of the mountain, which, being unable to bear the enormous pressure, give way, and allow the molten mass to escape.

Guides, provisions, and animals for the ascent of Maunaloa, can be obtained at the Volcano House, on the summit of Hilauea. In all excursions on rainy portions of the islands, the outfit should include plenty of waterproof clothing. In many parts, no day passes without a heavy rain shower, and there are localities where the rainfall exceeds 100 inches a year. It is also advisable to take, as part of the luggage, a saddle, bridle, and all the trappings needed for a horse. It is difficult to hire a saddle or saddle-bag, and sometimes even to buy one. Horses are more plentiful than men, and can always be purchased at a very moderate cost. It is one of the jokes in Hawaii to go to a horse auction, and buy an untrained colt for 25 cents.

Many travelers prefer to return to Honolulu in sailing vessels, which make the trip in almost the same time as the steamer, though requiring several days to beat up to Hawaii, on account of its lying to windward.

Kauai.—This island lies to the leeward of Oahu, and can be reached by steamer from Honolulu, or a passage may be taken by sailing vessel from ports in Oahu, Maui or Hawaii, and the return trip made by steamer. The boat leaves Honolulu on Monday afternoons, and after touching at Nawiliwili, the principal port in the island, and calling at Hanamaulu, Kapaa and Kilauea, proceeds to Hanalei, on the northern coast. The steamer fare from Honolulu to any part of the island is $6.

In Kauai the best mode of travel is to take a camp outfit. With the exception of restaurants at Waimea, Kilauea, Hanalei and Koloa, there are few conveniences for obtaining board, and apart from the houses of the natives, there is no sleeping accommodation on the island, outside of Koloa.

The sea near Waimea, a favorite landing place for schooners, abounds with sharks, and the natives make a business of catching them, when they are asleep in the sea caves. The Kanaka is an expert swimmer and diver, and can remain under water 5 minutes at a time. He will peer about cautiously until he discovers a shark asleep and in a suitable position—that is with his head in a cave. He then runs a noose around his tail, and the shark is pulled ashore, dispatched with spears and clubs, and boiled down for its oil. Many of the natives do not hesitate to fight the shark, and one man has been known to noose as many as ten at a time, and all in a single cave.

A short distance from Waimea are the "barking sands,"—a bank of coarse sand, 50 or 60 feet high, with a steep, uniform angle. If the sand be taken up in handfulls, and brought together with a sharp concussion, a sound is produced like the barking of a dog—hence the name. Sliding your horse down the bank, you hear a dull, subterraneous rumble, like the muttering of distant thunder. The sand is formed of decomposed lava, coral and shells, and the phenomenon is attributed to the action of electricity.

At a short distance from the sand-hill is a mirage, always visible at certain hours of the day. It is the apparition of a great lake, and the deception is so complete that visitors, who are not aware of the phenomenon, often attempt to ride around the phantom lake.

In Kauai, especially near Koloa, (a short distance from Waimea), are many beautiful ravines, in which are waterfalls and many-tinted woods festooned with ferns; but the most picturesque sight is the vale of Hanalei, 2 days ride from Waimea. Here the mountains, with the waterfalls streaking their wooded slopes, and the river Hanalei, narrowed into a gorge by the mountain barriers, but expanding into a stream over 2 miles in width, as it approaches the Pacific, form a scene that the tourist will not care to miss.

On the north-east corner of the island, at Haena, near Hanalei, is the "Wife of the Devil," a sea cave, the depth of which no one has yet been able to fathom; neither has its cave been yet fully explored. There are numerous legends extant about monsters that once inhabited this cave.

The climate of Kauai is much cooler than that of the islands to windward of it, and during most of the year there is a moist but enjoyable atmosphere.

The steamer leaves Hanalei for the return trip about noon on Wednesday, and after calling at the same points as on the outward voyage, touches at Nawiliwili, whence she sails for Honolulu, on Friday afternoons.

CHAPTER IX.

MINERAL SPRINGS.

Medicinal Value.—Our slope has thousands of mineral springs, which are not only far more numerous than those on the Atlantic side of our continent, but also more valuable for medicinal purposes. Among all the American Springs, east of the Rocky Mountains, there is not one of the first rank in the alkaline or purgative class; whereas, our slope has several excellent springs in each class. The prediction may be made with confidence, that when the qualities of these occidental springs are better known, many thousands of invalids will come from the Atlantic States every year to enjoy their curative influences.

Medicinal Waters are of two main classes, those for internal use, or drinking; and those for external use, or bathing. Some waters are used extensively for both purposes, but they are prized chiefly for one or the other use.

The waters for internal use are subdivided into two main classes, the alkaline, in which carbonates predominate, and purgatives in which sulphates predominate.

The solids found in mineral waters are either active or inert. Sulphate of lime, carbonate of lime, silica and chloride of sodium, are usually considered inert. When, however, the carbonate of lime is the predominant mineral, there are possibilities that it may be deposited in the bladder; and when water is strong with chloride of sodium, its use provokes an injurious thirst. Borax is usually an inert substance, but may be of service in some irritations of the throat. A difference of five grains in the quantity of the active salts in alkaline or purgative waters is not important, and, therefore, it is useless for the purposes of the physician to state fractions of a grain, unless in the case of iodine, bromine, phosphoric acid, or some mineral which is potent in small quantities. Such minerals however are very rare.

The term, mineral water, has no precise definition, recognized as correct, by general consent of the writers on the subject, and may be defined here, as any natural water containing more than 12 grains of solids in a gallon. No mineral spring with less than 50 grains of solid matter in a gallon, has a long established reputation for curative qualities, as an internal remedy. The Bethesda Spring, which has a reputation of recent date, contains 36 grains to the gallon.

Localities of Springs.—Among springs of which analytical tables are given in this chapter, the Adams Springs are in Lake County, California; the Aptos Spring, on the farm of B. C. Nichols, in Santa Cruz County; the Beer Spring in Oregon; the Bitter Spring at Mineral Park, Arizona; the Cabezon Valley Hot Spring, 10 miles south from White River, in Nevada; the Calistoga Springs at Calistoga; the Congress Spring, (not to be confounded with the Pacific Congress,) 5 miles north of Suisun; the Des Chuttes Hot Spring in Wasco County, Oregon; the Dos Palmos Spring in San Diego County, California; the Empire Spring, 5 miles north from Suisun; the Encino Spring, 14 miles from Los Angeles; the Etna Springs, 18 miles from St. Helena, California; Fulton's Sulphur Well, 13 miles from Los Angeles; the Geyser Springs in Sonoma County, California; the Gypsum Spring in northwestern Arizona; the Hot Borate Spring in Lake County, California; the Idaho Hot Springs in Clear Creek County, Colorado; the LeRoy Mineral Springs, 2 miles from LeRoy, Wyoming; the Litton Spring in Sonoma County, California; the Little Yosemite Soda Springs in Kern County, California; the Lower Soda Springs, 30 miles south from Salem, Oregon; the Napa Soda Springs, 6 miles from Napa City; the New Almaden Spring at New Almaden; the Pacific Congress Springs at Saratoga; the Paso Robles Springs at Paso Robles; the Saline Flats in the Mojave Valley; the Salt Lake Hot Springs, near Salt Lake City; the Salt Wells, near Stone's Ferry, in Nevada; the Sanel Spring in Mendocino County, California; the San Bernardino Hot Springs, 5 miles from the town of San Bernardino; San Fernando Sulphur Springs, near San Fernando; San Juan Capistrano Springs, 12 miles from San Juan Capistrano; Santa Barbara Thermal Springs, 5 miles from Santa Barbara; Skagg's Springs, 8 miles from Geyserville; Summit Soda Springs, near Summit Station; Virgin River Springs, Lincoln County, Nevada; White Sulphur Springs, 2 miles from St. Helena and Wilhoit Springs, 27 miles south from Portland.

Chemists.—Among the Chemists who have made quantitative analytical examinations of the mineral waters of our slope, are J. A. Bauer, Thomas Price, H. G. Hanks, B. B. Thayer, John Hewston, Jr., Edward Booth and L. Lanzweert, of San Francisco; John Le Conte and E. W. Hilgard, of Berkeley; the late John A. Veatch; C. T. Jackson, of Boston; and J. H. Hill, of London.

Alkaline Springs.—The following table shows the number of grains of each of the principal constituents in the Pacific Alkaline Springs, of which we have analytical figures. Less than half a grain is not counted: more than half a grain is put down as a grain. The asterisk (*) attached to a carbonate, indicates that it is a bicarbonate. The X means that the water sparkles with gas. The gallon of the Etna water, analyzed by Bauer, is a wine gallon; in all other cases it is, or is supposed to be, an imperial gallon.

ALKALINE SPRINGS

Spring	Carbonate of Soda	Carbonate of Magnesia	Carbonate of Iron	Carbonate of Lime	Chloride of Sodium	Chloride of Potass.	Sulphate of Soda	Sulphate of Lime	Sulphate of Magnesia	Biborate of Soda	Oxide of Iron	Silica and Alumina	Total Solids	Carbonic Acid Gas—cubic in.	Temperature
Skagg's Hot Springs. (Hilgard.)	*161	11		2	6					26		7	213	x	120
Empire Spring.—(Hewston.)	115	37	1	36	727	13				61		3	983	210	
(Congress Spring.—Hewston.)	53	10	1	48	215	6				21		3	359	210	
Summit Soda Spring.	10	4		*13	26					2		4	89	186	
Litton Seltzer Spring. (Hanks.)	16	11		5	8	129	4					3	229	384	
Napa Soda Springs. (Lanzweert.)	*13	26	8	11	5		2			1			66		
Lower Soda Spring, No. 3.	962		94	5	35								1096	x	
(Lower Soda Spring, No. 2.)	482		34		120								636	x	
Lower Soda Spring, No. 1. (Or. Medical & Surgical Journal)	120		38		24								182	x	
Wilhoit Springs.—(Veatch.)	88	85	7	32	201			6					422	338	
Little Yosemite Soda Spring. (Wheeler's Survey.)	122		6	93	29							41	291	52	
Geyser Spa.	*23	*10	4	4	10		3				2	57			
Pacific Congress.—(Thayer.)	123		14	17	119		12				50	336	50		
Sanel.—(Bauer.)	53	45		70	17								186		
Adams.—(Price.)	57	99	1	29	4						7	199	304		
Etna, No. 4.—(Bauer.)	*66	*14		*10	28	8							126	68	98
Etna, No. 3.—(Bauer.)	*69	*14		*10	28	8							129	58	98
Etna, No. 2.—(Bauer.)	*66	*14		*10	28	8							126	58	98
Etna, No. 1.—(Bauer.)	*75	*14		*10	29	8				1			137	58	98
New Almaden.	*200			*32	32		40	12	4				320	112	

For the purpose of comparison, the active constituents of the Vichy, Ems, and Apollinaris, are here given.

Constituents.	Vichy.	Ems.	Apollinaris.
Carbonate of Soda	208	84	70
Carbonate of Magnesia	11	7	25
Carbonate of Iron	..	..	..
Carbonate of Potash	16	..	..
Sulphate of Soda	18	..	17
Sulphate of Magnesia	..	..	..
Sulphate of Potash	..	3	..

The active substances which give character to alkaline springs are usually carbonate of soda, magnesia, and iron, with smaller proportions of sulphate of soda, magnesia, and potash. The alkaline waters are alterative and tonic in their effect, and are mainly valuable in diseases of the stomach and kidneys, in certain inflammations of the throat, and other internal organs.

The most famous alkaline waters of Europe are those of Vichy, Ems and Apollinaris, which bear a strong resemblance to one another in the proportions of their active constituents, though the number of grains in a gallon is considerably larger in Vichy than in Ems and Apollinaris. The New Almaden Spring closely resembles the Vichy, but has more carbonate of lime than is desirable; the Etna Springs closely resemble the Ems and Apollinaris, and are, by the combination of their medicinal qualities with their situation, better suited to become a great health resort than any other springs on our slope. The New Almaden Spring is in a narrow canyon, near the quicksilver mine, and will probably not attract many visitors so long as the miners occupy the surrounding ground. The Adams Spring is, next to the Etna, the one which will find most favor with physicians. The Skaggs Spring is good; the Little Yosemite and the Sanel have undesirable proportions of carbonate of lime; the Pacific Congress and the Willhoit waters are used extensively, and have some excellent features, though they would be better if they had less chloride of sodium.

The Lower Soda Springs, 1, 2 and 3, are remarkable for the suspiciously large amount of iron; it seems almost incredible that the water could hold so much.

The weaker alkaline springs, if they contain any iron, are sometimes classed as chalybeate. Their waters can be used in large quantity, without injury, as common beverages. Europe has nothing in this class equal to the Napa Soda, of which 700,000 bottles are sent to San Francisco and other places annually.

The Congress and Empire Springs are rather saline than alkaline.

Besides the constituents of the Litton Spring, ascertained quantitively by Prof. Hanks, he found that it contains 53 grains of boracic acid, alumina, organic matter, and carbonates of ammonia, potash and lithium. Until these constituents are ascertained, it will be impossible to determine the medicinal value of this water.

Edward Booth, chemist, who analyzed the water from one of the Etna Springs, for the State Mineralogical Bureau, found that it contained 162 grains of solid matter in an imperial gallon, including 46 of carbonate of potassium, 25 of carbonate of sodium, 20 of carbonate of magnesium, 4 of carbonate of lime, 3 of sulphate of lime, 25 of chloride of potassium, 14 of chloride of soda, 7 of silica, 11 of borax, and less than half a grain each of carbonate of iron and sulphate of sodium. This analysis is remarkable for the large amount of carbonate of potassium which it discovers—46 grains. That salt is not reported by any other analyst in California; and among 195 springs, of which the analysis is given in Blum's German Book on mineral waters, only one contains carbonate of potassium, and that has only about the twentieth part of a grain in a gallon. In those 195 springs, not one has so much chloride of potassium as chloride of sodium, and no flowing spring has one eighth so much of the former as of the latter salt. The exceptional character of the analysis suggests a doubt of its correctness; but Prof. Hanks, of the State Bureau, has full confidence in Mr. Booth's trustworthiness as a chemist, and the discrepancy seems to deserve further investigation.

The Etna Spring, No. 1, of the table, is the spring that rises through a mining shaft; No. 2, is the iron spout spring, or middle spring, on the southern bank of the brook; No. 3 is the eastern spring on that side, and No. 4 is the spring on the north side of the brook.

Purgative Waters.—Next in value to alkaline waters for medicinal use are the purgative springs, in which the leading constituents are sulphates of soda, magnesia and potash. The association with these of carbonates of soda, magnesia and iron, and chlorides of magnesia and lime are considered beneficial.

The Paso Robles Mud Baths, in San Luis Obispo County, California, according to the analysis of John Hewston, Jr., contains 5 grains of carbonate of soda; 3 of carbonate of magnesia; 96 of chloride of sodium; 41 of sulphate of soda; 18 of sulphate of lime; 4 of silica and alumina; total solids in a gallon, 167 grains; temperature, 140°.

The Volcanic Mineral Spring, in Death Valley, analyzed by Thomas Price, contains 345 grains of carbonate of soda; 368 of chloride of sodium; 26 of chlorate of potassium; 139 of sulphate of soda; 6 of silica and alumina, with traces of iron, bromine, iodine, and boric and phosphoric acids. Total solids in a gallon, 884 grains.

The water found 1,800 feet from the surface in the Gould & Curry Mine, at Virginia City, in 1877, contained 48 grains of soluble salts in a gallon, including 17 of sulphate of lime, 26 of sulphate of soda, and 1 of chloride of sodium; while the water on the 1,700 foot level had 14 grains of sulphate of lime, 6 of sulphate of soda, and 7 of alkaline carbonates. The water found in the lower levels of the Hale & Norcross Mine, in the same year, had 19 grains of sulphate of potassa, 23 of sulphate of lime, 8 of sulphate of soda, and 1 of chloride of sodium.

PURGATIVE SPRINGS.

Constituents.	Bitter Spring. (Wheeler's Survey.)	Gypsum Spring. (Wheeler's Survey.)	Aptos Spring. (Lange.)	Beer Spring.	Idaho Hot Spring. (Dohle.)	Encino Rancho. (Wheeler's Survey.)	Virgin River Spring. (Wheeler's Survey.)	Salt Wells. (Wheeler's Survey.)	San Bernardino Spring, No. 1. (Wheeler's Survey.)	San Bernardino Spring, No. 2. (Wheeler's Survey.)	Dos Palmos Oasis. (Wheeler's Survey.)	LeRoy Mineral Spring. (Smart.)	Saline Flats. (Wheeler's Survey.)
Carbonate of Soda						17						59	
Carbonate of Lime		8		15	31				8	8		51	120
Carbonate of Iron					10								
Carbonate of Magnesia ...			4	13	4	2	134	1287			16	270	
Chloride of Sodium		279		9	3		53	34	9	9	22		
Chloride of Magnesia				5	4		54	122			23	41	15
Chloride of Lime	4		92	5		22							
Sulphate of Lime		91	36	48	3		67	209	57	56		117	6
Sulphate of Magnesia	83	120		9	19	38							
Sulphate of Soda	45	36	38		20	8							
Sulphate of Iron							3		1	15	16	1	44
Sulphate of Potassa			336	3	4	87	311	1652	15		206		
Silica and Alumina				107	107	86		90	90	88	82	539	198
Total solids in a gallon.	132	534	506		115				172	172			
Temperature						x						x	
Carbonic Acid													13

The Boulder Mineral Spring, 12 miles from Boulder, Colorado, contains 7 grains of the bicarbonate of soda; 1 of bicarbonate of magnesia; 52 of bicarbonate of lime; 5 of bicarbonate of iron; 6 of chloride of sodium; 129 of sulphate of soda; 1 each of the bromide and the iodide of sodium; and 5 of silica and alumina. The total solids in a gallon, amount to 207 grains. The author of the analysis is not reported.

Owen's Lake Warm Springs, near Little Owen's Lake, according to Wheeler's survey, contain 1,733 grains of carbonate of soda; 1652 of chloride of sodium; 659 of sulphate of soda; 458 of sulphate of potassa; and 12 of silica and alumina; together with traces of boric, phosphoric and nitric acids. Total solids in a gallon, 4514 grains.

The Black Lake, near Benton, in Mono County, California, as analyzed by Wheeler's survey, contains 875 grains of carbonate of soda; 166 of chloride of sodium; 209 of sulphate of soda; 60 of sulphate of potassa; and 4 of silica and alumina; together with traces of bromine, iodine, and boric and phosphoric acids. Total grains in a gallon 1,314,

Of the Pacific Seltzer Spring, 10 miles west of Santa Clara, we have no information, save from a card purporting to give an analysis made by the late James Howden, who at one time held the title of State Chemist of California. He found 51 grains of carbonate of soda, 77 of carbonate of magnesia, 9 of carbonate of lime, 91 of chloride of sodium, 18 of chloride of magnesium, and 12 of chloride of potassium, besides 152 grains of free carbonic acid. This makes an excellent alkaline water, one of the best on the continent.

The Paso Robles Des Chutes, Santa Barbara, No. 1 and Owen's Lake Warm Spring, of which the figures are given under the head of Thermal Springs, have excellent alkaline qualities. The presence of a little sulphate of soda adds to their value. There are hotels at the Aptos and San Bernardino Springs.

The Atlantic Ocean contains in a gallon, 2,139 grains of solid matter, including 1,671 of chloride of sodium, 200 of chloride of magnesium, and 108 of sulphate of potash; the Dead Sea has 13,488 grains of solid matter, including 6,703 of chloride of sodium; 4,467 of chloride of magnesium; 1,376 of chloride of lime, and 683 of chloride of potassium; Owen's Lake has 7,005 grains of solid matter, including 2,942 of chloride of sodium, 2,914 of carbonate of sodium, and 957 of sulphate of sodium.

One of the best purgative springs in California is the Paraiso, 6 miles from Soledad, in a beautiful shady canyon, 1,000 feet above the level of the sea. According to an analysis made by Prof. A. Cichi, S. J., it contains in a gallon 59 grains of solids, including 36 of sulphate of soda, and 4 each of carbonate of soda, chloride of soda and sulphate of lime.

The typical purgative waters of Europe are the Pullna, Seidlitz, Friedrichshall, Hunyadi and Rakoczy. The following table shows the grains in a gallon of their chief constituents:

Constituents.	Pullna	Seidlitz	Fried'shall	Hunyadi	Rakoczy
Sulphate of Soda	990	136	372	1275	1170
Sulphate of Magnesia	745	600	316	1153	1410
Chloride of Soda			489	95	110
Chloride of Magnesia	132		242		
Carbonate of Soda				29	25
Carbonate of Magnesia			32		
Total Solids	1986	848	1553	2725	3196

Our slope has nothing to approach these waters in their purgative strength, but has several that may be equally valuable for medicinal purposes. Two tablespoonfuls of the Rakoczy or Hunyadi are enough for a patient in a day; but the large proportion of solid matter in the gallon, adds nothing to the value of the water, except for exportation. Some of the Pacific purgative waters are strong enough for efficiency. The best are the Beer, Encino, Idaho, Virgin River and San Bernardino, No. 1 and No. 2. The Bitter, Gypsum and Aptos are good, but have more sulphate of lime than is desirable. The salt wells are predominantly saline though rich in sulphate of soda. The Dos Palmos Spring is also predominantly saline and has no purgative quality. The San Bernardino Spring, No. 1, is near, and in front of the hotel; spring No. 2, is 200 yards distant and also in front of the hotel.

Thermal Springs.—The tables headed thermal springs and sulphur springs are miscellaneous in their character. The Hot Borate, on account of its large percentage of borate of sodium, and carbonate of ammonium, is not a medicinal spring. The Santa Barbara, Owen's Lake and Paso Robles, are predominantly alkaline springs, the last having an excellent combination of constituents, making it one of the best natural therapeutic remedies on our coast. Of the influence of minerals in bathing waters, too little is known to serve as a basis of comparison. The Salt Lake Springs, given in the table of sulphur springs, and the Paso Robles Mud Spring, are properly thermal springs, and among the most valuable for bathing purposes. A mud bath at the Geyser's, deserves to be counted in the same class with these; also the Gilroy Springs, and several other springs, from which we have no analysis.

Paso Robles, notwithstanding its remoteness from railroads and seaports, has been one of the most noted health resorts of California. Its mud spring, containing a little iodine, has the best water of its class on the coast. The hotel is well kept. There is a good hotel at the Santa Barbara Springs.

THERMAL SPRINGS

Constituents.	Santa Barbara, No. 1. (Wheeler's Survey.)	Santa Barbara, No. 2. (Wheeler's Survey.)	San Juan Capistrano. (Wheeler's Survey.)	Cabezon Valley. (Wheeler's Survey.)	Owen's Lake Warm Spr'gs. (Wheeler's Survey.)	Des Chuttes. (Dornbach.)	Hot Borate. (Moore.)	Paso Robles. (Hewson.)
Carbonate of Sodium	21	17	8	6	31	34	*77	51
Carbonate of Ammonia	....	....	....	....	....	....	*108	*
Carbonate of Magnesia	....	....	....	....	....	....	....	1
Carbonate of Peroxide Iron	....	....	....	....	8	....	....	....
Chloride of Sodium	6	5	8	22	19	20	85	27
Chloride of Magnesia	....	....	....	....	....	1	....	....
Chloride of Potassa	....	....	....	....	....	2	....	....
Sulphate of Potassa	....	....	....	....	....	....	....	1
Sulphate of Soda	3	....	....	....	6	9	....	8
Sulphate of Lime	....	....	....	....	....	2	....	3
Peroxide of Iron	....	....	....	....	....	....	....	1
Borate of Sodium	....	....	....	....	....	....	*103	....
Silica and Alumina	2	4	6	....	....	8	9	2
Total solids in a gallon	32	26	22	28	64	76	382	94
Temperature	114	117	120	100	96	145	104	140
Carbonic Acid Gas	....	....	....	....	....	....	23	36

Sulphur Springs.—Most of the mineral springs of our slope contain sulphur, and there are places where hundreds, if not thousands, of sulphur springs, or wells, can be found within a radius of five miles. The waters generally, however, have apparently little active influence on the human system, and few of the springs, containing sulphur, have been analyzed. As a general rule, the sulphur waters are prized mainly for bathing purposes. The Napa White Sulphur Springs are mild purgatives. They have a hotel which, for 20 years, was the most fashionable summer resort of California, but of late years it has suffered from the competition of many other places, and in 1881 the hotel was not open. Calistoga was also a favorite pleasure resort for years, and now has a relatively small patronage, but its hotel for the accommodation of guests is always open. The Lake Hot Springs have a hotel and bath house, and so have the Fulton Sulphur Wells.

The Harbin Sulphur Springs, 21 miles from Calistoga, and 1,700 feet above the sea, have enjoyed a large patronage for many years. A stage leaves Calistoga every morning for the springs, of which there are half a dozen, varying in their flavors, and called according to their temperatures and supposed constituents, the hot iron, hot arsenic, hot sulphur, cold iron, cold magnesia, etc. The hot sulphur has a temperature of 120°. A commodious hotel and bath houses are open for guests, and the surrounding country contains much game.

SULPHUR SPRINGS.

Constituents.	San Fernando. (Wheeler's Survey.)	White Sulphur, No. 2. (Le Conte.)	White Sulphur, No. 6. (Le Conte.)	White Sulphur, No. 7. (Le Conte.)	Calistoga. (Rudolph.)	Fulton Sulphur W'ls. (Hill.)	Salt Lake—Warm. (Jackson.)	Salt Lake—Hot. (Jackson.)
Carbonate of Soda........	4	....	....	....	3	*2	....	....
Carbonate of Iron....	....	....	....	....	....	*13	....	....
Carbonate of Lime........	*35	1	2	6	....	12	4	1
Carbonate of Magnesia....	....	1	1	4	....	*17	3	....
Chloride of Sodium........	....	22	23	14	22	10	182	26
Chloride of Lime..........	....	1	1	1	3	....	....	3
Chloride of Magnesia.....	....	1	2	1	....	....	32	1
Sulphate of Soda..........	17	8	11	13	2	1	....	....
Sulphate of Lime..........	....	3	2	2	....	....	39	....
Sulphate of Magnesia.....	....	....	....	....	1	....	....	....
Peroxide of Iron..........	....	....	....	....	....	....	1	....
Silica and Alumina........	....	....	....	....	7	....	....	....
Total solids in a gallon....	56	37	42	41	38	78	261	31
Temperature..............	....	90	86	70	97	....	100	200
Carbonic Acid Gas.......	x	....	....	....	....	7	....	....
Sulphuretted Hydrogen....	29	6	4	....	3	4	6	8

In reference to the constituents of the Fulton sulphur water (which comes from artesian boring, 350 feet deep), there is a discrepancy between J. H. Hill, of London, England, a man of whom we know nothing in California, and J. A. Bauer, a respectable chemist of San Francisco. Hill's figures are given in the table, and they bear a remarkable resemblance to those of Bauer, who, however, found half a grain of carbonate of iron, 17 grains of bicarbonate of lime, and 12 grains of bicarbonate of magnesia. According to Bauer's analysis, the water has little medicinal value.

Other Springs.—The Highland Springs in Lake county, 22 miles from Cloverdale by stage over one of the most romantic mountain roads in California, number 25 in all, of which 3, named the Seltzer, the Dutch, and the Magic, have been analyzed by Prof. W. B. Rising. The numbers of grains in a gallon in the Dutch are 68 of bicarbonate of magnesia, 18 of bicarbonate of soda, 1 of bicarbonate of potash, 2 of chloride of sodium, 1 of bicarbonate of iron, 57 of bicarbonate of lime, 7 of silica, and 88 of free carbonic acid, making a total of 242. In the Magic there are 70 grains of bicarbonate of magnesia, 22 of bicarbonate of soda, 1 of chloride of sodium, 1 of bicarbonate of iron, 1 of bicarbonate of potash, 50 of bicarbonate of lime, 7 of silica, and 74 of free carbonic acid, making a total of 227. In the Seltzer there are 35 of bicarbonate of magnesia, 13 of bicarbonate of soda, 1 of bicarbonate of iron, 52 of bicarbonate of lime, 5 of silica, 2 of alumina, and 100 of free carbonic acid, making a total of 209. All are good alkaline waters, the Magic, because of its smaller proportion of carbonate of lime, being the best.

Of the Saratoga (formerly the Pearson) Springs, 46 miles from Cloverdale and 14 from Lakeport by stage, 4 have been analyzed by the Selby Smelting and Lead Company. No. 1 contains 93 grains of carbonate of magnesia, 20 of carbonate of soda, 1 of carbonate of potassia, 1 of carbonate of iron, 5 of chloride of sodium, 39 of carbonate of lime, 6 of silica, and 84 of free carbonic acid, which last, however, was not determined at the spring, and is therefore probably less than the correct figure. It is a good alkaline water. The three other springs analyzed are weaker, but contain exactly the same materials, and in nearly the same proportions.

Garratt's Spring, in Mendocino county, as analyzed by H. G. Hanks, has 81 grains of carbonate of magnesia, 61 of carbonate of soda, 12 of chloride of sodium, 5 of silica, 5 of carbonate of iron, 16 of carbonate of lime, and traces of carbonate of lithium and boracic acid, making a total of 181 grains of solid matter, besides 170 grains of carbonic acid, free and semi-combined. It is a good alkaline water, but would be better with such a proportion of the aperient sulphates as is to be found in Vichy, Ems, and Apollinaris.

The Ukiah Vichy Spring, analyzed by John Hewston, 32 miles from Cloverdale by stage, contains in a gallon 198 grains of carbonate of soda, 23 of carbonate of magnesia, 18 of carbonate of lime, 28 of chloride of sodium, and 7 of silica, making 273 of solids, and 250 cubic inches of carbonic acid gas. It bears a close resemblance to the Vichy.

The best cathartic spring in California is the Paraiso, 7 miles by stage from Soledad. Its analysis by Prof. A. Cichi shows 36 grains of sulphate of soda in a gallon, 4 of carbonate of soda, 5 of chloride of sodium, 4 of sulphate of lime, 1 of carbonate of lime, 3 of silica, 2 of alumina and iron, and 5 of organic matter, making a total of 59 grains.

General Remarks.—In reference to the use of mineral waters, the following points deserve attention.

First.—An analysis does not deserve trust unless it comes from a respectable chemist. If anonymous it is suspicious. The proprietors of springs have strong motives for deception.

Second.—The chemist, in his analysis, does not find carbonate of soda, sulphate of magnesia, and chloride of lime, but he finds soda, magnesia, lime, chlorine, and carbonic and sulphuric acids, and it is his duty in making an analysis to combine these elements and tell the amount of the different salts. He may hesitate to make these combinations for fear that he will not get them right, but he is more competent than the physician to make them, and without them the analysis is worthless for medicinal purposes.

Third.—The cures attributed to mineral waters are in many cases affected by change in diet and mode of life, rest from labor and care, residence in a dry, warm atmosphere, at a considerable elevation above the sea, exposure to the sun and open air, or abundant exercise.

Fourth.—It is not safe for a physician to prescribe mineral waters of which he has no analysis by a trustworthy chemist.

Fifth.—The best way of ascertaining the value of a mineral water is by comparing its analysis with that of European mineral waters, the curative effects of which have been proved by long experience.

Sixth.—Invalids should not use strong mineral waters (containing 100 grains of solids to the gallon) in considerable quantity without medical advice.

Seventh.—As a general rule, those waters in which chloride of sodium (common salt) is the predominant mineral should not be prescribed.

Eighth.—It is an easy matter to find whether mineral water is strong by evaporating a pint of it in an enameled earthenware dish and weighing the solid deposit. A general idea of the constituent parts can often be obtained then by tasting the deposit. If the water contains two grains of iron to the gallon it will, if placed in an open plate, within two days throw down a brownish precipitate.

Ninth.—When a mineral spring commands an extensive patronage and the proprietor does not publish an analysis of it the presumption arises that he has had it analyzed, and has been advised that the publication would diminish his profits.

Tenth.—A qualitative analysis giving a list of the constituents of a mineral water gives no idea of its medicinal value; what is wanted is a quantitative analysis, showing the amount of each constituent.

CHAPTER X.

DISTANCES, PRICES, ETC.

Explanation.—The table on the following pages has been compiled for the purpose of showing, in the most convenient form, the name of the most notable points in California, Nevada, and Arizona, with the distances, routes, and prices, from San Francisco.

As there are frequent changes, it is well to consult the latest edition of the RAILROAD GAZETTEER, published by H. S. Crocker & Co., 215 Bush street, San Francisco, for the routes and prices from San Francisco, without forgetting, however, that that publication gives the routes forming part of the Southern Pacific system, or tributary to it, more fully than those competing with it. For the routes in Oregon, Washington, and Idaho, the best summary of information is given by the TRAVELLERS' GUIDE, published monthly by Lewis & Dryden, Portland, and obtainable at the office of the Pacific Coast Steamship Company, in San Francisco.

In condensing the information, it has been found convenient to use these abbreviations:

A. & P.—Atlantic and Pacific; Mojave to Albuquerque, 815 miles.
C. & C.—Carson and Colorado R. R.; Mound House to Keeler, 293 miles.
C. N.—California Northern R.R.; Marysville to Oroville, 28 miles.
Cal. P.—California Pacific R. R.; San Francisco to Sacramento, 90 miles.
Cal. P., K. L. B.—Cal. P. R. R., Knight's Landing Branch; Davis to Woodland, 9 miles.
Cal. P. N. B.—Cal. P. R. R., Napa Branch; Vallejo to Calistoga, 40 miles.
C. P.—Central Pacific R. R.; San Francisco to Ogden, 895 miles.
C. P. A.—C. P., Amador Branch; Galt to Ione, 27 miles.
C. P. & N.—C. P. and Northern Railway; Oakland to Suisun, 50 miles; and Woodland to Willows, 65 miles.
C. P. N. S. P. & T.—C. P. Northern Railway and San Pablo and Tulare R. R.; Port Costa to Tracy, 51 miles.
C. P. O.—C. P. R., Oregon Division; Roseville to Delta, 190 miles.
C. P. S. J. B.—C. P. Branch; Washington to San José, 14 miles.
C. P. & S. P.—C. P. and Southern Pacific, connecting at Goshen.
C. P. V.—C. P., Visalia Division; Lathrop to Goshen, 147 miles.

C. P. W.—C. P., Western Division; San Francisco to Sacramento, 140 miles.
C. S.—Coast Steamers, from San Francisco, north and south.
C. S. R. R.—California Southern R. R.; National City to San Bernardino, 130 miles.
E. & P.—Eureka and Palisade R. R.; Palisade to Eureka, 90 miles.
L. & I.—Los Angeles and Independence R. R.; Los Angeles to Santa Monica, 15 miles.
N.—Northern Railway; Woodland to Willows. 65 miles.
N. C.—Nevada County, Narrow Gauge R. R.; Colfax to Nevada, 23 miles.
Nev. C.—Nevada Central Railway; Battle Mountain to Austin, 93 miles.
N. P. C.—North Pacific Coast R. R.; San Francisco to Ingram's, 88 miles.
S. Cz.—Santa Cruz R. R.; Pájaro to Santa Cruz, 22 miles.
S. C.—Stockton to Copperopolis R. R.; Stockton to Oakdale, 34 miles.
S. F. & N. P.—San Francisco and North Pacific R. R.; S. F. to Cloverdale, 84 miles; Fulton to Guerneville, 16 miles.
S. L. O.—Pacific Coast Railway; Port Harford to Los Alamos, 68 miles.
S. P.—Southern Pacific R. R.; San Francisco to El Paso, 1,286 miles.
S. P. G.—S. P., Goshen Division; Goshen to Huron 41 mills.
S. P. N.—S. P., Northern Division; San Francisco to Monterey, 125 miles.
S. P. S.—S. P., Soledad Line; Castroville to Templeton, 33 m.
S. P. T.—S. P., Tres Pinos Line; Carnadero to Tres Pinos, 18 miles.
S. P. W.—S. P., San Diego Division; Los Angeles to Santa Ana, 34 miles.
S. & P.—Sacramento and Placerville R. R.; Sacramento to Shingle Springs, 48 miles.
S. P. C.—South Pacific Coast R. R.; San Francisco to Santa Cruz, 81 miles.
S. Q.—San Quentin Ferry; San Francisco to San Quentin, 12 miles.
S. V.—Sonoma and Santa Rosa R. R.; Sonoma Landing to Glen Ellen, 21 miles.
V. & C. L.—Vaca Valley and Clear Lake R. R.; Elmira to Madison, 29 miles.
V. T.—Virginia and Truckee R. R.; Reno to Virginia City, 52 miles.

Several roads which, though incomplete, have commenced to run trains to accommodate local traffic are omitted here, because no printed time-tables or other precise information about them is now obtainable in San Francisco.

[A continuation of these remarks will be found on page 258, after the tables.]

DISTANCES, ETC.

FROM SAN FRANCISCO.

STATIONS.	State.	County.	Railroad.	Distance by rail.	Distance by steamer.	Change to stage at	Distance by stage.	Total Fare.
Alameda	Cal	Alameda	C P	11				$ 15
Albion	"	Mendocino	S F & N P	84		Cloverdale	67	9 50
Alleghany	"	Sierra	C P O	142		Marysville	60	13 10
Allens	"	Shasta	"	260		Redding	22	12 35
Alma	"	Santa Clara	S P C	58				1 85
Alpha	Nev	Eureka	C P and E & P	576				27 65
Alta	Cal	Placerville	C P	159				5 75
Altaville	"	Calaveras	C P and S & C	122		Milton	22	7 00
Alturas	"	Modesto	C P O	260		Redding	180	24 50
Alvarado	"	Alameda	S P C	24				55
Amador City	"	Amador	C P & A B	140		Ione	14	6 35
Anaheim	"	Los Angeles	C P & S P	471				15 85
Angels	"	Calaveras	C P and S & C	122		Milton	24	5 70
Antioch	"	Contra Costa	C P W	55				1 50
Apache Pass	Arizon	Pima	C P & S P	1013		Benson		
Aptos	Cal	Santa Cruz	S P & S C	121				3 00
Arbuckle	"	Colusa	Cal P & N	114				3 90
Arcata	"	Humboldt	P C S	234				10 75
Argenta	Nev	Landers	C P	486				22 15
Arroyo Grande	Cal	S.LuisObispo	S P S	143		Soledad	128	8 25
Aubrey	Arizon	Mojave	C P & S P	720	255	Yuma		63 55
Auburn	Cal	Placerville	C P	126				4 10
Aurora	Nev	Esmeralda	C P & C C	386		Hawthorne	30	28 05

DISTANCES, ETC.   233

Place	State	County	Railroad	Dist	Nearest Point		Fare
Austin	Nev	Landers	C P & Nev C	567		1	$38 30
Bakersfield	Cal	Kern	C P & S P	302	Sumner	43	9 10
Ballards	"	Santa Barb.	P C S		Santa Barb.	43	15 00
Ballena	"	San Diego	"		San Diego	43	19 00
Bangor	"	Butte	C P O	142		20	7 10
Banner	"	San Diego	P C S		San Diego	50	20 00
Banning	"	San Bernard	S P	557	Marysville		17 65
Banta	"	San Joaquin	C P	74			2 20
Bartlett Springs	"	Lake	Cal P	73	Calistoga	46	7 30
Batavia	"	Solano	"	65			2 30
Battle Mountain	Nev	Landers	C P	474			21 55
Belleville	"	Esmeralda	C P V & T and C & C	436			26 50
Belmont	"	Nye	C P	474	Battle M'tain	170	44 05
Belmont	Cal	San Mateo	S P	25			1 00
Benicia	"	Solano	Cal P & N	33			70
Benson	Arizon	Pima	S P	1013			40 00
Benton	Cal	Mono	C P V & T and C & C	436	Belleville	40	32 55
Beowawe	Nev	Eureka	C P	507			23 20
Berenda	Cal	Fresno	C P V	167			5 00
Berkeley	"	Alameda	C P & N	11			15
Berry Creek	"	Butte	C P O & C N	170	Oroville	16	9 90
Bidwell's Bar	"	"	"	170		9	7 50
Big Meadows	"	Plumas	C P O	186	Chico	65	13 85
Big Oak Flat	"	Tuolumne	C P and S & C	122	Milton	44	8 70
Big Trees	"	Calaveras	"	122	"	47	8 70
Biggs Station	"	Butte	C P O	163			5 20
Big Valley	"	Lassen	"	186	Chico	80	15 90
Binghampton	"	Solano	Cal P	68	Dixon	7	3 45
Birchville	"	Nevada	C P O	142	Marysville	36	7 60
Bishop's Creek	"	Inyo	C P V & T and C & C	436	Belleville	80	35 05

234 DISTANCES, ETC.

FROM SAN FRANCISCO TO	State	County	Railroad	Distance by rail	Distance by steamer	Change to stage at	Distance by stage	Total Fare
Blacks	Cal	Yolo	Cal P & N	97				$3 46
Black Diamond	"	Contra Costa	C P & N	51				1 60
Bloomfield	"	Sonoma	N P C	63		Valley Ford	4	2 75
Blue Canyon	"	Placerville	C P	168				6 25
Boca	"	Nevada	C P	218				8 70
Bodega Roads	"	Sonoma	N P C	65				2 20
Bodie	"	Mono	C P V & T and C & C	386		Hawthorne	40	26 55
Bolinas	"	Marin	N P C	30		Olema	8	1 85
Boonville	"	Mendocino	S F & N P	84		Cloverdale	32	6 50
Borden	"	Fresno	C P V D	177				5 35
Bridgeport	"	Mendocino	N P C	79		Moscow Mills	70	9 00
Bridgeport	"	Mono	C P V & T and C & C	386		Hawthorne	62	32 55
Brighton	"	Sacramento	C P	134				3 30
Brooklyn	"	Alameda	"	9				15
Brown's Valley	"	Yuba	C P O	142		Marysville	12	5 90
Brownsville	"	"	"	142		"	33	8 60
Brunswick	Nev	Ormsby	C P and V & T	281				12 40
Brush Creek	Cal	Butte	C P O & C N	170		Oroville	25	11 10
Buckeye	"	Shasta	C P O	260		Redding	30	
Buck's Ranch	"	Plumas	C P O & C N	170		Oroville	44	14 10
Buena Vista	"	Nevada	C P & N C	155				6 75
Bullion	Nev	Eureka	C P and E & P	534				25 00
Bullionville	"	Lincoln	"	616		Eureka	204	65 10
Burgettsville	Cal	Shasta	C P O	260		Redding	80	19 05

DISTANCES, ETC. 235

Place	State	Railroad	Dist		Destination		
Cabazon	Cal	C P & S P	564				$17 95
Cahto	"	S F & N P	84		Cloverdale	76	11 00
Calahans	"	C P O	260				
Caliente	"	C P & S P	325				10 00
Calistoga	"	Cal P N B	73				2 30
Camanche	"	C P W	104		Lodi	20	4 40
Camp Bidwell	"	C P	245		Reno	245	20 00
Camp McDermitt	Nev	"	414		Winnemucca	75	30 55
Campo	Cal	P C S		480	San Diego	60	25 00
Campo Seco	"	C P	104		Lodi	25	5 40
Camptonville	"	C P & N C	167		Nevada	22	10 00
Candelaria	Nev	C P V & T and C & C	444				27 30
Carlin	"	C P	535				24 55
Carpenteria	Cal	P C S		288	Santa Barb	12	12 00
Carson	Nev	C P and V & T	276				12 05
Casa Grande	Arizon	C P & S P	902				34 90
Caspar	Cal	N P C	80		Duncan'sM'ls	80	11 00
Castle Dome	Arizon	C P & S P	720		Yuma	22	40 55
Castle Rock	Cal	C P O	260				
Castroville	"	S P R	110				3 00
Cave City	"	C P and S & C	121		Milton	32	7 00
Cayucos	"	C S					6 00
Cedarville	"	C P	245		Reno	225	30 05
Centerville	"	"	33	180	Niles	3	1 00
*Cerbat	Arizon	C P & S P	720	300	H'dyville, Yu	38	
Cerro Gordo	Cal	"	371		Mojave	135	35 05
Cherokee (Patterson)	"	C P & N C	166		Nevada	12	10 00
Cherokee Flat	"	C P O & C N	170		Oroville	12	9 10
Cherry Creek	Nev	C P	615		Wells	95	43 55
Chico	Cal	C P O	235				5 90

236   DISTANCES, ETC.

FROM SAN FRANCISCO TO	State.	County.	Railroad.	Distance by rail.	Distance by steamer.	Change to stage at	Distance by stage.	Total Fare.
Chili Bar	Cal	El Dorado	C P and S & P	138		Shingle Spr's	48	$13 00
Chinese Camp	"	Tuolumne	C P and S & C	122		Milton	26	7 10
Chualar	"	Monterey	S P S	128				3 60
Clipper Gap	"	Placer	C P	133				4 45
Clipper Mills	"	Butte	C P O & C N	170		Oroville	30	10 20
Cloverdale	"	Sonoma	S F & N P	84				3 50
Coles	"	Siskiyou	C P O	260				13 25
Colfax	"	Placer	C P R	144				5 05
Collinsville	"	Solano	B & R S		40			1 50
Coloma	"	El Dorado	C P	126		Auburn	22	6 60
Colorado Reserve	Arizon	Mojave	C P & S P	720	225	Yuma		60 55
Colton	Cal	San Bernard	"	529				16 75
Columbia	"	Tuolumne	C P and S & C	122		Milton	49	8 70
Columbia Hill	"	Nevada	C P & N C	166		Nevada	14	10 00
Columbus	Nev	Esmeralda	C P V & T and C & C	444		Candelaria	8	28 30
Colusa	Cal	Colusa	Cal P & N	125		Williams	10	5 00
Contention City	Arizon	Pina	C P & S P	1013		Benson	22	41 00
Copperopolis	Cal	Calaveras	C P and S & C	122		Milton	13	6 50
Cordelia	"	Solano	Cal P	49				1 45
Cornucopia	Nev	Elko	C P	558		Elko	80	
Corralitos	Cal	Santa Cruz	S P	99		Pajaro	6	3 50
Corte Madera	"	Marin	N P C	13				35
Cotate Ranch	"	Sonoma	S F & N P	51				1 50
Cothrins	"	El Dorado	C P & S P	124				5 35

DISTANCES, ETC.

Cottonwood	Cal	Shasta	C P O	242			$6 95
Coulterville	"	Mariposa	C P V	141			8 75
Courtland	"	Sacramento	B & R S		46		1 50
Crescent City	"	Del Norte	C S	95			10 00
Crescent Mills	"	Plumas	C P O	186			16 60
Cross Creek	"	Tulare	C P V	274		Chico	6 75
Crystal Springs	"	San Mateo	S P	224	64		1 25
Cucamonga	"	San Bernard.	C P & S P	21		San Mateo	16 30
Cuffy's Cove	"	Mendocino	N P C	513	4		9 00
Darwin	"	Inyo	C P & S P	80		Duncan'sM'ls	35 05
Santa Cruz	"	Santa Cruz	S P	325	80	Caliente	6 00
Davenports Landing	"	Yolo	Cal P	21	106	San Mateo	2 75
Davisville	"	Butte	C P O	77	53		6 40
Dayton	"	Alameda	C P	186		Chico	6 70
Decoto	"	Eureka	C P and E & P	27	6		27 90
Deep Wells	Nev	Kern	C P & S P	573			8 15
Delano	Cal	Solano	B & R S	271			2 70
Denverton	"	Eureka	C P and E & P		14	Rio Vista	31 40
Diamond	Nev	El Dorado	C P and S & P	604			7 20
Diamond Springs	Cal	Solano	Cal P & N	48	7	Shingle Spr's	2 45
Dixon	"	Butte	C P O & C N	69			9 60
Dogtown	"	Sonoma	S F & N P	170	32	Oroville	1 25
Donahue	"	Nevada	C P	35			8 00
Donner Lake	"	Los Angeles	C P & S P	195	2	Summit	15 40
Downey	"	Sierra	C P & N C	473			13 05
Downieville	"	Amador	C P A B	167	45	Nevada	6 85
Drytown	"	El Dorado	C P & S P	140	16	Ione	5 90
Dugans	"	Sonoma	N P C	132			3 50
Duncan's Mills	Nev	Humboldt	C P	80	20	Mill City	21 10
Dun Glen	Cal	Yolo	Cal P K L B	386			3 60
Dunnigan				104			

DISTANCES, ETC.

FROM SAN FRANCISCO TO	State.	County.	Railroad.	Distance by rail.	Distance by steamer.	Change to stage at	Distance by stage.	Total Fare.
Durham	Cal	Butte	C P O	180				$5 70
Dutch Flat	"	Placer	C P	157				5 65
Eberhardt	Nev	White Pine	C P and E & P	616				40 35
Egan Canyon	"	"	C P	615		Wells	90	
Ehrenberg	Arizon	Yuma	C P & S P	720		Yuma		50 55
El Casco	Cal	San Bernard	C P & S P	493	175			17 20
Elk Grove	"	Sacramento	C P	123				3 30
Elko	Nev	Elko	C P	558				25 70
Ellis	Cal	San Joaquin	C P	70				2 05
Ellsworth	Nev	Nye	C P	279		Wadsworth	100	2 10
Elmira	Cal	Solano	Cal P	60				1 20
Ely's	"	Sonoma	S F & N P	39				6 50
Emigrant Gap	"	Placer	C P	174				1 50
Enumaton	"	Sacramento	B & R S		56			12 30
Empire City	Nev	Ormsby	C P and V & T	280				32 10
Eureka	"	Eureka	C P and E & P	616	225			10 00
Eureka	Cal	Humboldt	P C S					25 60
Evans	Nev	Eureka	C P and E & P	538				
Fairfax	Cal	Marin	N P C	19				1 70
Fairfield	"	Solano	Cal P	50				3 30
Farmington	"	San Joaquin	C P and S & C	112				2 65
Felton	"	Santa Cruz	S P C	74				15
Fernside	"	Alameda	C P	12				
Fiddletown	"	Amador	C P A B	140		Ione	22	7 25

DISTANCES, ETC.

Firebaughs	Cal	Fresno	C P V	196		Fresno	$7 25
Fisk's Mills	"	Sonoma	N P C	80		Duncan's Ml'ls	6 60
Florence	Arizon	Pinal	C P & S P	902		Casa Grande	39 90
Florin	Cal	Sacramento	C P W	130			3 30
Folsom	"	"	C P & S P	112			4 60
Forbestown	"	Butte	C P O & C N	170		Oroville	9 10
Forest City	"	Sierra	C P O	142		Marysville	13 10
Forest Hill	"	Placer	C P O	126	60	Auburn	7 10
Forest Home	"	Amador	C P A B	140	22	Ione	5 00
Forestville	"	Sonoma	S F & N P	69	4		2 45
Fort Jones	"	Siskiyou	C P O	260			20 00
Fort Mojave	Arizon	Mojave	C P & S P	720			
Fort Ross	Cal	Sonoma	N P C	80	16	Duncan'sMl's	5 50
Fort Yuma	"	San Diego	C P & S P	720			25 75
Freeport	"	Sacramento	C P and S & P	97			3 55
Freestone	"	Sonoma	N P C	67			2 35
French Corral	"	Nevada	C P O	142	33	Marysville	8 10
Fresno	"	Fresno	C P V	196			5 90
Gabilan	"	Monterey	S P S	118	11	Salinas	3 80
Galena	Nev	Landers	C P & Nev C	485			22 55
Galt	Cal	Sacramento	C P W	113			3 25
Garcia	"	Marin	N P C	35			1 45
Garden Pass	Nev	Eureka	C P and E & P	595			29 55
Garden Valley	Cal	El Dorado	C P	126	25	Auburn	6 50
Garrotte	"	Tuolumne	C P and S & C	122	37	Milton	7 50
Gaviota	"	Santa Barb	P C S		230		10 00
Genoa	Nev	Douglas	C P and V & T	276	12	Carson	13 55
Georgetown	Cal	El Dorado	C P	126	18	Auburn	7 50
Geyser Springs	"	Sonoma	S F & N P	84	15	Cloverdale	7 50
Geyserville	"	"		74			3 50

240 DISTANCES, ETC.

FROM SAN FRANCISCO TO	State.	County.	Railroad.	Distance by rail.	Distance by steamer.	Change to stage at	Distance by stage.	Total Fare.
Gibsonville	Cal	Sierra	C P O & C N	170		Oroville	28	$16 10
Gila Bend	Arizon	Maricopa	C P & S P	839				31 75
Gilroy	Cal	Santa Clara	S P	80				2 20
Gilroy Hot Springs	Cal	Santa Clara	S P	80		Gilroy	14	3 70
Glenbrook	"	Lake	Cal P N B	73		Calistoga	29	6 30
Glenbrook	Nev	Douglas	C P and V & T	276		Carson	14	12 50
Globe City	Arizon	Pinal	C P & S P	913		Casa Grande	125	49 90
Golconda	Nev	Humboldt	C P	431				19 35
Cold Hill	"	Storey	C P and V & T	295				13 05
Gold Run	Cal	Placer	C P	155				5 55
Gonzales	"	Monterey	S P S	134				3 75
Goodwins	"	Sonoma	S F & N P	40				1 30
Goodwin	Arizon	Pima	C P & S P	902		Casa Grande		
Goshen	Cal	Tulare	C P V	230				6 90
Grand Island	Cal	Colusa	Cal P K L B	95	36	Knight's Ldg		5 50
Graniteville	"	Nevada	C P & N C	167		Nevada	28	11 00
Grant's Station	"	Sonoma	S F & N P	64				2 40
Grantville	Nev	Nye	C P V & T and C & C	411		Luning	53	34 30
Grass Valley	Cal	Nevada	C P & N C	161				6 00
Green Valley	"	Sonoma	S F & N P	65				2 55
Greenville	"	Plumas	C P O	186		Chico	60	9 60
Greenwood	"	El Dorado	C P	126		Auburn	13	5 35
Gridley	"	Butte	C P O	160				5 10
Guadalupe	"	S. Barbara	S L O	11	199	Port Harford	13	

DISTANCES, ETC. 241

Gualala	Cal	Mendocino	N P C	80		Duncan'sM'ls	44	$8 00
Guerneville	"	Sonoma	S F & N P	71				2 85
*Hackberry	Arizon	Mojave	C P & S P	720	300	Yuma	65	37 30
Halleck	Nev	Elko	C P R	582				26 90
Hamilton	"	W. Pine	C P and E & P	616		Eureka	40	38 60
Hanford	Cal	Tulare	C P & S P	252				7 30
Harbin Springs	"	Lake	Cal P N B	73		Calistoga	24	5 00
Hardyville	Arizon	Mojave	C P & S P	720	300	Yuma		38 95
Harford	Cal	S. Luis Obispo	P C S		199			8 00
Havilah	"	Kern	C P & S P	325		Caliente	29	14 00
Hawthorne	Nev	Esmeralda	C P V & T and C & C	386				22 05
Hay Ranch	"	Eureka	C P and E & P	545				25 80
Haywards	Cal	Alameda	O P	21				65
Healdsburg	"	Sonoma	S F & N P	66				2 50
Henly	"	Siskiyou	C P O	260				
Highland Springs	"	Lake	S F & N P	84		Cloverdale	22	6 25
Hollister	"	San Benito	S P T	94				2 65
Homcut	"	Yuba	C P O & C N	154				5 50
Hookton	"	Humboldt	P C S		222			10 00
Hornitos	"	Mariposa	C P V	141		Merced	22	6 75
Hot Springs	"	S. Luis Obispo	S P S	143				
Howland Flat	"	Sierra	C P O & C N	170		Oroville	55	16 50
Hueneme	"	Ventura	P C S		321			12 50
Humboldt	Nev	Humboldt	C P	424				16 55
Humboldt Bay	Cal	"	P C S		216			10 00
Huron	"	Tulare	C P & S P	259				8 10
Hydesville	"	Humboldt	P C S		222	Eureka	25	12 00
Independence	Cal	Inyo	C P V & T and C & C	436		Belleville	120	35 05
Ione	"	Amador	C P A B	140				4 35
Iowa Hill	"	Placer	C P	144		Colfax	8	7 05

DISTANCES, ETC.

FROM SAN FRANCISCO TO	State.	County.	Railroad.	Distance by rail.	Distance by steamer.	Change to stage at	Distance by stage.	Total Fare.
Iron Point	Nev	Humboldt	C P	442				$19 95
Jacinto	Cal	Colusa	C P O	186			15	8 25
Jackson	"	Amador	C P A B	140			12	6 35
Jacksonville	"	Tuolumne	C P and E & C	122		Chico	29	6 70
Jamestown	"	Tuolumne	C P and S & C	122		Ione	31	6 75
Janesville	"	Lassen	C P	245		Milton	80	18 00
Jenny Lind	"	Calaveras	C P and S & C	122		Milton	4	4 20
Jewells	"	Marin	N P C	32		Reno		1 40
Jolon	"	Monterey	S P S	143		Milton		6 65
Julian	"	San Diego	P C S		480	San Diego	65	20 00
Junction	"	Placer	C P	108				3 60
Kelsey	"	El Dorado	C P	126		Auburn	28	7 50
Kelseyville	"	Lake	S F & N P	84		Cloverdale	24	6 50
Kernville	"	Kern	C P & S P	325		Caliente	40	15 00
Kingsbury	"	Fresno	C P V	216				6 50
Klamath Ferry	"	Siskiyou	C P O	260		Redding	128	
Knight's Ferry	"	Stanislaus	C P and S & C	126		Oakdale	12	5 00
Knight's Landing	"	Yolo	Cal P K L B	95				3 35
Knoxville	"	Napa	Cal P N B	73		Calistoga	28	7 70
Korbells	"	Sonoma	S F & N P	68				2 70
Kress Summit	"	Nevada	C P & N C	157				7 00
La Graciosa	"	S. Barbara	S P S	143				8 45
La Grange	"	Stanislaus	C P N	103		Modesto	32	5 60
La Porte	"	Plumas	C P O & C N	170		Oroville	45	12 60

DISTANCES, ETC.

Laguna	Cal	Sonoma	S F & N P	61			$ 2 35
Lagunitas	"	Marin	N P C	28			1 20
Lake City	"	Modoc	C P	245	Reno	220	20 00
Lake City	"	Nevada	C P & N C	167	Nevada	12	8 05
Lakeport	"	Lake	C P & N P	84	Cloverdale	32	7 00
Lakeville	"	Sonoma	S F & N P	35			1 25
Lancha Plana	"	Amador	C P A B	113		27	4 90
Lang	"	Los Angeles	C P & S P	428			14 15
Langville	"	Yolo	Cal P K L B	86	Woodland	16	4 60
Lathrop	"	San Joaquin	C P	83			2 50
Latrobe	"	El Dorado	C P and S & P	127			5 50
Lexington	"	Santa Clara	S P	47	Santa Clara	12	3 00
Lincoln	"	Placer	C P O	119			3 90
Linden	"	San Joaquin	C P	92	Stockton	14	5 30
Little River	"	Mendocino	N P C	80	Duncan'sMl's	93	10 90
Little York	"	Nevada	C P	157	Dutch Flat	4	9 00
Litton Springs	"	Sonoma	S F & N P	70			2 75
Livermore	"	Alameda	C P	48			1 25
Lockford	"	San Joaquin	C P W	104	Lodi	9	3 65
Lodi	"	San Joaquin	C P W	104			2 95
Lompoc	"	S Barbara	P C S	325	La Gaviota	14	12 00
Lone Pine	"	Inyo	C P & S P	230	Caliente	145	35 05
Lorenzo	"	Alameda	C P	18			40
Los Angeles	"	Los Angeles	C P & S P	471			15 00
Los Banos	"	Merced	S P	80	Gilroy	45	6 60
Los Flores	"	San Diego	P C S	480	San Diego	58	20 00
Los Gatos	"	Santa Clara	S P C	56			1 75
Louisville	"	El Dorado	C P	126	Auburn	29	8 75
Lovejoys	"	El Dorado	C P	126	Auburn	7	5 50
Lovelocks	Nev.	Humboldt	C P	341			14 85

DISTANCES, ETC.

STATIONS.	State.	County.	Railroad.	Distance by rail.	Distance by steamer.	Change to stage at	Distance by stage.	Total Fare.
Lower Lake	Cal	Lake	Cal P N B	73		Calistoga	35	$6 30
Lowes	"	Monterey	S P S	143				5 75
Luning	Nev	Esmeralda	C P V & T and C & C	411				24 30
Lyfords	Cal	Marin	N P C	10				35
Madera	"	Fresno	C P V	174				5 25
Madison	"	Yolo	Cal P & V and C L	89				3 60
Manchester	"	Mendocino	N P C	80		Duncan's M'ls	66	8 50
Maricopa	Arizon	Pinal	C P & S P	876				33 85
Mariposa	Cal	Mariposa	C P V	141		Merced	41	9 25
Markleeville	"	Alpha	C P and V & T	276		Carson	39	20 50
Mark West	"	Sonoma	S F & N P	57				2 10
Marshalls	"	Marin	N P C	48				1 60
Martinez	"	Contra Costa	C P W	36				1 00
Marysville	"	Yuba	C P O	142				4 60
Maxwell	"	Colusa	Cal P & N	134				4 50
Mayfield	"	Santa Clara	S P	35				1 00
Mayhews	"	Sacramento	C P and S & P	100				3 80
McCracken	Arizon	Mojave	C P & S P	720	250	Aubrey	25	
Meachems	Cal	Sonoma	S F & N P	57				2 15
Meadow Valley	"	Plumas	C P O & C N	170		Oroville		16 00
Melrose	"	Alameda	C P	12				25
Mendocino	"	Mendocino	S F & N P C	90		Duncan's M'ls	75	9 50
Menlo Park	"	San Mateo	S P	32				95
Merced	"	Merced	C P V	141				4 25

DISTANCES, ETC.

Merced Falls	Cal	Merced	C P V	141	Merced	23	$8 50
Meridian	"	Sutter	C P O	142	Marysville	17	5 60
Michigan Bar	"	Sacramento	C P and S & P	127	Latrobe	6	7 00
Michigan Bluffs	"	Placer	C P	126	Auburn	30	8 10
Middletown	"	Lake	Cal P N B	73	Calistoga	18	4 30
Milbrae	"	San Mateo	S P	17			45
Milford	"	Lassen	C P	245	Reno	67	17 00
Mill City	Nev	Humboldt	"	436	"		17 10
Millerton	Cal	Fresno	C P V	177	Borden	20	10 85
Millerton	"	Marin	N P C	43			1 55
Millville	"	Shasta	C P O	260	Redding	15	9 50
Milpitas	"	Santa Clara	C P W	42			1 10
Milton	"	Calaveras	C P and S & C	122			3 70
Mineral	Nev	Eureka	C P & S P	157			27 45
Mineral City	"	W. Pine	C P and E & P	616	Eureka	80	
Mineral Hill	"	Elko	"	564	Mineral	5	
Mineral Park	Arizon	Mojave	C P & S P	720	Yuma	43	
Minturn	Cal	Fresno	C P V	157			
Mission San Gabriel	"	Los Angeles	C P & S P	480			4 75
Modesto	"	Stanislaus	"	103			15 30
Mojave	"	Kern	"	371			3 10
Mokelumne Hill	"	Calaveras	C P A B	140	Ione	18	11 85
Monitor	"	Alpine	C P and V & T	276	Carson	36	6 40
Monte	"	Los Angeles	C P & S P	484			20 25
Monticello	"	Napa	Cal P N B	46			15 40
Monterey	"	Monterey	S P R N	125	Napa	27	4 60
Montezuma	"	Tuolumne	C P and S & C	122	Milton	28	3 00
Moore's Flat	"	Nevada	C P & N C	167	Nevada	20	8 00
Morrano	"	San Joaquin	C P V	89			11 50
Morro	"	S. Luis Obispo	P C S	166			2 70

246   DISTANCES, ETC.

FROM SAN FRANCISCO TO	State.	County.	Railroad.	Distance by rail.	Distance by steamer.	Change to stage at	Distance by stage.	Total Fare.
Mosquito Gulch	Cal	Calaveras	C P W	105		Lodi	50	$7 40
Mound City	"	San Bernard.	C P & S P	532				16 85
Mount Eden	"	Alameda	C P	21			8	65
Mountain City	Nev	Elko	"	608		Haywards	75	35 70
Mountain House	Cal	Butte	C P O & C N	170		Elko	24	10 60
Mountain Ranch	"	Calaveras	C P W	105		Oroville	43	7 40
Mountain View	"	Santa Clara	S P N	39		Lodi		1 40
Mud Springs	"	El Dorado	C P and S & P	138		Shingle Spr's	5	7 25
Murphy's	"	Calaveras	C P and S & C	122		Milton	33	6 70
Nacimiento	"	Monterey	S P S	143				
Napa	"	Napa	Cal P N B	47				1 50
Napa Junction	"	"	"	38				1 25
Nashville	"	El Dorado	C P and S & P	138		Shingle Spr's	4	
National City	"	San Diego	P C S		480	San Diego	3	15 00
Natividad	"	Monterey	S P S	118		Salinas	7	4 00
Navarro Ridge	"	Mendocino	S F & N P	84		Cloverdale	60	9 00
Nevada	"	Nevada	C P & N C	167				7 30
New Almaden	"	Santa Clara	S P C	47				1 80
New Idria	"	Fresno	S P T	100		Tres Pinos	40	10 80
New York Landing	"	Contra Costa	B & R S	39				1 50
Newark	"	Alameda	S P C	30				75
Newcastle	"	Placer	C P	121				3 95
Newhall	"	Los Angeles	C P & S P	441				14 65
Newville	"	Colusa	Cal P K L B	125		Williams	65	6 95

DISTANCES, ETC. 247

Nicasio	Cal	Marin	N P C	25			$1 10
Nicholaus	"	Sutter	C P O	130		Wheatland	4	5 00
Niles	"	Alameda	C P	30				75
Nord	"	Butte	C P O	193				6 10
Nordhoff	"	Ventura	P C S		311	San Buen	12	13 25
North Bloomfield	"	Nevada	C P & N C	167		Nevada	15	9 00
North San Diego	"	San Diego	P C S		480	San Diego	4	15 00
North San Juan	"	Nevada	C P & N C	167		Nevada	12	9 00
Nortonville	"	Contra Costa	C P & N and B D	56				2 00
Norwalk	"	Los Angeles	C P and S & P	488				15 55
Novato	"	Marin	S F & N P	25				75
Novo	"	Mendocino	"	84		Cloverdale	85	12 00
Oakdale	"	Stanislaus	C P and S & C	126				3 85
Oak Grove	"	Sonoma	S F & N P	54				1 60
Oak Knoll	"	Napa	Cal P N B	51				1 65
Oakland	"	Alameda	C P	7				15
Oakville	"	Napa	Cal P N B	59				1 85
Ocean View	"	Sonoma	N P C	80		Duncan's M'ls	14	4 00
Olema	"	Marin	"	39				1 75
Omega	"	Nevada	C P & N C	167		Nevada	20	6 25
Ophir	"	Placer	C P	121		Newcastle	2	4 50
Orange	"	Los Angeles	C P & S P	503				15 95
Oreana	Nev	Humboldt	C P	403				15 45
Oregon House	Cal	Yuba	C P O	142		Marysville	23	8 10
Oro Fino	"	Siskiyou	"	260				14 25
Oroville	"	Butte	C P O & C N	170				6 60
Osceola	Nev	W. Pine	C P and E & P	616		Eureka	110	52 10
Otay	Cal	San Diego	P C S		480	San Diego	12	17 00
Pacheco	"	Contra Costa	C P W	36		Martinez	5	1 50
Pac. Con. Springs	"	Santa Clara	S P C	44		Santa Clara	11	2 50

DISTANCES, ETC.

FROM SAN FRANCISCO TO	State.	County.	Railroad.	Distance by rail.	Distance by steamer.	Change to stage at	Distance by stage.	Total Fare.
Pages	Cal	Sonoma	S F & N P	43				$1 40
Pajaro	"	Santa Clara	S P	99				2 75
Palisade	Nev	Eureka	C P R	526				24 10
Pantano	Arizon	Pima	C P & S P	995				39 55
Paso Robles	Cal	S. Luis Obispo	S P S	143				6 20
Patchin	"	Santa Clara	S P C	44		Santa Clara	17	9 75
Pearson's Springs	"	Lake	S F & N P	84		Cloverdale	46	1 25
Penn's Grove	"	Sonoma	"	40				3 85
Penryn	"	Placer	C P	168				7 60
Pentz	"	Butte	C P O & C N	170		Oroville	12	3 55
Perkins	"	Sacramento	C P and S & P	97				3 10
Pescadero	"	San Mateo	S P	21		San Mateo	32	1 00
Petaluma	"	Sonoma	S F & N P	36				3 10
Peters	"	San Joaquin	C P and S & C	107				3 00
Phœnix	Arizon	Maricopa	C P & S P	876				37 00
Pigeon Point	Cal	San Mateo	S P R	21		San Mateo	38	4 25
Pike City	"	Sierra	C P O	142		Marysville	50	10 00
Pilot Hill	"	El Dorado	C P	126		Auburn	7	6 00
Pine Flat	"	Sonoma	Cal P N B	73		Calistoga	18	3 80
Pine Grove	Nev	Esmeralda	C P and V & T	276				
Pioche	"	Lincoln	C P and E & P	616		Eureka	180	58 35
Placerville	Cal	El Dorado	C P and S & P	138		Shingle Spr's	11	7 75
Plainsburg	"	Merced	C P V	150				4 70
Pleasanton	"	Alameda	C P	42				1 10

DISTANCES, ETC.

Pleasant Valley	Cal	El Dorado	C P and S & P	138		Shingle Spr's	21	$9 75
Pleito	"	Monterey	S P S	143				9 00
Plymouth	"	Amador	C P A B	140		Ione	18	6 85
Point Arena	"	Mendocino	N P C	80		Duncan'sMl's		7 00
Pomona	"	Los Angeles	C P & S P	503				16 00
Port Harford	"	S.LuisObispo	P C S		199			8 00
Poway	"	San Diego			480			18 00
Prairie	"	Yolo	Cal P K L B	97		Blacks	2	3 65
Prattville	"	Plumas	C P O	186			40	12 90
Prescott	Arizon	Yavapai	C P & S P	876		Chico		46 60
Princeton	Cal	Colusa	Cal P & N	143		Norman	10	7 00
Puente	"	Los Angeles	C P & S P	490				15 60
Purissima	"	San Mateo	S P R	21		San Mateo	17	1 50
Quaker Hill	"	Nevada	C P O & N C	167		Nevada	7	9 00
Quincy	"	Plumas	C P O & C N	170		Oroville	65	14 05
Railroad Flat	"	Calaveras	C P A B	140		Ione	29	8 90
Ravena	"	Los Angeles	C P & S P	420				18 90
Red Bluff	"	Tehama	C P O	225				6 45
Redding	"	Shasta	C P O	260				7 50
Redwood City	"	San Mateo	S P	29				80
Reno	Nev	Washoe	C P	245				10 05
Reveille	"	Nye	C P and E & P	616		Eureka	160	75 30
Reynold's Ferry	Cal	Calaveras	C P and S & C	122		Milton	20	7 00
Rich Bar	"	Plumas	C P O & C N	170		Oroville	69	17 00
Rio Vista	"	Solano	B & R S		89			1 50
Ripon	"	San Joaquin	C P & S P	94				2 85
Riverside	"	S Bernardino	"	529		Colton	8	17 25
Rocklin	"	Placer	C P	112				3 99
Roseville	"	Placer	C P	108				3 80
Rohnerville	"	Humboldt	P C S		223	Eureka	20	12 00

250 DISTANCES, ETC.

FROM SAN FRANCISCO TO	State.	County.	Railroad.	Distance by rail.	Distance by steamer.	Change to stage at	Distance by stage.	Total Fare.
Rough and Ready	Cal	Nevada	C P & N C	161		Grass Valley	4	$7 00
Routiers	"	Sacramento	C P and S & P	102				3 90
Ruby Hill	Nev	Eureka	C P and E & P	616		Eureka	2	33 10
Ruby Valley	"	Elko	C P	558		Elko	35	40 30
Rutherford	Cal	Napa	Cal P N B	61				1 90
Rye Patch	Nev	Humboldt	C P	363				15 95
Sacramento	Cal	Sacramento	C P	90				3 00
Sacramento Ferry	"	Sacramento	C P O	260				10 00
Salida	"	Stanislaus	C P V	97				2 90
Salinas	"	Monterey	S P S	118				3 25
Salmon Falls	"	El Dorado	C P and S & P	112		Folsom	9	5 60
Salsbury's	"	Sacramento	C P and S & P	106				4 30
Salt Point	"	Sonoma	N P C	80		Duncan'sMl's	25	6 00
San Andreas	"	Calaveras	C P and S & C	122		Milton	22	6 00
San Anselmo	"	Marin	N P C	17				50
San Antonio	"	Monterey	S P S	143				6 65
San Benito	"	San Benito	S P	95				6 80
San Bernardino	"	S Bernardino	C P & S P	529		Colton	3	16 85
San Bruno	"	San Mateo	S P	14				40
San Buenaventura	"	Ventura	C P & S P	441		Newhall	50	12 00
San Diego	"	San Diego	P C S		480	San Diego		15 00
San Dieguito	"	San Diego	P C S		480	San Diego	24	17 50
San Felipe	"	Santa Clara	S P	80		Gilroy	10	4 00
San Fernandino	"	Los Angeles	C P & S P	450				14 90

DISTANCES, ETC.

Place	State	Railroad	To	Miles		Fare
San Gabriel	Cal	C P & S P	Los Angeles	480		$15 30
San Gorgonio	"	C P & S P	S Bernardino	552		25 45
San Gregorio	"	S P	San Mateo	21		2 50
San Jose	"	S P	Santa Clara	47		1 25
San Juan	"	S P	San Benito	87		3 10
San Juan Capistrano	"	C P & S P	Los Angeles	504	6	18 05
San Leandro	"	S P C	Alameda	15	28	35
San Luis Obispo	"	S P	S Luis Obispo	143		6 50
San Luis Ranch	"	S P	Merced	80	40	6 00
San Luis Rey	"	C P & S P	San Diego	504	59	19 00
San Marcos	"	S P S	S Barbara	143		
San Marcos	"	S P S	S Luis Obispo	143		6 20
San Mateo	"	S P	San Mateo	21		60
San Pablo	"	C P	Contra Costa	18		45
San Quentin	"	S Q F	Marin	15		35
San Rafael	"	B & R S	Marin		12	35
San Ramon	"	C P	Contra Costa	7	14	1 65
San Simeon	"	P C S	S Luis Obispo		160	6 00
San Ysidro	"	S P	Santa Clara	80	3	2 50
Sanel	"	S F & N P	Mendocino	84	17	6 25
Santa Ana	"	C P & S P	Los Angeles	504		16 05
Santa Barbara	"	C P & S P	S Barbara	441	78	10 00
Santa Clara	"	S P C	Santa Clara	44		1 25
Santa Paula	"	C P & S P	Ventura	441	40	15 00
Santa Cruz	"	S P C	Santa Cruz	80		3 00
Santa Inez	"	P C S	S Barbara		40	14 00
Santa Margarita	"	S P S	S Luis Obispo	143	38	
Santa Maria	"	P C S	San Diego	480		18 50
Santa Monica	"	C P S P & L & I	Los Angeles	486		15 50
Santa Rita	"	S P	Monterey	118	3	3 80

DISTANCES, ETC.

FROM SAN FRANCISCO TO	State.	County.	Railroad.	Distance by rail.	Distance by steamer.	Change to stage at	Distance by stage.	Total Fare.
Santa Rosa	Cal	Sonoma	S F & N P	51				$1 75
Saratoga	"	Santa Clara	S P C	44		Santa Clara	10	2 75
Sargents	"	"	S P	86				2 35
Saucelito	"	Marin	B & R S		6			15
Savanna	"	Los Angeles	C P & S P					15 40
Sawyer's Bar	"	Siskiyou	C P O	471				17 00
Schellburn	Nev	W. Pine	C P	260		Wells	107	55 30
Scott Bar	Cal	Siskiyou	C P O	615				18 00
Searsville	"	San Mateo	S P	260		Redwood	7	1 55
Sebastopol	"	Sonoma	S F & N P	29		Santa Rosa	6	2 75
Shasta	"	Shasta	C P O	51		Redding	6	8 50
Shaw's Flat	"	Tuolumne	C P and S & C	260		Milton		6 75
Shelter Cove	"	Mendocino	P C S	122	167			10 00
Sheridan	"	Placer	C P O					4 10
Sherwood Valley	"	Mendocino	S F & N P	126		Cloverdale	63	10 25
Shingle Springs	"	El Dorado	C P and S & P	84				6 20
Sierra City	"	Sierra	C P O	138		Marysville	79	16 50
Sierraville	"	"	C P	142		Truckee	30	12 00
*Signal	Arizon	Mojave	C P & S P	210		Yuma	28	
Silver City	"	Pinal	"	720	95	Casa Grande	60	23 00
Silver Mountain	Cal	Alpine	C P and V & T	902		Carson	54	33 30
Silver Park	Nev	Esmeralda	C P V & T and C & C	276		Candelaria	47	12 00
Simi	Cal	Ventura	C P & S P	444		Newhall	35	4 50
Skagg's Springs	"	Sonoma	S F & N P	441		Geyserville	8	
				74				

DISTANCES, ETC.

Place	State	Route	Dist	To	Dist	Fare
Slate Creek	Cal	C P O	260			
Smartsville	"	"	142	Marysville	18	$6 60
Smith's River	"	P C S		Crescent City	15	14 00
Snelling	"	C P V	141	Merced	16	6 00
Soda Springs	"	Cal P N B	47		7	2 50
Soledad	"	S P S	143			4 00
Somersville	"	Cal P & N	56			2 00
Sonoma	"	Cal P N B	47			1 00
Sonora	"	C P and S & C	122	Milton	35	7 70
Soquel	"	S P & S C	115			3 00
Southern's	"	C P O	260			
Spadra	"	C P & S P	500			15 90
Spanish Ranch	"	C P O & C N	170	Oroville	57	16 00
Spanishtown	"	S P	21	San Mateo	13	1 55
Spring Valley	"	Cal P & N	125	Williams	12	6 00
Springfield	"	C P and S & C	122	Milton	31	6 75
Sprucemont	Nev	C P	615	Wells	35	36 00
Stanwix	Arizon	C P & S P	805			30 00
Starveout	Cal	C P O	260			
Steamboat Springs	Nev	C P and V & T	256			10 80
St. Helena	Cal	Cal P N B	64			2 05
St. John	"	Cal P & N	125	Williams	50	10 00
St. Louis	"	C P O & C N	170	Oroville	51	16 00
Stockton	"	C P	92			2 50
Sugar Pine	"	C P and S & C	122	Milton	49	8 50
Suisun	"	Cal P	50			1 70
Sulphur Creek	"	Cal P & N	125	Williams	40	10 00
Summit	Nev	C P and E & P	589			29 90
Summit	Cal	C P				7 60
Sumner	"	C P & S P	303			9 10

DISTANCES, ETC.

FROM SAN FRANCISCO TO	State.	County.	Railroad.	Distance by rail.	Distance by steamer.	Change to stage at	Distance by stage.	Total Fare.
Sunol	Cal	Alameda	C P	37				$ 95
Susanville	"	Lassen	C P O	186			85	18 00
Sutro	Nev	Lyon	C P and V & T	297			5	14 05
Sutter Creek	Cal	Amador	C P A B	140			12	6 35
Swansea	"	Inyo	C P & S P	371			130	28 35
Sweetland	"	Nevada	C P O	142			37	9 10
Sweetwater	Nev	Esmeralda	C P and V & T	276		Mojave	73	22 05
Table Bluff	Cal	Humboldt	P C S		222	Marysville	15	11 50
Tahoe City	"	Placer	C P R	210		Carson	14	10 80
Talmapais	"	Marin	N P C	15		Eureka		35
Tamarack Flat	"	Mariposa	C P and S & C	122		Truckee	70	1 35
Taylorsville	"	Marin	N P C	31				18 00
Taylorsville	"	Plumas	C P O	186		Milton	85	31 65
Tecoma	Nev	Elko	C P	726				11 05
Tehachapi	Cal	Kern	C P & S P	351		Chico		6 10
Tehama	"	Tehama	C P O	213				5 55
Telegraph City	"	Calaveras	C P and S & C	122			5	18 00
Temecula	"	San Diego	P C S		480	Milton	60	20
Temescal	"	Alameda	C P	8		San Diego	2	7 00
Thompson's Flat	"	Butte	C P O & C N	170		Oakland	3	5 50
Timber Cove	"	Sonoma	N P C	80		Oroville	20	7 10
Timbuctoo	"	Yuba	C P O	142		Duncan's Ml's	18	30 35
Toano	Nev	Elko	C P	701		Marysville		7 00
Todd's Valley	Cal	Placer	C P	126		Auburn	20	

DISTANCES, ETC.

Place	State	County	Railroad	Dist	To	Dist	Fare
Tomales	Cal	Marin	N P C	56			$1 70
Tombstone	Arizon	Pima	C P & S P	1013	Benson	31	45 00
Tower House	Cal	Shasta	C P O	260	Redding	18	12 20
Town Talk	"	Nevada	C P & N C	165			9 75
Tracy	"	San Joaquin	C P W	72			2 10
Treasure City	Nev	W. Pine	C P and E & P	616	Eureka	42	
Tres Pinos	Cal	San Benito	S P T	100			2 80
Trinidad	"	Humboldt	P C S			242	10 00
Trinity Center	"	Trinity	C P O	260	Redding	51	15 00
Troy	Nev	Nye	C P and E & P	616	Eureka	116	52 10
Truckee	Cal	Nevada	C P	260			8 30
Truitts	"	Sonoma	S F & N P	86			3 90
Tucson	Arizon	Pima	C P & S P	967			38 15
Tulare	Cal	Tulare	C P & S P	240			7 25
Turlock	"	Stanislaus	C P V	116			4 45
Tuscan Springs	"	Tehama	C P O	225	Red Bluff	7	8 00
Tuscarora	Nev	Elko	C P	585	Carlin	44	32 70
Tustin City	Cal	Los Angeles	C P & S P	498	Anaheim	7	17 00
Tuttletown	"	Tuolumne	C P and S & C	122	Milton	26	6 75
Twin River	Nev	Nye	C P	474	Battle Mt'n	43	
Two Rocks	Cal	Sonoma	S F & N P	36	Petaluma	8	2 50
Tybo	Nev	Nye	C P and E & P	616	Eureka	100	47 10
Ukiah	Cal	Mendocino	S F & N P	84	Cloverdale	31	6 75
Uniontown	"	El Dorado	C P	126	Auburn	17	7 00
Unionville	Nev	Humboldt	C P	363	Rye Patch	30	18 95
Upper Lake	Cal	Lake	S F & N P	84	Cloverdale	42	7 50
Vacaville	"	Solano	Cal P and V & C L	64			2 35
Vallecito	"	Calaveras	C P and S & C	122	Milton	29	8 00
Vallejo	"	Solano	B & R S			27	1 00
Valley Ford	"	Sonoma	N P C	63			2 25

DISTANCES, ETC.

FROM SAN FRANCISCO TO	State.	County.	Railroad.	Distance by rail.	Distance by steamer.	Change to stage at	Distance by stage.	Total Fare.
Valley Springs	Cal	Calaveras	C P and S & C	122		Milton	14	$ 4 30
Virginia	"	Placer	C P O	119		Lincoln	6	4 90
Virginia City	Nev	Storey	C P and V & T	297				13 05
Visalia	Cal	Tulare	C P V	238				7 40
Volcano	"	Amador	C P A B	140				8 35
Wadsworth	Nev	Washoe	C P	279				11 75
Walker's Landing	Cal	Sacramento	B & R S		92	Ione		1 50
Walnut Creek	"	Contra Costa	C P	7		Oakland	17	1 65
Ward	Nev	W. Pine	C P and E & P	616		Eureka	120	1 00
Warm Springs	Cal	Alameda	C P	37				19 00
Warren's Ranch	"	San Diego	P C S		480	San Diego	65	9 00
Washington	"	Nevada	C P & N C	167		Nevada	21	3 30
Washington	"	Yolo	Cal P	96				48 55
Washington	Nev	Nye	C P	474		Battle Mt'n	130	85
Washington Corners	Cal	Alameda	C P	34				4 00
Waterloo	"	San Joaquin	C P	92		Stockton		2 80
Watsonville	"	Santa Cruz	S P & S C	101				11 00
Weaverville	"	Trinity	C P O	260		Redding	47	50
Webb's Landing	"	Contra Costa	B & R S		53			12 50
Webber Lake	"	Sierra	C P	210		Truckee	24	28 55
Wells	Nev	Elko	C P	615				15
West Oakland	Cal	Alameda	C P	7				8 00
West Point	"	Calaveras	C P A B	140		Ione	38	16 25
Westminster	"	Los Angeles	C P & S P	498		Anaheim	4	

DISTANCES, ETC.

Wheatland	Cal	Yuba	C P O	130	$ 4 20
Whiskey Hill	"	Santa Cruz	S P & S C	101	3 05
Whitley's Ford	"	Modoc	C P O	260	
Wickenburg	Arizon	Yavapai	C P & S P	720	
Wilbur's Springs	Cal	Colusa	Cal P & N	125	
Willards	Nev	Eureka	C P and E & P	541	
Willcox	Arizon	Pima	S P	1053	
Williams	Cal	Colusa	Cal P & N	125	
Williamson's	"	Sacramento	C P and S & P	104	
Willows	"	Colusa	Cal P & N	151	
Wilmington	"	Los Angeles	C P & S P	493	
Windsor	"	Sonoma	S F & N P	60	
Winnemucca	Nev	Humboldt	C P	464	
Winters	Cal	Yolo	Cal P and V & C L	77	
Woodbridge	"	San Joaquin	C P W	104	Lodi	3	10 00
Woodford's	"	Alpine	C P and V & T	276	Carson	30	25 50
Woodland	"	Yolo	Cal P K L B	86			40 00
Woodside	"	San Mateo	S P	29			4 25
Woolsey's Flat	"	Tulare	C P V	238	Redwood	17	4 20
Yankee Hill	"	Nevada	C P & N C	167	Visalia	21	5 00
Yankee Jim's	"	Butte	C P O & O N	170	Nevada	16	15 50
Yosemite	"	Placer	C P	126	Oroville	18	2 25
Yosemite	"	Mariposa	C P & S P	141	Auburn	18	18 55
Yosemite	"	"	C P & S P	141	Merced	88	3 10
Yosemite	"	"	C P & S P	174	Merced	100	3 45
You Bet	"	"	C & S and S & C	122	Madera	100	19 50
Yountville	"	Napa	C P	157	Milton	147	3 05
Yreka	"	Siskiyou	Cal P N B	55	Dutch Flat	7	1 55
Yuma	Arizon	Yuma	C P & P	260			11 00
				720			10 00
							12 00
							8 00
							6 65
							1 75
							13 20
							25 75

9

The summer resorts of California are generally crowded during the June vacation of the schools; and the best accommodations are usually engaged far in advance for that month, and prices are also higher then than when business is dull. It is always well, especially when there are several in a party, to write for terms, and if the house is not very near the station, about conveyance.

Information is here given as to a few of the summer-resort houses.

Angwin's Summer Resort, Howell Mountain, 8 miles by stage from St. Helena; fare from San Francisco, $3.20; charges, $10 per week. E. Angwin, proprietor; address Angwin post-office, Napa county.

Etna Springs, 18 miles by stage from St. Helena; fare from San Francisco, $4.20; charges, $10 to $12 per week, baths included. Camping ground free. Proprietor, W. H. Lidell; address Lidell post-office, Napa county.

Atlas Peak, East Napa ridge, 12 miles by special conveyance from Napa City. A. P. Evans, proprietor; Napa City post-office.

Wright's Arbor Villa, Santa Cruz mountains; two miles by stage from Wright's Station; fare from San Francisco to Wright's Station, $2.65; charges, $2 per day, and from $10 to $16 per week. Proprietors, Wright Brothers; address Wright's post-office, Santa Cruz county.

Mountain House, 2 miles by stage from Wright's Station; charges, $8 to $10 per week. Proprietor, R. Jeffries; Wright's post-office.

Ocean View Fruit Farm, 4 miles by stage from Wright's; charges, $8 per week. Proprietor, Mrs. C. C. Slaughter; Wright's post-office.

Hillside Cottage, 4 miles by stage from Wright's; charges, $7 to $8 per week. Proprietor, H. J. Gray; Wright's post-office.

Hotel de Redwood, 2½ miles by stage from Highland Station; fare from San Francisco to Highland, $2.75; charges, $8 per week. Proprietor, M. S. Cox; Laurel post-office, Highland, Santa Cruz county.

Glenwood Springs, near Glenwood Station; fare from San Francisco to Glenwood Station, $2.85; charges, $10 to $12 per week. Proprietor, J. N. Luff, Glenwood, Santa Cruz county.

Soda Bay Hotel, on shore of Clear Lake, 29 miles by stage from Cloverdale; fare from San Francisco, $7. Proprietor, John Behr.

Highland Springs, near Clear Lake, 22 miles by stage from Cloverdale; fare from San Francisco, $6.50. Proprietor, Dr. C. M. Bates.

Napa Soda Springs, 7 miles by stage from Napa City; fare from San Francisco, $2.50. Board, $15 per week. Proprietors, A. Jackson and F. L. Wooster, Napa Soda Springs post-office.

Del Monte Hotel, Monterey. G. Schonewald, manager.

Blue Lakes, 44 miles by stage from Cloverdale; fare from San Francisco, $8. Charges, $2 per day, $12 per week. Theodore Deming, proprietor. Address, Bertha post-office, Lake County.

Sisson's, at foot of Mt. Shasta, 39 miles by stage from Delta. Round trip from San Francisco in season of 1885, $30. Board, $10 per week.

The summit of Mount Diablo can be reached from either Haywards or Martinez, the distance from the former being 24, and from the latter 20, miles. As the round trip from San Francisco cannot be made in a day, tourists who wish to see the mountain advantageously should pass the night at the hotel, 2 miles from the summit by the road and 1,500 feet below in elevation, with opportunities to see the sun rise and set. About 3,600 feet of ascent are made in 6 miles, the road being very steep; and not less than 6 hours should be given to the ascent. Parties of seven or more are taken up by special stages—there is no regular stage line—for $5 each; and if the number be smaller the charge is more. Stages, rockaways, and buggies can be had at the livery-stables of Bennett and of Ward in Martinez, and of Hayward and of Geary Grindell in Haywards.

The only livery-stable in San José of which we have the address is that of Welch, who supplies teams to make the ascent to Mt. Hamilton.

Teams for the ascent of Tamalpais can be had in San Rafael from Jewel Brothers or from Murray.

The ordinary price for a rockaway holding four persons with two persons in the smaller towns is from $6 to $8 for a day; for a buggy holding two, with two horses, from $4 to $6 for a whole day, and with one horse $3 to $5, and two thirds as much for a half day. The prices vary, however, greatly with the quality of the horses and vehicles, and with other circumstances. A person known as a careful and kind driver can get lower rates than a stranger.

The best season for going to Southern California is in February, March or April; to Yosemite in May or June; to Strawberry Valley in June or July; to the High Sierra, August or September; to the Summit of Mt. Diablo, Mt. Hamilton or Tamalpais, any time shortly after a rain, when the barometer has set fair, from January to April; and Alaska from June to August inclusive. Tourists to Alaska should have two Coast Survey Charts showing the channels from Victoria to Harrisburg. These charts, costing about 50 or 75 cents each, can be obtained from C. Pace, 418 Battery street, or from S. Arnheim, 8 Stewart street, San Francisco.

The Yosemite season is indicated by the statistics. Of 2,831 persons who visited the Yosemite valley in 1883, 301 went in April, 728 in May, 576 in June, 428 in July, 416 in August, 219 in September, 99 in October, and 64 in other months. Of the total, 817 were residents of California, 1,625 of other parts of the United States, 254 from Great Britian and Ireland, 42 from British Colonies, and 93 from other foreign countries. Of the 817 Californians, 133 went in May, 291 in June, 207 in July, 103 in August, and 89 in the other eight months; and most of these 89 went on account of business or to accompany friends from the Eastern States or Europe.

The tolls on the various wagon roads leading into Yosemite Valley are so high that they are serious items in the expense of camping parties. The rates can be obtained by writing to Washburn & Co., Clark's Station, for the Mariposa road; to Mr. Priest, of Big Oak Flat, for the Oak Flat road; and to Dr. John T. McLean, of Alameda, for the Coulterville road.

The mountainous surroundings of San Francisco, Berkeley, Piedmont, and Saucelito abound with picturesque walks, some leading to commanding peaks and others into wild cañons.

The pleasure of visiting the Chinese Theater, or making a tour through the Chinese quarter in San Francisco, is much enhanced by the company of a good interpreter, and guide; and the most competent person for that service is an Englishman known as Ah Lim, who may be found at the northwest corner of Dupont and Clay treets. He spent many years in China and is familiar with its language. His charge is $1 for each person.

Relatively little use is made of cabs in San Francisco, because their charges are so high, and such comfortable, speedy, and cheap conveyance can be had in the street-cars to nearly every part of the city. The United Carriage Company and the Pacific Carriage Company have uniform rates; their charges are $1 for one person or two within the district bounded by Broadway, Gough, and Twelfth streets, and the bay, or for one mile; and 25 cents for each additional mile. Call for card with schedule of fares.

After a guide, interpreter, or hackman agrees to perform a certain service for a stipulated sum, he will often claim that the price mentioned was to be for each person, though the understanding on the other side was that it should be for the whole company. The tourist who makes the bargain for his associates cannot be too explicit in his contract, since the party on the other side frequently prefers to leave the matter in doubt at first, trusting for final success to his own insolence, and the anxiety of strangers to escape from noisy controversy and possible litigation.

Steamboat Routes.—The leading steamboat routes on our coast, are those by sea southward, from San Francisco to Panama; northward from San Francisco by sea to Harrisburg, Alaska; eastward from the Columbia River Bar, up the Columbia River; and eastward from Victoria, across the Gulf of Georgia and up Fraser River.

The distances south, from the foot of Market street in San Francisco, by steamship, are to Point Lobos, 7½ miles; Point Pedro, 19; Pillar Point, 26; Pigeon Point, 46; Point New Year, 51; Santa Cruz, 70; Monterey, 85; Point Cypress, 88; Point Sur, 104; Cape San Martin, 136; Piedras Blancas, 154; San Simeon, 160; Leffingwells, 166; Cayucos, 180; Morro, 185; Point Bouchon, 193; Port Harford, 201; Point Sal, 217; Point Argüello, 236; Point Concepcion, 248; Gaviota, 260; Santa Barbara, 288; Carpenteria, 296; San Buenaventura, 311; Hueneme, 321; Point Duma, 344; Santa Monica, 361; Point Vincent, 377; Wilmington, 382; San Pedro,

387; Anaheim Landing, 396; Point Loma, 475; San Diego, 482; Mazatlan, 1,194; San Blas, 1,519; Manzanillo, 1,685; Acapulco, 1,836; Port Angel, 2,043; Salina Cruz, 2,124; Tonala, 2,204; San Benito, 2,306; Champerico, 2,349; San Jose de Guatemala, 2,425; Acajutla, 2,485; La Libertad, 2,523; La Union, 2,627; Amapala, 2,648; Corinta, 2,711; San Juan del Sur, 2,817; Punta Arenas, 2,973; and Panama, 3,427 miles.

The fares to places of importance are as follows: Santa Cruz, $2.50; Santa Barbara, $10; San Diego, $15; Mazatlan, $75; Acapulco, $100; San Jose de Guatemala, $115; Panama, $125.

The distances north, from the foot of Market street in San Francisco, by steamship, are, to Point Bonita, 7 miles; Bolinas Point, 17; Point Reyes, 33; Point Tomales, 49; Bodega Head, 52; Point Arena, 100; Cuffey's Cove, 112; Little River, 119; Mendocino City, 122; Shelter Cove, 167; Point Gordo, 184; Cape Mendocino, 195; Cape Fortunas, 200; Eel River, 205; Hookton, 209; Table Bluff, 212; Humboldt Bay, 216; Eureka, 222; Arcata, 234; Trinidad, 242; Crescent City, 274; Cape St. George, 276; Chetco, 291; Rogue River, 313; Port Orford, 336; Cape Blanco, 341; Coquille River, 360; Cape Gregory, 372; Coos Bay, 378; Empire City, 383; Umpqua River, 394; Cape Perpetua, 433; Yaquina Bay, 454; Cape Foulweather, 464; Cape Lookout, 486; Tillamook Bay, 499; False Tillamook, 511; Tillamook Head, 522; Columbia River Bar, 540; Cape Disappointment, 545; Shoalwater Bay, 569; Gray's Harbor, 588; Destruction Island, 634; Flattery Rocks, 667; Cape Flattery, 680; Port Townsend, 773; Seattle, 809; Tacoma, 830; Steilacoom, 836; Olympia, 855; Victoria, 750; Nanaimo, 833; Seymour Rapids, 907; Cape Fox, 1,306; Fort Wrangel, 1,434; Sitka, 1,596; and Harrisburg, 1,726 miles.

The fares from San Francisco northward, are, to Humboldt Bay, $10; Astoria, and river ports to Portland, $20; Cascade Locks, $23.50; the Dalles, $25; Lewiston (Snake River), $40; Port Townsend, Seattle, Tacoma, or Olympia, $20; Victoria, B. C., $20; Nanaimo, $25; New Westminster, $22; Fort Wrangel, $45; Sitka, $55; and Harrisburg, $70.

The distances on the Columbia River from the Bar, are, to Astoria, 15 miles; Cathlamet, 43; Oak Point, 55; Ranier, 71; Kalama, 80; St. Helen's, 91; Willamette, 109; Portland, 121; Cascade Locks, 58; the Dalles, 98; Ainsworth (mouth of Snake River), 239; Priest Rapids, 314; and Lewiston (Idaho), 390.

The distances on Fraser River from Victoria, are, to New Westminster, 75 miles; Maple Ridge, 87; Langley, 92; Riverside, 106; Matsqui, 108; Sumas, 116; Chilliwhack, 122; Hope, 160; Yale, 175; Boston Bar, 125; Lytton, 157; Cache Creek, 210; Clinton, 236; Kamloops, 260; Lillooet, 283; Soda Creek, 368; Quesnelle, 429; Stanley, 463; and Barkerville, 475 miles.

General Rules for Travelers.—*First.*—Carry your funds, except so much as you want to use on your journey, in the form of a draft or letter of credit. If you have no friend at your place of destination to identify you, let the banker who gives you the draft send your photograph and signature to the drawee.

Second.—Remember, that thieves along leading routes of travel, obtain most of their plunder from men who drink strong liquor, show their money and gamble among strangers.

Third.—Look with suspicion on strangers who claim to be old acquaintances.

Fourth.—When you stop on the road, prefer a reputable hotel, and in a small town take the best.

Fifth.—Buy your railroad or steamboat tickets at the main office, not from runners in the streets. If you are going a long distance, have a wallet for your ticket, and keep it in a special pocket where you can reach it at any moment. Inexperienced travelers often forget where they have put their tickets.

Sixth.—If you are to occupy a particular berth, section or room, examine the car or boat beforehand if possible, and select the place best adapted to your wants.

Seventh.—When you have baggage to be delivered or checked, you can generally trust the companies or firms which are associated with the railroads or steamboats, and a stranger should deal with them rather than with individuals who have no fixed place of business or responsibility.

Eighth.—When your baggage is to be checked, have your ticket ready to show, deliver to the baggage man only the packages that are to be checked, and be careful to tell at once the point to which your baggage is to go. If the baggage is left where you can examine it, you can see whether the numbers attached to the packages, correspond with those given to you.

Ninth.—If you intend to stop over for a day on your way, it is the safer plan to have your baggage checked to that point.

Tenth.—When you change cars, see that your baggage is transferred, that should be your first care, and attend to your meals afterwards. This is especially important if your baggage is checked to the point where the change of cars occurs.

Eleventh.—Before starting, enquire how much baggage you can carry through free, and do not put anything in a bag, barrel, box or bundle, to be checked, unless you know that all the companies on your route will give checks for such packages.

Twelfth.—Unless your trunk is of extra strength, put a stout rope in it, of sufficient length to tie it up in case it should be broken. The baggage smashers frequently make a considerable profit by selling ropes to travelers, whose trunks have been broken by needlessly rough usage.

Thirteenth.—If baggage is to be checked, you snould be at the office half an hour before the train starts, so as to have abundant time for seeing that all is right.

Fourteenth.—Before starting, get a map and time-table, which all steamboat and railroad companies should furnish to every patron, to give him information about distances and stopping places. Some of the railroad time-tables on our coast give the elevations, which are often of much interest in a mountainous region. The companies which have the most attractive routes and the best management, have also, as a general rule, the most complete time-tables and maps.

Fifteenth.—Provide yourself with small change for use along the road.

Sixteenth.—A long journey by rail, through a sparsely settled region, demands a lunch basket, which will give wholesome and palatable meals, at regular hours, with abundant room and time for eating. A little padlock should protect its contents. The provisions generally should be solid, dry, simple in their nature, free from grease or semi-fluid material, nutritious and varied in their flavors. Fresh bread, graham crackers, hard boiled eggs, cheese, of several qualities, roast beef, (cross rib, having no bone or waste, is excellent for the occasion,) dried figs, prunes and dates, are excellent staples. Roast chicken or turkey occupies more space than an equal amount of nutriment in boneless roast beef. Canned meats can be used after the others have been exhausted. Fresh bread and cheese should be enclosed in tin, or carefully wrapped up to keep from drying out. Tea can be made before starting with such strength, that a table-spoonful will be sufficient in a cup of hot water, which can be bought at the stations. Borden's condensed coffee makes a passable drink, when mixed with either hot or cold water. The lack of conveniences for washing dishes on the cars should be taken into account, before jellies and greasy mixtures are put into the basket. The plates, however, can be covered with Japanese paper, or thin wooden platters can be used and thrown away after every meal. The butter should be in a tin cup, without a handle. Bottles containing liquids should have the best of corks, so that there shall be no leakage.

Seventeenth.—The stranger in California should learn to recognize the poison oak, and then avoid it with care. Many persons can handle it, and even eat its leaves and buds with impunity; others, by touching it, catch a troublesome inflammation, accompanied by an intense itching, sometimes by swellings, which are followed on very rare occasions by loss of sight or hearing. Many remedies are used, and what has cured one sufferer may be of little service to another. For the average sufferer, there is no better remedy than concentrated spirits of ammonia, applied as a wash. It is most effective when used immediately after a good scratching. The application causes acute pain for a few moments, but this is a trifle as compared with the long worry of the poison if not checked. Other remedies are saltpetre, common salt, and carbonate of soda, applied in strong solution as washes. Steam baths and plasters made of muslin covered with vaseline, have also been recommended.

www.ingramcontent.com/pod-product-compliance
Lightning Source LLC
Chambersburg PA
CBHW032134230426
43672CB00011B/2338